# LOVE AND ETHICS

# love
## and
# ETHICS

## A NOVEL
## BY IVAN HILL

Inquiries should be addressed to Barlina Books, Inc., 7405
Colshire Drive, McLean, Va. 22102
Printed in the United States of America.

Library of Congress Cataloging in Publication Data

Hill, Ivan.
  Love and ethics

  "The story of a man who played God and a divorcee
who played married men."
  I. Title.
PS3558.I389L68   1986   813'.54      86-3627

ISBN 0-937525-00-6

# Author's Note

The characters in *Love and Ethics* are fictional, although they may bear resemblance to the writer and to those the writer has observed. The actual issues confronting the characters, however, are real. One expert who read the original manuscript thought that what was utterly fictional was fact and that what was derived from fact surely was fiction. But what we see and hear in everyday life often leaves us uncertain as to what is fact or fiction.

Nevertheless, some readers may detect similarities between my public life and philosophy and those of Jonathan Barron. I acknowledge that I was inspired by and drew upon my own background and experiences, as many writers do. More importantly, Jonathan Barron shares my lifelong dedication to the advancement of sound ethics within our contemporary society.

*Love and Ethics* has been written with the belief that there are many men and women, especially women, who are intellectually and emotionally mature enough to gain some pleasure and much benefit from reading it.

# 1

Even for Washington, it was a big reception and dinner party. Over two thousand guests gathered in the Sheraton Washington ballroom, quite a gathering for a thousand-dollar-a-plate affair. The occasion was the announcement of a Congressional Educational Awards program, supported entirely by private funds. Senate and House leaders were there, along with more than three hundred of their colleagues. Hundreds of lobbyists, lawyers, and trade association executives were also on hand. Just about everyone came, to see and to be seen, to help and to be helped. In politics, the only thing you can do by yourself is fail.

Jonathan Barron was there. He was not a politician, lobbyist, or lawyer. And certainly he was no cocktail party aficionado, but he knew and was known by many of those present. He was there because of his high regard for the major sponsor of the awards program, a wealthy, well-intentioned man, who was, Barron thought, unjustifiably discounted by the press.

Whatever the party, Barron could usually be found on the edge of the crowd looking on. This night was no exception. He saw the scene as if it were a grand dance, with the crowd waltzing back and forth, around and around, with glasses in their hands. He seldom joined the dance, but he usually held a glass of scotch and water as a prop. Now and then someone would waltz over to him, grab his hand, and take him to one of the "dancing" circles that kept forming and changing. This time it was Barbara Ballinger who wanted him to meet a group of congressmen.

Barbara was an attractive, quick-moving widow, about fifty-two, slender and blond, and always beautifully dressed. Her husband had been a successful businessman, but most of Barbara's money she herself had earned in real estate. If anyone wanted to buy a home in the million-dollar-and-up range in the Washington area, Barbara was the one to see. Barron had first met her when he spoke to a conference held by a religious foundation. She was a member of their board of directors. Barbara knew Jonathan well enough to know that she could count on him to be interesting and often surprising at cocktail parties. That was one of the reasons she liked to introduce him to her friends. She also knew that politicians liked to be seen with him, because as founder of the Ethics Inquiry Group in Washington, Jonathan was sometimes referred to as Mr. Ethics.

On this occasion when Barbara introduced him to a small group of congressmen and their wives, the conversation was going rather slowly. Jonathan began talking casually to one of the women, Mrs. Ehlers, an elegant brunette.

"I believe you have two young daughters, Mrs. Ehlers," he said, looking directly at her.

"Oh, yes—two very lively ones, thirteen and fifteen," she responded as she turned toward him. "I was just thinking about them."

"Do they celebrate their birthdays together? I believe they were born in the same month—August, perhaps?" Jonathan speculated.

"Why, yes, they were! But how could you possibly know that?" Mrs. Ehlers asked, looking startled.

Barbara was listening and smiling. Jonathan was up to his old tricks again. Mrs. Ehlers turned to her, "I've heard of Mr. Barron's work in ethics, but I didn't know he was a psychic."

"That's one of the reasons I like my friends to meet him. One never knows what he's going to come up with next."

Keeping her composure, Sally Ehlers said, "I think that's a wonderful talent, Mr. Barron. What else can you tell me?" She sounded enthusiastic, but her husband cut short the conversation. He said, "Come on, Sally. It's time to go to our table."

As the congressman and his wife departed, Barbara took Jonathan's arm. Her eyes were sparkling. "Jonathan," she said softly, "you observe the craziest things. Did you notice how eager Congressman Ehlers was to get away! Your insight seems to make him uncomfortable."

"I don't blame him," Jonathan said. "I shouldn't make these presumptuous observations."

He smiled at Barbara and said, "That kind of thing wouldn't bother you, would it? You're so self-assured and ornery."

"Oh, Jonathan, thank you—I think." She smiled again. "By saying that, you just showed me that your ESP isn't perfect. Let's look for your wife. I haven't seen Rene for weeks."

With that, Barbara took him by the hand, and they started through the crowd.

"There she is, Jonathan, as bright and beautiful as ever."

Rene Barron was never alone at a cocktail party. The usual number in her lively circle of conversation was anywhere from five to eight men and women. It didn't matter to Rene who she was with; she could talk to anyone. Of course, there were always a few men who would have preferred to monopolize her attention. And who could blame them? When she looked at a man with her large, quite beautiful brown eyes and listened intently to what he was saying, the man couldn't help believing that she understood and shared his views.

Rene Barron was a journalist who specialized in feature stories and special reports. She had worked in public relations, as a member of college and foundation boards, as a real estate corporation executive, and even as a cattle farm manager. She was five feet eight inches tall, stately and distinguished looking. She appeared to be in her late thirties but was, in fact, fifty. However, she always seemed to be at the peak of attractiveness. Her blonde hair was softly coiffured at just the right length for ballroom, boardroom, or bedroom. Whatever she wore, she looked stunning.

Jonathan Barron made a strange partner for Rene. He was as detached and reserved as she was outgoing. He dressed unnoticeably well, wearing suits simple in style and solid in color. His hair was black and curly, his face tan and earthy. His nose was short and straight. He had a generous, rather sensuous mouth that rarely revealed an impish grin. He was a well-proportioned, muscular man, slightly less than six feet tall.

As for his age, it never occured to people, even to his friends, to think of him in terms of any given number of years. If they were specifically asked, "How old do you think that guy with the pretty blond is?" they usually answered that they had no idea, but would guess that he was somewhere in his early fifties.

Just as men found Rene attractive, many women thought her husband appealing or perhaps just different, and sometimes disconcertingly candid in his comments.

As Barbara and Jonathan wound their way through the crowd toward Rene, she saw them, excused herself from those around her, and came to embrace Barbara.

"Barbara, I'm so glad to see you," she said. "It's been months!" Then as she took Jonathan's hand she said, "Congratulations on

3

pulling my husband out into the crowd. He often just looks on until he sees someone interesting—usually a pretty woman."

Looking at Jonathan, Rene said, "Have you been up to any of your mind-reading tricks or have you been converting someone to good ethics?" Turning to Barbara she said, "You know that's the way he avoids the usual Happy Hour chatter."

Barbara responded in his defense, "He's been on his best behavior, Rene. Only once did he let his personalized insight dart out. The woman was intrigued, but her husband wasn't."

"Isn't it funny," Rene observed, "that men are so cautious about their personal lives?"

"Oh, is that ever true," Barbara replied. "Most men just prefer talking about business; one wonders why they're so self-conscious about other things in life."

As the two women chattered, Jonathan Barron listened and looked around at the crowd. "The truth is," he interjected, "women like you are so attractive that you make men happy just by letting them look at you and listen. Rene, do you remember our table number?"

"It's number 38." Turning to Barbara, she asked, "Where are you sitting? Could you join us?"

"I'd like to, but I'm the hostess at my table. I really should find it now." Barbara gave Jonathan a smile and said, "I hope I'll see you both again soon."

Jonathan and Rene found table 38, and the rest of the dinner party proceeded uneventfully. In fact, the audience was in such a happy mood they even applauded a senator who insisted on playing his fiddle.

Shortly after the party ended, Jonathan and Rene were seated in their car. When they arrived to attend the dinner, Jonathan had found a parking place in the small lot near the entrance, so they were able to drive out quickly onto Connecticut Avenue, ahead of the crowd. In fifteen minutes they were parked in their space in the Watergate garage, near the elevator that took them up to their apartment. Despite all the Nixonian-era publicity, the Watergate complex remained one of the most desirable close-in places to live in Washington.

The Barrons' apartment was located in the newer Watergate South building. From its balconies they could look over the Potomac River and the Kennedy Center, a restful bit of scenery. As soon as Jonathan opened their door and followed Rene into the reception area, he told her that no matter who else had attended the party, he knew he had brought home the most attractive woman he had seen all evening.

"That's what you always say," she replied, never tired of hearing him say it. "But what about Barbara? You and she seem to hit it off well—very well, in fact."

"Sure we do," Jonathan said as he pulled Rene into his arms and kissed her. "But Barbara is one of the rare women with whom a strictly platonic relationship is a sufficient reward."

Rene moved away and walked on into the living room and toward the hallway leading to her bedroom. She was almost out of sight when Jonathan called to her, "I think I'll get a brandy and go out on the balcony for a while. Care to join me?"

Rene came back into the living room. "Thank you, darling, but I'm tired, and I want to go to bed. I'm always exhausted after these things. Why don't you come and sleep in my room tonight?"

Jonathan was pouring his drink. "I like that idea, but I'm feeling rather restless. You go on to bed, and maybe I'll slide in with you later. If I do, I promise not to wake you."

"You shouldn't stay up too late. We're having cocktails and dinner tomorrow evening at the Kennedy Center with Ralph Lawton. He has tickets for the National Symphony concert with Rostropovich and Perlman. And after that, we go up to the Golden Circle to a reception for the maestro."

"You know, I'd just as soon skip it. For some reason, when I go to the Kennedy Center I feel like I'm attending a promotion, not a concert or a play. Ralph is a charming, party-loving fellow. Why don't you just go with him?"

The tone of Rene's voice didn't change. "Honey, I know how you feel, but as nice a fellow as Ralph is, he's not my husband. I hope you'll go."

"Of course, I'll go," Jonathan assured her. "But one of these social affairs a week is enough. The idea of a surrogate to attend any more than one a week may be worth considering."

"In that case, who would take your place next Saturday night when we're hosting a party for the directors of my journalism society? But you may not mind that affair so much—there are some very smart young people in the group."

"Have a good night's sleep," he said, and kissed her lightly as he walked by and went out to sit on the balcony.

It was rather quiet at this time of night, with no airplanes flying over from National Airport. He sipped his brandy and began to lose himself in the soft moonlight, watching a small yacht glide down the Potomac River. The scene was so different but it reminded him of another river and another boat that he saw when he was a child.

Jonathan's birthplace was far back in the woods among the bayous of southern Louisiana near Catahoula Lake in Catahoula Parish, across the Mississippi River, about forty miles west and south of Natchez. It was a peaceful place. Back in the bayou country when he was a child, only about once a month did he see anyone other than a member of his family, usually a hunter friend of his father, or possibly a group of four or five hunters and fishermen seeking his father's services as a guide. His father had been a hunter and a trapper, an erect, muscular man, six feet tall. Even in his sixties, his father had been lean and handsome. Maybe he was handsome because he was rugged and free and proud—a real man, despite his lack of money.

His family lived in a large cypress clapboard house built on cypress blocks two or three feet wide and five or six feet high, high enough to keep ordinary flood waters from rising into the house. Under the house was a wonderful place where he and his two youngest sisters played. There were seven children in his family; Jonathan was the youngest, then his two youngest sisters, Dora and Hazel, who were two and four years older than he. There were three older sisters: Stella, who was ten, Sylvia, who was almost fifteen, and Jennie, who was seventeen. His brother Wayne was thirteen. There had been eleven children in the family, but two died early and the two oldest children, Paul and Horace, had long since left home for the outside world. They were about fourteen or fifteen when they left. As a child, he never knew them.

He had been glad one brother was still at home, because this big thirteen-year-old brother would put him behind the saddle on a lanky sorrel horse, and they would ride into the woods to hunt. Jonathan was good at spotting animals, and one day his brother shot a big panther he had pointed out. He remembered that as an exciting hunting day. They had to struggle to put the dead panther on the horse. They dragged the animal up a leaning log and pushed him over onto the horse, behind the saddle, where Jonathan usually rode. On the return trip, he rode in front of his brother in the saddle. That was the last hunting trip he ever took

6

with his brother, who soon moved on into the outside world, probably using money he had earned from selling his own furs. When Jonathan visited his birthplace many, many years later, he learned that coyotes had virtually replaced panthers in the area.

All of his sisters and brothers were attractive, and except for the two younger sisters, not one of them ever attended school, not even one day in their entire lives. Yet, incredibly, all were reasonably successful, and never could anyone tell they lacked any formal education. They had learned on their own. Good character is more important than a good education, he thought, though both are desirable.

He never knew a mother at all. His mother died giving birth to him. Yet he rarely thought about his being a motherless child. In later years, even now as he sat on the Watergate balcony, he wondered if his not having had a mother might have contributed to his being so detached, so isolated. Had he needed more of a sense of belonging a mother might have given him? Would he have been gregarious instead of aloof?

He recalled that his family had lived "high on the hog" in their cypress house in the woods. They had had a smokehouse full of meat, cattle and hogs that roamed freely through the woods, and several big hounds to help round up hogs, coons, and possums. There were quail, squirrels, fish, and wild berries. His sisters canned fruits and vegetables. Apples, turnips, and sugary sweet potatoes (real yams) were stored. About all that was needed in the way of "boughten" stuff was salt, sugar, flour, baking powder and soda, calico and gingham, needles and thread, and occasionally pants and shoes. Of course, his father bought guns and ammunition and nails and such. He used to cut his shotgun shells so that the whole charge would come out, because it often took a full load to kill a wild hog or a big panther. His sisters made clothes out of flour sacks. Sister Jennie was a great seamstress, and Sylvia was a wonderful cook. Cooking was done on a big iron range, and plenty of stove wood was always stacked up. He remembered pleasantly that he had helped carry stove wood into the house from the time he could walk.

Yes, he thought, as he looked at the Kennedy Center and the yacht in the moonlight, that was a wonderful way for a kid to grow up. But by his sixth birthday a great flood engulfed the whole Mississippi Valley from well above St. Louis down to the Gulf of

Mexico. Many people and hundreds of livestock were drowned. As the waters kept rising, his father was tempted to try to stay, but Jennie persuaded him to take the family and leave the area forever. When the waters and fish filled the lower level of the house, the family left in a big skiff, powered by an early edition of an outboard motor attached to the skiff's flat stern.

Sadly he recalled that the day before they left, he had failed to hear the distinctive tinkle of the bell on Rosie, his very own big Guernsey-type milk cow. The waters had covered her final refuge on high ground. Rosie had been the lead cow, and he knew that if she was gone, all the cows were gone. As their skiff chugged over the top of their orchard trees, he saw another skiff towing a couple of drowned people, a rope tied to their feet and hitched to the back of the boat.

His father knew exactly where to take the family: to the highest point of a nearby levee on a Black River tributary. When they got there, his father saw a paddle-wheel cottonboat steamer coming their way, headed north to much higher ground. Recognizing the boat, his father yelled loudly to the captain, "Captain Swayze! Oh, Captain Swayze!" His voice echoed across the waters from the woods. Captain Swayze pulled up and hauled everyone aboard the little steamer and lifted the skiff aboard, too.

Jonathan interrupted his musings and went to the living room bar. He returned to the balcony with another brandy.

Captain Swayze's boat was headed for Harrisonburg, the county seat of Catahoula Parish. The courthouse and the buildings immediately surrounding it were situated on a small hill, and that was where everyone in that area was being taken.

At the time his family arrived at the courthouse, Jonathan learned years later, there were about fifteen hundred flood refugees on the courthouse hilltop. About all he could remember was that he had enjoyed the ride on the cottonboat and the sound of the paddle wheel.

In those days, he had learned from his recent visit, Harrisonburg was an important crossroad town, with roads and railways leading west to Texas from Natchez and the Mississippi River traffic. One way or another, Jonathan's family got on a train heading west and north. Apparently his father had almost run out of money and had asked the conductor to take the family as far as his money allowed. Jonathan found out later that his father had sold his dearly loved

8

violin to get extra money for the train fare. Without any idea of the town or place, one morning the Barrons got off the train in Cotton Creek, Arkansas.

Fortunately, Cotton Creek was a friendly and prosperous sawmill town with a population of about twenty-five hundred. Jennie was feeling a little sick when they got off the train, and the telegraph operator, who tripled as station manager and porter, told them to go see Dr. Hastings, whose office was only four blocks away from the station. They found Dr. Hastings in his office at the back of Hastings' Drug Store. Fate had certainly directed them to a great man, a very competent and compassionate doctor. Not only did he give the entire family some medicine, but he told Johnathan's father that he could take his family to a three-room pine clapboard house, located behind the doctor's own house, on the edge of his pasture. He asked Jonathan's father if he had any money left, and the answer was, "Eighty cents."

Dr. Hastings asked him what kind of work he had been doing. Jonathan's father answered, "Hunting and trapping, but I'm all right with a hammer and saw and nails. And I sure do enjoy making a pretty garden. Down in Louisiana we had *some* garden." Dr. Hastings said, "Okay, fellow, you're in business. My lazy son doesn't like gardening or cutting the lawn and weeds. What's your first name, Mr. Barron?" "John," his father answered.

"Well, John," Dr. Hastings said in a very kindly voice, "let's you and I and your ailing daughter and young son go out back and get into my surrey and we'll drive to your house. Rent will cost you nothing. Just repair the house and keep it up. We'll drive very slowly, and the girls can walk along. Do you have any more baggage besides the two cases and sacks?" John Barron said he didn't. "Then put everything in the surrey, and let's go get you settled. Welcome to Cotton Creek. Here's five dollars advance payment on your keeping up my lawn and gardens." Dr. Hastings handed John Barron a five-dollar bill.

As he sat on the balcony, recalling Dr. Hastings, Jonathan began to cry. He had long ago left the church. He respected its raison d'etre but did not wish to be a part of religion as an institution. Yet, as he rose from his chair to stroll back and forth on the balcony, he could believe that fate, or whatever one may call the gathering of events, must have led him and his family to Cotton Creek. He remembered so well how various residents of the community had

9

brought them pieces of furniture and bedding. The hardware store gave them a used kitchen stove and a heating stove. To top it all, within a couple of days after they had settled in their little house, one of the deacons of the local Baptist church, where Dr. Hastings was a member, brought out a buggy-load of assorted foods and told Jonathan's father that the Blair Lumber Company's big company-owned store had asked the church to pick it up and bring it out.

Within a few weeks, the community of Cotton Creek had become Jonathan's surrogate mother. His sister, Jennie, soon married a young farmer, and his next two sisters went to work in foster homes. His two youngest sisters started to school, and Jonathan helped his father in his gardening jobs, except for the time he spent roaming the nearby fields and woods.

One day two local boys just a little older than Jonathan stopped him and asked why he didn't go to school. He asked them lots of questions, and the next day he showed up in the first grade. He soon became an "A" student in everything. All the townsfolk complimented John Barron on his son. Jonathan graduated from high school at sixteen, eight years from the time he had entered the first grade. As the school janitor through grade school and high school, he not only earned his way but had money left over to travel around the state, speaking in churches and schools as a young evangelist for high school YMCA's.

Jonathan loved learning, attended good colleges, and had many successes in business, but he never lost the unconscious identification with nature that he had acquired in his childhood. He had been unhampered by the cultural habits that usually imprint, restrict, and cover over the delicate sensibilities of the unconscious. It was this unfettered, innate ability to sense others that enabled Jonathan to be so strangely perceptive. It was this perception that became his ESP.

After a long while on the balcony, his brandy was exhausted, and so was he. Reviewing one's own history can be as tiring as it is revealing. He went inside, rinsed his brandy glass at the bar, and left a note on the breakfast table for Rene: "Honey, I went back home to Louisiana last night and stayed late. I should be up by eight. Didn't want to risk waking you, so I went to my own bed."

Rene woke up early as usual, around six o'clock. She showered and went into the kitchen to make some coffee. She and Jonathan preferred percolated coffee; maybe the percolating sound increased the pleasant anticipation of a fresh cup of coffee. She saw Jonathan's note, and as soon as the coffee was plugged in, she read it. She went to the apartment door and opened it, but the *Washington Post* hadn't arrived yet, so she sat down at the breakfast table and waited for the coffee, thinking about what Jonathan might have found on his memory trip to Louisiana. She thought that if ever a husband and wife had different childhood environments, she and Jonathan certainly did.

Rene was born in the densely populated Chicago Southside area. She and her parents lived in a one-bedroom-and-den apartment on the seventh floor of a nine-story apartment building near 67th and Halstead Streets. Several businesses were on the first floor of their building—a three-chair barber shop, a delicatessen, and a cleaning and pressing shop. A movie theater was in the same block. Almost as many people lived or worked in the one block where her apartment was situated as there were in all of Catahoula Parish.

She had no brothers or sisters until she was almost sixteen, when her red-haired baby brother was born. Her mother worked part-time as a telephone operator, and her father was a traveling salesman who was home only on the weekends. In that environment, Rene easily learned to make friends and to get along with all kinds of people. She loved listening to music on the radio and learned all the songs. She was at the movie theater every time the picture changed and went home afterward to dance around the apartment, doing the dances she had seen in the movie musicals and singing the songs.

By the time she was eight years old, the family had moved into a small brick bungalow in nearby Riverside, and she had begun a career as a child model, appearing mostly in magazine ads for a nationally famous soap. Her mother was her manager, and Rene was a fairly successful child model for a period of three or four years. It came naturally for her. She had self-discipline and followed the photographer's instructions precisely. Her childhood was a strange contrast to Jonathan's—at eight years of age he was just getting out of the woods and fields, while at eight Rene was modeling, singing, dancing, and going to the movies every week.

In later years when Rene thought about her adolescence, she remembered little about her high school career but a great deal

11

about the feelings she had experienced as her body moved through its changes from girlhood to womanhood. When Rene's breasts had begun to enlarge noticeably in her freshman year, her mother bought heavy, uncomfortable, flattening bras for her to wear. At the time, Rene didn't question her mother, nor did she protest. Only later did she realize how clearly those tight, binding bras had represented her mother's sexual fears and attitudes and how subtly they had contributed to her own feelings that it was wrong to be proud of her breasts, proud of her total body.

After high school she attended an excellent small college in southern Indiana, where she joined a sorority. In the easy camaraderie of the sorority house, Rene learned a great deal about the backgrounds, lives, and values of the girls she lived with. She was amazed by their knowledge of sex and in some cases, by their apparent lack of inhibition. So many of the girls seemed to be able just to accept their bodies and to experience sex as a natural, normal part of life. After two years in college, Rene decided to leave school and to take a job as a secretary in Chicago's downtown Loop area.

She was a good secretary, but one Sunday her mother saw an interesting help-wanted classified ad in the *Chicago Tribune.* Television programming was beginning to expand rapidly in Chicago, and the most active producer of daytime shows had advertised auditions for a young woman to co-emcee a two-hour daily talk show, then a pioneer move in television. Her mother called the producer, a woman, and arranged an audition for her daughter. Rene went along with her mother's idea and won the job over many competitors. Jonathan owned the show. She met him after the auditions, because he had to approve the person selected.

Her recollections ended when the coffee stopped percolating. After pouring herself a cup of coffee, she went to the apartment door again and found that the *Post* had arrived. Back in the kitchen she sat at the table, slowly drinking her coffee as she read the *Post.* By the time she had finished, she heard Jonathan's shower running. After almost thirty years together she didn't need to ask what he wanted for breakfast. She scrambled two eggs, toasted English muffins, and set the table for two. She poured a small glass of orange juice and also a glass of milk, sure that he would prefer his coffee after breakfast.

Still in her breakfast gown, she went into the dressing room and quickly arranged her hair. As usual, her husband would come to the breakfast table shaved and fully dressed, ready to meet the day.

As he walked into the kitchen Rene said brightly, "Good morning. I found your note. How was Louisiana?"

"Oh, it was all right," he replied, "but California wasn't."

"Did you visit California, too?" Rene asked with curiosity.

"Not in my balcony recollection, but later in a nightmarish dream. It seemed that I was walking along a beautiful boulevard bordered with tall palm trees—like in Beverly Hills. It was about dusk, and I saw a man and woman come out of one of the buildings, a hotel or apartment. They were dressed for a black-tie affair. The doorman waved his hand toward someone up the street, as he would for a taxi or limousine. Instead of a cab or car, a woman in blue jeans and red-checkered shirt rode up on an Arabian horse, stopped, pulled out a pistol, and yelled at the couple to dance, while she shot at their feet. After a few shots, she rode swiftly away. Two ambulances came up. The man was wheeled into one and the woman into the other. They didn't appear to be seriously injured, but each one had a towel wrapped around their feet."

"Well, the California scene must have been more exciting than Louisiana. What did *you* do all this time?" Rene almost demanded to know.

"I just stood there wondering why the doorman was laughing, and I awakened before I could ask him. Now, the storytelling is over. So, how are you this morning?"

"Until I heard your California dream, I was okay. What do you make of it?"

"Nothing, just as I make nothing of other dreams, except that I drank too much brandy before going to bed." He glanced at the kitchen clock. "Sorry I'm a little late, but it's only a quarter of eight. Looks like you've been up for a while. Do you go to the *Post* today?"

"No, I have no assignment this week. What about you? Are you going to the Ethics office today? Or need I ask?"

"Yes, I've got to, honey. At this stage it doesn't move much by itself. I hope we'll soon be staffed well enough for me to 'retire' from this everyday kind of participation."

"That day can't come too soon for me," Rene declared. Her husband's obsessive commitment to his Ethics group was overshadowing his commitment to her.

# 2

Saturday night came too soon for Johnathan, but he didn't complain. He would have preferred watching the news and the "Agronsky and Company" talk show. But when Rene came into his room to announce it was almost time for the guests to arrive, he was ready.

"Am I not always on time for cocktail parties? The sooner they start, the sooner they're over—sometimes." He adjusted his new silver-white bow tie with navy and gray polka dots and turned around for Rene's approval.

"You are indeed ready—and handsome. Look at that tie! Have you invited someone I don't know about?" she added.

"No. You told me to put on my cocktail greeting clothes, and I did."

"When you want to, Jonathan, you can be a fascinating, even charming, host. I really appreciate your getting in the mood to greet my friends tonight."

She turned to walk out of the room. "There's the phone now for the first guest. I think I'll tell Robert at the reception desk to send all the guests right up."

"My mathematical probability synthesis," Jonathan said with a touch of humor, "tells me the first guests will be two women and one is the vice-president of your group, who wishes to be next year's president."

They were both at their front door, and Jonathan went down the hall to meet the guests. As Rene waited, she could see him happily greeting two women as they got off the elevator. One was indeed the current vice-president of the chapter, Ethel Gordon.

Ethel was a tall, thin, unmarried brunette, editor of a large trade association's monthly magazine. She appeared to be in her early thirties. Susan Clark, just married, was brownish-blonde and quite attractive, probably twenty-seven or twenty-eight. She edited a scientific newsletter. Her husband, Ward, was in banking, whatever that is nowadays. He was delayed parking his car on the street instead of downstairs in the Watergate garage.

Since moving to Washington, the Barrons had given only small parties. Jonathan didn't like overcrowded gatherings of any kind, and Rene didn't like to entertain large groups because she truly enjoyed preparing her own hors d'oeuvres and dinners. She was a superb gourmet cook. When they were first married, Jonathan owned, among other TV shows, a daily one-hour cooking show that featured three French-Italian chefs. Rene watched the show every day to check the commercials. While doing so, she became fascinated with the creativity of gourmet cookery. For this party she had included two of her husband's favorite hors d'oeuvres— a caviar roulade crepe and a cheese and mushroom puff, which she served hot. She usually brought in a couple of college students to serve and to watch over the guests' needs.

In addition to being a cocktail party and dinner, this gathering had been scheduled as a business meeting, so eventually the directors got down to business. Jonathan excused himself from the group, explaining that he knew they could solve their own problems and that he would go to work on a task of his own—writing a speech he had reluctantly agreed to give to the Women's Advertising Club.

As he walked down the hall to his study, he thought that his problem was complicated because he wished to open his speech by recommending to the club that it disband. Considering that the advertising business has always welcomed women, he wondered why these club members wanted to be self-appointed segregationists. He also understood that many special-interest groups are kept active, not for the benefit of all the participants, but as power bases for one or two individuals to get personal publicity and influence. Historically, he concluded, individual personal ambitions often nurture the diversity that societies need to grow. But as he sat down at his desk, he asked himself why he felt compelled to be so analytical and didactic in whatever he did. In a way he envied speakers who just got up and told funny stories, glorified the past, ignored the present, and sketched an overly optimistic future.

The business session of the journalism meeting didn't last long, and Rene asked her husband to rejoin the guests who had accepted her invitation to stay for a brandy. Jonathan hated speech writing

—or any kind of writing—more than cocktail party conversation, so he didn't mind the interruption.

As soon as he rejoined the group and sat down for a leisurely glass of brandy, Ethel Gordon, the up-and-coming chapter vice-president, asked him, "How's your speech for the Women's Ad Club coming along?"

"Very slowly, Miss Gordon."

"You've given thought to lots of questions women may be asking," Ethel continued. "Will you tell me, Mr. Barron, why is it that strength in men is called aggressiveness in women?"

"May I call you Ethel?" Jonathan asked with a slight smile. "Did someone say you are aggressive?"

"Please do call me Ethel, but also do answer my question, because more than one man has called me aggressive.

"Well, congratulations, Ethel. Aggression implies that someone's territory is being invaded. In many aspects of our culture, males have enjoyed 'territorial rights' for so long they feel endangered by a wave of women crossing the 'old boy' frontiers. However, I think that the more secure males welcome a show of initiative and aggression by women as well as by men.

"What bothers people, women as well as men, is a display of assertiveness rather than aggression. Persons entering a new territory for the first time, whether that territory represents another community, county, culture, business or country club, should guard against being dogmatic and insistent. Such conduct is rightly called assertiveness and usually reflects fear and defensiveness on the part of the newcomer.

"But as our society matures, more and more women and minority groups are showing *aggressiveness* in moving forward and upward, a characteristic that indicates confidence and determination. However, women and minorities who are moving into new and higher levels of business and professions should avoid being *assertive,* because that often reveals an insecurity that indicates they feel out of place, possibly inferior. Assertiveness suggests that a person is saying 'I declare and I insist that I belong here'—but at the same time is questioning whether or not that's true. If you are on the outside looking in, being *aggressive* is often necessary and helpful. When you get inside, being *assertive* is usually harmful and often becomes abrasive."

Ethel started to reply, but hesitated. The others looked at her.

She seemed to be thinking about Johnathan's statement; then she said, "I believe I agree with you. I never thought about the practical implications of assertiveness, nor did I contrast such reactions with aggression. It does seem reasonable that since more males occupy 'territories' where women want to be, should be, and will be," she added emphatically, "as newcomers, women might well recognize the vestigial network of pathways and not try to jump the fences and arouse the guard dogs of habit." She laughed. "How's that, Jonathan, for a professorial response?"

"Not bad, Ethel. You're almost as pedagogical as I am. There are still lots of guard dogs, in different sizes and places. For example, young executives, especially young women—MBAs, lawyers, accountants, and doctors are often much better qualified than some of their older associates, male or female. But the newcomers need to be understanding and tolerant of those who have come before them. These older professionals can read the signs of the future. The younger folks should be respectful, courteous, and cooperative. Then those already inside will help and not resist the ambitious newcomers. In today's super high-tech, increasingly complex service economy, men and women, old and young, must learn to accept that the key words to success are cooperation and sharing, practicing the Golden Rule."

Jonathan stood up and asked, "My God, how did we ever get into this press-interview type of discussion? You guys are journalists, but I'm not a senator up for reelection."

"But you still give funny answers, Jonathan," Ed Harkness spoke up from outside the square circle of sofas. The smooth-faced, heavy-set young man had been aggressive enough to get himself a scotch and soda. "I'm a staffer for the Senate Foreign Relations Committee. Yesterday, after a very heated, partisan committee meeting, one of the senators casually asked me, if I could change one thing in the world, what would it be? I told him, my job for his. He said one more day like that one and we would have a deal."

Everyone laughed.

"But seriously," Ed began again, "how would *you* answer that question, Johnathan?"

"Ed, I'll bet you get to the Senate without having to replace your senator friend." Then Johnathan said pensively, "You ask, if I could change one thing in the world, what would it be? Well, as an old actor used to say, considering mankind's desire to survive and assuming that one good thing begets another, let the world destroy all weapons that can kill more than one person at a time."

"That's a good answer, but it doesn't sound like the old actor I think you had in mind." Ed laughed and finished off his scotch.

Ward Clark, Susan's husband, had been walking around the living room listening to the conversation. He stood behind the sofa where Susan was sitting and said to the group, "Before we end this discussion, I'd like to ask Johnathan what he thinks makes a person successful."

Rene jokingly warned Ward, "You don't know what you're letting yourself in for when you ask Johnathan such an open-ended question."

"Ward, my wife warned you, but I'll try out an observation or two, if the others will blame you for asking the question and not me for trying to answer it.

"Success and happiness may be harder to define than to achieve, because they don't necessarily go together. The prime obligation of a man or a woman is to strive for a high measure of his or her human potential. As a single goal, or as a primary goal in life, materialism is destructive of our most meaningful and cherished human values. What I'm saying is, love of things can destroy love of others. When one puts money ahead of everything else, then everything else doesn't mean a lot. As a secondary goal, however, materialism can be enormously beneficial to the individual and to society. You need a certain amount of material success to have the leisure, education, and opportunity to develop a high degree of your human potential."

Jonathan continued to talk as he walked over to the floor-to-ceiling windows facing the Kennedy Center. "You know, Ward, you can make physical sacrifices, get ulcers, and take risks that endanger health and life in order to make more and more money. But once you take spiritual risks, commonly called 'selling your soul,' for money, even if you are very successful financially and professionally, you will fail as a human being.

"As we look around us, as we look at television talk shows, so many men and women we call successful, who possess the usually required attributes of money, fame, and high peer status, may be very much alive and yet forever dead in terms of achieving their human potential."

18

Sitting back down again on the sofa he added, "But you only asked what makes a person successful. Let me say what I should have said in the beginning—it takes luck, often called fate, and hard work, self-discipline, dogged perseverance, courage, and a firm belief that life, your life, has a purpose. To all of these blessings, add compassion and the practice of the Golden rule—the oldest of all formulas for success. And sometimes it helps to have someone to act as a mentor, someone who has traveled the road ahead of you, to guide you, to warn you about the detours.

Jonathan paused, "Well, now, I've justified Rene's warning. She invited me to join you in relaxing, and I've kept you from it. It's hard to relax and think, too." Noticing a continuing silence from the group, Jonathan added, "But if we don't think, how can we know when we're relaxing?

"So much for this surfeit of seriousness. To hell with thinking! Let's check the end of the eleven o'clock news to get the latest in sports."

The group laughed and began to talk with one another. A few drifted down the hall to the bathrooms. Within a few minutes the chapter president, Marilyn Escobar, a strong prototype of the efficient executive, who had worked her way up to owning her own public relations firm, spoke up for the group.

"Rene, you've been the perfect hostess, in addition to being the best chef we've been around for long while. Next year we hope you'll let us meet here again. We'll invite your husband to be an ex-officio member."

Turning to Jonathan she added, "I appreciated your comments. They were very timely for me." Then Marilyn led the way to the entrance foyer. Everyone was talking happily and saying goodnight.

When all the guests were gone and the door was closed, Jonathan and Rene returned to the living room and sat near one another on the sofa. They were quiet for a while. "Darling, wouldn't it be nice if we were once again in our Illinois farm home," Jonathan asked, "sitting on that curved brown sofa in front of our fireplace? Even in May we once had a little snow. Remember?"

"Whatever made you think of that? Yes, I remember that fireplace. I loved the beige marble that framed it. There was plenty of room on the long mantel to hang three Christmas stockings for the children and two for us. But I liked our big fireplace in North

Carolina even better. When the light flickered up to the cedar beams of the ceiling, it seemed to join the warmth of the wood. That was a great house."

Jonathan was quiet for a while and then said apologetically, "I'm sorry about my wet-blanket seriousness tonight. But your guests did seem to enjoy the food and drinks—and you. You looked very pretty. You're always such a beautiful and joyful hostess. I wish that I could be relaxed and light-spirited like you are. Nowadays, I relate more to abstractions than to people. In fact, I'm duller than dishwater.

"I should have passed over the questions quickly and jokingly. But I can't do that. I feel a compulsion to answer a serious question seriously. I know better. For pleasant conversation, I guess one should try to avoid serious replies to serious questions."

"No, no, Honey." Rene said earnestly. "Everyone wanted you to speak your mind. They expected you to be as you are, and I think they all appreciated your comments, just as Marilyn said she did."

Her voice became more gentle. "I feel sorry for you, not for those who hear you. I know how tense you've been. Really, it's been that way ever since you quit using your creativity and dynamism to sell products for your advertising agency clients and to sell real estate. You did so enjoy all that, especially the farmland sales. For such a strong and active man, I guess you retired from business too soon. In retiring to your ethics work, you retired from action to abstraction.

"Your efforts to sell honesty and ethics have been more successful, though, than you could reasonably have hoped. But you see only the little that has been done, in contrast to the urgent need. You don't seem to get any satisfaction out of what you've accomplished. Darling, it sounds selfish, but I wish that your commitment to improve ethics in America hadn't absorbed you so completely."

She realized that she had said enough, that she should bring her husband around to her, if not to her diverging world. With a definite change in her tone of voice she jumped up and said, "Let's have music and champagne. Tomorrow is Sunday, sleep-in time. I'll change clothes. You get the champagne?" On her way out she turned "Nadia's Theme" on the stereo.

Earlier, Jonathan had put a bottle of champagne on ice and two long-stemmed champagne glasses in the refrigerator. He hastened to his room to put on the blue and burgundy velour robe Rene had made for him. It was a symbolic mood modifier. He returned, placed the glasses on the long coffee table in front of the sofa, opened the champagne, and had it ready to pour when Rene came back.

She was wearing a gold satin wrap-around robe with a Japanese-style sash for a belt. Jonathan immediately poured the champagne, carefully handing a full glass to Rene. As they touched glasses, he said, "May the future protect the joys of our past."

"I like that wish," she said. "I'll make an addition. Whatever our futures, wherever we are, may there be peace and love for each of us."

They listened to the music. In between sips of champagne they kissed, more fervently as their thoughts deepened, not from the champagne itself, but from a sense of their being separated by a long, long journey.

"That Marilyn Escobar, a fine woman," Jonathan said rather absentmindedly.

"Yes, are you thinking of her hope that the group would meet here again next year?" Rene thought she detected a little catch in his voice.

"Yes, I was," he said firmly, "but no more. Let's move our glasses to the other end of the table. I want to hold you. That robe is falling open delightfully." Then he kissed and embraced her, firmly and exploringly.

She pulled gently away. "I want to come up for air and more champagne. I'll set the music again. Maybe I should dance for you," she said as she moved gracefully around the room.

"God," Jonathan said to himself, "this woman needs to live her own life, a fuller life, her own way—with a more kindred soul."

He danced a circle or two with her, then picked her up in his arms and carried her to the sofa for the champagne she had requested. As Rene settled back on the sofa she reached for him. For a few seconds, he still possessed rational thoughts. He knew that no matter how much their guests had admired her spontaneous hospitality, her lively conversations, and her creative cookery, very few could have imagined how otherwise wonderfully creative Rene Barron could be.

21

# 3

It was almost ten o'clock when Rene awakened. She lay quietly for a few minutes, knowing that if she got out of bed, her husband would wake up. After a while she guessed he might already be awake, simply keeping his eyes closed. She leaned over him and asked, "Are you awake?"

Since she slept nude and was still propped up on her elbow, leaning over closely, Jonathan proved he was quite awake by kissing the breast nearest his mouth. She paid no attention.

"Do you know what time it is?" She seemed to feel guilty for waking up so much later than usual.

"No, but I think it's Sunday," he remarked sleepily, happy that he felt no sense of time, a rare mood for him.

"It's ten o'clock already!" she exclaimed.

After a few moments of thought Jonathan asked, "Why do you wear your watch to bed, Honey?"

"I like to."

"But, Darling, you can't tell the time when you are asleep."

"No, but when I wake up, I know what time it is." She lay back down.

"Rene, if you keep thinking so deeply, you'll really wake up. So, be quiet. Go back to sleep—if you're not already asleep again." He noticed that her eyes were closed. He was fully awake.

"I'll get up and fix us a Sunday brunch—bacon, scrambled eggs rosemary, and pancakes with real Vermont maple syrup, the kind we bought in Canada. I'll serve you fresh orange juice in bed. It'll be so fresh, you'll smell the orange blossoms and wake up. Okay?"

Jonathan took his shower, hot, then cold, and shampooed his head to wake up the inside of it as much as to cleanse the outside. Then, to confirm that the world was still going around he went to the hall door to pick up the paper. Now he knew it was Sunday. It took two hands to pick up the thick *Post*. The headline for June 27 revealed no new impending disaster, just follow-up reports on the usual ones.

With that, he turned his attention to the task at hand, preparing breakfast. When everything was almost ready, he took a glass of cold, freshly squeezed orange juice to Rene and announced, "Breakfast awaits my lady's convenience."

He put the juice glass on the nightstand, where he knew she would find it before she headed for the shower. Seeing her eyes open, he went back into the kitchen to glance at the sports section. Soon Rene came breezing in with her pretty pool robe on. She looked lovely. Her robe was aquamarine, slightly fitted with a coral sash, and it was more attractive than many evening dresses. Jonathan had selected it for her because he was tired of looking at all the sloppy beach robes women usually wore to the pool. It was the kind of special thing Rene was too practical to bother to get for herself and that he so enjoyed buying for her.

After breakfast they settled down with the *Post.* Jonathan thought to himself, "One of the really happy hours of the week is this peaceful period following Sunday brunch when we sit comfortably, hot coffee within easy reach, and read the Sunday paper." Then a somewhat painful thought occurred to him: "I will miss this."

As usual, Rene included the funny papers in her reading, and Jonathan gave a careful reading to the sports section. He thought about the similarity between comics and sports—aside from the fact that both occupied a lot of print space. They were both changing in their basic thrust. Comics were becoming more political, and sports more financial. To Jonathan, the philosophy dispensed by some of the cartoon characters was of a much higher order than that expressed by some of the owners, managers, coaches, and millionaire ballplayers.

However relaxing the Sunday reading session, Rene and Jonathan soon became a little restless—waiting and hoping for a phone call from one or all of their three children. To reach out and touch any of their children, young adults out on their own, meant a phone visit to New York or Los Angeles.

For someone outside the family, a description of the Barron children would seem rather idealistic, but the success of their lives, so far, was very real. All three were quick learners; all had graduated from college at only eighteen or nineteen years of age.

Ellen, at twenty-nine, was the Barrons' oldest child. She had moved through college and law school easily and rapidly, graduating from Wellesley and Harvard Law School. By age twenty-two she was a trial lawyer with a prestigious Chicago law firm and by twenty-five, the wife of Anson Folsom, a fellow lawyer she had come to know when they worked together on two difficult cases. Anson was a graduate of UCLA and Stanford University Law School. And it didn't take him long to persuade his new wife that they should live in southern California. After moving to Los Angeles, Ellen joined a top law firm, and Anson joined the legal staff of a major California corporation. They were living in their first home now in Santa Monica and were looking forward to the arrival of their first child.

Bruce, the Barrons' second child, was a musician—he played the piano and string instruments and was a composer. He was also a writer, a linguist, an amateur physicist, and most of all an able young executive. By age nineteen he had finished college and was a creative supervisor in one of Chicago's largest ad agencies. Now, at twenty-seven, he was in New York as the youngest creative supervisor in one of the world's largest advertising agencies. In addition to all his professional talents, Bruce was a very sensitive and compassionate person.

Susan, the Barrons' youngest child, had majored in journalism, graduating from Carolina State University in North Carolina. After college she, like Bruce, went to Chicago to work in advertising. But since she didn't immediately find a job as an agency copywriter, she went to work for one of the large graphic arts firms. In the course of her four years in graphic arts, she supervised the production of so many corporate and bank financial statements that she decided to switch her career to finance. After checking with advisers and deans at the University of Chicago, Sanford, Berkeley, and Northwestern, Susan chose New York University as the place to get her MBA in finance. Now, at almost twenty-four, she was finishing up her master's program at NYU.

On this particular Sunday, it was Susan who phoned home first. She shared all her school news—courses in finance, computers, mathematical theory, investment analysis, statistics, and so on. She was making good grades, but she said there were some very smart students in her classes and she really had to study hard. She said that the cost of books and supplies was increasingly high, adding that she would need money within a few days for summer-session tuition and for rent. The kind of schooling she was getting was very high-priced.

After Susan's call, Rene walked out on the balcony and when she came back in reported it was so nice outside she thought she would go down to the pool for a while.

"What if Ellen calls?" Jonathan inquired. "Maybe we should go ahead and call her now."

"That's a good idea, because I certainly do want to talk with her. I want to know how her pregnancy is coming along. It's two-thirty now, so that makes it eleven-thirty in Santa Monica. She should be up and around, maybe out by their pool. I'll call her." Rene was sharing with Ellen the happy anticipation of the baby.

Ellen answered the phone quickly and said that she had been about to call them. Her doctor thought that she might have a premature birth, but he didn't think that she and her family should be overly concerned at this time. Ellen discussed the possibility of her mother's coming out for a visit, but before making definite plans, she wanted to talk with her doctor again. Her next appointment was Tuesday. Jonathan, not wishing to indicate to Ellen any special concern, mentioned during their conversation that a trip to California might be good for her mother.

As he hung up the phone, he recalled that the first week in June of the previous year, he had casually predicted that Ellen would have her first child about fifteen months later. That would be the first week of September of this year. He remembered that Ellen had thought her father was carrying his crystal ball act too far when it came to telling when her first baby would be born—long before it was even conceived.

After talking with Ellen, Rene turned to her husband and asked, "Didn't you say you were going to Chicago tomorrow for an Ethics Group board meeting Tuesday and that you'd stay over a couple of days to close the sale of our last piece of farm land?"

"Yes, what's on your mind? Want to go with me?"

"No, but since I don't have any assignment at the *Post* for at least ten days, I think I'll fly to Los Angeles tomorrow and visit with Ellen. If it develops that her doctor thinks she should have someone stay with her until the baby arrives, I'll go back."

"I think that's a good idea," Jonathan quickly agreed. "Why don't you go on down to the pool, and I'll take my beach chair out on the balcony."

Rene knew there was no need to ask her husband to join her, because he didn't care much about sitting around a fancy pool with an assortment of people too old or too young. He wasn't much of a swimmer, anyway.

But Jonathan had another reason or two for not going to the pool with Rene. On more than one occasion, he had observed that when a couple went to the pool and had chairs alongside one another, others at the pool were not inclined to break into their pair. Since Rene enjoyed meeting people, as well as sunning and swimming, he thought she would have more fun going down alone. Then many of her friends would ask her to join them, or would stop by to visit with her.

He took his beach chair and went out onto the balcony, but he didn't attempt to read. He was thinking about Rene's trip to Los Angeles.

For several years, it had seemed increasingly evident that his friends and his thoughts and Rene's friends and her thoughts were coming from two different worlds. While they had discussed the differences in the kinds of friends and interests each found satisfying, discussion had not solved the problem.

He thought that now might be a good time, if ever there was a good time, for the two of them to begin living separate lives, lives apart. All the children were aware of the divergent interests of their parents. Four or five years earlier, before Susan had graduated from Carolina State University, a rumor had spread through Church City that Rene and Jonathan Barron were going to be divorced. It seemed that someone had heard Susan mention it.

Rene and Jonathan talked with Susan and asked if she had said anything that could have been misinterpreted to mean that her parents were getting a divorce. Susan said, "You know, folks, that's possible. At the last big cocktail party you gave for some of the university people, I heard a professor telling another professor and his wife that you two were so different you couldn't possibly stay married. And I told my roommate, who had classes with both professors, what I had heard them say. Maybe my roommate figured you were getting a divorce because I admit that I agreed somewhat with the professor's observations. For example, it hasn't been unusual for Dad to get bored at a country club dance and go home and read while you, Mom, stayed through the last dance."

Jonathan remembered that he and Rene had smiled and told Susan that they understood what had happened, that no harm had been done, and that many people might wonder how two such different personalities could long find enough in common to remain together.

It was a strange dilemma of love and ethics. Jonathan believed that most people would feel that love and love alone must rule, as an old song suggested. Is love a part of ethics, or is ethics a part of love? He believed that love is a part of ethics—indeed, the foundation of ethics, that "Love thy neighbor as thyself" and the Golden Rule are both ethical imperatives. Looking at the totality of life, to love is to survive.

For more than twenty years their married life had been full and mutually rewarding. Their marriage had worked phenomenally well. Then Jonathan had retired from business to devote his time to the task of ethics, to trying to help keep the country honest enough to function efficiently and be manageable as a free society. At the same time, the children had grown up and had gone their separate ways. So it was little wonder that Rene might want to go out and be on her own—maybe have "her turn" as head of the household. Jonathan reflected that many able women seemed to feel this way as their husbands, children, and home patterns changed, presenting a situation in which both husband and wife must try to be objective and considerate of what is, as well as of what might be. It wasn't just Rene who was changing, but all of society.

He cared for Rene very much indeed. He had encouraged her to keep learning, to move out into business and politics. In Illinois, when she had decided not to run for the college board of trustees, saying that the men on the board were more able than she, it was he who had told her that she was smarter than any of them. She was elected and had proved to be the dominant leader of the board. In North Carolina, when she was offered an excellent position at Carolina State University, he had told her to take the job that very day, even though the offer had come just as they were moving into their big new home. She had always been happy that he had insisted she go ahead and take the job. She had loved it.

And always she had more than justified his confidence in her. She succeeded at every task. She was not only a good businesswoman, journalist, and public official, but she was also a good mother and a challenging wife. As she grew and grew professionally, she had become even prettier and sexier.

Notwithstanding all the wonders of his wife, Jonathan believed they should separate. Rene was twenty-three years younger than he; realistically, according to life expectancy statistics, she would outlive him by at least twenty to thirty years. He believed she should be prepared for that eventuality. Further, although Rene had told him she would stay with him forever if he wished, he knew that after he was long gone, she would wonder what her life would have been, had she lived on her own sooner. True, she had traveled to public relations and academic conventions and seminars. However, Jonathan thought she should be free to be what she could be. He knew he would miss her greatly, but he felt that her life fulfillment was a better choice than for both of them to level off and accept less. Nor did he believe Rene would ever be proud to see him adjust to the academic and party-going crowd. He hated to act nice to everyone when he didn't think he should. And for Rene's part, he didn't want her to live a life of "what if's."

Jonathan became very fidgety, restless. He knew he had always been a strangely objective person. He wasn't that way on purpose. He had just grown up as an isolate, a very detached person. Paradoxically, his natural detachment and objectivity enabled him to identify with one he cared for, especially with one he loved. He would act on the basis of what he thought best for Rene and perhaps, secondarily, for himself, especially his work. In thinking about this dilemma, he became aware that in reality there are actually very few ethical dilemmas for anyone. One or the other party—or both—usually knows what the ethical decision should be. The problem is having the strength and courage to do what you believe is the right thing when you doubt that anyone will believe you did the right thing for the right reason.

But all these thoughts weren't Jonathan's alone. Just recently in their apartment, he had sensed Rene's thoughts. He had asked her if she was sitting there thinking that here she was, almost fifty years old, with three kids who had lived all over half the world on their own, yet she had never lived alone anywhere. She had replied, "That's exactly what I was thinking. I was about to rent an apartment just before we married. I wonder if I would have liked that?" She was silent for a while, then spoke out dramatically, "But you know, if you wanted me to give up all my outside work and stay home and be your mistress, I'd do it."

He had quickly replied, "You're a wonderful mistress now because you have kept yourself growing and learning and living a challenging professional life. If you were merely a beautiful woman whose primary task was to be a good mistress for her husband, you would soon cease to be so attractive; you'd wither and die—spiritually and mentally, like a rosebush that hasn't been properly watered and nurtured. No, you're so much just as you are—beautiful, intelligent, capable and strong. And incidentally, because you are all of these, you can sexually glorify the ego of an intelligent man. Maybe other women are almost as good as you are now, though I doubt that any are better, but what turns a man on is to have such an able and beautiful woman honor him with her playful kisses— particularly where he doesn't expect them."

Jonathan was getting more restless at this stage of his thoughts, and he jumped up and welcomed Rene back from the pool as though she had just arrived from Rome.

"It was wonderful at the pool today. Some of our most prominent Watergate residents showed up, including a couple of senators and their wives. I enjoyed our discussions, and I think you would have, too." Then, seeing the strained look on his face, she asked, "What have you been doing—worrying about you and me?"

"Exactly. I've been trying to find my way out of the labyrinth. But I know what'll help now. Even my doctors say one or two martinis a day won't hurt and may help. I'll fix some while you take your shower. Then let's talk about Los Angeles and you and Ellen."

Rene said teasingly as she went off to shower and change, "I know something else that helps you, but we'll do something about that later."

When Rene returned, she was dressed in her beige satin cocktail lounging robe that connected only at the waist. Jonathan brought in the cocktails and some cheeses and chips.

"What have you been thinking about?" she asked as soon as they were seated in the living room.

"I've been thinking about railroad tracks," he replied.

"Railroad tracks? Whatever for?" Rene's surprise was genuine, but so was the tinge of uneasiness that she was feeling.

"When I was a boy, down in Cotton Creek, Arkansas, I often stood outside the train depot on the railroad track, looking for miles up the track, northeast toward Little Rock. The tracks

29

seemed to come together in the distance, but my friend, the telegraph operator assured me that those tracks were strictly parallel to one another and would never merge."

"It's a wonder you didn't get run over by a train," Rene said absentmindedly.

"Oh, no," he replied. "There were only two trains a day that passed through, a slow one that stopped for passengers and a fast one, old Number Seven, the mail train that stopped for nothing."

As he looked at her glass he asked, "Is your drink okay, honey?"

"Yes, it's very good. You'd think that after twenty-five or thirty years of marriage I'd be able to make as good a martini as you do, but mine never seem so smooth."

"Thanks. It's compliments like that that have kept me making martinis for you for so long.

"But let's get back to the depot in Cotton Creek. There were freight trains that came rumbling and shaking through town, but we didn't count them because they didn't think we counted for anything. I remember best the mail train, old Number Seven. I used to get up early and go down and wait for it. Number Seven stopped for no one between Little Rock and Texarkana. It carried a special postman who used a mail crane to hook on a new bag of mail and hook off mail for Cotton Creek. The train didn't even slow down. I was there every day to pick up the *Arkansas Gazette,* which they kicked off in a well-tied bundle. I checked and counted the papers. They always seemed to survive, and I would get on my bicycle and rush delivery, because the *Arkansas Gazette* subscribers were Cotton Creek's leading citizens. You know, I had an important responsibility. All those people waited for me to deliver their papers. Come to think of it, my always delivering the Gazette on time must have helped to build my reputation in Cotton Creek."

Rene was looking out the window.

"Is this train of conversation too slow arriving for you?"

"No, no," she assured him. "It's good background for my martini. But what are you arriving at, Jonathan?"

"I've been thinking how far into the distance those rails seemed to go without ever coming together. We have both hoped that our lives could come together; but maybe we knew if they did we would have a train wreck."

"Yes," she said, "I see what's been in your mind. You love me,

30

and I love you, but we're running on separate tracks—in fact, we've finally reached a junction point."

"I was thinking," Jonathan said slowly, "that while you're in Los Angeles you might look at rental apartments. You may need one from month to month in case things don't go well with Ellen. At least, check out a sample of what's available. Then while there you might get a feel of the job market, especially at the universities and newspapers where your experience would count."

"You mean," Rene said quickly, "where my experience would offset the disadvantage of my being fifty when they want someone twenty-five or thirty? But if I went to Los Angeles and found a nice apartment and a good job, what would you do?"

"Well, I've already notified the directors that I wish to resign as president of the Ethics Group, although I may continue on the board if they want me to. Monday, I'll go to Chicago for the meeting. I'll ask them to make my resignation effective immediately, because I've already discussed this with George Gregson, the executive director. Of course, I'll remain available to him, should he wish to consult with me from time to time."

"That's a step I wish you'd taken five years ago. Your dedication to the ethics program is an obsession. No wife can fight a mistress who is an abstract, consuming obsession."

"Rene, you're very prescient. Remember our first board meeting when the small group of original directors asked you if you favored my becoming the full-time unpaid president of the Ethics Group? You said you wouldn't object if I wished to do so, but you doubted if I could find the support of the business community that I would need. They seemed to know you were right. But I had to try."

"Why did you have to try, honey? Why so hard?"

"After retiring from several businesses, I didn't wish to go into any other business. Yet, I had to do something meaningful, or staying alive might not have had much appeal for me. I anticipated the different set of problems that dishonesty, corruption, and lack of loyalty and responsibility would bring into our increasingly dominant service and technical economy. Each day's events have confirmed the urgency of our task. Of course, the directors had the challenge of getting someone who could afford to work for nothing and provide the original financing, who had management and marketing skills and was also stupid enough to undertake the task. That last qualification left only me to do it."

He smiled at Rene, but he knew he was being honest with himself and with her. Then he asked quietly, "Honey, may I have a little more watery martini? I want to drink to our future, which for you I hope will bring nothing but blessings. As for me—in this case I'm not so stupid that I don't realize that without you, there can be no great number of blessings for me."

"Oh, let's wait and see. Right now, I'm ready for lots of things, including less watery martinis for us both."

As she left to get new ice and new glasses, Jonathan wondered if anyone could possibly understand why a man who cared so much for a woman would give her up voluntarily for what he, more than she, perceived to be her own happier future. The answer seemed to lie in understanding that a mature, intelligent, capable woman, no less than a man, would at some point in her life want the experience of living on her own, making her own day-by-day decisions. Jonathan deeply regretted that Rene had missed out on that and other experiences in her younger days.

Rene returned with the fresh drinks, gave Jonathan his, and told him she would be back in a minute. "I'd better make my plane reservation and call Ellen and tell her I'll be there tomorrow."

"Great," Jonathan said, "but do hurry back."

## 4

On Monday morning Jonathan took Rene to Dulles Airport to catch an eleven o'clock flight to Los Angeles. Nothing was said about the real purpose of the visit. Perhaps both were thinking what a joyous occasion the birth of their first grandchild should be for them, and yet how their personal lives were overshadowing the impending event. From Dulles he drove to Washington National Airport, parked his car in the long-term lot, caught the shuttle bus to the terminal, and arrived just in time to catch a luncheon flight to Chicago's O'Hare Airport.

As he was walking down the boarding ramp he saw an old friend, Fred Osborne, entering the plane ahead of him. Fred was a well-known Washington vice-president of one of the world's largest banks. He and Jonathan had been friends for years, since the days they were in Chicago together.

While Jonathan tended to avoid large gatherings of people, he did enjoy one-on-one conversations with intelligent friends. He hoped Fred wouldn't be riding in the first-class section, as he himself always rode coach, and he looked forward to visiting with Fred during the flight.

As he passed through the first-class section, he was pleased to see that Fred had gone on into the coach area and was putting his coat in the overhead rack. Jonathan nudged him in the back and greeted him.

"Did some of your bank's Third and Fourth World countries default on their loans, making it necessary for even an important vice-president to ride coach?"

"Why, hello, Jonathan." Fred was pleasantly surprised. "No, I often ride coach, unless I have a lot of work to do en route." Fred inched his way out of the aisle and into his seat. "Anyway, this is a vacation trip, and I couldn't possibly justify charging the plane ticket to the bank although, come to think of it, I *am* making a speech for them tonight at a Chicago financial editors' dinner."

Then he smiled. "I've talked ethics with you for so many years, I decide all borderline cases totally in favor of ethics." He gestured to Jonathan. "Here, take this seat. The flight doesn't seem too crowded."

Jonathan looked at his boarding pass and then at Fred's row number. "I'm a row or two behind you. Just let me check with the flight attendant to make sure I can switch."

The flight attendant was very obliging and said there would be no problem. As Jonathan sat down, he resumed his conversation with Fred.

"So you're going on vacation. To your usual fishing spot in northern Minnesota?"

"That's right. Dina and our youngest son, Bret, are driving out to Chicago. We'll spend a couple of days at my parents' home and then go on to Minnesota. You know, Bret now has his driver's license. He welcomed the chance to drive out from Washington with his mother. I took the plane so I could speak at this dinner tonight."

"What are your older boys doing this summer?"

"Well, both are busy. Larry's interning at the Supreme Court. He was lucky to be selected. He's really happy about it. And Fred junior is working in a law firm for the summer. He'll be getting his law degree from the University of Virginia next spring. So only Bret has time to vacation with us this year."

As Fred hooked his seat belt, he added rather wistfully, "The total family life of the past has to yield to the less total family life of the present as the children go out on their own."

"I know all too well what you mean," Jonathan responded.

"What takes you to Chicago? And how's Rene?" Fred inquired.

Jonathan was hooking his seat belt and didn't look up.

"Oh, I just put Rene on a plane out of Dulles to Los Angeles. She's on her way to visit Ellen, our oldest. I'm going to Chicago for an Ethics Inquiry Group board meeting tomorrow. Tonight I'll have dinner with Ken Rush, emcee of Chicago's top-rated TV show for children. When you lived in Chicago, your kids were probably regular fans of Rush and his Gargoyle puppet. I know mine were."

"Jonathan, my kids, especially the two older ones, loved that show. Not only did they watch Ken and Gargoyle, but Dina and I frequently shared the show with them. Didn't you start the show years and years ago, when you pioneered so many television shows in Chicago?"

"Yes, I owned the show by contract with Ken Rush. The program was his creation. Rush has always been a man of such high principles. I believe he does more to help and to inspire children toward better values than some parents do."

The plane was soon up and away. The sun was shining, and the sky was clear except for a few white, puffy clouds. It was a beautiful day.

Fred leaned back in his seat and closed his eyes for a minute. Then he asked, "What's new with the Ethics Group? I've kept up with it somewhat, through your speeches and writings, and also through our bank. You know, we've become a regular contributor to the group."

"Yes, I know, and I personally appreciate your support." Jonathan paused. "The Ethics program is developing slowly, but satisfactorily. The young man I brought in five years ago as executive director is proving to be one of the most competent and pragmatic ethicists in the country. At the last director's meeting, I advised them that I wished to resign, effective the date of tomorrow's meeting. In cooperation with one of the best executive placement firms and through our directors, we've been searching for a retired, successful businessman or woman who would be willing to do as I've done the past few years—work full time at no salary. Strangely, in this land that has benefited so many with so much, men and women with millions of dollars they'll never use are unwilling to work at no salary—not even in an effort to keep this country honest enough to stay free."

He frowned and continued. "Incredibly, so many who shout for free enterprise do not seem to be able to understand that without strong ethical underpinnings, a free market economy cannot function efficiently. Too few business leaders seem to fully realize this."

Fred leaned forward in his seat. "Jonathan, let's face it, ethics frightens a lot of people. But times are changing. The problem is that perhaps they're changing too slowly." He continued encouragingly, "I know that our bank is very actively upgrading its code of ethics and is instituting a continuing series of ethics seminars at all levels of management. You should feel that your efforts have had considerable effect. The Ethics Group has been an important factor in stimulating many corporations to develop similar programs in ethics." "Of course," he added understandingly, "I know you're concerned that business and the professions may not be moving fast enough in this direction."

Jonathan shifted in his seat.

"I believe yours was the first big bank to recognize that fostering ethics might be as important as fostering art. Much of corporate America seems to be gung-ho for the opera and the arts. Interestingly, great art often derives from poverty and persecution, whereas great freedom can only derive from ethics. What I mean is that great art can result from the compulsion to express oneself in the absence of freedom."

Fred quickly replied with a smile, "People can understand art a hell of a lot easier than they can understand you." Then he added seriously, "Keep in mind that many corporate executives have come into their companies ready to market their MBA degrees to the highest bidder. It's doubtful that one out of ten graduates of business schools has had a course in ethics, except, possibly, as a sideline to some other course. Many business leaders have been trained to revere the concept of management by objective. When that concept is put into operation, the results are often that sales and profit targets are set so high that ethical values have to be sacrificed in order to meet short-term goals. And those values that fall by the wayside include even those declared in a company's own code of ethics. Jonathan, what do you say to corporate chief executive officers who wish to satisfy both the goals of business and the goals of ethics?"

"Well, Fred, I believe that the ultimate goal of ethics is the moral and spiritual perfection of individuals. The ultimate goal of business is to provide the opportunity and the means for individuals to achieve their ethical goals. History suggests that achieving ethical goals prepares the way for more business and more profits."

After a pause Jonathan began again. "I do not believe the ardent free-enterpriser understands the political and social significance of making profits. He seems to understand only his short-term personal benefits. Profit in a social system is an activating force without the *sanction of death.* In essence, where there is no profit there is no freedom."

Fred didn't reply. Instead, he reached for a magazine in the seat pocket in front of him. Jonathan figured he had said enough about ethics, so as Fred was leafing through the magazine, he leaned over and said, "From the way the couple in front of us just turned around and looked at me, I believe they think we've been talking about AIDS instead of ethics."

Fred laughed. "Jonathan, a lot of people feel as uncomfortable talking about ethics as they do AIDS. And I'll bet we find a cure for AIDS before we find a cure for dishonesty."

"I think we'll find a cure for AIDs if we put the money and effort into the task," Jonathan replied, "but I don't believe we'll ever eradicate dishonesty. However, that doesn't mean we shouldn't put the money and effort toward controlling the disease of dishonesty. We need to keep it at a low enough level to enable society to function. We haven't eradicated cancer. But our efforts have helped to control it and even to reduce it. Greed and violence, to my way of thinking, are very pernicious social diseases.

"If we spent in the promotion of better ethics just a fraction of the amount of money spent on any one of dozens of diseases and causes, we might save more lives and improve all our lives. We need strong media campaigns to debunk dishonesty. We should quit using media to make heroes out of bums and to glorify violence."

"Well, Jonathan, why don't you do it?"

"Fred, the simple fact is we have written radio spots, prepared and tested TV storyboards, and developed in detail a marketing campaign to promote better ethics and reduce dishonesty and corruption, but we have not been able to get the money to carry out market tests."

Fred shook his head as Jonathan continued. "We have raised enough funds, including contributions from all our directors and the organizations they represent, to work only at the level of influencers—the trade associations, government agencies, corporations, and other organizations. These efforts have been increasingly successful. But eventually we're going to have to use mass media massively to make the public as a whole understand that honesty and good ethics mean good business and a better life for everyone."

"So what are you going to do now," Fred interjected, "since you'll not be working full time on ethics?"

"Well, perhaps for a starter, I'll research the literature on the effects of human behavior that may result from the habits of parents during the first twenty to thirty months of a child's life. I think we should consider more thoroughly the possible imprinting of the human personality by parental activities early in their children's lives."

"Jonathan, don't tell me you're interested in astrology."

"Astrology? No! Imprinting! Consider that a child born in Minneapolis in January when it's cold might be exposed to fewer people for longer periods of time because the parents' living pattern is influenced by weather conditions. The same genetically identical child born in Minneapolis in July when it's warm might be taken out in a baby carriage more often. As a result, this summer-born child might be exposed to more people for shorter periods of time. We might wonder if the genetically identical child would be different at twenty or thirty years of age. It's possible that weather and different exposures to people may have influenced the personality permanently during the first few months of the child's life. We'll never know, because the child can't be born twice, but we might find out something by studying correlations. Some research on identical twins has been interesting."

Fred asked, a little amazed, "You mean that a kid born in Minneapolis in January might be more of an introvert than the same kid born in July? I don't know, Jonathan. There are so many other factors to consider."

"Possibly, Fred, although I doubt that behaviorists would give as much credence to human imprinting as they have to Lorenz's imprinted goslings. I've also considered a series of correlation studies that might statistically reveal variations in human behavior sufficiently significant as to suggest niches open for basic research."

"Jonathan, have you ever actually considered retiring and taking life easy? You've been working on what the corporate world calls social responsibility projects for many years on an unpaid basis. Why don't you quit and do nothing for a while?"

"Oh, I've thought about quitting, but visits to Florida, Arizona, Palm Springs, and other retirement areas gave me a touch of nausea." Jonathan grimaced. "I hate to see men and women who have benefited so much from living in our free, competitive society do nothing to try to preserve for their children and their children's children the freedom and opportunities they have enjoyed.

"Recently, I followed a couple of my rich friends around Palm Springs for a day of 'rest,' which included nine holes of golf in the morning (sometimes it can be eighteen if they play well and bet on the score), a sauna, a jacuzzi, and a few hands of gin rummy, followed by a well-deserved nap. Later there were cocktails and dinner at the currently 'in' club or restaurant to see if any celebrities and new starlets were around, and an exchange of comments with friends about their mutually 'busy' days until it was time to get in line for a piece of Lillie's banana pie. What a day! For grown men and women! For multi-millionaire leaders! Duller than hell!" Jonathan said emphatically. After a moment's reflection, he added, "But sitting on the benches in Florida or playing shuffleboard and bridge on your fourth round-the-world cruise isn't a very stimulating alternative."

"What would you consider a good alternative, Jonathan, if you decided not to keep thinking and working?"

"Well, there are many good alternatives to what we call working. There are reading and other forms of learning. Exercise, games, making love—they're all good alternatives to working. But I can't think of a good alternative to thinking except death. That's why when one's brain has ceased to function and one survives only as a so-called 'vegetable,' death might be considered the correct alternative."

"Jonathan, you look twenty years younger than I know you must be, and you're certainly as vigorous, creative, and quick-thinking as you were when I first knew you in the Chicago advertising agency and television business. What's your advice to senior citizens?"

"I think they should disinvent the term 'senior citizen.' When does one become a senior citizen? At thirty-five, as some do? At forty-five, fifty-five, sixty-five, seventy-five, eighty-five, or maybe for sure at one hundred? If we're going to use the term 'senior citizen,' let's apply it to those of any age who have decided to let the mainstream of life flow by while they sit on the bank under a tree—a tree, I might add, that also has moss on it."

"Of course," Jonathan continued as he readjusted his seat belt, "I respect some of the changes of advancing age, such as being beaten in a game of tennis by my son. But I don't believe we should run down life's road looking for age limitations and drag them into our mind and body before they even get to our block. Let these often-identified signs of old age chase us, search for us, and then let them go on their way after they find us doing business-as-usual at a new task in a new service to others. A person should retire *to* something, not just *from* something."

Fred leaned forward in his seat. This was of obvious interest to him, because he knew that someday he too would be a "senior citizen," and Jonathan seemed to be a good model for anyone who was even thinking about growing older.

"Go on," Fred encouraged him. "I want to learn as much as I can from you before those senior years catch me."

"As the years pass, Fred, I believe older humans build up a greater equity in life than the young. This investment in life should carry with it the responsibility of increased stewardship. No matter how narrow and shallow, or broad and deep our individual assets, each of us has something to give. Each of us owes something to the future. We're in an everlasting relay, and we should hand on to the next runner a fair chance to win the race."

Fred was nodding his head in agreement with every word Jonathan said. "I hear you, and I wish all senior citizens could take your message and act upon it. They would live longer, richer, happier lives. They could do so much for the young people of this country and for the disadvantaged, especially the virtually unemployable groups. They could help their fellow senior citizens who might have irremediable handicaps. Why don't the retired healthy people, rich or poor, take a look at Bob Hope, a very wealthy man who keeps working and doing good at eighty or more, or George Burns, or Congressman Claude Pepper, or some of the Supreme Court Justices? All over the country there are businessmen and farmers who pay no attention to their eightieth birthday, as they go to the office or plow the fields."

Jonathan smiled. He knew when he was with a kindred soul. It was good to talk with someone who believed as strongly as he did. "Recently," he continued, "I visited a friend who lives in a California leisure home community. Nice place, but when I went into the restaurant to wait for him, I saw rows of sad, blank faces that said 'Hello' or something. They wanted someone to pour a little faith in the future into their coffee cups. So many were bored, when they could be serving and going strong. But then, many people achieve senility long before they achieve maturity."

As Jonathan looked up, he saw the flight attendant standing

beside his seat with their lunch trays. "Lord, Fred, aren't you glad they're serving us lunch? What a pleasant interruption."

They lowered their serving tables, and the flight attendant placed dishes of chicken Kiev in front of them. For a moment, Jonathan's thoughts flashed back to a similar lunch many years ago. He remembered a certain London restaurant and Rene. They were so happy that day, and the chicken Kiev was better than any he had tasted since then. That was twenty-five years ago. Perhaps this was just the first of many things that would cause him to think of Rene as though she were gone forever.

"Looks good," Fred said. While working to get out the knife, fork, spoon, pepper, and salt, he continued, "You know, my father has been retired twenty years. He's reasonably healthy and looks fine. He was a top-flight executive, a very successful banker, and he still has a keen mind. Although he's done some financial consulting, he hasn't elected to undertake specific and productive projects that would give him the genuine satisfaction and pride in accomplishment that he deserves. Several of his friends believe they've accomplished enough. Maybe they have."

The lunch turned out to be as tasty as it looked. As they finished eating, the seat belt sign came on. The pilot announced that they were descending into Chicago's O'Hare Airport and expected to be at the gate on time.

As they prepared to leave the plane, Fred said, "You'll get to see my father again, Jonathan, because he'll be meeting me at the gate. I noticed that you and he were having quite a laugh at our last Christmas party."

Jonathan smiled. "Wherever your father goes, he's prepared to tell a joke or come up with something about politics that he knows will evoke a response. I'll be glad to see him again. Your father's impressive appearance and gentlemanly bearing remind me of distinguished Southern bankers and judges I met as a boy in Arkansas when I was the janitor in the governor's hometown law office."

Bob Osborne was at the gate to meet his son. He and Jonathan greeted one another enthusiastically. There was no need for Bob to delay, because his son had brought only a carry-on bag. Nevertheless, true to form, Osborne pulled Jonathan over to the wall out of the passenger traffic and asked him if he knew how to tell when he was getting older. Knowing what was expected of him, Jonathan answered, "No, Bob, I guess I don't. Do you have a formula that would help?"

"Do I have a formula, the man asks! How many do you want?"

"Well, I'll settle for three."

As Bob reached into his vest pocket, he said, "I always come prepared for guys like you—I'll give you three times three." His son winked at Jonathan and put on a patient grin. He suspected what was coming.

"What's the first way you suggest that I can tell I'm getting old, Bob?" Jonathan asked.

Bob took out a black notebook and replied, "Your little black book contains mostly names ending in M. D."

Jonathan grinned and said, "You must have been looking at my book of frequently called numbers. Go on! Let's have them all."

"Okay, Jonathan. See if these don't puncture your ego." Bob read the list with feigned pedagogical authority.

"Your children begin to look middle-aged." Bob glanced at his son.

"You regret all those mistakes you made resisting temptation."

Jonathan interrupted, "Whatever else you may say, Bob, that one hit me."

"You look forward to a dull evening," Bob continued.

"You join a health club and don't go."

"You're getting personal again," Jonathan joked.

"You feel like the morning after, and you haven't been anywhere the night before.

"You turn out the lights for economic rather than romantic reasons.

"You get winded playing chess.

"You decide to procrastinate, but then never get around to it.

"Now, of course, Jonathan, I tell you these things for your future use." Then he added mockingly, "In fact, I just happen to have an extra copy for you. I don't see many people to whom these apply."

Jonathan took the list from Bob and said, "I know they'll come in handy for me, but I wonder what stranger gave them to you."

Fred looked at his watch and said, "Come on, fellows, I've a speech to make this evening, and I need to get going."

Bob gave Jonathan a conqueror's smile. They shook hands and exchanged good wishes all around. Jonathan sent his regards to Bob's wife, Ellie, and wished Fred and his family a happy vacation.

The Osbornes went over to the parking garage to get their car, and Jonathan took the escalator down to pick up his baggage. It occurred to him that Bob Osborne certainly wasn't wasting all his time in retirement. He was going around making people laugh, and it was a real trick to get old people to laugh at themselves.

He had fond memories of Bob and the jokes he had for every occasion. Bob's favorite trick at cocktail parties and other gatherings was to pounce on his liberal friends, tell them a funny story, and while they were feeling good, preach his favorite conservative doctrine to them.

Shortly, Jonathan picked up his Hartman three-suiter and went outside to wait for the airport bus marked "Gold Coast" that would take him directly to the Drake hotel at Lake Shore Drive and Michigan Avenue.

# 5

Having a few minutes to spare before boarding the plane for Los Angeles, Rene went to the newstand and purchased a copy of the *Washington Post* and a current, best-selling paperback. In recent years, she had found herself reading novels about the "new" woman. After reading several of the nonfiction books and research reports on contemporary women, she doubted that they were more valid sources for information than the current fiction best-sellers. However, she still couldn't believe that some women, according to what she had been reading, accepted sex as a casual, but most satisfying, thing to do with a man—and not just one particular man.

Rene's timing was perfect. She arrived at the gate just as the first call for boarding was announced. Fortunately, she had been assigned a window seat, and the woman sitting next to her couldn't speak English. Rene settled in for an enjoyable flight. She read the *Post,* had a martini and lunch, and was deep into her novel when she arrived at the Los Angeles International Airport. She survived the crush of passengers at the baggage claim carousel, rented a car, carried her case outside, and caught a shuttle bus to the rental car lot. Soon she was on her way to Ellen's via the Santa Monica Freeway.

Traffic was light, and in what seemed a very short time, she was negotiating the residential streets close to Ellen and Anson's house. No sooner had she pulled into her daughter's driveway and parked the car than Ellen, eagerly anticipating her mother's visit, opened the front door and yelled, "Hello, Mom!" As Rene emerged from the car her daughter said, "Mom, you look great!" Rene laughed as she rushed along the walk to the door and hugged and kissed Ellen.

"You look so pretty, Ellen, that special pregnant prettiness. And your eyes just glow. I'm so happy for you and so glad to be here." Ellen did indeed look happy. She patted the baby who was resting under her light-blue sleeveless maternity dress and who was, apparently, a bit too eager to be born.

"And I'm sure happy to see you," Ellen said. "Maybe you can go with me to the doctor's office tomorrow morning."

"I'd like to, Ellen. You know, this may be your first baby, but it's also my first grandchild. It's exciting for both of us." Rene and Ellen stepped just inside the front door.

"Mom, I don't know what the doctor will be telling me tomorrow. He seems to think the baby will arrive well before it's due. He says I may have to stay home and lie on my back for three weeks." She paused. "And that's going to be tough for Anson, as well as for me." Ellen smiled at her mother. "But I'm going to do everything possible to protect the baby and to make sure it has a healthy start in life. And I'm going to need someone to stay here with me and keep house and do all that sort of thing. Do you think you could possibly do it, Mom? I mean, would you be willing to stay with me until I'm all right?"

Rene moved closer to Ellen, put her arms around her, and assured her that she would be happy to help her in any way she could. As the two women walked on through the entry hall and into the living room, Rene said, "Ellen, it just so happens I want to get out of Washington for a while, so I'll welcome a chance to stay here with you as long as I'm needed."

Ellen's living room was homey and very inviting. The afternoon sun was coming in through the windows facing the pool, and Ellen moved a few plants out of the direct rays. "Why are you so eager to get out of Washington? I thought you loved living at the Watergate and working on your assignments for the Post. What will Dad do with you out here?"

She hesitated and asked softly, "Are you and Dad finally going to try a separation?"

Rene looked at her daughter, so lovely and so eager to begin her own family, and thought to herself, "What a shame this all has to come to a head at this time."

"Well," she answered, "we're going to talk about that when I get back to Washington. Your father seems to believe that it would be best for me to pursue my career almost any place other than Washington. He thinks that before I lose what he calls my attractiveness and distinctiveness, I should go to a place where there are more entrepreneurs and fewer lobbyists, lawyers, politicians, groupie journalists, and bureaucrats. These days I don't know where that would be. But I do know I'm not getting any younger. And man or woman, when one is fifty, it's hard to get the job you want.

"But let's wait and see what the doctor tells you tomorrow. If it turns out that you're going to need me for a fairly long time, then, when I come out to stay with you, I'll look around southern California for a job."

"Mom, what if the doctor tells me I need someone to stay with me for four or five weeks?" Ellen was trying to plan for the worst, but she knew she could count on her mother for help.

"Let's see what he says, first. Then we'll worry about time. But I promise you I'll stay as long as you need me. After the baby arrives, you and Anson will have all your time taken by the baby, especially if it's anything like you were." Rene smiled at Ellen knowingly. "Babies are so much fun, but they need a lot of attention.

"Now," she said as she stood up and looked at her watch, "I'd better get my things out of the car. I'll have dinner started by the time Anson gets home."

"I can still get around pretty well, Mom, but you're welcome to help in the kitchen anytime you want. You're still the best cook I've ever known."

"Well, thanks. But now that we don't have even one of you three children around, I don't cook very much. Daddy likes hamburger steaks or bacon and eggs better than the finest entree any chef can cook up."

As Rene reached the front door, she said, "I'll get my things. Where do you want me to put them?"

Ellen smiled at her whole new way of thinking about her home. "In the baby's room, right in here." And she pointed to an open doorway a few steps down the small hallway.

Ellen and Anson had been lucky to find a home they liked in Santa Monica with three bedrooms, a nice swimming pool off the living room-dining area, a grape arbor, and a pleasant, fenced-in side yard. The front lawn was large enough, considering the price of homesites and homes in southern California. Actually, they had paid much more than they had wanted to, but there was no choice. Every home in southern California cost too much.

Ellen hadn't wanted her pregnancy to be a big deal, but it was turning out that way. In fact, she had hoped to keep going to her law office in downtown Los Angeles until four or five weeks before the baby was due, and even that was longer than she wanted to take off from work. But she certainly wasn't going to take any chances. If the doctor told her not to go back to work at all, she would stay home. The doctor had suggested she take off the Monday before her Tuesday examination; that's why she was home when her mother arrived.

Rene brought her luggage in, unpacked, changed her dress, and asked Ellen if she needed anything from the store. Ellen said she certainly did, because she hadn't really felt like shopping. She was more worried than anything else. She mentioned to her mother that she remembered her Dad's telling her a year ago that she would be having a baby the first week of September, 1982.

"I know Dad is uncanny at guessing the darnedest things," Ellen said, "or, maybe I should say, he's a good prophet, but how could he guess my baby's birthday long before I was even pregnant?"

Rene answered Ellen as they were walking out to the car to go shopping. "I've lived with your father for about thirty years, and I still don't know how he reads people and makes these strange predictions. But he is so often annoyingly right!" She unlocked the car door on the passenger side and started around to the other side. "Maybe you had better take a cue from Daddy's forecast and not worry so much about the baby arriving prematurely." Ellen was quiet. She believed in her father, but she thought naming the time of her baby's birth fifteen months in advance was a little too much. She would be sure not to mention to her doctor what her father had said.

"Mom, let's go to Golden's. You've been there before. Do you remember the way?" Ellen said as her mother backed out of the driveway onto the street.

"Yes, I like that store," Rene replied. "Let's celebrate and have some nice big lamb chops. Anson likes lamb, as I recall."

"Lamb chops would be great. Lamb's my favorite meat, too."

"Now, Ellen," her mother chided, "you know your very favorite is the juicy, medium-cut prime roast beef that I used to cook. But we can have that tomorrow night."

"Anson and I will be living high on the beef while you're here," Ellen said with gleeful satisfaction. Ellen had always enjoyed shopping with her mother.

They didn't do a lot of shopping, because they wanted to get back and have dinner started before Anson came home. Rene was also eager to relax with a martini and talk more with Ellen.

Rene enjoyed the creativity of cooking, but she was not a guesswork-type cook. She searched for good recipes, and when she found them, she followed them precisely. For that Monday night's dinner she told Ellen that vegetables mornay a la Pope would be a perfect accompaniment for the lamb chops. Ellen thought no other vegetables mornay ever tasted as good as her mother's. While cooking, Rene was slowly working on her martini, into which she had put a couple of extra little green olives.

Her son-in-law came home earlier than usual and rushed in, threw off his jacket, kissed his mother-in-law, went into the kitchen, kissed Ellen, asked how she was doing, and grabbed a beer out of the refrigerator. Anson moved around any room as if he were returning a kickoff for the Rams.

Rene was fond of Anson, and he was especially partial to Rene because he could never quite get into sync with his father-in-law. This condition wasn't due so much to Anson as to the fact that long before Anson came along, Jonathan thought his son, Bruce, the most wonderful man in the world.

But Jonathan did appreciate Anson because, as Ellen's father, he knew she was a challenge to the most secure of husbands. He wondered how Ellen had come by such a strong will and such diverse interests. Ellen didn't hesitate to let her father know that he was responsible. However, she was like her mother in her fondness for parties and people.

Anson took his beer and went back to the living room, and Rene and Ellen chatted in the kitchen as they prepared dinner.

"Has Anson expressed a desire for a boy or for a girl? Of course, I know you both just want a healthy baby, but I have an idea that Anson would really like a little girl."

"Mom, we would welcome a boy, or girl, or both. But I think Anson might be very happy with a girl. There were only boys in his family."

"The happiest moment of your Dad's entire life," Rene said, "was the moment he saw you, his first baby, a blonde girl. You were just as he had always pictured a baby should be, but never really hoped to have. In the first few minutes after your birth, you looked at the bright lights around you and screamed like hell. Your dad thought he saw you point at the lights and tell the doctor to "Turn those damn lights down.' " Rene smiled.

After dinner Anson asked Rene when she thought she might come out.

Rene replied very seriously, "I really don't know what I shall do or what Jonathan and I will do. Everything is uncertain." She took a sip of brandy.

"When I ask Jonathan where he would like to live, he says, 'Nowhere, really.' During the past five or six years he's suggested any number of times that I leave him and marry a man more my own age, particularly a man who would share my current interests and who liked people and parties."

Anson and Ellen just listened. Some of this they had heard before, but their interest was no less intense.

"One of your father's doctors told him he should not expect to live much longer. You remember when he just about killed himself doing so much heavy manual labor during the construction of our house. Your father says longevity figures suggest that I should live twenty-five or thirty years longer than he, and he wants me married again and happy before he dies."

Ellen and Anson glanced at each other, and then both looked back to Rene. They knew Jonathan's logic was sound, but perhaps they were thinking that there is more to life than logic. At any rate, they didn't say anything, so Rene continued.

"I keep telling him that no matter what the life expectancy figures indicate, he'll probably out live me."

Sitting in a straight, dining-room chair was becoming uncomfortable for Ellen, so the three of them got up and cleared the table. As Rene and Ellen worked, cleaning up the kitchen, they continued to discuss Jonathan's attitude.

"You know, your father has been depressed for several years— ever since we left the farm, ever since he retired from active business. The ethics project has been very burdensome to him. He is terribly angry, even furious, that there isn't greater acceptance of his crusade to make America more honest, although he's realistic enough to understand the reasons why."

By this time the dishwasher was loaded, and Ellen and Rene walked through the dining area and into the living room to join Anson around the coffee table.

Rene talked softly as they walked. "Your father is also often angry with me for not being as kind and warm and loving as he needs me to be."

"But, Mom," Ellen said sympathetically, "you've done what you could. Why hasn't Dad consulted doctors who know about depression?"

Rene took a seat at one end of the sofa and Ellen the other. Once down in the cushions, Ellen became uneasy almost at once. She looked across the room at Anson, and they both laughed. She laboriously lifted herself off the couch and sat down in a straight chair between her mother and her husband.

"Your father understands a great deal about depression and its causes," Rene continued. "You were away at Harvard at the time, but he and I did a lot of research on the subject. I even wrote a long feature article as a summary report of our research. Your father called numerous medical authorities all over the country to determine who might be considered the greatest expert on depression. The highest vote favored a neuropsychiatrist in Chicago, a professor at Northwestern University Medical School. Jonathan made appointments with him and with a European doctor who was temporarily in Chicago. They gave him tests, had several visits, and finally, after a two-week interim period for summarizing their conclusions, they sent him a report."

"What was in the report?" Ellen asked with concerned curiosity. "Or should you tell me?"

Her mother laughed and reached over to touch Ellen's arm.

"The report simply stated that he had what the doctors described as 'ethical depression.' They said they would advise no medicine and no treatment. He would just have to deal with it. They did suggest that giving up the day-to-day work at the Ethics office would help. Even your father laughed at the conclusion of the experts, but he said he had gone to the best and to the honest. He agreed with their conclusion. He recalled that their report fitted in with what Dr. Erich Fromm had told him—your father hated the fact he was human. Personally, I think he hated the fact he couldn't move the ethics program along faster."

Rene gave Ellen a knowing look. They both knew Johnathan so well. "Anyway, Ellen," Rene continued, "he doesn't just sit around when a problem comes up. He actively seeks a solution.

"Johnathan's been very sad about the diverging pattern of our interests since we left the farm and the real estate business."

"Mom," Ellen said in a motherly manner, "you must be very tired from your trip, and it's late by your time. Perhaps we should all go to bed."

"Yes, Dear," Rene said, realizing she was thinking about her upcoming discussion with her husband. She really shouldn't have been talking about her personal problems with her daughter and son-in-law. Yet, maybe her problems would cause Ellen not to think so much about her own. Rene knew Ellen was doing everything she could to make sure the baby would be healthy. Rene wasn't sure she was doing everything she could to handle her own problem.

Anson, who had been sitting quietly, just listening, spoke up. "Rene, whatever you and Jonathan decide, I think your coming out here and staying with us for a while will be good for you as well as for Ellen. Anyway, thanks for helping prepare such a wonderful dinner."

Ellen picked up the few glasses they had missed in their clean-up and started for the kitchen. She called over her shoulder to Rene, "Mom, I think you'll find all the towels and things you need in the hall bathroom. If there's anything else I can get for you, just call me."

"Everything will be fine. I think I'll take a glass of brandy with me and sip it while I finish a novel I've been reading."

Ellen came back into the living room. "Remember, my doctor's appointment is at 9:30, so we'll want to leave here at nine. And if the doctor approves, I'll want to go on to the office. I have a big bankruptcy case. So maybe you can follow me in your car."

"But I'll see you for breakfast," she added. "Good night."

"Rene," Anson said, "I'll see you tomorrow for dinner. I leave the house about seven in the morning, so I won't see you for breakfast. Good night."

As the two women went down the hall to their rooms, Anson turned out the last light in the front hall and followed them.

Rene was glad to get to bed. She felt that perhaps she shouldn't have discussed her plans or lack of them with Ellen and Anson.

But why not? she asked herself. They're family. They both know that Jonathan and I aren't looking at life with the same goals or even with similar immediate needs in mind. Furthermore, Ellen is not only my oldest daughter, she's also an understanding friend.

Then she thought, Jonathan will be objective, and he'll have a

51

recommendation, now that we've both come to the point of doing something. It'll be good for both of us.

With that bit of self-consolation, Rene undressed and went to bed to finish reading her novel. Since she slept nude, she kept her robe over her shoulders, placed her brandy glass on the bedside table, and between sips resumed reading about the torrid affairs the forty-seven-year-old female protagonist was having. Rene flipped back through several chapters she had already read and counted five different, overlapping sexual affairs this fictional woman had experienced within a period of six months.

Are there women like that? Rene wondered to herself. And are they happy and exhilarated, or sad and debilitated?

This heroine, if one could call her that in view of her conquests, had two successful, grown-and-gone children. She had divorced her husband, with his ready consent, when he switched from his regular practice of medicine to medical research, which seemed to occupy him too intensely, as far as his wife was concerned. When her husband became absorbed in his research, the heroine returned to school and obtained her MBA. Within five years she was vice-president for corporate loans in a big bank. What had happened to the doctor husband of the heroine reminded Rene of her own husband's abstraction.

Rene had been a young and inexperienced virgin when she had married. Now she wished to supplement in a vicarious way, perhaps, what she had learned about sex and life from her husband by reading novels and reports written by and for women.

One particular novel, written by an English woman, had had a great influence on Rene. It told of women who could live exciting lives and take sex when and where they happened to find it, without any seeming harm to themselves. The women described in the novel seemed to resent the fact that men, especially the ex-husband of one and lover of both, had much more money, but less strength than the women—or so they thought. That kind of situation apparently made characters in the book combative and defensive. Reading about them had affected Rene.

When she and Jonathan had their evening martinis, he often accurately observed that she had been reading "that book" again. It was a well-written, successful novel, but he doubted that the writer had ever understood the message it conveyed.

Rene felt very confused about her life. Like the heroine in the novel she was just finishing, she had been almost forty-six years old when her last child had left home. Her husband was involved in a very abstract commitment like the research-doctor husband she was reading about. But the more she read, the more confused she became. The culture had changed the rules on her since she was sixteen.

Although she was already an experienced journalist, she had decided five years earlier to go back to college and qualify for a degree in journalism. At that time, Jonathan moved to Washington and suggested that Rene go ahead on a full-time basis at Carolina State, finish her degree program, and come to Washington after the one final semester that she needed. She had easily earned her degree, and four months later she joined her husband in the Watergate apartments.

But there was a problem. She had brought with her some of the mores of her twenty to twenty-two-year-old classmates—an unsettling influence for a forty-six-year-old woman. She had gone to class with these younger women and men, studied with them, became friends with them. Some of the young girls had already lived with three or four different lovers since entering college. Rene felt left out in that area of her education.

Now on this summer evening, as she read in bed in her daughter's home, she was fifty years old and about to become a grandmother, and she was contemplating separation from her husband of almost thirty years.

She finished her brandy and the last chapter of the novel. Tomorrow she and Ellen would find out how the baby was doing. When Ellen went to her office, Rene planned to look around at rental apartments and maybe explore job opportunities. In all her fifty years, she had never lived alone. The one time she had lived away from home had been in college, but one would certainly not call living in a college sorority house being on one's own. Maybe she wanted what she had missed when she was twenty—something her young classmates weren't missing now.

She put her book and her thoughts to rest and went to sleep.

The following morning Rene and Ellen arrived at the doctor's office on Wilshire Boulevard a few minutes early, and the doctor told his nurse to bring Ellen right in. He didn't expect the examination to take much time.

"Ellen," the doctor said, "I think you can go on working, if you don't overdo it at home or at the office. But you must get plenty of bed rest.

"If you reduce your working and commuting day, you'll probably be all right for two or three weeks. Perhaps today you can arrange to work half-days only, or two or three full days a week.

"I want you to come in at nine o'clock next Tuesday and let me take another look at you. You don't smoke or drink, which is fortunate for you and the baby, so just reduce your workload and eat properly, as we've discussed. You may be able to carry your baby almost, if not all the way, to full term."

Ellen was pleased. "Thank you. I'll call you if I don't feel right. Otherwise, I'll see you next Tuesday morning."

As Rene and Ellen walked out of the building Rene said reassuringly, "Ellen, the doctor certainly didn't seem alarmed. That's a relief to me. While you go to the office, I'll begin to look for a rental apartment right here in the Westwood area."

Ellen felt some concern, but it was for her mother, not for herself. "Mom, you may have to take a full year's lease."

"I'll go and see a couple of real estate brokers, and I'll also go up and down the streets that appeal to me and stop at apartment houses. I'm going to look several blocks away from the university area."

Giving Ellen a goodbye hug, she said, "In any case, I'll see you tonight."

As Rene slid in behind the steering wheel, Ellen said, "Good luck, Mom."

Rene stopped at the first real estate office she saw. It was south of Wilshire on Westwood Boulevard, and she figured the apartments there might be less expensive. She wanted a two-bedroom, two-bath unit. The length of lease didn't worry her, because she could always sublet it, or perhaps find an apartment now that she herself could sublet for a few months. The agent had no rentals, so Rene continued to look at apartments on her own.

At one building the owner happened to be in the manager's office, and he seemed impressed by Rene. He told her he could show her an apartment that would be available September 1.

She thought he was a nice fellow, and he seemed to think Rene might make a good tenant, in addition to being pretty. He was so pleased with the good things she said about his building and the apartment he showed her that he readily agreed to hold it for her until after her daughter's next visit to the doctor. Rene said she would let him know and would send him a check for one month's rent and the equivalent amount as a security deposit if she decided to rent it. The location on Malcolm Avenue, five minutes from Westwood Village, was perfect for her.

She stopped for hot tea and a tuna salad lunch at one of the attractive restaurants in Westwood. She wasn't sure what she and Jonathan would agree to do, either in the short or long run. But she was sure that he wanted her to come out to California and be with Ellen when she needed her. That would take care of the short-run plans.

As these thoughts went through her mind, she watched the students and shoppers who strolled past the restaurant. She would wait until she returned to Washington before making any firm decisions on her own. Her long-term decision would be based primarily on what her husband wanted to do and what he wanted her to do. She couldn't break the habit of asking Jonathan even about her own desires.

She thought of the past. They had had so many happy years together. What was it about those times that had made them happy? They had both been busy, especially the first few years when they were working in television and then when the children were small. Later, there was the farm life and their work as a team in real estate. Jonathan's many careers had been challenging for both of them. They had both moved into the future with interest, expectancy, and zest, always moving to a different home, a different occupation. Even when he had retired from the advertising agency business and followed her into the real estate business, they had been able to keep the momentum going. Now they were both floating free amid uncertainty. They weren't helping each other.

Rene finished her lunch, feeling that perhaps she should return to Ellen's to make some phone calls regarding a job.

# 6

As she left the restaurant, Rene decided it was such a pretty day she would walk the three blocks up to Bullock's and look for a bathing suit. She hadn't brought one with her, because she hadn't expected to have any time to use Ellen's pool. Bullock's Westwood was more a fine speciality shop than a department store, so she was sure she would find something suitable.

Rene loved shopping and, if she needed nothing specific, she often bought small gifts for people whose birthdays she noted and kept on file. She loved to surprise her friends and acquaintances with little gifts. The fact that she remembered their birthdays endeared Rene to many men and women in all walks of life. She had found that top executives were usually the most surprised and pleased to be remembered with a simple birthday card.

She browsed around Bullock's, bought a few greeting cards, and went to look at bathing suits. She thought that she might buy a new one-piece suit, cut a little higher on the thighs and maybe with lower-slashed armholes than the ones she had.

She found a beige-brown suit with a touch of light orange trim and tried it on. Her long legs, thirty-seven inch hips, and thirty-seven-inch bust made the high-on-thigh, one-piece suit look quite interesting, she thought. As she paid the salesclerk, it occurred to her that it was the kind of swimsuit a woman character in a novel she had been reading would choose.

Resisting the temptation to shop more, she walked back to the restaurant where she had lunched, checked her car out of the nearby parking lot, drove down to Wilshire, and turned west toward Santa Monica and Ellen's house. She didn't feel as if she were in a strange place; in fact, she felt quite at home in southern California.

Rene had always enjoyed her visits to southern California. She and Jonathan had visited their daughter and son-in-law several times. They usually stayed at the Bel Air Sands Hotel, because its location was convenient to Ellen's house and also to a number of Jonathan's friends, who were in the creative areas of the television and motion picture business.

As soon as she arrived at her daughter's house, she picked up the key from its hiding place, entered the house, and went to Anson's desk to begin making phone calls.

The first call was to Dr. Arnold Spirrison, whom she had met about a year before at a public affairs seminar at Carolina State University. Dr. Spirrison had moved up through public affairs and administration to his present position as president of Southland University. Rene's boss at Carolina State, Vice-Chancellor Harold Otis, a long-time friend of Dr. Spirrison, had invited her to sit with them at the seminar dinner.

Because Rene had learned a great deal about public relations through her position as a college trustee and through her close association with television and other media, Dr. Spirrison had been impressed with her professionalism. He seemed to be rather fascinated with her personality, also. He was first on her list, and she dialed his direct number from the business card he had given her at the Carolina State seminar.

"Is Dr. Spirrison available? This is Rene Barron of Washington calling."

"I'll see if he is in, Miss Barron. Does he know you?"

"Dr. Spirrison is a friend of Dr. Harold Otis of Carolina State University. If you'll check, I think he'll remember Mrs. Barron."

Rene doodled on a pad of paper while she waited. A long time seemed to pass.

"Mrs. Barron, he's on the phone right now, but he asked if you could hold for just another minute. He will be happy to talk to you."

"I'll be glad to wait," Rene replied, relieved that she would be able to speak with him today.

"Hello, Rene, this is Arnold. So glad you called. Are you in Los Angeles now?"

"Yes, I'm here for a couple of days, but I plan to return, perhaps to stay. That's why I called you. I may be looking for a job. Do you have any leads, by chance?"

"By chance, Rene, I do. We're making some changes here at

Southland. Perhaps you could come out and talk to me tomorrow."

"I certainly could. What time and where should I come to see you?"

Spirrison was apparently looking at his calendar. "Well, up to about four-thirty tomorrow I have a number of appointments and a couple of faculty committee meetings. Would you mind coming to my office tomorrow at four forty-five?"

"No problem. I'll be there."

"You know where the university is located. Well, my office is on the second floor of the Administration Building, Room 200."

"I'll find it, Dr. Spirrison. I'm looking forward to seeing you again. Thank you very much. Goodbye."

Rene hung up the phone slowly and gently. Was she likely to be offered a job? What was in his mind?

Oh, well, she thought, we shall see.

Then she called Howard Culbertson at the *Los Angeles Chronicle,* to whom she had been referred by Ralph Lawton.

That Ralph knows everybody, she thought to herself.

She dialed the number Ralph had given her. A woman answered, "Mr. Culbertson's office."

"This is Rene Barron from Washington. I'm in Los Angeles for a couple of days. Mr. Ralph Lawton suggested that I try to see Mr. Culbertson while I'm out here. Would he be available for a brief appointment in the next day or so?"

"Mrs. Barron, I recall seeing the letter from Mr. Lawton mentioning your name. I'm sure Mr. Culbertson would like to see you if he can. Let me check his calendar. Could you come in tomorrow afternoon at two-thirty?"

"Yes, I can be there. Where is Mr. Culbertson's office?"

"It's in the *Chronicle* building on the sixth floor, Room 601. We'll look for you at two-thirty, Mrs. Barron."

"Thank you. I'll be there."

Rene replaced the phone and lit a cigarette. Ralph Lawton really did seem to know everyone, or at least a lot of people. As vice-president and assistant to the chairman of Homeland Corporation, he handled the public affairs programs and also influenced their rather substantial grants program.

Executives of big corporations often remembered those who had given to the favorite charity of the wife of their chief executive officer. Mr. Culbertson, a vice-president, and Mr. Lawton had probably arranged an art gift in exchange for an opera gift.

Who knows? Rene said to herself. Whatever the reason, I'm glad to have such contacts when I'm looking for a job. Her phone calls completed, she decided to spend the rest of the afternoon swimming and reading.

She drove to a nearby drugstore and purchased a novel she had heard about on television. Returning to Ellen's, Rene changed into her swimsuit and went out to the pool. She thought her new suit would be all right for the home pool, although it was a rather more daring style than she had worn before.

Well, she thought, might as well wear it and get used to it.

Her figure was not bad for fifty—or thirty, for that matter. She knew she had to watch her weight; one hundred twenty-two to one hundred twenty-four pounds and no more. Her breasts were large and firm enough to look good with or without a bra, although she usually wore one except with her evening gowns. She was in good shape now, but as Jonathan said, "You should go get a new husband while you're so pretty and sexy."

Rene didn't know whether Jonathan was tired of her or if he was genuinely concerned about leaving her unprepared for the many years she would be likely to live after he was gone. She wished he were not so willing to give her up, whether or not it was best for her.

She dismissed these thoughts as she went outside to enjoy the sunshine and the clear, inviting pool. She jumped in and swam vigorously. In her younger days Rene had taught swimming, so she was confident in the water. When she climbed out of the pool a short time later, she felt so good in her new suit she wished she had an audience.

She found that she really didn't want to read. Stretching out in the warm sunshine, Rene felt her body and her mind begin to relax.

Her thoughts drifted back to the beach in southern Portugal and the lovely Hotel Dona Felipa in the Algarve where the Barrons had once vacationed. It was there, while swimming in the ocean, that a big wave had caused her to lose her brushed gold wedding ring. When she came back to the hotel to report its loss, Jonathan was skeptical. She remembered his asking, "How in the world could a wave take off your wedding ring and not take you down with it?"

"I honestly don't know," she had replied, "but Susan was sitting right there on the beach watching me, and she can tell you it was a big wave."

Jonathan said no more. She didn't know if he believed her, and she didn't know if the event was an omen. It had happened about ten years ago. Was that the beginning of their taking different paths instead of the one they had traveled together? It could have been, Rene supposed. Their lives often seemed to be directed by some chance occurrence—a newspaper ad for a TV person or for a farm.

Rene's thoughts went from that day on the beach to Church City, North Carolina, where the Barrons had decided to live after returning from their stay in Portugal. It was at that time that Jonathan had designed and supervised the construction of their "dream home." She knew then, as she knew now, that never again would she love a house as much as she had loved that one. Her husband had carefully landscaped it with azaleas, pink dogwoods, gardenias, magnolias, and a border of white pines to screen in the entire yard.

He had decorated the home using carefully selected grasscloth wall coverings, teak panels, and magnolia burls. The living-room ceiling was twenty feet high and covered with three-inch-thick knotty cedar, supported by long, smooth, wood beams. It was an incredibly personal home. Rene participated in the discussions and design, but her husband had been the creative one, the conceptualizer. She had planned the packing and had made arrangements for the mover.

It was the day before the movers were to bring their furniture that Paul Ashley, the public affairs director of Carolina State, had walked across the yard to where Jonathan and Rene were standing and asked her if she could help with some of their journalism commitments while one of the staff was on leave having a baby.

"Paul," she recalled saying, "I would certainly like to, but we're just ready to begin moving in tomorrow." Paul stood and looked at the big new home. "I'm so sorry you can't. I certainly understand. But you could do so much for us right now. I need a mature, responsible assistant so badly."

Rene remembered Jonathan's looking at her. Of course, he knew she thought she couldn't possibly start a full-time job on the very day they were to move into their new home. But he had said,

"Paul, Rene is obviously right in not accepting your offer. You were so thoughtful to come over. But if you will hang around and let me show you more of our new home, she can walk up to the house we've been renting in the next block and change into something suitable to go back to the office with you to start work; that is, if it pleases both of you."

Rene was absolutely amazed. "Jonathan, I would like the job, but I can't leave all this moving to you."

"Well, you've just said you'd like the job. I think it's the best opening for you that's likely to show up in this area for a long time. As for moving, I know exactly where everything goes, and we do have a good set of local movers. So come on Paul," Jonathan said, "I'll show you inside our new home, while Rene goes back to the house for her journalism clothes."

Those memories were pleasant for Rene. The job turned out to mean a great deal to her and her career. Ashley proved to be a wonderful man who challenged her to become a much better writer and an all-around journalist.

Less than two years later, Paul Ashley had died of a heart attack, only a week after she and Jonathan had given a big party to celebrate his twenty years with Carolina State. The chancellor of Carolina State University, as well as all the former chancellors who were still living, came to the party. She was glad they had given Paul that additional recognition. The office staff had wanted to postpone the party for a month, so the date would coincide exactly with his twentieth anniversary, but Rene had insisted on going ahead with it. How fortunate for all of them that they hadn't missed the chance to honor Paul.

After Ashley's death, the job hadn't been the same. Rene had been offered his position, but she didn't wish to be the boss and handle administrative functions. She simply wanted to write. Jonathan, observing that the staff standards were rapidly declining, told Rene that she was not being challenged and was adjusting downward, professionally and personally.

As she remembered the situation, the quality of the entire staff's work hadn't been good, but she didn't think her personal standards had declined. However, she did start smoking again, excessively. Her voice didn't seem so clear, and Jonathan had considered some of her new expressions a little on the vulgar side. She

61

had to admit that she had started dressing more casually and that she hadn't been particularly inspired by her job. She hadn't been as proud of her writing, either.

At the same time, Jonathan's activities in the ethics field had expanded into publishing books and newspaper and magazine articles, giving numerous speeches, and making television appearances.

She recalled that even then, he had emphasized to her that they were following separate paths. He had said that sooner or later their divergent interests might overcome their common interests.

He had scarcely been able to tolerate her new friends. To him, they seemed boosters of mediocrity and were annoying as hell. He resented them, not so much because of his disregard for them, but because they were tearing down the pedestal he had built for his wife.

She believed he had grown antagonistic toward the world and women. He had grown up in a world that put women on pedestals, his early world of the South. She felt constrained by Johnathan's high ideals for himself and for women. She seemed always to be on stage, when she wanted to be in the balcony.

About that time she decided to reenter the university and take special courses in journalism, psychology, and economics. An offer to teach in the school of journalism had inspired her to finish the requirements for a degree in that field. Johnathan had encouraged her to stop everything and go to school full time, telling her that too many reentry women wasted their time dragging a few courses out over many years. Rene, of course, was free to attend classes full time, whereas many women could not. At the end of the semester, she had accomplished what she'd set out to do but was exhausted, mentally and physically.

Meanwhile, Johnathan had moved the Ethics Group to Washington and had rented a small apartment for himself. She joined him in five months, right after Christmas, and they moved into a large apartment in the Watergate.

Before leaving their Church City home, they celebrated Christmas with all the children around the biggest Christmas tree they had ever had. Rene remembered the beautiful gold necklace Jonathan had given her.

A little breeze was coming in from the ocean. Soon it would be too cool to stay out by Ellen's pool. Although she didn't wish to end her meditations, Rene realized she was becoming sad recalling all these memories of Church City and her work at Carolina State. She turned over onto her back and began to think of things that had happened before the move from Church City. Some of those things she had orchestrated herself.

Since she simply couldn't persuade herself to join in her husband's more complicated and abstract endeavors, and with all the children gone, she started on a methodical campaign to conquer Jonathan with a major sex breakthrough. She felt that possibly sex could hold them together until he gave up on his ethics obsession. She remembered that Jonathan hadn't kidded her about her home study course on the arts of sex. He told her that learning about making love could be helpful, but learning to love loving was the prime essential.

Jonathan knew that her mother had created barriers to restrain Rene's sexual impulses. For example, she called Rene Ray—maybe because the baby her mother had lost had been a boy. Jonathan thought that such culturally male or female names could cause girls or boys to visualize themselves differently, especially if their peers picked up the nickname used by the parents. Some parents name their daughters Patricia, Joan, or Alison and end up calling them Pat, Jo, or Al. Their children's friends follow suit. Rene remembered Jonathan telling her that he had made a superficial check of the "Pat and Jo effect" on young women he had known, and not always, but often, there appeared to have been a correlation between a masculine self-image and girls whose names had been abbreviated to what are usually masculine first names. Of course, in some cases it wasn't the effect of the nickname but the result of a parent, usually the father, wanting a boy.

Rene never forgot the tight bras her mother had forced her to wear in high school to keep her growing breasts as flat as possible. To this day, she thought, she didn't have the responsiveness in her breasts that so many women seemed to enjoy. But her husband had convinced her that her pretty nipples paid no attention to her mother's discouragement. He demonstrated that, when they were properly attended to, they responded wonderfully. He understandingly and enthusiastically helped Rene to appreciate her full femininity.

For most of their married life, sex had been reasonably good, mainly she admitted to herself, because Jonathan was incurably romantic. She realized she had not been as sexually expressive and impressive as Jonathan's first wife, Mindy. She remembered asking Jonathan how his first wife had done it. He told her gladly. She read and she practiced on him. And she definitely remembered the first time he told her she was just as exciting as Mindy. Her husband—yes, her husband—had told her that she was far more sexy than she realized. Jonathan had been the only man in her life, and she sometimes wondered if she was truly as satisfying as he said she was.

The current best-selling novels had awakened her to a new kind of woman and had given her a whole new idea of sexual freedom. The crowd at the university, her peers, many half her age (and half as beautiful, she thought to herself) seemed to enjoy sex with a capital S.

With her usual thoroughness and discipline, attributes Jonathan readily confirmed she possessed to a high degree, she focused on her sex education. She read every how-to book she could find, and they were all readily available in a college town. She thought her husband sexy, and now her own feelings told her that she was, too.

But it appeared that all her studying, all her practicing, and all her sexuality were not going to preserve her marriage.

# 7

Rene left the pool and her reveries to go to her room. She checked over her clothes and laid out a comfortable brown knit dress with a small stand-up collar and narrow V neck. After a leisurely shower, she brushed her hair, put on a touch of make-up, dressed, and went out to the kitchen. She wanted to see what Ellen had on hand so she could plan dinner.

After completing her shopping list, she drove up to Golden's. She liked Golden's because it was a genuine California-style supermarket, with a full line of everything, especially in meats, fish, and fresh fruits and vegetables. She felt that even the supermarkets were tempting her to come to California, but she wasn't sure about it. She didn't want to lose her husband, but she did want to find herself.

Rene didn't analyze things as objectively as Jonathan did. She knew that he thought things out very carefully, perhaps unemotionally, and then acted. But that wasn't her way. She decided to fall back on her old standby approach to life: live from day to day and see what develops.

The shopping task was a pleasure. It was something that she could do immediately and make decisions about, with the certainty that it would all end well in the harmony of a good meal. As the bags of groceries were being placed in her car, she decided that she liked her rental car. Soon she might have to buy her own automobile for her life in California.

All kinds of things, average decisions, in a way, would bunch up to make big ones. Rene wanted to try living entirely on her own because she had never done it. Yet, she didn't want to be entirely on her own, again because she had never done it. It was all rather confusing.

Well, she summarized as she drove back to Ellen's place, I don't have to decide anything right now. I'll just enjoy creating a nice dinner for Ellen and Anson.

Once home, she put away the groceries and got herself and the ingredients organized for the dinner preparation. She familiarized herself with the kitchen so fixing dinner wouldn't be such a chore.

Ellen came home shortly afterwards, feeling fairly well, with no problems. Soon Anson came in. They sat talking for a while, Rene with her martini on the rocks and Anson with his beer. Ellen usually didn't drink much of anything besides water, milk, and tea. But today she propped her feet up and sipped a low-calorie soft drink. The conversation was mostly about the activities around the law offices, with occasional references to the soon-to-be-born baby. When Rene told them during dinner that she had rented an apartment near Westwood, they were surprised and pleased that she had found one so quickly.

Rene recommended to her daughter that she go to bed early, reminding her of the doctor's suggestion that she get plenty of rest. Ellen said she believed she would do just that. Saying goodnight, Rene went to her own room, although she wasn't tired or sleepy. She wanted to read and meditate.

She undressed for bed and began reading the new novel she had purchased at Golden's. She just skimmed through it first, noting the first chapter and scattered paragraphs in some of the others. Again, the story was about a woman whose children were grown and gone, a woman who was restless, one who had caught the "self-fulfillment fever," the yen for freedom.

After reading for a while, Rene threw her newly purchased novel on the floor and decided that she already knew too many stories about women wanting fulfillment and freedom. She wondered what kind of freedom they were looking for—these fictional and non-fictional characters about whom she had read so much in magazine articles and so-called research reports.

She began to think about herself.

"What kind of freedom do I want that I couldn't have with Jonathan?" she wondered.

She continued to consider her own situation in contrast to that of women described in both fiction and non-fiction. None of the fictional husbands were like Jonathan, but then nobody was. Her husband, from the very beginning of their marriage, had always helped her to grow, to accept more responsibilities, to move into business opportunities.

In Wood Lake he had encouraged her to give up volunteer work with women's groups and go into business, into real estate. He had encouraged her to run for the college board of trustees and to become a real estate appraiser, in addition to being a broker.

And she would always thank him for telling her to go with Paul Ashley when he asked her to join the public affairs office of Carolina State.

Yes, her husband was very different from the husbands described in the novels. She wondered if there were actually many women like those in the novels. She thought there must be, because she had met several of them when she'd gone back to college to get her degree in journalism.

Rene's brandy was gone. She didn't want any more, but she was thirsty. She put her robe on and went to the kitchen for ice water and then back to bed. She was still wide awake.

She thought there must be thousands, maybe hundreds of thousands of married women, many who didn't really have to work, who felt compelled to get whatever it was they hadn't gotten before they were married, or while they were married. The most acceptable object of their desires was a degree or advanced degrees. These were the reentry women whose numbers made it necessary for universities to set up or enlarge their women's studies departments. From her own observations, she knew that many of these women were choosing more education, not just for economic reasons, but to get out of their houses to find out what they could do —and would do—on their own.

But, Rene wondered, does it have to be a case of degrees and divorces?

Prompted by all her thinking about others, she asked herself, just exactly why did I want the journalism degree? I had already been offered a teaching job in the journalism department because of my experience.

Maybe I wanted the degree for symbolic proof of my career achievement. I also studied hard and made all A's to prove to myself and to my children that not all their brilliance came from their daddy's side.

I got a kick out of taking twenty-one credit hours in one semester and making all A's. My young classmates were impressed, too. We became pals. Most of them weren't even half my age, but they accepted me as just another classmate, all calling me Rene, and often asking me about an exam coming up.

Thinking of her journalism classmates reminded her of a happening, as she identified the event to herself, that she wasn't sure she wanted to remember. What she was sure of was her wish to have had when she was nineteen or twenty at least one or two experiences some of her classmates accepted now as part of their education, as well as part of their pleasure. The event Rene remembered was a party given by one of the popular journalism professors, Dr. Catalan.

Johnathan had moved to Washington in August, right before the fall semester started. Rene was determined to finish her credit requirements in one semester. She studied hard and by midsemester break was exhausted.

Professor Catalan's party was a good excuse to celebrate and relax. She was fond of both Catalan and his wife. She knew they loved parties, but she was surprised that his party turned a little wild, by her standards. The professor's blue jokes set the tone, and the alcohol heightened it.

When the party was over, five of her young fellow guests insisted that she show them her home. They had heard it was an impressive place, inside and out.

The group came over, and she gave them a tour of the house, upstairs and downstairs. Two couples went out on the large deck that overlooked the yard and forest behind it. One young man couldn't resist the grand piano. To Rene's surprise and delight, he played very well, almost as well as her son, Bruce.

When the other four were ready to go, Rene invited Billy, the pianist, to continue playing. She said she would drive him home afterwards. So he stayed and asked her to name her favorites. Rene first requested "Yesterday," the beautiful number by the Beatles, then "Autumn Leaves." As Billy continued to play, she was surprised at the number of songs he knew.

"I earn most of my way through college by playing cocktail parties," he explained. "You wouldn't believe how many parties they give around this town."

She got a beer for Billy and another martini for herself and sat on the bench with him, singing almost every number he knew how to play. She had long ago recognized and developed her knack for recalling the name of a song, the basic melody, and the lyrics.

Billy was happy to find such a talented musical partner, one who could really sing. Rene thought she might further surprise and please him by showing him how well she could dance. She slipped off her shoes and danced to Billy's tunes.

Billy picked up the tempo, but Rene went back over to sit on the piano bench with him, sipping her martini. She was wearing a soft, medium-long, green silk crepe dress, slit up the left side to a little above the knee. The top was low-cut and was held together at the waist with a wide brocade belt. She had worn no bra that evening because, she remembered saying to herself, she was part of a young crowd. But when she stopped dancing and rejoined Billy at the piano, every time she leaned over, one breast or the other was almost fully revealed.

Yes, she remembered the midsemester break of her one semester back in school all too well. The absence of Jonathan, the party that was a blur, and Billy's good music had all contributed to her "I don't care" spirit. Now, in bed at her daughter's California home she remembered her encounter with Billy.

On the night of the party she had kissed Billy from time to time, to congratulate him for an especially pleasing rendition of a song she liked. Finally, Billy could stand it no longer. He slowly brought her to him, with both arms around her, and kissed her fully and deeply. He was excited and so was she.

Billy said, breathing faster, "Rene, you are really some woman. Lord, you are unbelievably appealing. Let's go see your bedroom again. On the tour I didn't get a good look at it."

As he spoke, his hand sought her breasts.

Rene moved away to the end of the bench. "Billy, you're a darling young man. I would enjoy having you visit my bedroom, perhaps as much or more than you would."

Then she had quickly risen from the piano bench. "I need some hot tea right now. And I think some hot tea would dampen your desire for any more playing." She laughed softly and looked at him sympathetically, as she headed for the kitchen. "Perhaps I shouldn't have used the word 'dampen.' "

Billy laughed. "It's okay, Rene. I'll take some tea. Got any cake or cookies?"

Rene disappeared into the kitchen. "You're in luck, Billy. I have some Sara Lee carrot cake that's almost as good as my Pope cookbook recipe. But maybe you don't care about cooking."

Billy followed her into the kitchen. "I don't care much about cooking, but I sure do care about carrot cake."

*Love and Ethics*

Rene served the tea and cut off a big slice of cake for Billy. She took a smaller one for herself. They discussed Professor Catalan's party and, she remembered, Billy wondered why such a smart professor felt he had to tell dirty jokes. Rene suggested that Dr. Catalan might be having a problem with impotency and used the jokes to substitute for virility, or maybe it was just the opposite. Billy was thoughtful.

"Rene, I don't ever remember wanting to make love to a girl as much as I did tonight with you. You and I worked up to the right mood through our love of music. I don't know exactly how old you are, but if I had a choice of a weekend partner, you'd be the one."

Rene remembered being comfortable with his honesty. "That's a very nice compliment, Billy. I'm sure the music helped. You got to me, too."

"However, if any medals were earned tonight, I won one when I went to the kitchen instead of to the bedroom. That's advice I would give to many lovers who shouldn't be lovers."

She smiled at him.

"I do love your music, Billy, and I'm glad we both settled for that —and tea."

"I'm glad, too, Rene, and I'll tell you why. My mother is forty-seven years old and has been a divorcee for three years. She's almost as pretty as you are and also has a nice figure. For some reason or other, perhaps to get back at my father . . ." His voice trailed off.

"My father left her," he continued, "after twenty-four years of marriage, for a twenty-five-year-old graduate student at the University of Illinois. He teaches there now. He still lives with his girlfriend, and they're still not married. She gets her Ph.D in psychology this year, and you can bet my father will soon be without his mistress.

"Anyway, my mother has a thing for young men as lovers."

Rene remembered being a lot more understanding of Billy's mother at that point than she would have been an hour before.

"I mean fellows no older than I am," Billy said. "Twenty to thirty is her normal age range. I even think some of my own friends have slept with her, although they haven't told me.

"I don't know what happened to her, because she's been a good mother to me and my older brother. I think she must have been a virgin when she married Dad, and now she's making up for lost opportunities."

Now the similarities are getting a little too close for comfort, Rene thought.

"Anyway," Billy added, "I don't like what she's doing to herself or to me and my brother. We've talked with her. We want her to marry someone—he could be fifteen years younger or fifteen years older—but marry she should.

"One good thing, we think she is getting over her high-frequency affairs." Then Billy sighed rather noticeably.

"So, Rene, I'm glad you got up and came to the kitchen. As much as I wanted you, I was happy that you didn't take me."

"Billy," Rene said, "maybe your mother is dating all these young men just to taunt your father, to let him and his friends know that she's not sitting at home mourning his rejection of her."

"Maybe so. But my father doesn't have enough pride in himself to be taunted. He has no reaction at all," he said sadly, "except to indicate that her post-marital conduct proves he was right in leaving her."

Rene remembered thinking she should give Billy the other side of the story. "Billy, you know there are several professors and high administrative officials, men in their fifties around this university, who are notorious for making love to women students who may not even have reached their twentieth birthdays. No one seems to condemn them, apparently not even their wives.

"So, why shouldn't your mother sleep with young men? She is divorced and free."

Billy thought about the comparison and then said, with a great deal of honest innocence, "I don't know much about men."

He seemed to want to confess. "Rene, I get around to adult parties by playing the piano. I've been seduced by several women —I don't know how old—anywhere from thirty-five to fifty-five, I'd guess, more or less." He thought a minute before continuing. "Frankly, I never realized before I had these experiences how much more accepting and soft and kind older women can be. To be honest with you, young girls around my age, which is twenty— going on twenty-one—seem to come on too strong, they're too competitive."

"Who wants to make a contest out of loving?" he asked in

exasperation. "I think young women take the initiative to satisfy themselves. Older women take the initiative to satisfy the man."

By this time the first serving of carrot cake and tea was gone, and Rene wondered if she should put an end to the evening at this point. But Billy had started her thinking, and she wanted to continue the conversation. She offered him more tea and cake. He brought his cup to the counter for a refill.

Standing beside Rene he continued, "Most older women I've made love to, or rather, most older women who have seduced me, always seem to feel a sense of guilt. It seems to me, if you feel guilty after loving, you shouldn't have done it. I guess when these women move outside their own cultural group, their age seems to bother them. But after they've made love, they seem to want to erase the guilt feeling by doing it again."

Billy smiled at Rene and kissed her gently on the cheek. "I noticed that you sure don't seem bothered, though."

Rene thought, we didn't make love, either. No telling how I would have felt if we had ended up in the bedroom instead of the kitchen.

"But, Billy, wouldn't the same culture or age gap bother men? It certainly doesn't seem to. Men boast about having a girl who's half or even a third their age.

"I'm now almost forty-six. You're twenty. My husband was only three years younger than I am now when he married a twenty-year-old girl—me!"

"I don't know, Rene. I don't know. All I know is what I've experienced. It seems to me that older women may not be getting all the sex they want.

"I used to think young people were the highly sexed group. These women in their forties may have been slower getting there, but as far as sex is concerned, they have it all put together now."

Rene thought about Jonathan's telling her over and over how very satisfying she had become. But then she also thought that he was probably just partial to her—or very used to her.

"Older women really know how to entertain a guy."

As Rene joined him again at the table, Billy said, "As for oral sex, they must have specialized in that to offset being fearful without the pill. I don't know when the pill came in. All I know is that the older woman can really turn a guy on." Then he added very softly, "But Rene, believe me, I haven't had to say this to the other older women I've met and loved. You're the only one with whom I've had to take the initiative."

"Oh, Billy." She recalled how difficult it was at that moment to refrain from losing herself in his apparently waiting arms. "I probably provoked you, and I shouldn't have. If I weren't married I believe our tea would have been delayed an hour or two."

Rene knew it was definitely time to change the subject. She asked him how he had liked the cake.

"Wonderful, although I've been so wrapped up in talking with you, I didn't notice how good it really tasted."

Standing up, Rene said, "Let me take you home now."

She didn't want to test her resistance any longer. Billy was an attractive male, very attractive, but he was also sensitive and sweet. Maybe all piano players were like that.

Billy took his plate, cup, and saucer over to the sink. "I have my own car. I parked it on the street."

They walked down the hall to the front door and into the foyer. Before opening the door to go home, Billy leaned over and kissed her briefly and warmly. "Goodbye, Rene, my beautiful lady of song."

Rene had just stood there, wishing that she had made love with a boy like Billy when she had been twenty.

When she was a young girl, she had dated several young men, especially to go dancing. She knew she was probably the best dancer any of the boys knew. The boys had asked her to do lots of things, but she had remained a virgin. Now she thought how ridiculous it was for her not to have gone to bed with Hudson, the Notre Dame boy to whom she had been engaged for seven months. Why hadn't she? She believed now that if they had gone to bed, they would probably have married. Instead, she had broken off the engagement. What was her reason? Had she feared sex?

As she lay in bed she thought about her school days in North Carolina and Indiana. There were school days after spending over twenty-five years with Jonathan and school days before she had ever met him. In some ways they were the same, but in other ways they were very different.

She wondered why and how she and Jonathan had decided to get married. He had never propositioned her, had never asked her to go to bed with him before their marriage. She had wanted him to make love to her, but he had kept his distance, despite the fact that she knew he had slept with many beautiful girls.

She recalled she'd often heard models who appeared on the TV show she co-emceed talking about Jonathan. Two of the six on the show one day had bragged about having spent weekends with him. Yet, he had never tried to seduce her.

She has asked him point-blank one evening before they were married, "Why do you want to marry me, Jonathan?"

He hadn't replied romantically, but very seriously. "Because of your high degree of self-discipline and perseverance. I need a woman with those rare qualities."

Of course, the question she kept asking herself was, "Why did I want to marry Jonathan?" that one was not so easily answered. Perhaps she had intuitively known that only an older man would be knowledgeable enough to bring her out of herself.

They married exactly sixty days from the day they first met (September 6 to November 6)—she hadn't felt as romantic as a woman should. But maybe she was smarter than Jonathan with regard to the marriage. She knew he could have married any one of at least a dozen girls. They were all prettier, some much better educated, and all were sexier than she was at the time. Now, thirty years later, she was careful to qualify her self-assessment. She knew she could have married one of two or three very fine young men, too, especially her fiance from Notre Dame.

But what made her marry Jonathan? She again pondered the question.

Yes, she believed only a strong man could have broken her out of the influence of her strong Catholic upbringing and her mother's constant warnings about sex. She was then, by her own admission, what one might now call inhibited, if not fairly frigid.

She had worshipped Jonathan. She didn't know whether worship was a form of love or stronger than love, but he was her god. She knew he could do everything for her. In return, she knew she would try to do everything for him.

After a while she fully understood that she was his protegee and he was her mentor. He gave to her what Mindy had given him— except that Rene had also needed sexual awakening and release. But perhaps Jonathan had, too, before Mindy.

As Rene reminisced about her marriage, she became a little sad.

For so many years every expectation of her marriage to him had been fulfilled. She had thoroughly enjoyed the luxurious apartment they had had on the lake front in Chicago the first three years of their marriage. Ellen and Bruce were born during those years, and she had never seen or heard of any father who enjoyed his children as much as Jonathan did.

The move to the Winnetka home was like a dream. She loved the home and the community. She had been younger than most Winnetka wives, but she was invited into all the clubs and community activities just the same.

And the farm! She had not been able to imagine how it would be. She remembered not being able to believe that any place would be as wonderful as Winnetka. But the farm was. The ten years there with the children, dogs, cats, and cattle were truly wonderful—what a rich life! She still thought the farm life had been the greatest thing possible for the children.

In Wood Lake she felt she had really arrived in her own right. She became successful in real estate and in politics. She was still pleased about having gone into real estate before her husband, although he did push her into it, in a way.

When had things begun to change? Was it when Jonathan retired from business and sold the farm? Was it when they returned from Europe to Church City, North Carolina, where Jonathan designed and built their wonderful big house? It was a perfect house, maybe too perfect—a tangible monument to a love that was dividing.

Was it when Jonathan became so involved in the formation of the Ethics Inquiry Group? From the very beginning she knew that she was seeing her husband become the victim of an obsession. Yet, she had joined him, taking a six-month leave of absence from the university, during which time she helped to get out two important books. But she hated all the things that depressed her husband.

Rene thought about their three children, who had been a source of common joy and excitement and pride from the day each was born. She and Jonathan, whether the marriage continued or not, would always know they had been good parents. They had great children to prove it.

That was one thing she had given Jonathan that no one else ever had—children. Then she smiled; she was also the only one who had ever given him milk left over from the babies. Rene accepted Jonathan's inordinate fondness for women's breasts, which probably came from his never having had a mother of his own. At least, that was his justification for admiring pretty bosoms.

They had had a great marriage for a long, long time. Now, for the welfare of each, she supposed she would have to agree with Jonathan. She should be given a chance to be on her own and choose her own friends—and a new husband if she so desired. She didn't know for sure that she would ever wish to marry again.

She remembered that Jonathan had once told her, shortly before they married, about Florence Hopkins, a rich, attractive forty-five-year-old divorcee. Florence had commented to him then that when his twenty-year-old-wife-protegee became a brilliant forty-five-year-old woman, she would feel compelled to try being on her own. Now they seemed to be fulfilling that prophecy.

Rene did know that their separation, for whatever reasons and however beneficial it might happen to be for each, could possibly be a tragedy for both.

What a strange man Jonathan was. She wished she could make him happy. She wished someone or something could.

Rene was aware that she was suddenly very tired of recollections and anticipations. She liked to play life from day to day and not judge or prophesy. Tonight she just wanted to go to sleep and awaken in the morning to another fresh new day.

# 8

For thirty years or more the Drake hotel had been Jonathan's campground in Chicago. Since it was only about three in the afternoon, he sent his baggage up to his room and decided to walk down Michigan Avenue. He went out the Lake Shore entrance so he could stop by the Cape Cod Room to make dinner reservations. He had invited two old friends to join him that evening.

Jonathan had lived on Chicago's Near North Side for many years, throughout the forties. Living in Chicago during those years had been like living in a small town. Even after he had moved away, he could come back and, generally, meet a friend or two walking along Michigan Avenue. Now most of his friends had retired to the sunbelt or were hibernating in the suburbs. Some were dead.

He continued his walk, stopping for a minute to look at the woman's wear displayed in an exclusive shop. He had purchased many fine blouses and dresses there for women he had known during his seven years as a widower.

He understood those women and consequently had never cared to give just any gift. He bought things that made them feel especially pretty and proud—things they hadn't realized would be so becoming or do so much for their total personality. He believed that many women underestimated the totality of their personality and do not dress to enhance or inspire dignity and distinction.

After their marriage he had purchased most of Rene's better clothes and jewelry. Unlike some wives, Rene was a very thrifty person, and she would forego buying for herself the more expensive items. For whatever reasons, she always seemed to be pleased and proud when she wore what her husband had chosen.

When the children were young, he had purchased clothes for them wherever he happened to be. In Dallas he shopped in the children's department of Neiman-Marcus. In Austria he bought lederhosen for his son and dirndls for the girls. As the children had grown up and become successful, things hadn't changed. He still purchased very special items for them from time to time, such as distinctive suits and blouses.

Recently he bought his son a particular sport coat to match his advertising agency life-style and brilliance. His daughters welcomed suits which were perfect for a lawyer or banker. For Ellen's last birthday he had purchased a soft green silk blouse with a double collar and pleated sleeves to go with her navy or white suits. He thought it an ideal combination for a distinguished young lawyer. He loved beauty and brains and dignity—all in one woman.

He looked across the street at the John Hancock building. Whether or not one liked the diagonal crosses it had to bear, the one-hundred-story, black obelisk-like building was an impressive structure. He remembered the night one of his corporate executive friends who had an apartment on the ninety-first floor took him up to the next floor to meet another corporate chief executive and his wife. Several guests were there, and in the discussions the question came up about getting rich and staying honest. The best-known and richest man present said, "Of course one can be honest and rich—no conflict." His wife had stared at him for a quiet moment or two and had said, "Now Abner." The subject was changed rather hastily. Jonathan recalled an old saying that the normal progression of a successful businessman was first to get on, then to get honest, and finally to get honor (by giving a new building to a college or hospital, for instance).

Continuing his walk down Michigan Avenue, past the Chicago water tower, he thought that that structure was still the most beautiful building on the avenue. Before reaching the Wrigley Building he ran into Mark Aaron, a Chicago Tribune columnist. He had first met Mark when he was writing for another Chicago paper. He had told Mark then that he would outlast all his advertising and marketing column competitors. He had forgotten that prediction, but Mark, now a little gray, balding and overweight, recalled Jonathan's early confidence in him. It occurred to Jonathan that one never knows how important a word of encouragement and an expression of confidence can be to a young person—and to some older ones, too.

The encounter with Mark made Jonathan feel that he had a good reason to drop in and see if any old advertising comrades happened to be in the Wrigley restaurant bar. It wasn't a big bar—it probably had no more than twenty or twenty-five seats at the bar counter. There may have been four or five small tables, but mostly there was just standing room, which made the place feel as intimate as a home cocktail gathering.

No one he knew was there and he learned that the last of the old-time bartenders had retired. For Jonathan, the only old friend he met at the bar was loneliness.

He ordered a martini on the rocks with no fruit to see if they still served great martinis. It looked good, served in a deep straight-up glass. He studied it, thinking he had never had a good martini on the rocks in a tapered glass. He took a sip. It was dry and satisfying, just as they had always been.

While enjoying his martini, he thought how the bar might pick up extra volume, profits, and publicity by serving what Jonathan called a Martini Split—equivalent to one-and-a-half regular martinis. The split would be for the fellow who likes a bit more than one martini but didn't want to move up to the two-martini bracket, certainly not at lunch.

In his days in Chicago, he had considered it the most dynamic big city in the world. They used to do big business so quickly and simply. In London, New York, Tokyo, and especially in Los Angeles, they made such a big deal out of a big deal. People would be kept waiting and procedures were slow. Chicago, in the forties and fifties, had a yes-or-no attitude, and it didn't take you long to find out where you stood. They took their cue, perhaps, from the simple, unquestioned authority of the old Chicago political machine.

Jonathan thought the early-day crooks in Chicago were dependable and predictable. They weren't nearly as flighty and unreliable as many modern politicians, gangsters, and their sympathetic business friends. When betting on potential winners, he considered genuine, dependable crooks were safer bets, and the most socially destructive crooks were the dignified hypocrites who committed sins of omission. Far too often, he thought, they are seated in tower suites.

Jonathan wandered north on Michigan, noting the new buildings and continuing improvements. Yet, it still felt like the old Michigan Avenue. The Michigan Avenue business leaders deserved a good deal of credit for protecting the avenue's intimacy.

He began to walk a little faster. After a time the pleasant memories penetrated so deeply they became painful—caused by the irreplaceability of past reality.

He returned to the Drake and looked in on what had been the Camellia Room. He remembered it as delightfully intimate. A design of camellias on a background of green and white appeared on the linens, the matches, and the swizzle sticks. As he stood there, it seemed like yesterday that he had responded to a phone call from an acquaintance who was president of the Drake at the time. He had heard that Jonathan knew a fellow who was an artist at the piano.

"Yes," Jonathan had replied, "I do. He's a fine gentleman and plays beautifully."

"If he's free," the hotel president said, "send him over tomorrow and have him start playing during the luncheon period in the Camellia Room. Tell him to see Franco."

"I think Franco will like him," Jonathan said. They liked him. Their customers had liked him, too. The pianist played during the Camellia Room luncheon period every day for the next twenty years. Every time Jonathan had come into that beautiful room for lunch, his grateful friend had played some of his favorites—Chopen, Liszt, and Scarlatti.

Jonathan strolled over to look around the Gold Coast room. It was in this room four years earlier that Ellen had married Anson Folsom. The Gold Coast was a large room, elegant without being rococo. The floor was marble, old and beautiful. Fortunately, the various owners and managements had left in place all the twenty or more multi-tiered crystal chandeliers. The great sixteen-foot windows faced Lake Michigan.

Ellen and Anson needed a big room because they had invited so many of their college friends from San Francisco to Boston. Ellen's childhood and high school friends drove in from Wood Lake and Winnetka. Of course, many friends of the Barrons came to see the first Barron child married. Knowing Rene and Jonathan, they anticipated plenty of good champagne and good food, but they couldn't have guessed there would be anything new about the wedding ceremony itself. Judge Austin Barton of the Federal Court of Appeals performed the wedding. Ellen had been his law clerk. The judge spoke eloquently, but it was what he said that caught the audience by surprise, including the parents of the bride and groom. The two young lover-lawyers had written their own vows. And the audience seemed pleased to hear them, enhanced by the marvelous way Judge Barton spoke them.

"Dear Ellen and Anson, today you are surrounded by your friends and family, all of whom are gathered to witness your marriage and to share in the joy of this occasion.

"As you know, Marriage is that relation between man and woman in which the independence is equal, the dependence mutual, and the obligation reciprocal. As you enter this relationship, I should like to speak of some of the things which many of us wish for you.

"First of all, we wish for you a love that makes both of you better people, that continues to give you joy and zest for living, and that provides you with energy to face the responsibilities of life.

We wish for you a home—not a place of stone and wood, but an island of sanity and serenity in a troubled world. We hope that this home is not just a place of private joy and retreat, but serves also as a temple wherein the values of your life are generated and upheld.

"We wish for you children—who will acquire your best traits and will go forth to re-create the values you shall have instilled in them. We hope you will pass on to your children, just as your parents have to you, the concept of family as a transcendent force which brings people close in time of joy and in time of need.

"Finally, we wish that at the end of your lives you will be able to say these two things to each other:

'Because you have loved me, you have given me faith in myself; and because I have experienced the good in you, I have received from you faith in humanity.' "

Judge Barton spoke to the audience: "Today's celebration of human affection is the outward sign of a sacred and inward commitment which religious societies may consecrate and states may legalize, but which neither can create or annul. Such union can only be created by loving purpose, be maintained by abiding will, and be renewed by human feelings and intentions. In this spirit these two people stand before us."

To Ellen and Anson: "Will you now please clasp your hands."

To the groom: "Do you, Anson, take Ellen to be your wife, to love and respect in your life together:"

"I do."

To the bride: "Do you, Ellen, take Anson to be your husband, to love and respect in your life together?"

"I do."

To the best man: "May we have the ring?" The best man presented the ring to the groom.

To the groom: "In offering this ring, which marks your desire to share your life with Ellen, repeat after me: With this ring I marry you and join my life with yours."

To the maid of honor: "May we have the ring?" The maid of honor presented the ring to the bride.

Judge Barton spoke to the bride: "In offering this ring, which marks your desire to share your life with Anson, repeat after me: With this ring I marry you and join my life with yours."

Judge Barton spoke to the company: "In the presence of this company, Ellen and Anson have joined in marriage and have pledged themselves to each other. May they now go their ways together as husband and wife in happiness and peace."

Jonathan remembered that he had listened very carefully to Judge Barton's reading of the vows. He liked the idea of mutual obligations. Everyone had been very attentive, some of them may have wished they had taken vows "according to Ellen and Anson."

The screaming sirens of an ambulance going down Michigan Avenue blasted him out of his deep reverie.

He walked through the wide doors of the Gold Coast Room that opened into the adjoining French Room where Ellen and Anson had held their big reception, with a dance band, plenty of champagne, and all kinds of food—even a wedding cake that actually tasted good. The French Room was subdued by its baroque pillars with scrollwork in gold and turquoise. Yes, he and Rene had done their part to help their daughter and new son-in-law have an impressive, happy, memorable wedding—so satisfying.

He glanced at his watch and saw that it was time to go unpack, shower, and dress for dinner. He walked around through the lobby to the information desk and picked up the key. His room was on the ninth floor at the opposite end from the suite where he and Rene had been married thirty years ago.

Their wedding had taken place in Suite 910. In contrast to Ellen and Anson's wedding, only the minimum number of family members and two outsiders, the best man and maid of honor, had been invited. The noted judge who performed the simple ceremony had at first refused to proceed with the marriage, because he had discovered the groom was forty-three and the bride only twenty. His reason was that, in all his life, he had never yet married a couple who had not remained married and he wasn't going to start now. But a good friend of the judge, one of the country's eminent lawyers and Jonathan's best man, persuaded him that the bride and groom were responsible persons whose age difference was not *prima facie* evidence that they would not stay married. The argument had been logical, although not necessarily valid, and the wedding quickly proceeded. The judge conducted the briefest ceremony the law allowed. There were quick thank you's and good-byes as Jonathan and Rene rushed off to catch a plane to Los Angeles for a honeymoon night in the bridal suite of the Town House Hotel. The next day they rented a car and drove to Palm Desert.

Ah, Palm Desert. How lovely and sparse it was when they had honeymooned there at an intimate little lodge. After thirty years of marriage, he supposed he and Rene had earned the judge's approval. But Jonathan wondered if they would, after all these years, disappoint the judge and themselves.

Marriage! Marriage! he thought, almost aloud. What constitutes a marriage? Two lovers living together isn't marriage. Nor is marriage two people carrying out their own commitment to one another. It takes more than persons to make a marriage.

Marriage is one plus one—plus something else. It is an entity, an institution. It is a cell in a cohesive social body, a cell that may become cancerous when divided.

Marriage takes two persons plus—society, the dynamic feeling of a third element, possibly spiritual. It was this indeterminate, but strong, third presence that he hated to disturb, over and above his love for Rene—and his concern for her future health and happiness.

# 9

When Jonathan arrived at the Cape Cod Room, Ken and Lois Rush were talking with the maitre d', who wanted them to know how much his six-year-old daughter enjoyed Ken's program, featuring his puppet Gargoyle. Ken and Gargoyle had been on TV daily for thirty-four years, so almost everyone knew them. Ken was sixty-five but looked a well-fed forty-five—effervescent and delightful. He still had all his hair, although it was mostly gray. A sophisticated stranger would have guessed that Ken was a very successful and happy banker whose golf score always hovered close to par. And Lois Rush, despite her natural reserve and dignity, looked much younger than her sixty years.

After they were seated at a quiet, comfortable table, Jonathan asked Ken why he hadn't brought Gargoyle. "Doesn't he like fish?"

"Oh, no, Gargoyle never eats out," Rush said as he leaned back and shook his head emphatically. "He absorbs a special puppet food. Anyway, Lois says I eat enough for two. Gargoyle likes to stay home and read. Tonight he's studying the relationship of a philosopher to a psychoanalyst."

"Dare I ask if he's found any relationship?" Jonathan asked cautiously.

"Yes, indeed. The first thing he discovered was that psychoanalysts and philosophers take turns on the couch."

"A plain case of not overlooking the obvious," Jonathan observed with a shrug of his shoulders.

"That's right," Ken quickly agreed. "And Gargoyle is also trying to determine how psychoanalysts and philosophers view the current surfeit of sex movies."

Jonathan played straight man and asked, "How does Gargoyle say they view them?"

"In disguise," Ken reported with a "you-should-know-that" smile.

"I never thought a puppet would drive me to drink," Jonathan remarked as he motioned for the waiter. Then he asked Lois, "What'll you need to survive Gargoyle's research?"

"I'd love a good white wine. What would you recommend?"

"There's one that's so good I seldom drink it, Berncasteler Doctor."

"I've had that wine only a few times, but it is wonderful."

"Now, for Gargoyle?"

Ken shook his head. "No, no, Gargoyle doesn't drink, but I'm sure he would want me to do a little research on that Berncasteler wine."

"And for me," Jonathan said to the grinning waiter, "I'll have a gin martini on the rocks with no fruit."

"Ken, you must be the first puppeteer to set such high standards for your puppet that the master must live the way the puppet does —exemplarily. And I know where you and Gargoyle found your moral and ethical principles—in Rosston, Indiana. I visited that little community when I went down that way searching for good dairy cattle. One of the finest purebred Holsteins I ever owned came from a farm near Rosston. That cow was later classified 'Excellent,' the highest classification for a cow."

"That's Rosston for you," said Ken. "Cows and people there *are* excellent. It was a fine community. And those wonderful summers I spent with my grandparents. I wish every boy and girl could spend some time in an old-fashioned little country town, walking in the nearby woods and fields. Perhaps, if they are real lucky, they might have grandparents who take time to love them a lot and teach them a lot, like my grandmother did for me. In a way, on our TV show, we try to express love for the children who tune in to our TV house to have fun and to learn good things from Gargoyle. They listen to him. They can imagine him to be whatever good friend they want and need. Didn't you once tell me that you grew up in a small country town in Arkansas? Or were you born full grown? And how did you ever become so interested in ethics?"

"Yes, I grew up in a small southern Arkansas town. It's still small, and they want to keep it that way. I spent lots of time with my father, because he was a gardener and I could work with him when I wasn't mowing lawns or doing janitor work in the Baptist church. As for my interest in ethics, I think it derived from my work —not what they call the 'work ethic,' but from doing something useful with somebody and for somebody.

## Love and Ethics

"Unlike some processes of getting religion, one doesn't become ethical by conversion, but primarily by absorption and development. You can't be ethical and lazy. You must do for yourself and for others. Ethics is our way of being human, having concern for others and for those who come after us. No, you can't be or do good by doing nothing—whether you're very rich or very poor. The essence of ethics is action.

"Economically speaking, I guess I was one of, if not the, poorest kids in town, my father and family having arrived there with eighty cents. I remember the first piece of waffle I ever tasted. It came out of the local bank cashier's garbage can. For a long time I wondered how the hell they got those little squares in that dough. But never did I think I was poor. You know, there is such a thing as 'pretty' poor and 'dirt' poor. We were a clean, neat, hardworking and very proud family. I lived in the poorest house, but it was on the *right* side of the tracks. In retrospect I realize what real estate people mean by the value of "Location, location, location." Before I was ten years old, I became an entrepreneur—I bought a brand new Pennsylvania brand lawnmower, the best there was. I financed it with my janitor work and credit from the local hardware store, where my Sunday school teacher was bookkeeper. Oh, heavens! Sorry for the digression. Let's order dinner."

They did, and it was delicious.

Before the coffee arrived, Ken, on behalf of his philosopher puppet Gargoyle, no doubt, pursued the conversation by asking Jonathan who his hero was when he was growing up. Jonathan was quiet for a moment and replied, "I suppose I had three heroes. One was my father, because of his kindness and selflessness. One was the local general practitioner, Dr. Hastings, and again, because of his kindness and his learned ability to do so much for others. Then, and this may surprise you, Jesus Christ as the man, not as the Son of God. Jesus as the man spoke out against evil and evildoers. He had courage. He had guts—enough to throw the money-changers from the temple. I'm not a member of any church —used to be a Southern Baptist—but I implore those who do believe in Christ, who believe in God, to believe also in the works that faith demands of honest believers."

"Well," sighed Ken, "anyone who picks Jesus for a hero must believe in the perfectibility of man."

"No, Ken, I do not believe in the perfectibility of man. Man's

86

task is to strive to be as good as he knows how to be and as good as his gumption and courage will allow. Perfectionistic policies for individuals or groups, especially in business corporations, can be a deterrent to growth."

"Jonathan, it's too bad Gargoyle isn't here now, because you and he seem to think much alike."

"Ken, thanks for the compliment. That's the nicest way anyone has ever called me a 'dummy'—my apologies to Gargoyle. However, Gargoyle's comment on psychoanalysts and philosophers reminds me of a couple of days I once spent with Erich Fromm, who was, in my opinion, the greatest psychoanalyst. After Mindy, my first wife, died I considered leaving business and going to medical school to prepare for a career in psychoanalytic research. So I went to see Fromm, not long after his book *Escape from Freedom* was published. I saw him in his New York apartment, and after visiting a while he called in his friend, a Swiss professor then teaching at nearby Columbia University. His friend was a famous expert on the Rorschach test and all sorts of thematic apperception approaches, all of which he tried on me.

"They asked me to come back the following afternoon. I found them looking quite satisfied with their conclusions. They made several very interesting observations, but Dr. Fromm's central comment touched the core of my thoughts and feelings.

" 'Mr. Barron,' he said, 'you will not learn to be more perceptive or to "read" people by going to any medical school. We don't know that anyone can teach anyone to perceive the thoughts and feelings of others. But I do know the personal problem that you now face and may face all through your life.' "

I just sat and looked at Fromm, patiently and quietly. " 'Mr. Barron, our tests and our conclusions clearly indicate that you hate the fact that you are human. You forgive others because you know that they are human.

" 'But you must learn to forgive yourself because you are human, too!' "

"Ken, the older I get the more critical I am of my own human limitations and of the danger of my being engulfed by society, of my being tempted to adjust to the mores of the group. However, I realize there is the possibility that if one wins his fight to remain apart from society, he may not have enough in himself alone of what Dr. Schweitzer called the 'will to live' to want to continue living. Life, like beauty, if not shared, loses much of its glory.

"In that case a man must identify his own life with all life. The conflict may be one of getting along with people without having to become dependent on being a 'nice guy' for one's happiness. So, I guess that's why years and years ago a teacher from Denmark called me an isolate."

Once again there was silence. Perhaps Ken and Lois were thinking about Jonathan's seriousness and about what he had just said. It was Lois who broke the silence this time.

"Jonathan, as a mother of two grown children, I think your childhood sounds like it may have been lonely, but rich. I haven't seen Ken sit that still and listen so intently since I first told him I was pregnant. In those days such an event was news—even after two or three years of marriage."

Ken looked surprised. "Lois, I sat still and speechless even before that—when you said 'Yes' to my marriage proposal. I couldn't believe I was so lucky—still can't, but I'm not speechless any more. Jonathan, the dinner was superb, even for perfectionists like you and me.

"But before we leave," Ken added, "may I ask you to do something else for me? Tell me how you see your role as an isolate, or rather, let me test my idea of the isolate's role.

"It appears to me that an isolate plays a part in life somewhat like the scouts who used to serve the early wagon trains that crossed the prairies and mountains. The scout was not an integral part of the wagon train, which we'll say represents society, but he felt responsible to it and for it. It was the scout's job to be the advance observer for the wagon train, to search for places where the rivers were shallow enough to ford and to find the mountain passes that could be negotiated.

"The scout's task was not only to find the best route for the wagon train to travel toward its destination, but also to watch out for and warn of other dangers. He could not be caught up in the politics and minutiae of the group that he guided.

"Am I on the right trail?"

"Indeed you are, Gargoyle! The isolate may always be lonely, but his loneliness is his protection from dependence."

"Jonathan, we've had a very different kind of conversation," Ken said as he got up slowly from his chair and pulled it aside for Lois. "But then, we always do."

Jonathan walked ahead a couple of steps to sign the check and then said, "Thank you both so very much for coming in from Winnetka to have dinner with me." As they walked out of the Cape Cod Room he added, "Please drive carefully and buckle up. You are worth so much to so many. Good night." They shook hands warmly, and Lois leaned over and kissed him lightly. The Rushes went to the Walton Street entrance to pick up their car, and Jonathan returned to his room in time to catch part of the ten o'clock news before going to bed. Since the meeting of the Ethics Inquiry Group was not scheduled until eleven o'clock the next morning, he could look forward to getting up at a reasonable hour, having a leisurely breakfast, and reading the *Sun Times, Tribune,* and *Wall Street Journal.*

Jonathan enjoyed the morning as planned and then packed his case, checked it downstairs with the bell captain, and signed his bill.

It was a delightful, sunny June morning—a very pleasant seventy degrees. He walked down Michigan Avenue to the Loop at Madison and Dearborn Streets. Max Elson was hosting this Chicago meeting in his big law firm's headquarters, located in the First National Bank Building.

Elson's firm was one of the few Chicago law firms that had its own kitchen and could serve luncheon to three or four different client meetings or conference groups. Elson had inaugurated the in-house food service because he believed it was about time for law firms to start catching up with the bankers, accountants, and corporations when it came to such conveniences. The meeting was held in a conference room with a single large directors' table. The lunch would be served in an adjoining meeting room.

Ethics Group board meetings generally started at eleven and continued through lunch until three. Usually about fourteen to sixteen directors attended the meetings, along with the executive director and treasurer. Often, a couple of special guests, perhaps university professors or government specialists, also joined the group. Since several of the group's directors were chief executive officers of major companies, a member felt honored to host a board meeting.

When Jonathan arrived at the conference meeting room, four or five directors and two staff officers were already there, chatting quietly among themselves. Soon all those who had indicated they were coming had arrived. More than the required quorum were present. The Ethics Group board meetings were businesslike but more informal than the usual corporate board sessions.

Jonathan had spoken to the chairman and to George Gregson, the executive director, earlier in regard to his desire to make his resignation as president effective immediately. Although he wished to relinquish his duties now, he emphasized that he would continue to be available to George and to the group for any special task or for consultation, should they need him.

On this day the chairman called the meeting to order promptly at eleven and proceeded through the *pro forma* part of the agenda. The minutes of the last meeting were duly read by the executive director. The treasurer read the always gloomy report of how difficult it was to raise funds for the increasingly important and growing number of ethics projects being considered. There were often new funding activities that looked promising and some of these, fortunately, were realized.

The chairman spoke to the board about Jonathan's letter of resignation as president, a letter they had all received. Then the chairman asked for board approval and received it, along with customary thanks for the five years of long hours, six days a week, that Jonathan had given without charge to the Ethics Inquiry Group. In addition, grateful mention was made of the substantial money grants he had made over the past several years since he and four of the present directors had founded the group.

The chairman announced that Jonathan wished the board to consider his resignation from the board of directors. He had submitted this letter to the chairman individually. As soon as the chairman mentioned this possibility, one member of the board, a nationally prominent black leader, jumped up from his chair and stated that if the board accepted Jonathan's resignation, they could also have his. Immediately, the director with the longest service on the board addressed the chair. He said that if Jonathan's resignation was accepted, he too would resign. The chairman had not believed the board would accept Jonathan's resignation, but apparently the distinguished black leader did not want anyone even to consider the idea.

After the remarks by his outspoken supporters, the board voted unanimously to reject Jonathan's letter of resignation from the board. Thereupon, the chairman initiated a motion to name Jonathan president emeritus of the Ethics Inquiry Group and a member of the executive committee of the board. The motion passed unanimously, and Jonathan thanked the board for their actions.

The chairman continued with the meeting agenda throughout lunch. All the board members were busy leaders, and the time they gave to the Ethics Group was helpful, but high priced. Because the chairman was also the chief executive officer of a large multinational corporation, he appreciated the demands on his fellow executives and moved the meeting right along. All went well. Two or three new committees were appointed, and the meeting ended about 2:45, fifteen minutes ahead of schedule.

Jonathan quickly said goodbye to each of the board members and staff. He had something planned for the remainder of the afternoon, and he was eager to get started.

As soon as he reached the street floor, he hastened out of the building and walked rapidly north on Dearborn Street to one of the car rental agencies.

# 10

Jonathan drove from the car rental agency over to Michigan Avenue, went south on Michigan to Congress Street, and then turned west on Congress to hit the Eisenhower Expressway. He was going to the Forest Home Cemetery, about sixteen miles west and a mile south of Chicago's Loop. It was there that his first wife, Mindy, was buried.

He remembered that sad day in his life very well. As soon as the hearse had pulled out of the funeral home parking lot the driver had said, "Guess if we drop down to the Eisenhower Expressway we should make it in twenty-five or thirty-minutes." There was no funeral cortege. Jonathan's wife, Mindy, in a soft fuschia suit with a little matching orchid in her hair, rode along with them in her coffin in the back.

As he drove to the cemetary this afternoon, so many years later, he could still visualize her perky, brownish-blonde curly hair, her mischievous blue eyes, and her absolutely darling little nose. He could think of no better way to describe Mindy's nose. That was the type of nose that came with Mindy's one-hundred-two-pound, five-foot-one-and-one-half-inch, perfectly configured body. All of which went with the picture-book, sample-size-three shoes she wore.

Jonathan arrived at the cemetery, checked through the iron-gated entrance, and drove to the open park section. He stopped the car on the edge of the small, curving roadway, got out, quietly closed the door, and walked about fifty yards to her grave site. He found the marble marker easily. Bending to one knee, he brushed the freshly cut grass off the ivory-colored stone. He remained in that position for a while just looking at the inscription.

Mindy Barron
October 9, 1901
September 5, 1944

All the words in the dictionary could say no more to him.

After a while, he rose, walked over to a big tree, sat down, and leaned against the tree, just as he had following her burial almost thirty-eight years ago. He thought to himself, "Mindy, how wonderful you were. How wonderful you were. I knew you so briefly, but I remember you so well."

After a breast removal, Mindy Barron had fought a two-year battle against the ravages of cancer. Following the operation there had been a period of optimism, then doubt, and eventually hospitalization again. But neither Mindy nor Jonathan had ever given up all hope.

Only three weeks before she died, Dr. Ernest Edwards, an eminent specialist and the senior doctor attending Mindy, asked Jonathan to meet with him and two associates at the hospital. The moment they met, Dr. Edwards told him that Mindy also had pneumonia and, inasmuch as the cancer was so far advanced, it might be best to allow Mindy to die quickly by simply letting the pneumonia run its course. He estimated that this would probably be within twenty-four hours.

Jonathan was surprised to hear about the acute pneumonia and was somewhat shocked that the doctors would suggest not treating the disease. However, since he had long known and respected Dr. Edwards, Jonathan accepted that for certain terminal cases this was an appropriate suggestion. Nevertheless, he asked Dr. Edwards, "If you arrest the pneumonia, can you continue to alleviate Mindy's pain?" Dr. Edwards assured him that Mindy was responding well to their schedule of treatment and that they believed they could continue to keep her comfortable.

Then he had directed an inquiry to all three doctors. "Is Mindy's space here in the hospital in such demand that her presence is keeping out curable patients? Can any one of you give Mindy the needed attention without being unavailable to serve other patients whose lives you might save?"

After looking at his colleagues, Dr. Edwards had stated, "The demands are always great for hospital space, and the cost is high. But we can continue Mindy's treatment without depriving another of a chance to live and without turning away any urgent cases. However, we must all realize that Mindy's chance for survival is virtually zero. In fact, it is zero. We feel that it is our ethical obligation to tell relatives of terminal patients of any alternatives open to them."

Jonathan remembered that he had remained calm, but also that his reply had been quite firm.

"Gentlemen, your deep personal as well as professional interest has kept Mindy alive and in reasonable comfort. You have kept her as free from pain as possible. She has remained rational and alert. She's always been courageous, and she seems determined to live as long as she can. Please continue to do everything you can to keep her alive."

As they walked away, he wondered if the doctors thought him selfish in wanting to keep Mindy alive longer. He knew very well that experience and the evidence clearly indicated she had no chance to survive. But he also knew this was his wife and the dearest person in the world to him. No one could rightfully blame either one of them for wanting to spend as much time together as possible, even if it was to be such a short time.

Mindy had fought desperately to free herself to live longer. For months, after it had been quite apparent that the breast operation had not stopped the spread of the cancer, Mindy knew that death had a tight hold on her. But she never gave up. Her strong hope for more life undoubtedly postponed her death.

Jonathan also knew that Mindy would have been extremely surprised if he had given up or failed her in any way. Surely, he thought, no man was ever more complimented by a woman's love than he was by Mindy's fight to remain alive one more month, one more day, one more hour.

In the end Mindy showed no fear. She looked death right in the face when the doctor last checked her blood pressure and tried to feel her pulse.

"How long will it be, doctor?" she asked in a soft, clear voice.

"Probably within the hour, Mindy," the doctor answered with tender admiration.

After the doctor had left, she asked Jonathan softly to prop her up in the bed so she could see and talk with him more easily. He remembered how he had held her right hand as she talked about friends and relatives. She told him what he should tell them for her and how he should say her goodbyes.

What Jonathan remembered most vividly was how she had looked at him and smiled while telling him, "Since I'm leaving, you will have more time for work—you've spent so many hours just being with me and taking care of me. You've given me so much love, and I have loved you so very much. You've been a wonderful husband. You have also been a patient teacher and a kind doctor. I want you to be like that to others."

He recalled that she had remained silent for a few minutes, had seemed to be able to speak only with her eyes, but finally managed to whisper, "I love you so terribly much."

Thus had she used her last words and Jonathan had said aloud, just as the nurse came in, "If there are angels in heaven, they now have a new queen."

He remembered the day of her burial was cool for September, and how short, much too short, the drive out to the cemetery in the hearse—his final trip with Mindy—had been. To him it seemed that the driver made the trip in five minutes, not twenty-five.

Only a few of Mindy's closest friends were invited to the cemetery, and by the time Jonathan arrived with Mindy, the guests were waiting. Most of the mourners were neighbors from Winnetka, where the Barrons had lived until Mindy's illness made an apartment near his office in Chicago more desirable. The Reverend Paul Conklin, the young pastor of the Cherry Street Bible Church, was there too. Mindy had liked him and his small, fundamentalist church, because she preferred to attend a church "where at least the pastor believed in God."

Mindy had enjoyed a wonderfully satisfying, simple faith. She could never figure out what the popular community church in Winnetka was all about—unless it was to bring together preachers and parishioners who were equally uncertain of their faith. Of course, as she had explained uncritically to her husband, "The big community church did conduct fantastic rummage sales." Jonathan also remembered agreeing with Mindy that participation in a rummage sale—giving to the church your unneeded clothes, furniture, and such other items—really didn't require any special commitment to God.

In his recollections of Mindy's faith and her burial, Jonathan was sure that Mindy would have liked the simple ceremony the Reverend Conklin had conducted in the rustic chapel, situated in the center of the very old, tree-covered cemetery that had once been used as a burial ground by Indians.

As Jonathan remembered that day, he also remembered that when the service was over, he had remained at the cemetery alone, after everyone had gone. Now, after all the years, he could almost see himself walking alone to the burial place and watching them lower the coffin into the grave. When they covered the casket with the fresh earth, then, and only then, did the full finality of Mindy's death possess him.

"Oh, Mindy, Mindy, Mindy," he had murmured softly. "Without you I'm so much less. Because of you I'm so much more."

As he remembered his words, he thought to himself, "That's all still true today." He realized that he was sitting under the same tree he had sat under on the day of her funeral. The tree appeared not to have noticed the passing of so short a time in its life—so long in years, yet, through the vividness of memory, just yesterday for Jonathan.

With that ambiguous concept of time he rose, as he had on the day of the funeral, and walked through the stillness of the cemetery woods. As he moved on through the woods that beautiful late summer afternoon, he meandered like a stream that knew only vaguely that he had to keep going somewhere. When he came to a small ditch he paused, thinking, if Mindy were walking with me now, she would just naturally expect me to lift her across. She could jump the ditch, but she would know how much he liked to pick her up. Whether it was a brook in the country or an alley in the city on a rainy day, Mindy waited for her husband to put one arm around her and ferry her across. She usually paid him a kiss for his services. So it was that as husband and wife, they had remained lovers throughout their marriage.

Amazing woman, Mindy, Jonathan thought. She was mature, independent, intelligent, and capable. She did a good job as assistant manager of a large Los Angeles hotel and even succeeded as a dispatcher in Milwaukee for a railroad when she was only seventeen. In her day it was a great compliment from that traditionally male group for her to be allowed to work as a dispatcher. But despite all her marketable skills, to Jonathan, Mindy was a pretty woman, a very feminine person, and, most of all, a very kind and loving person.

Jonathan always had to smile whenever he remembered how he and Mindy had met. He had had a small studio apartment in the big Los Angeles hotel where she was assistant manager. One day he left his office early to go to his apartment to shower, shave, and change clothes for a dinner appointment with a client of the radio broadcasting station where he worked. As soon as he went into the apartment bathroom, he saw there were no towels. He called the housekeeping department, and they promised to send towels up right away. He waited ten minutes. He was annoyed to begin with, and now he angrily went directly to the manager's office to demand towels. The manager was out of the city, but the young lady who came out to see him identified herself as Mindy Clark, the assistant manager. She could see that Jonathan was quite upset, so when he told her about the towels, she acted very quickly and strongly for, as he thought, such a petite, charming woman.

"It's outrageous, Mr. Barron, that one of our permanent guests would be neglected—no towels!" she said.

She dialed the housekeeper and said, "Mrs. Spenkelhauser, this is Mindy Clark. Mr. Barron of 1410 is in my office. By the time he gets back to his room will you have someone waiting at the door with a set of towels. Or to make sure, you might take them up yourself. Also, please let us know who it was that cleaned his apartment today."

Miss Clark hung up quickly. "Sorry, Mr. Barron, to have inconvenienced you, but I'm glad you reported it directly to this office. Have a good evening."

"Thank you, Mrs. Clark—or is it Miss Clark?" Jonathan was really interested, but he asked hesitantly.

"Either one, Mr. Barron."

The next evening, when he came home, there was a basket of fruit on his table, compliments of the hotel, with a card from Miss Clark. The following day he called and asked Mindy Clark if she would have lunch with him someday.

"I'd be glad to, Mr. Barron," she said quickly.

"Would tomorrow at noon here at the hotel coffee shop be all right?" he asked just as quickly.

They met for lunch. Jonathan knew he needed her, wanted her, but he was frightened. He had never really had a regular girlfriend.

Soon afterward he moved to New York, going from there to Washington, then to Memphis, and on to Oklahoma City. He spent a few months in each place, easily finding jobs because of his background in broadcast sales. During those two years, he wrote just one letter to Mindy. He knew that he was running away from a relationship with her, but her very presence in California was like a magnet, always pulling him westward.

Two years after he had left, he arrived back in Los Angeles, checked into his old hotel, and went to the manager's office to see if Mindy was still there. She was. She almost fainted when he came into her office. She had just had her hair dyed a light red the day before, and it looked awful. She was normally a brownish blonde. It was about noon, and Mindy said nothing more than, "Let's get out of here and have lunch somewhere where I can't be seen."

The first thing she said after they sat down at the luncheon table was, "You could have told me. I wouldn't have dyed my hair. I've just been desperate. I'm so glad you're back."

Jonathan was embarrassed—and very ashamed of himself for not having contacted her. He had known he needed her since their very first luncheon date, but his own fears had kept him away. He knew that being with Mindy would change his life. He would no longer be free. He would be hers. He had been foolish in fighting his need for her. He realized as he gazed across the table at her that she would not restrict his freedom. She would open up for him a whole new world.

They were married within two months, but not before Jonathan went to San Francisco to catch a boat to Australia. She wrote him such a wonderful and understanding letter before the boat was to leave that Jonathan knew he absolutely could not leave her. Australia would have to wait. Mindy had loved him enough to undertake the task of breaking him out of his mold of isolation. She had captured a loner with her love and kindness. Jonathan was thirty-two when he married Mindy. She was thirty-seven.

Her hair returned to its normal color before long. But Jonathan never returned to what had been normal for him, even though their almost seven years of marriage was so fleeting.

As he walked back to his car he thought, "There can be no love without kindness, and Mindy was so very kind."

But Mindy could also be mischievous. On his birthday, the second year of their marriage, he returned from work at the usual time. He grabbed up Mindy and kissed her and carried her over to a big chair. He sat there, holding her on his lap, and talked about his day at the office. He wondered what she had been doing.

"Oh, the usual, except I did go over to Helen's house for a visit. Then I came home and worked on the flower beds. You know, we have a lot of petunias. They look nice alongside our white picket fence." Then she innocently changed the subject. "When will you be ready for dinner?"

98

Jonathan couldn't believe it. She had forgotten it was his birthday. "Honey, how could you forget? This is my birthday!"

"Oh, I'm sorry, Darling. I don't know what came over me. I am so sorry."

Tears leaked down her cheeks. She kissed him very sweetly. He kissed her and kissed her tears away. When she heard a noise at the double doors leading from the patio into the dining room, she jumped up as if frightened and rushed to the door. In came all five of Jonathan's fellow broadcasting sales staff and their wives. Mindy had completely fooled her husband. All of them sang "Happy Birthday" to him, and Jonathan was a very happy man.

He smiled in remembrance of that day. After that he had always been a bit wary of his wife's ready tears—but he always kissed them away.

Lord, he said to himself, she was an incredible, delightful, adorable, ornery, edible, wonderful woman.

Then he wept.

Jonathan left the cemetery in his rented car and drove a roundabout way to Chicago's Lincoln Park. He parked the car in a Clark Street garage and walked over to the park. He was hoping to find a certain park bench from which he could see the Lincoln Park West apartment where he and Mindy had last lived. The bench was still there, so he sat down. It was old and very sturdy. It could have been the same one on which they had often sat to enjoy a box of popcorn.

Jonathan thought about the experiences of his day. Since leaving the board of directors' meeting about four hours ago, he had been transported to a strange land of memory where all around was sadness. But in the center of the sadness were so many visions of Mindy—an ecstasy of reverie. He still wanted to look back to that afternoon of many years ago when his spirit must have joined Mindy's.

He remembered that when he had returned from her funeral he had not gone directly to their apartment, but had instead come to this bench. A few days before her death he had sat there and watched the first pre-autumn leaves float gently down from their life on the trees to another destiny. The falling leaves, some of them still half green in color, had reminded him of the life that was slowly, prematurely, but inexorably, leaving Mindy.

Despite the fact that the day of Mindy's funeral was long ago,

Jonathan felt compelled to reconstruct that day and many episodes in his life with Mindy. He got up from the park bench and walked the short distance to the apartment building on Lincoln Parkway where he had lived with Mindy the last two years of her life, until her final trip to the hospital. It was a sturdy, seven-story structure that time had made more attractive. It was a gracious, modest Gothic building in design—a satisfying contrast to the cold, flat sheets of glass that stared defiantly at him from some of the new high-rise apartments. He and Mindy had appreciated the nine-foot ceilings, the big, wide windows, and the spaciousness everywhere —closets, baths, kitchen, bedrooms, and living room. The sofa and chairs had not all been Baker, but they were of fine quality and were upholstered in soft-toned prints that said hello when you approached them. They reflected Mindy's charm.

After the funeral Jonathan had returned to their apartment. He remembered how noisy the door had been, its opening and closing echoing throughout the apartment. How strange, it seemed to him, that a place so recently redolent of love and laughter could now feel like an empty cavern. Without the hope of Mindy's return, there was only nothingness.

He went to a hotel that night and never again stayed in the apartment. He quickly sold the lease and all the furnishings to a rich dentist who found it handy to his North Michigan Avenue office.

All that was so long ago in time but so close in memory. On this Tuesday afternoon, Jonathan walked away from the apartment on Lincoln Park West. He went up to Fullerton Avenue, over to Clark and then a couple of more blocks north to the garage where he had parked his car. As he walked he tried to recall if he knew anyone still living in the area who had known both Mindy and Rene. It was then that he thought of the Brysons in Barrington.

Herbert and Millie Bryson, though often tempted to move to Arizona, where one of their daughters lived, had remained in their lovely Barrington home, with its five acres of lawn, flowers, gardens, and trees. In June they weren't likely to be in Arizona visiting, so Jonathan called them from the pay phone in the garage.

"Hello, Millie, how are you and your squirrels and the golfer?" he asked, knowing she detested the army of squirrels encamped about her place.

"Oh, Jonathan," she exclaimed after recognizing his voice, "are you in Chicago?"

"I came in yesterday for a board meeting of the Ethics Inquiry Group and thought I would stay over a day or so. I'm on the Near North Side picking up my car. I thought I'd drive out to Wood Lake and stay tonight. Is Herb home?"

"He's out hitting a few golf balls, and our dog, Bogie, is still shagging the balls for him. He'll be in soon. Why don't you come by for cocktails and dinner and plan on staying with us, unless you have a commitment in Wood Lake?"

"Check with Herb first, Millie. Perhaps we could have cocktails at your place and then go out to that fish place in Algonquin for dinner."

"I know Herb will be happy to see you, Jonathan, so come on out. What time do you think you'll be here?"

"Well," Jonathan said as he looked at his watch, "it's about ten of seven now. Possibly in an hour or less."

"We'll be looking for you then. Herb will be showered and ready for his second scotch by the time you arrive."

"Sounds good, Millie. See you soon." Jonathan paid his parking ticket and drove to the Walton Street entrance of the Drake, where he could park long enough to go in and get his case out of the checkroom. From the Drake he drove south on Michigan to Ontario, and on Ontario to the Kennedy Expressway. The rush-hour traffic was almost over, so the driving was easy. His thoughts, once again, returned to Mindy.

Mindy, Mindy, he thought to himself. She was my mystery woman—always dressed so demurely. She was so modest, so dignified, and never, no never, he recalled, did she use a vulgar word. Once in the bedroom, however, with the door closed, Mindy was delightfully explosive, totally loving, incredibly satisfying.

Yes, Mindy had been Jonathan's kind of woman. For a man who tended to idealize women, that said a lot about her. Such common things as dirty language, sloppy dress, and coarse laughter shocked and repulsed him. And he had long ago observed that those to whom sex meant the most used four-letter words the least. Mindy fit his ideal perfectly.

But their relationship surpassed the physical joy they had given each other. After Mindy's operations, when her body was too fragile and sensitive to pain even to be picked up and held, he told her that for him, their love was a twenty-four-hour-a-day experience and leaving out a few moments of peak excitement was not important. Actually, as he recalled, with the growing but unexpressed awareness of the scarcity of time they might have been together, intimate physical love had been absorbed in the totality of their deeper spiritual relationship.

Love thrives on the satisfaction of mutual needs. Although most lovers think they are made uniquely for one another, rarely, he believed, could this be so true as it was for Mindy and himself. He did for Mindy spiritually what Mindy did for him in totality. He gave her a reason for living. She showed him by example how to live in a sharing way with others.

Yes, Jonathan said to himself, as he turned off the Kennedy Expressway onto the Northwest Tollway, Mindy was an angel, but if she had been only an angel she wouldn't have been such a fascinating, absorbing woman.

He remembered telling her sometimes that if she weren't so distractingly tantalizing, he would be more successful. He would work at the office longer, attend more business dinners, take more important trips, and attend more committee meetings and conventions. He would do all the things a businessman was supposed to do to maximize his economic opportunities. Instead, he couldn't resist coming home to see her. Often he teased, "What a waste of time—leaving meetings early, not going to every client dinner—all just to run off to be with my own wife."

But she didn't mind the teasing. Instead, she would ask, "Why live just for the next rung up the ladder or sacrifice human fulfillment for unneeded dollars?"

But he was remorseful, wishing he hadn't teased Mindy, wishing he had only told her a simple fact: she had been a greater magnet for him than all his business activities. She must have been pleased in a way, though, he consoled himself. She knew how hard he had worked all his life, and she knew what a compliment it was to her for him to have given up that extra effort.

He soon turned off the tollway and headed north on Barrington Road. The Brysons' home was directly west of Barrington on Larkspur Lane, off County Line Road.

Jonathan was bewildered by the intensity of his remembrances during the afternoon. Yes, he had gone looking for them, but why? Why—after all these years? Was it possible that after almost forty years he was looking to Mindy again, for himself and for Rene?

Rene had never been jealous of Mindy's place in Jonathan's life. In fact, she had been glad he had been married to Mindy. Rene doubted that Jonathan, without Mindy's help, would ever have moved out of his extraordinary isolation. From the very beginning of their marriage, Rene had encouraged him to talk about Mindy, to tell her what he thought Mindy would have said or done. Many times she wished she could have known Mindy; through Jonathan, Rene learned so much from his first wife.

This evening Jonathan wished he could talk with Mindy. He thought of her as the only mother he had ever had. But she had also been a good friend. He was uneasy about the possibility of experiencing another loss, but not because of death. This loss might result from separation and divorce.

# 11

Jonathan turned on Larkspur Lane and saw the Brysons' home, a long, low, brick ranch trimmed with cedar, on top of a small hill. All the homes in the area were situated on five or more rolling acres. They were easy to see, because much of the acreage looked like well-kept golf course fairways. When he pulled into the Brysons' driveway, he was greeted by Bogie, a handsome border collie with a black, furry coat and a touch of white around his neck that looked like a clergy collar.

Herb Bryson was standing near the driveway, throwing an old golf ball for Bogie to fetch. He greeted Jonathan, who shook hands with both Herb and Bogie. Jonathan had owned several border collies in his life, and he preferred them to all other dogs as an all-around friend and helper, perhaps because he thought them to be proud, beautiful, kind, and intelligent—the characteristics he also liked in human beings.

Herb was a consistent nineties golfer who was always trying a new grip, a new club, or another instructor. What he got out of the game was lots of fun. After watching his master's hitting and putting for so many years, surely Bogie understood why his name wasn't Birdie.

Jonathan looked around the yard. "Herb, do you still do all the mowing and trimming yourself? It certainly looks nice."

"Yes, I keep at it, but I never quite catch up." Herb gestured toward the road. Then with a goodbye pat on Bogie's head, Herb said, "Come on in. I've been waiting for my scotch. Will you have one, or could I fix you your favorite martini?"

"I think I'll join you with a scotch and water," Jonathan replied. "Where's Millie?"

"Here I am, Jonathan, in the kitchen preparing one of Rene's recipes, sausage skillet. I know both you and Herb like it. I think Herb took three helpings of it out at Wood Lake the last time we had dinner there."

Millie was smiling, genuinely glad to see Jonathan.

"How's Rene?" she asked. "Couldn't she make this trip with you?"

She greeted him with a hug. Jonathan looked at her. "Now, that's the kind of dress I like to see a woman wear." He was referring to Millie's blue dirndl sprinkled with small buttercup blossoms. Around the collar and cuffs were two rows of buttercup —yellow rickrack trim. The dress reflected Millie's warm, smiling personality—not sophisticated, not reserved, not shy. Her brown hair was losing out to grey, but not before its time. Millie was a delightful, lovely woman who was pleased with being a good wife, a marvelous homemaker, and the adored mother of two grown daughters.

"Rene is in Los Angeles, checking up on Ellen's condition. Ellen's about to have her first baby, our first grandchild, maybe prematurely."

"Ellen's having a baby? That's wonderful! There's nothing like a first grandchild. When is the baby expected?"

"Her doctor thinks the baby might be as much as six or eight weeks ahead of schedule. He isn't sure yet. I told Ellen not to worry, though," Jonathan said casually. "I predicted fifteen months ago, before she decided to have a baby, that her first child would be born the first week of September. We have a little ways to go till then."

"Jonathan, do you think your ESP works that far ahead? I thought you specialized in guessing or telling people their birthdays and how many brothers and sisters they have."

"Well, Millie, I hope she goes full term—whatever works for Ellen's health and happiness and for a strong, healthy baby."

"How's your ethics project coming along?" Herb asked as he went back to the kitchen to strengthen his scotch.

Since they were sitting in the living room, Jonathan raised his voice so Herb could hear his reply. "Oh, the project is moving along-and after today it may move along even better. I've just resigned as president. I'll still remain on the board of directors, though, and serve as president emeritus; that is, on call as a free consultant."

Herb had returned from the kitchen and was putting fresh ice in Jonathan's glass.

"You know, Jonathan, before you arrived I was thinking about you. Some of us who knew you thirty-five or forty years ago and have kept on doing our jobs in the same field—well—we hardly know you any more. You have had so many different careers."

Jonathan was a little surprised. "That's an interesting observation, Herb, but changing interests shouldn't cause changes in basic attitudes. True, a corporate president who retires to Longboat Key, Florida, to fish for the rest of his life may not keep up with his old friend who retires to open a chain of massage parlors in Austin, Texas. It may be a matter of one fellow idling his motor and the other trying to rev his up.

"The most noticeable differences may not be those that originate within the individual, but those that result from new peer influences—from the different behavioral patterns and attitudes expressed by the new groups he learns to know."

Jonathan turned to Millie. "What do you say, Millie?"

"I think I agree with you. All I need do is look at the differences that exist among women who were my sorority sisters in college. Through the years many have had children and stayed at home. Others have gone back to college for advanced degrees, have become professional women at forty-five years of age. And some of them have acquired the moral standards—especially the sexual freedom—of their twenty-two-year-old classmates.

"And I should know. I've remained home with the usual club and episodic 'do-gooder' jobs, while Lydia Gorham and other friends are making big money, becoming mayors and bankers; and, I might add, more than a few don't hesitate to admit that they enjoy the freedom to sleep around with their different 'friends,' as they call them."

Millie waited for the men to enter into the conversation, but they remained quiet, sipping their drinks and listening to what she had to say. "The so-called 'new' woman," she continued, "calls her lovers friends, because she wants sex without love. Apparently, she thinks that makes her more like a man, more independent.

"Actually, some of the women are, indeed, afraid to fall in love —so they say. They're still vulnerable to earlier home influences that are in conflict with the new demands for self-sufficiency. Many are uncertain and unhappy.

"We all still belong to the same sorority," Millie added. "But our annual round-robin letters now appear every ten years or in the form of newspaper clippings mailed around."

106

"Millie, what you've been observing may be part of nature's plan to balance population with productivity. Nature seems to function in strange ways for not so strange reasons. Sex without love and a neuterized comradeship may be nature's way of downgrading effective sexual intercourse, placing the emphasis on friendship and recreation instead of on love and procreation. And man is helping nature with pills and pollution," Jonathan said.

Herb invited Jonathan to have another scotch and asked, "Have you heard from any of our old poker-playing friends lately?"

"Herb, the one that I hear from most is Jack Kildare." Jonathan smiled as he got up to have his scotch replenished. "Jack has liked me since the night he astounded me by throwing in his hand with four fives and a ten of diamonds. I happened to have drawn an ace and a deuce of clubs to go with the three aces in my hand. He sure read me. And, there's Wally Horton down in Durham, who always wants me to give him at least three-to-two odds on all Duke-Carolina State football and basketball games.

"Speaking of old friends," Millie interjected, "what is Rene going to do with her career?"

"Millie, neither Rene not I really knows what she will do, what I will do, or what we will do," Jonathan answered slowly.

Sensing a touchy subject, Herb said, "Mill, how about that sausage skillet? Talking about Rene brings her recipe to mind!" Both men got up and headed toward the kitchen to help serve dinner.

"I don't remember if you ever knew the Arthur Ashenbaums. They lived in Barrington Hills for some years," Herb said to Jonathan as he placed the silverware on the table.

"I didn't know them, but their son, Roger, came out to look at farm properties with me one time. What about them?" Jonathan asked.

"The old man and I have played a lot of golf. We've known the family rather well. Yesterday we had a very sad journey to the Forest Home Cemetery, where Roger is buried. There's been a lot of progress in treating leukemia, but Roger finally lost the battle. His parents and his wife and two children have been terribly demoralized. They wonder why so good a son, such a kind and attentive husband and father, had to be taken from them so early, so mercilessly."

"Herb, you and Millie knew my first wife, Mindy. I visited her grave in Forest Home this afternoon. Then I stopped by the apartment building on Lincoln Park West where we last lived together.

"When I lost Mindy, the inevitable question came to me, as it must have come to the Ashenbaums: Why did someone so needed and with so much to give, have to die so soon? Why does death often claim earliest the kindest and dearest?

"There is no answer, but it may be that the better the person, the more kind and loving, the more his or her death is a challenge to those remaining. Perhaps the purpose of death is growth. As time passes, those who miss and mourn the good may feel obligated to live richer, more serviceable lives in order to fulfill the mission of the one who was called away.

"The Ashenbaums have been a very religious family, haven't they?" Jonathan asked Herb.

"Yes, they have great faith, and they've been very active in their church," Herb affirmed.

Jonathan nodded. "Those who genuinely believe in God and in the ultimate beneficence of all that happens are fortunate. If they believe, the Ashenbaums will accept that in going about His task and in bringing the whole of mankind to a greater realization of Him and His purpose, the God of their faith surely expects mankind to see the challenge that each good life, such as that of their son, Roger, creates."

Millie motioned for him to be seated for dinner and said, "I never knew you had any religion, Jonathan."

"I'm aware of religions and their benefits and limitations as institutions, as structures. But if I were religious, I would want my religion to derive from faith in God rather than from faith in any institution.

"Mindy, for example, found more comfort and kindness in the small, shall I say, unfashionable little Cherry Street Bible Church in Winnetka than in one of the big churches where she had to listen to the indeterminate ramblings of a New England-educated doctor of divinity."

"We didn't realize that you'd just visited the cemetery where Mindy was buried. But Roger's funeral was in the back of our minds. I think I'll pass along to Arthur the gist of your comments."

Millie was a marvelous cook. She didn't have to tell Jonathan and Herb to quit talking and start eating. As soon as he tasted the food, Jonathan said, "Sausage skillet may not sound so great, but it sure tastes good."

"I'm glad you like it, Jonathan. I followed Rene's recipe."

"Didn't Rene get her coffeecake recipe from you, Millie?"

"Yes, and is that a hint you'd like fresh coffeecake for breakfast?"

"It did sound like a hint, didn't it? If you'll make the coffeecake in the morning, Herb and I will prepare the rest of the breakfast."

"You mean to tell me that you like Millie's coffeecake better than my popovers?" complained Herb.

"Your popovers are a close second."

Millie warned Jonathan and Herb that she had a surprise dessert, a lemon custard pie she made that afternoon.

"I have to play a lot of golf to offset the good food around here," Herb said with a chuckle.

"I probably shouldn't mention this, Herb," Millie remarked as a reminder to her husband, "but I've found that plenty of yard work also goes well with lemon pie."

The three old friends laughed, and the dinner proceeded enjoyably. Jonathan and Herb cleared the table, rinsed the dishes, and put them in the dishwasher. It was pleasant outside, so Millie served coffee on the patio.

Jonathan asked Millie and Herb about their two daughters.

"Oh," Millie replied joyfully, "the girls are fine. Both are out on their own now, and we sure miss them, don't we, Herb?" As she smiled warmly at her husband, he nodded.

"Beth is with the State Agricultural Department in Arizona and is quite happy there," she continued. "Her husband, Jerry, is doing well in the real estate business in the Phoenix area. Lorrie is involved in theater projects in Colorado. They get home for most holidays, and when they can't make it here, we gladly go there."

Millie asked about the Barron children. "We need to catch up on the whereabouts of your children. You've said that Ellen is in Los Angeles and expecting a baby soon, but what are Bruce and Susan doing?"

"Bruce is a creative supervisor for a New York advertising agency, and Susan is in graduate school at NYU and getting her MBA in finance. They're all happy, working hard and learning a lot."

"As I recall, they all finished college early . . ."

"Before they were nineteen," Jonathan answered quickly.

"That's really amazing! What do you know about raising and

educating children that so many other parents apparently don't know?" Millie asked.

Jonathan thought a moment before he replied, "Oh, I'm really not sure, Millie. Perhaps if there was any secret to their rapid advancement, it was that they learned to love learning from the day they were born. They grew up in a learning environment. Each of the children had his or her own library in their own room.

"But I think another thing that helped was that both Rene and I believed our children could be successful. So often, you know, parents greatly underestimate a child's capacity for learning and the satisfaction children find in being responsible—particularly their satisfaction in being treated as individual persons with responsibilities and rights. We also helped them to understand that a good education without good character was no good."

After coffee, Jonathan said he would like to phone Rene to see how she and Ellen were doing. He used his telephone credit card for the Los Angeles call.

Rene answered, and immediately after greeting her he asked about Ellen and the baby.

"The doctor is still uncertain when the baby will arrive. He told Ellen this morning that he wants her to come back again Tuesday. In the meantime, she is to stay home and get plenty of bed rest. Next week he may tell her to remain in bed. I've told Ellen, I'll be glad to come right back out and help her until after the baby arrives."

"What are your immediate plans, pending word from the doctor next week?"

"I'll check with a couple of my friends in the universities out here and also with the *Los Angeles Chronicle* about possible job opportunities. You'd suggested that I do this, remember? But I'll be back in Washington Friday night to see you and Bruce."

"When does your plane arrive? I'll meet you."

"I'm on United, arriving at Dulles Friday evening at eight-thirty."

"Okay, I'll meet you at the gate to the general lounge area. The eight-thirty arrival is good, because I can meet Bruce at National when he arrives at seven o'clock on Friday. Don't call Ellen to the phone now, but reassure her that the baby will arrive in good shape.

"Now, here's Millie—and Herb—at whose resort home I am staying tonight."

110

As soon as the conversation ended, Millie couldn't resist asking Jonathan if he and Rene really did plan to live apart.

"Millie, I don't know. Both of us are exploring our futures."

"Half the businessmen I know," Herb said, "are separated from their wives and families half the time. So a period of separation for you and Rene would be doing as lots of people do anyway for a variety of reasons."

"With that observation, Herb, let's let Jonathan go to bed. He must be tired."

"That sounds good to me, Millie," Jonathan quickly agreed, "so I'll see you in the morning; the evening has been very pleasant. Goodnight, all."

"Goodnight," Millie said. "I believe everything you need is already in your room."

"Goodnight, fellow. See you at breakfast. Remember, we'll have homemade coffeecake," Herb added.

# 12

Jonathan awakened early. He showered, shaved, dressed, and went outside to walk around. Soon Bogie came rushing out of his home in the garage, grabbed a stick along the way, and placed it at Jonathan's feet. Jonathan took it and threw it down the hillside.

The Barrons had had two border collies, Preacher and Carla, when they lived on the farm in Wood Lake, so Jonathan felt right at home with his friend Bogie. The main problem was when to quit throwing the stick, because Bogie was tireless in retrieving it. Jonathan changed his tactics and threw the stick into the bushes where Bogie had to search around for it—an enjoyable thinking and sniffing task for him.

After a half hour or more of walking and playing with the dog, Jonathan returned to his room to wash. Then he went to the kitchen to assist Herb in preparing breakfast.

Millie was up and had already mixed up the coffeecake and placed it in the oven. Herb soon joined them and took his place at the bacon-griddle. Jonathan beat the eggs, putting in his customary sprinkle of rosemary. They drank their orange juice while working, and soon breakfast was on the table. The air was filled with the country-kitchen fragrance of the freshly baked coffeecake. For Jonathan, no meal at any time of the day was better than bacon and eggs and fresh coffeecake, and he told Millie, "No breakfast anywhere could beat this one."

"Thank you, Jonathan. I've always said men should help with the cooking," Millie said, smiling over Herb.

After breakfast Jonathan thanked Millie and Herb for their warm hospitality, put his case in the car, waved goodbye to everyone, including Bogie, and drove away. Instead of going west to Algonquin and north to Wood Lake, he drove back to County Line Road.

Rene and Jonathan had moved to Winnetka from the lakefront apartment in Chicago, where they had first lived after their wedding. Mindy and Jonathan had moved from Winnetka into Chicago about ten years before he returned to Winnetka with Rene.

Jonathan wanted to see again the house on Locust Street where he and Mindy had lived. He also wanted to look again at the Williamsburg colonial house on Edgewood Lane that he had purchased and remodeled for Rene and their young children.

He wondered why he was looking at houses. He supposed he was researching himself, looking back at his track record, looking not for facts, but for enlightenment, for a guideline. He wanted the past to throw him a lifeline for the present, possibly for the future. He was seeking a solution to the growing, intensifying conflict he had been experiencing during the past several years.

Arriving in Winnetka, Jonathan drove to the house on Locust Street first. He parked his car a block away and walked slowly to the house. It had not changed much except in paint and price. He figured the house would now sell for five or six times what it had been worth when he lived there with Mindy.

No one seemed to be home, so Jonathan felt comfortable standing on the sidewalk near the long side yard. For several minutes he gazed at the row of windows that were above the sink in the kitchen. He remembered fondly that he had often found Mindy in the kitchen, working happily at the sink and adjoining counters when he came home from the office. She had loved the creativity of cooking. After leaving her business career, she had found being a homemaker not a bit dull. She had worked from the age of seventeen, so her home was like a resort to her.

From Locust Street, Jonathan drove about a dozen blocks to the place on Edgewood Lane where he and Rene had lived. The house was located on a dead-end block of Edgewood, and he walked quickly over to his old home.

He was pleased to see that the attractive, sturdy, white picket fence he had built around the back yard had not been torn down. When his family lived there, the house had been surrounded on three sides by three or four acres of woods with only the front lawn area open. Now several very expensive houses surrounded his former home, instead of the woods that had once been part of an estate. But his old home still looked good—far more livable than the expensive development—type houses around it.

Jonathan studied the Edgewood Lane home. Here he had lived a different life with a very different kind of wife. He believed that when a widower remarries, he should never try to duplicate his first wife, no matter how much he cared for her. A man changes; he should marry a woman to suit those changes. He should marry a woman for her own characteristics and values, not as a replacement for a previous wife or for a mother. The differences between his two married lives reflected his beliefs, he thought.

The family living in the Edgewood Lane house was at home, so he just walked on by, going up to the cul-de-sac and returning slowly. The yard was not quite as well manicured as he had kept it, but the place still looked invitingly attractive. For a moment, Jonathan imagined he could see their small children running around the back yard. He was tempted to stand across the street from his former residence and look at it for a while, but someone opened the garage door to take the car out, so he walked back to his own car.

He decided to drive out to Marriott's Lincolnshire Resort Hotel, located on a hundred or more acres about halfway to Wood Lake. He could have a pleasant luncheon there and walk around the grounds for exercise and meditation. He wanted to call his attorney, Carl Cochran, about the real estate closing session, which was set for the next morning at eleven o'clock in Wood Lake. He also wanted to find out if Cochran would be available for lunch after the meeting. Jonathan knew that Cochran, a member of a family long prominent in the area, could bring him up to date on what was going on in Wood Lake.

He drove west to Edens Expressway, north to Highway 22, and then west to the Lincolnshire. The hotel had a room available, so Jonathan went right up and made the call to Cochran, who readily agreed to lunch after the meeting.

Jonathan thought a good martini might supply a little solace for the loneliness that now fully possessed him. For two or three hours he had vividly recalled so much joy and love, how else could he feel but full of loneliness, once he had closed the door on the memories of his two happy homes in Winnetka?

He unpacked his case, hung up his suits, and went back to the lobby. He decided to take a walk around the hotel before having lunch. Strolling by the swimming pool, he stopped and looked around for a minute or two, then moved over to a nearby picnic area about half the size of a football field. No one was picnicking, so he sat at one of the tables under a tree—a quiet spot that was conducive to reminiscing.

The year following Mindy's death had been a busy one for Jonathan. In addition to his advertising agency business, he'd experimented with other ventures. Television had been in its infancy, and he'd set up a small television-program production firm, along with a talent booking agency. There was no Mindy in his life to hasten home to, so he needed and found more things to do, new things. He had even purchased one of the very best Michigan Avenue beauty salons, the most fashionable shop of its day. In addition, he had gone to the West Coast and has purchased a proprietary pharmaceutical product, which years later became a best seller in its classification.

He had returned, to a degree, to the aloofness that had characterized him before he met Mindy. And the loss of Mindy had made him more hesitant to become dependent on anyone for anything. This resultant state of mind may have made his choice of his second wife, Rene, a predominantly rational and objective one, rather than a subjective, emotional discovery and response to a spontaneous romantic love. Jonathan wondered as he walked back to the hotel what the outcome would have been, had he been able to analyze the situation so clearly thirty years ago. But he had never regretted choosing Rene to be his wife.

# 13

During his period of renewed isolation following Mindy's death, Jonathan had come to know many women professionally. A few of them had been kind enough to be objectively concerned about his personal life. They thought that for his own good he should have women friends who could break him out of his prison of memories. After a year or so, even his male business associates said that he should certainly start moving into a new personal life.

Now, more than thirty-five years later, he was trying to recall the path he had followed from Mindy to Rene.

As he sipped his martini, he remembered one woman who had seen him frequently on a non-social basis. Sue Elliott was the manager of his Chicago beauty salon. He occasionally went to the shop around five o'clock, closing time, to check operations, to get a manicure, or perhaps without realizing it—to see Sue Elliott.

One day she had called him before five and said she would like to talk with him about the shop operations. She requested, however, that they meet outside the shop. Jonathan suggested that they meet at his nearby apartment at five-thirty. He knew Sue well enough to know that she wouldn't call just to discuss routine matters of the salon. *She* managed the shop, he didn't. He was curious, not only about the business matter, but about the woman herself.

Sue was thirty years old and very attractive. However, one scarcely noticed her pretty face and figure, because she had acquired a cold veneer, like a freshly ironed white sheet over a designer silk dress. Jonathan attributed this to her five-year career as a manager in the better salons. He imagined that anyone, man or woman, who long attended to the beauty therapy of so many neglected, upper-middle-class women might find it desirable to wear a duster over one's soul.

Her fine features were often tightly drawn from stress, but Jonathan had admired her lovely eyes. They were clear, greenish-grey, with naturally long lashes and beautiful eyebrows. He suspected that if her protective shell were removed, one might discover a very lovely woman. Her choice of clothing reflected professional strength, while retaining a feminine delicacy. She dressed properly and becomingly. As Jonathan thought about Sue, he wondered why—with all these pleasing characteristics—she had never been in his apartment.

At the sound of the apartment doorbell, Jonathan hastened to greet her. He anticipated seeing Sue, even though their past contacts had been only pleasant business meetings. On two or three occasions, when he had visited the shop, she had noticed that he needed a manicure and had reminded him that she could still give a good one. She teased him into the manicures, because, as she said, he'd spent so much money on the shop already that he might as well get a tax-free benefit.

Sue arrived and after her hello, said jokingly, "And I didn't forget my manicure kit."

"Maybe I do need a manicure," Jonathan replied, "but I run a very modern salon here. With every manicure we serve cocktails. What's your choice?"

"A plain gin and tonic would be nice, thanks." She laughed and said, "You don't know it, but one of our girls has a little drink before each manicure."

Sue followed him into the kitchen and sat down in the adjoining dining alcove. He served the drinks there.

"Oh, I'm so glad to get out of that shop," Sue began. "Today was really bad. Business was good, but Francois came to me and said that he and the other stylists wanted more vacation time and all sorts of additional benefits that I've never heard of in any beauty shop."

She frowned. "It made me so mad, because you've given everyone more money, better facilities, and more vacation with pay than any other shop in town. And worst of all, this happened the very day that I was finally getting up enough courage to tell you I wanted to leave for California and get out of this business.

"Now I must stay and work out these matters for you. I'd like to shoot Francois," she said emphatically as she drank her gin and tonic.

"California sounds good, Sue. What kind of opportunity do you have out there?"

117

"One of the cosmetic and pharmaceutical firms—you know them, Wellington, Inc.—has asked me to represent them in southern California. They want me to be their actual manager in southern California, not just someone who trains and contacts demonstrators. I can't believe it. It's such a good job and they've actually offered it to me!"

Jonathan smiled. "It's too late now for you to telephone anyone, but no later than ten o'clock tomorrow morning their time, you call and tell them that you've discussed the matter with me. Tell them that while I will certainly hate to lose you, the salon is in the process of being sold and you are free to join Wellington at whatever time you and they agree upon. Okay?

"Let me congratulate you on the new life ahead of you—and on the new job. And let's switch to champagne to celebrate this good news!"

"But what will you do about the hair stylists and the immediate problems of running the shop?" she asked.

"It's typical of you to be unselfishly concerned," Jonathan responded, while getting the champagne glasses and the champagne from the refrigerator. "Not many left of your type—what corporations call 'company minded.' No wonder Wellington wants you.

"As for the shop, your previous assistant, Gretchen, may be wishing to amuse herself differently for a few weeks with something other than simply being a rich mistress. I'll bet she'd be glad to take your place temporarily. And I'll bet, too, that she knows just how to handle every man in the shop." He smiled a very knowing smile.

Jonathan had a little trouble getting the champagne cork out in one piece, but Sue was too preoccupied to notice. He poured the cold champagne into the refrigerated glasses, which he always kept "on ice" with the bottle.

"In reference to the employees' demands, you and I have long realized that, when a company voluntarily takes the lead in upgrading working conditions and gives wage increases beyond previous industry levels, employees are often tempted to figure that management is either naive or getting rewards the workers don't know about. So they place pressure on the spot that gives most easily. That's why I believe that, even when a company is very small, owners or management should still negotiate changes—and not just be socially conscious Santa Clauses.

118

"Employees prefer to negotiate. That's what I should have done. Come to think of it, that's one reason I don't favor our government's making unilateral concessions to other nations. The other country thinks we're stupid or deceptive."

He paused for a moment, laughed, and interrupted himself. "Anyway, don't worry about it because, with our location and patronage, I can easily sell the shop to one of the large chain operators. Let's drink a toast to your future with Wellington and southern California."

They touched glasses, and both took good opening drinks.

"In a way, your going solves a problem for me, because I had been thinking that, if you wanted the shop, you could buy it with nothing down at your own price and pay me for it as profits permitted."

Jonathan had another thought. "But acquiring the shop would have married you to the business, and you really should get out of it."

"Thank you so much for the offer," she replied, "but I stayed this long only because of you. And, in another way, because of you I've been prompted to want to leave this business. Confusing, isn't it?

"Now, I also came up here to give you a manicure, remember?" She was feeling that she had better have something to do, or she might drink too much champagne.

"May I now have the honor of being your very last customer, until someday, you give your husband a manicure?" Jonathan asked.

"Didn't you tell me, Mr. Barron, that Mindy used to give you manicures?"

"Indeed she did, and they were wonderful. You probably wouldn't wish to give me a manicure, though, like she used to." Jonathan picked up the drinks and was moving toward the sofa. "But let's sit in here where we can be more comfortable. And, Sue, please call me Jonathan. 'Mr. Barron' seems so formal."

He placed the drinks on the table in front of the sofa. He hoped she might sit beside him, so he put the glasses close together.

Sue followed him.

"I'm sure I can trim your fingernails the way Mindy did, Mr. Barron—I mean, Jonathan."

"You're sure?"

"Of course."

"Let's have a little more champagne." He refilled the glasses, and both of them looked at the bubbles, perhaps wondering what the other was thinking. Jonathan knew what he was thinking. "She is so kind. And she'd be far prettier if she could just relax and gain a certain confidence and pride in herself. Getting away from the beauty shop business, not having to deal with so many neglected, unloved, and now probably unloving women would help her most of all."

He believed that when a girl is young and growing up, she learns how to be feminine from other girls, but when she is a grown woman she learns to be feminine from men. When a woman is grown, he philosophized, if she's kind and has remained pretty, she should avoid spending very much of her time with women who have become jaded, women who are wasting their lives. Jonathan felt that when Sue moved into another environment, she would blossom.

Sue was quite perceptive. She sensed that Jonathan liked her very much but that he hadn't wanted her. She also knew herself and her own possibilities.

True, she had remained longer in the shop business than she should have, but that evening she was free. She thought that perhaps she could help Jonathan break out of his past. The girls in the shop talked about his still being married to Mindy, even though more than a year had passed since her death. One of the girls, who thought she could get any man she wanted into bed with her, had met her first failure trying to seduce Jonathan.

Sue knew he was much too sensitive to settle for just a lovely body. As they sipped the last of the champagne, Jonathan asked, "Do you really want to give me that manicure?"

"Sure I do. I'd be disappointed if you were unwilling to be my last customer," Sue responded a little flirtatiously.

"Then please move over here, because Mindy always sat in my lap while she talked and manicured."

"I did say that I would try to do it as Mindy did, didn't I?" she said hesitantly, as she casually placed her manicuring tools on the table near him. Then she went into the kitchen and returned with a cup of hot, soapy water.

"Please put your left hand in the water and hold me on with the other." Sue was trying to position herself, but the manicure was becoming less professional.

120

also have set free her own emotions for a rich love in the future."

He kissed her and got out of bed and dressed. Sue lay in bed daydreaming, feeling good all over. When she arose, Jonathan slowly helped her dress. She was in no hurry and was probably thinking it would have been nice to go back to bed. So was he. But he handed her skirt to her, and she put it on. He picked up her shoes and kissed each one as he gave them to her. He wanted Sue to know that after loving, he adored her even more than before.

When they were dressed, their conversation became light, reflecting the joyous mood of two people who had something to celebrate. Indeed, they did. Their warm, intense loving, founded on mutual respect and admiration, served to satisfy their strong emotional needs and dissolve their stress and loneliness.

Jonathan and Sue walked over to the Singapore Restaurant for a steak sandwich, holding hands, swinging along—two different people, both so much happier.

The following week, Sue went to California and accepted the job offer. Before she left for Los Angeles, she and Jonathan had lunch in the garden room of Jacques's Restaurant. Sue was eager for the challenge of her new job and thanked Jonathan for having helped her feel more confident, professionally and personally.

Jonathan smiled at Sue and said that he would be forever grateful to her for reaching in to his isolation and drawing him back into the world of partnership, communication, and sharing. They parted with a gentle kiss, knowing that they had had a very special, very loving relationship—one each would long remember.

Jonathan finished his martini and ordered lunch. As he ate slowly, sitting alone in the hotel dining room, he thought about another fine woman he had known during the years between Mindy and Rene.

Marie Warren had been chairman and chief executive officer of a profitable manufacturing company—the leader in its field. She was seventeen years older than Jonathan, but she had been one of his more frequent dinner dates.

He learned a great deal from Marie. She was clever, in the best sense of the word, in handling people of many ages and types under different conditions. He saw her in many business and social situations. Whether talking to one of her major distributors about pricing and discounts, or to the wife of an employee about a sick child, Marie was considerate, composed, and gracious. If someone had tried to convince her that women had to be assertive, autonomous, and more or less androgynous to succeed in business, it might have baffled her. Marie never entertained any notion that she should act like a man.

At national trade conventions, no major competitor failed to show up at Marie's big hospitality suite. So many conventioneers came that she often rented a ballroom. She sat and stood with dignity. She wasn't slender, but she looked like a stately queen in her carefully selected, specially made clothes. She wore expensive, carefully chosen accessories. Her coiffure was always perfect except for a few stray wisps of hair on each side. At sixty years of age, she didn't mind if these selected strands of hair chose to be gray.

In thinking about what had made Marie so special, Jonathan recalled that she had radiated a sense of sureness and inner peace which drew people to her. And she knew a lot. She wasn't just intelligent, she was "street smart"—the Michigan Avenue, Rodeo Drive, K Street, and Wall Street type of street. She usually spoke and laughed softly, a trait, Jonathan reflected, many professional women hadn't mastered or had simply never acquired. Marie also had a wonderful sense of humor, springing from her ability to laugh at the incongruities of life.

Jonathan finished his lunch, wishing that all women who reach the age of fifty-five could know a Marie Warren. It seemed to him that fifty-five had become a watershed age for contemporary women—too often an age of resignation. While many are highly sexual and quite attractive, some move toward neuterization of gender, compulsively, defiantly, demonstrating their self-sufficiency and independence. These attitudes often show up in harsher looks and lack of care in dress, and horrible hair styles, he had observed.

Marie Warren had passed through her fifties, retaining her charm and grace and pride. She didn't have to "prove" she was capable of being self-sufficient. She didn't need a ready comeback line when a man challenged her. Marie knew her strengths, and she knew that the male combatants knew her strengths, too. She let such people express their own inadequacies. As to men at fifty-five, Jonathan had often thought that many were so hung up on demonstrating their virility with women under thirty that they had little time to do much more than seek the power and money to make up the difference.

When Jonathan first recognized that he and Rene might marry, he talked with Marie about her. "Well," Marie had said, "if you're asking me what I think about the young lady, I'll at least have to meet her. I'll give you and Rene your first engagement celebration —at the Drake in the Camellia Room. Let's set a date now."

About mid-morning on the date Marie had chosen for the luncheon, she died of a heart attack. Rene hadn't known Marie Warren, but she felt a deep personal loss. Jonathan knew that from what he had told her about Marie, Rene believed she had missed meeting and talking with a woman whose life would have been especially inspiring to her.

Jonathan sat at his luncheon table, gazing into space, absorbed in wondering if all their lives would have been different, had Marie and Rene met.

"Sir, is anything the matter?" the waitress asked. "Are you ill?"

"No, no, thank you," Jonathan said, coming back to life. "Did I order coffee?"

# 14

There is a saying, not heard often enough, in Jonathan's opinion: "One's friends make one cry; one's enemies make one laugh." In his relationships with women, for his own short-term benefits or joys, Jonathan might have found it advantageous to tell his date of the day or evening nothing but nice and happy things. She might well have been quite pleased and cooperative. Instead, he told each woman with whom he spent much time what he thought would be helpful to her.

Why he felt this obligation to help and to bear the truth, as he objectively perceived the truth to be, he didn't really know. Now, as he looked back over the years since Mindy's death, he realized that, to a considerable extent, he had been unconsciously carrying out her last wishes. How had she said it?

"You have given me hope in the future and inspiration to want to do better. I want you to be like that to others. One reason I was attracted to you was because you didn't just tell people what you knew they wished to hear. You said what you thought a person should hear. Please keep on being you."

Maybe he had taken Mindy's admonition too seriously.

He realized that during his years of widowhood he had increasingly taken the role of mentor to his women acquaintances. Filling that need in their lives had given him a great deal of personal satisfaction. Mindy had been the female-to-male mentor for him. He became the male-to-female mentor for others.

Eventually, Jonathan's mentor role and the end of his personal loneliness had coincided in one woman. Her name was Rene Hamilton.

Surprisingly, he had met Rene through an advertisement in the *Chicago Tribune.* No, it had not been like one of the contemporary ads in the personal columns. He had advertised for a female co-emcee for a two-hour daily TV interview show.

The ad copy specified an attractive young woman, prefereably around twenty-five years of age, with a good speaking voice and at least two years of college. There were numerous replies. A very high percentage of the replies came from women working with building and construction companies. Jonathan concluded that men in that industry must convince their female employees they are attractive, no matter what the actuality.

Rene, with her mother's encouragement, applied for the TV position. She always loved change but usually had to be pushed into it.

Freda Jackson, the producer of the TV show, sat very patiently through numerous auditions and talked to the applicants. She finally selected four girls she liked best and arranged for Jonathan to audition these finalists.

Freda's first choice for the job was Rene, whom she said was handsome, if not cute-pretty.

"Rene," Freda had told Jonathan, "looks resourceful, responsible, and credible."

"If she is going to go on TV at nine every morning," Jonathan thought, "reliability must be a prime requirement."

He asked Freda to bring Rene into the private audition room so he could talk with her.

As Rene seated herself in the chair offered her, Jonathan sat down across from her. Freda stood by the door.

"Are you working now, Miss Hamilton?" he asked.

"Yes, I'm a secretary at the General Furniture Company."

"Why would you wish to give up a good, steady job for a TV program trial? We can't guarantee how long the show will be on."

"Oh, the answer to that is simple," Rene said quickly. "Surely your TV show will be far more interesting than typing."

Jonathan shifted in his chair. "Has Miss Jackson told you that you would have to work a nine-to-five day and, when you're not appearing on TV, you'll be typing up interview material, program data, and whatever the job demands?"

"Yes, she told me all that," Rene replied promptly, "and because I do type very fast, an accurate seventy or eighty words a minute, that might be a big help."

Jonathan felt that her qualifications were good, but he had one reservation. "Miss Hamilton, two of your front teeth are not as perfect as they should be for TV closeups. If Miss Jackson selected you for the job, would you agree to have them capped?"

"Sure, Mr. Barron. That's a good idea. I wonder how much the capping job would cost?"

"You talk to Miss Jackson here," Jonathan said as he stood up. "As far as I'm concerned, Freda, you can go ahead and hire Miss Hamilton, and we'll pay for capping her teeth—these two teeth, right here." He put a finger very close to Rene's mouth and indicated the teeth he had in mind. Rene didn't move.

"Jonathan," Freda said, "I'll go ahead and work out the starting date and other job details, but first I want to thank the other girls for coming in. Perhaps you should come with me, Rene."

Two or three weeks after Rene Hamilton started to work, Jonathan asked Freda how her new girl was doing. "Rene is not only looking good on the show, especially now that all her teeth are perfect, but in the office she does a thorough job and keeps everything on schedule.

"I think she's one of the best employees we've ever had. Perhaps you should take her to lunch sometime. You seem to enjoy prophesying for women under twenty-five." Freda was familiar with Jonathan's perceptiveness and weaknesses.

"Okay, but it will be strictly a business luncheon to give me a chance to assess her future," Jonathan replied with a grin. He knew Freda was needling him about some of his younger dates.

A couple of days later Jonathan stopped by the production office. Freda was out of her office, but Rene Hamilton was at her desk. Since the show was on from nine to eleven in the morning, Rene and the other participants usually returned to the Michigan Avenue office by eleven-thirty to prepare for future shows.

Rene looked up and gazed at Jonathan, giving him plenty of time, he assumed, to notice her beautiful brown eyes.

"Freda has told me you're doing a good job on and off television," Jonathan began. "I told her I'd like to learn more about you and your plans, maybe at lunch. Would that suit you?"

Rene had such a ready response, it was as if she were expecting his invitation. "Sure. And if you're talking about today, it should be very pretty in Jacques' garden. I'll go ask Freda. She's in Frank's office." She was on her way out the door in a flash.

"Well," Jonathan thought, "I guess I don't have to go to that ad club meeting today, so why not take her to lunch?"

He called after her, "Miss Hamilton, I'll wait for you in the reception room."

In three or four minutes Rene returned and said, "It's fine with Freda. Shall we go?"

Jacques' Restaurant was in the center of the 900 North Michigan building with no direct street entrance to the restaurant. In addition to the regular dining room and bar lounge, there was an open court atrium area surrounding a delightful fountain, where Jonathan preferred to eat on pretty days. One always found large vases of fresh roses all around the restaurant, for Jacques loved these beautiful flowers. He was about as demanding and independent as Jonathan, so they got along quite well after the first stand-off meeting. Jonathan learned later how much Jacques appreciated pretty women, but he had already suspected as much because of Jacques' deep love for the velvet-petaled roses with delicate fragrances, so like beautiful women.

As Jonathan and Rene entered the door to the garden dining area, Eddie, a long-time waiter at Jacques' motioned to Jonathan that the table he usually preferred was available. It was in a quiet spot not far from the center fountain. Jonathan indicated that Rene should follow Eddie's lead, and the couple wound their way through the maze of tables.

All the while, Jonathan was studying Rene. There was something about her that he liked, but he hadn't decided what it was.

"Maybe she isn't pretty," he thought to himself, "but she is attractive."

Rene, however, didn't project the same feeling that some of his differently-pretty girl friends did. She didn't radiate sensuality and femininity, as some of the others, but the others didn't quite reflect the stately dignity and arithmetical soundness of Rene. She was pretty enough in her own way.

Eddie stood quietly watching as Jonathan enjoyed looking at Rene.

After a few minutes Eddie approached the table, and Jonathan introduced him. "Miss Hamilton, this is Eddie Hudson, a part-time yachtsman and the best retired waiter who ever kept working."

Eddie beamed. "So glad to see you here, Miss Hamilton. Mr. Barron will continue his entertaining conversation as soon as I bring him his martini on the rocks. What would you like?"

Rene smiled pleasantly. "I'm so glad to meet you, Eddie. I don't care for a cocktail, thank you."

Eddie handed her the large menu, passed one to Jonathan, and said to Rene, "I'll just bring his martini before he complains."

As Eddie walked away from the table, Rene looked at Jonathan instead of at the menu.

"He seems to know you well," she observed.

"You mean people have already been telling you that I'm a little impatient." Jonathan smiled as he waited for Rene's reply.

She was adjusting the brown scarf at her neck, and for a minute he didn't think she was listening to him. Then she looked across the table and said laughingly, "Yes, that's what I've heard, but I don't believe you are when you get what you want when you want it."

"So, Miss Hamilton has been here less than a month and she knows me well," Jonathan said as he leaned back in his chair. "Perhaps I should know more about her. Let's see, when would you have been born? What time of year? It seems to me it should be about December sixth or seventh."

"It's December sixth. But how could you possibly guess my birth date?" Rene was astonished. She had heard that Jonathan could tell people a lot of things about themselves, but now she had become uncomfortable wondering what else he knew about her.

Jonathan reassured her. "Really, Rene, I don't guess on many of these things. Sometimes I just sort of pick up the information from the storage bin in the other person's brain. They usually dig the information out of storage when I ask the question; that is, if they're not defensive and haven't fenced in their feelings.

"Anyway, you don't have sisters, but maybe a younger, much younger brother."

Rene was quick to present a logical answer to Johnathan's ESP performance. "Mr. Barron, have you looked up all this stuff about me? If so, I'm complimented by your interest. If not, I'm afraid to think, even to myself."

"No, Rene, I didn't look up your vita—and I'm often wrong about people." But the tone of his voice was confident and suggested he didn't make very many wrong guesses.

"But," Rene persisted, "you must admit that telling me when I was born and that I have a much younger brother is pretty good for me the first five minutes of conversation."

Jacques' was filling up with customers. As quiet conversations mingled with the tinkle of water pitchers and glasses, the atmosphere was becoming almost festive. Jonathan's interest in Rene Hamilton was increasing.

"I'm sure there are lots of things I don't know about you, and I think I'd like to know more," he said quite frankly. "What do you plan as a career? You're just twenty now."

Rene arranged the napkin on her lap and glanced around the room. "Actually, I haven't planned a career. I just live, more or less, from day to day, year to year. I like almost every task I undertake, but I like best of all working here with Miss Jackson."

Jonathan looked up as Eddie approached their table, martini in hand. "Here's Eddie. It's time to order." Without looking at Rene, he said to Eddie, "I think Miss Hamilton has been thinking about fish. Do you recommend the filet of sole or the lake perch?"

Rene, a bit flustered, spoke up quickly, "I'd like the sole, if you please." Looking at Jonathan, she said, "And what kind of dressing am I having on my salad?"

Jonathan had a ready reply. "Vinaigrette would be nice, but why not try their house dressing as a surprise?"

"Which dressing do you recommend, Eddie?" Rene asked.

In a low voice Eddie replied, as if he didn't want Jonathan to hear him, "Let him have his fun, Miss Hamilton. He means to get all the information about a pretty woman that he can. In this case, if you like a light roquefort dressing, ours is delicious. And Professor Barron, here, never guessed it."

"Thank you, Eddie," Rene said. "I do especially like roquefort. Glad you recommended it."

Jonathan grinned slightly at Eddie and Rene and ordered his own lunch. Then he changed the subject to the TV show, as Eddie walked away.

"I saw the show yesterday, and I think you and David are doing a good job with the interviews, but some turn out to be pretty dull. Why don't we put a nice, funny character on the show?"

Surprised, Rene said, "The program does have slow spots, but two hours is a long time. It would be difficult and expensive to get the additional talent to speed up and lighten it, don't you think?"

"No," Jonathan said matter-of-factly. "I was thinking about a character that might help and would cost nothing."

Rene laughed. "Who would work every day for nothing?"

"Believe me, you'd love him. I think we should get a frisky, mongrel puppy and let him grow up on the show. People like dogs and monkeys. Some even like cats. What do you think?" Rene thought Jonathan actually sounded like he wanted her opinion.

She was enthusiastic. "I'd love to have a dog on the show," she said eagerly. "When can we get one?"

"After lunch, let's talk with Freda and then call David. If they're both agreeable, I'll go out and find one tomorrow."

"May I go with you?" Rene asked with a little plea in her voice. She leaned over, greatly aided in her appeal by her big brown eyes.

"Yes. You should be introduced to a new partner before you're stuck with him. I have a friend who publishes a magazine for dog fanciers. I'll ask him to refer us to a reliable pet shop. We'll go as soon as I locate a good shop. Maybe we can go tomorrow about four o'clock."

Rene was obviously excited at the prospect of helping Jonathan choose her new television partner.

"This will be fun!" she said. "What kind of dog were you thinking of selecting?"

Rene's eyes were sparkling, and Jonathan thought this dog idea of his was one of the best he had ever come up with. Rene's genuine enthusiasm about the puppy would make the whole situation appealing to most viewers. He was beginning to enjoy Rene's company, as well as her enthusiasm.

"I rather prefer a spunky but loving dog. Maybe we can get a border collie, but he might be too dignified." Jonathan leaned forward. "We don't want another dignified personality on the show."

Rene was caught off guard. "And who's the other dignified personality, Mr. Barron? I think David is just right as emcee."

Jonathan smiled. "I had you in mind."

"I'm dignified? She laughed. "We do need some comic relief on the show."

Their food arrived, and they spent the rest of their lunch chatting comfortably. Eddie was his usual attentive self, and the food was delicious. Rene declined dessert, as did Jonathan, so as soon as the dishes were cleared, he signed the check and helped Rene with her chair. Eddie had seen Jonathan with many young women, but he couldn't remember when his friend seemed to be so pleased. As they left the restaurant, Eddie told Rene that he hoped he would see her again soon.

When Jonathan and Rene returned to the office, they met Freda in the hallway, and he said nonchalantly, "I've decided to add another personality to the show, if you and David approve."

"Do you know someone who'll work for nothing?" Freda asked. "The budget we've agreed on can't stretch enough to add another personality. What would this person do?"

"I wasn't exactly thinking of a person," Jonathan said, wondering how Freda was going to receive his suggestion. "How about a cute dog?"

Freda thought a minute and said, "I think a dog might be a good addition—if he behaves. You remember the day we had the chimpanzee as a guest on the show? He almost tore Rene's blouse off."

Jonathan smiled and looked at Rene. "I don't think a dog is that much like a human. What do you really think about our adding a dog?"

Freda just looked at Jonathan. Rene didn't bat an eye.

"We do need some help filling out the two-hour show and a dog, if he's a real character, could add warmth and humor."

"Okay, then, if it pleases you, why not phone David and get his approval, too. And, incidentally, ask him if he would like to have the dog as his own, for his kids. They might like having a well-known playmate in their home."

Within an hour, Freda received David's enthusiastic approval. Rene was very pleased, so Freda asked Jonathan if he would find the dog.

"I think I know where we can get one, Freda. And, since Rene would be one of his masters, I think she should go along to help me pick out the dog."

"Yes, of course. And I might add that I never thought I'd live to see the day when Jonathan Barron had to pick up a dog as his excuse for developing his acquaintance with a young lady." She and Jonathan smiled at each other, but no more needed to be said.

That same afternoon Jonathan called his friend, the publisher of a magazine circulated to pet dealers, and asked him to recommend a good pet shop in Chicago. His friend named a shop on North Clark Street near Howard.

Jonathan called the local pet shop and spoke to the owner, who seemed to know everything about dogs and was very happy to hear that Jonathan planned to put a dog on television every day. In fact, the owner said he would supply the dog free, if he could find one

Jonathan liked, just to be able to appear on the show to present the dog to David and Rene.

The pet shop owner told Jonathan that one of his customers had a female cocker spaniel who had three puppies that were now about six months old. The puppies were half chow, an unusual combination. Jonathan knew enough about dogs to comment that the chow-cocker cross might produce a dog with real individuality —the gentleness of a cocker and the gumption of a chow.

They arranged to meet at the pet shop the next afternoon at four-thirty.

Rene was so keyed up about getting the dog, Jonathan thought that he was merely acting as her chauffeur. They weren't disappointed. The three puppies were little clowns with pretty brownish-tan coats. Their heads were especially distinctive, shaped like that of a smaller and more finely chiseled Alaskan malamute.

One of the puppies acted as if he wanted the job more than his sister or brother did. He put on the best tail-wagging act. Jonathan and Rene were sold. They asked the pet shop owner to bring him down to WBKB studios about nine-thirty the next morning. Everybody and the dog were happy.

"Well, Miss Hamilton, have you picked out a name for our dog?" Jonathan asked as soon as they were back in the car.

"No, not yet. I'm just thinking what an original little character we found. We're so lucky. What are we going to name it?"

"First, let me call you Rene," Johnathan began. "As to the newest addition to the show, let's think about names. I started off with Caleb, but I don't think that name fits an urban youngster."

"Oh, no, no," Rene said spontaneously.

"I thought you might like Caleb, Rene. It's a dignified name," Johnathan said with a smile.

"I didn't think you wanted any more dignity on the show. And our dog simply wouldn't consider being a 'Caleb.' "

"Seriously, Rene, I think I do have a name that will work and will fit his mischievous personality. The name will be a joke that even the dog will enjoy, because he'll be too sophisticated to be like his name."

"What name have you come up with?" she asked.

"How do you like Macho? Most of our daytime viewers are women, and they'll think some of the macho husbands act as silly as our dog will act, we hope."

Rene was a little reluctant. "Maybe. But I'll bet Freda won't like it." Then she paused. "On the other hand, she might. She thinks you're a little macho yourself."

Rene saw the look on Jonathan's face and had second thoughts about what she had just said. "Oh, I shouldn't have said that. I don't really know what Freda thinks about you."

Jonathan didn't react. "If Freda and David say Macho is okay, we'll go with Macho. Meanwhile, it'd be a shame not to celebrate this occasion with dinner. Don't you think?"

Rene seemed surprised and asked, "Are you inviting me to dinner?"

"Yes, I am. But it's a little early now. So let's go to my apartment and wash our doggy hands. Then we can go have a cocktail and dinner."

"That's fine with me," Rene said in a voice displaying a little concern. "But I should call my mother from your apartment and tell her I'll be catching a late train."

"No," Jonathan said, "tell your mother I'll drive you home."

"But I live in Riverside, that's a forty- or fifty-minute drive."

"That's okay, Rene. I'll take you home," Jonathan said as if his driving her home should be taken for granted.

Rene was the first woman to enter his apartment without making a comment about its simplicity or some other aspect of it. This indicated to Jonathan that she was accustomed to accepting things as they were, not thinking about them one way or the other. He directed her to his guest powder room.

"Rene, if you don't mind, I'll change into a dark suit. It will only take a minute. This week's *Time* is on the table near the windows. I won't be long."

Rene went into the powder room and Jonathan into his bedroom. Normally, he might have welcomed an attractive young lady visitor with a greeting kiss or might even have suggested they have a cocktail at the apartment, but he didn't feel intimate toward Rene.

In a few minutes they were both ready. Rene made no comment about Jonathan's smoky blue, double-breasted suit. He habitually noted all reactions shown by his women companions to any change of clothes or manner. Rene fooled him by being so blasé.

Just before leaving the apartment, he gently stroked Rene's strawberry-blonde hair and said, "Your hair is such a beautiful color."

But he added to himself, "Now I'll test her smug little aplomb."

"We should celebrate our luck in getting Macho with a good-luck kiss—a macho kiss. Don't you think that's a proper way to express our success?"

By this time she had stepped out the door. She turned toward him and didn't hesitate. She kissed him.

"Yes," she replied as they walked toward the elevator, "this has been a lucky day."

Jonathan hoped her comment included more than the dog.

Even though he had met Rene so many years ago, Jonathan remembered how pleased she had been when he took her that evening to the Yar, a Russian-style restaurant that used to be on Lake Shore Drive near the Drake hotel. They arrived early for dinner and took a table for two near the far corner. Jonathan always tried to avoid being parked too close to his fellow diners. He liked to have his back to a wall or to be placed in a corner with two walls to protect him from close neighbors who might be noisy.

It turned out to be a slow night at the restaurant. As soon as they were seated, Jonathan suggested a champagne cocktail to celebrate their lucky day. When the champagne arrived, so did the two violinists who were part of the ambience.

He remembered how Rene had seemed to love the whole idea. The total package, including Jonathan, finally elicited approval from her. She appeared to lose her sense of being with her boss's boss and with an older man, one known for having had many pretty women friends. She began to speak and act more confidently and freely, like a sophisticated older woman. Jonathan had always found that good music and good champagne seemed to please most women, whatever their age.

The dinner was excellent, and Rene became more relaxed. She began to accept him as a friend. He suggested that too many people already called him Mr. Barron and asked her to call him Jonathan.

Rene thought about this development and gave a studied reply. "That's fine, Mr. Barron, or rather Jonathan, but you can be sure I'll call you Mr. Barron in the office."

"Call me Jonathan anywhere. Most people in the office call me Jonathan—unless they're calling me somewhat uncomplimentary names."

"Doesn't anybody ever call you Jon?" Rene asked a little cautiously. "Perhaps your mother?"

"I never had a mother, but my guess is, if she had lived, she would have called me Jonathan."

After dinner he drove her home for the first time. He had been driving about thirty minutes when it dawned on him how far away from work Rene lived. "You sure live to hell and gone a long way south," he said long before they were even close to her home. "How far is it from the office?"

"I usually take the train, so I'm not sure what the driving distance is. It's probably thirty miles, maybe more." Her voice was very soft, almost apologetic.

She was beginning to be sorry she had let him drive her home, thinking that she should have taken the Illinois Central south and just walked the four blocks to her house. But Jonathan had been so insistent about taking her home. On the way they talked, mostly about her.

Rene had been engaged to a young Notre Dame graduate but had ended the engagement just a couple of months before going into television. He asked her why she had stopped dating the young man and why she had broken off the engagement.

"Bob is a very wonderful young man, but he was a little young for me," she said.

"Rene, he must be a precocious young man to have graduated from Notre Dame at nineteen or twenty," Johnathan said, as he wondered what "too young" meant to Rene.

"Oh, no. Bob is almost twenty-three, but I feel that for me, that's still a bit young, even though we liked each other very much. Besides, I like working, and I don't want to get married too young." She had apparently thought the situation through quite thoroughly.

"You're probably right about waiting to get married. However, actual age doesn't really mean too much. I have a twenty-year-old girl friend who is more mature and more sophisticated than some women I know who are thirty—or older."

"Maybe you're right, Johnathan. It probably isn't the number of years that makes a difference, but the individual and her experiences," Rene said thoughtfully.

Johnathan turned his attention back to the road. "Now, just where do we turn along here to get to your house?" But while he was asking directions, he was wondering what she had meant by her experiences. In a couple of minutes she was pointing to her house.

137

When Johnathan parked the car in front of her home, he noticed a light in the house. He asked if her mother might be up, since it was not quite ten o'clock. Rene started to answer but realized that he was already out the door and halfway around the back of the car on his way to open her door.

As she got out of the car, she said rather quickly, "Yes, my mother is probably still up. But I think it would be better if you met her next time."

She stopped his reply by kissing him rather fully.

Jonathan settled for that. He thanked her for having helped select Macho, and she thanked him for dinner. Then she gave him another kiss and started toward her doorway. Jonathan walked with her and touched her hand goodnight as she went up the steps to the door of her house.

All of this had been a long, long time ago. Jonathan finished his third or fourth cup of coffee, signed his check, including an extra large tip for "waiting time," and left the dining room.

# 15

In Los Angeles, the next morning was sunny and clear. Rene awakened early enough to precede Ellen into the kitchen to prepare breakfast. Anson had already left for his long commute. Ellen was so busy on major law cases that she really appreciated a "free" breakfast and being able to walk out of the kitchen, knowing that everything would be put away.

Rene wasn't planning to do all the cooking and housework, but she did want to help her daughter, and Ellen was very grateful. They talked for a short while about the problems of keeping house and working at the same time. Then Ellen was off to her car pool. And Rene went out to the swimming pool.

She lounged in the sun, looking stretched out and comfortable, but there was uncertainty in her mind and in her body. She was thinking about her two-thirty appointment with Mr. Howard Culbertson of the *Los Angeles Chronicle.* However much Mr. Culbertson might respect Ralph Lawton's recommendation, her experience in journalism made Rene believe that the *Chronicle* would probably favor younger journalists. She was told that she appeared to be around thirty-five to thirty-eight, which was old enough, but her resumé showed that she was fifty. That didn't help in applying for any job. But she would make a try; she thought it might at least be worth her while to meet Mr. Culbertson, because she did plan to continue in public relations or feature writing.

She believed her chances for employment with Dr. Spirrison were very good, because she knew that Dr. Otis of Carolina State had strongly recommended her to his friend, Spirrison, after they had met at the Carolina State seminar. Dr. Otis later told Rene that Dr. Spirrison had said he needed a good public relations person who could handle interviews and write feature stories. Furthermore, Rene sensed that Dr. Spirrison had liked her personally, and she had subtly let him know that she liked him, too. She was pretty sure he would offer her a job, but it might take a while for him to work it out. She didn't mind waiting, though, because Ellen might need her for several weeks. She was looking forward to her four forty-five meeting with Dr. Spirrison.

Rene decided to leave Ellen's house about one-thirty to go to the *Chronicle* office. She would then go directly from Howard Culbertson's office to Dr. Spirrison's. But she had plenty of time now to meditate, so she relaxed into her lounge chair, closed her eyes, and began to recapitulate recent developments in her relationship with Jonathan.

The new crop of novels she had been reading certainly carried the message that women, especially those in their forties and early fifties, were trying to make up for lost time and to use their new freedom. Rene was wondering what it would be like to be the heroine of her own novel. She thought about the kind of sex life she would have if she were separated and living in Los Angeles.

If there had been another woman, she believed she could have won, but there was no other woman—only the devilish discontent of Jonathan's deep depression.

Rene sat quietly by the pool, looking at a few leaves floating on the water. She had never been one to dwell on the past or the future, but now she had to tie past and future together in trying to find herself, in trying to be honest with herself.

Did she really want to leave Jonathan?

She was convinced that Jonathan wanted her to leave, for her own future. He had told her that more than once. Was his depression caused by the deep conflict between his respect for the institution of marriage and his deliberate encouragement of her to find another husband? Or were his problems temporary, a result of his retirement from business and his subsequent commitment to the ethics project?

She admired, respected, and, in her way, loved Jonathan. But she could not help feeling that she was still his protegee. Their children were living quite well on their own. Her husband had been everywhere and had done so many things, and in the course of so doing had had many women. There was nothing wrong with that—he had been free.

But here she was, a woman of fifty, who had never lived alone, free to make all her own decisions, little and big. She wondered if she could persuade Jonathan to agree to a separation. He had indicated that he considered the extended separation agreements of some of their Washington friends cowardly contrivances to avoid divorce and to open the door for open marriages. All the separated men and women he knew seemed to date frequently.

Jonathan believed that when a married couple is so free to have lovers, they should no longer call it separation but an open marriage. When a couple lives with that kind of arrangement, the marriage has ceased.

True, Rene thought, few open marriages ever do become closed again.

But separation does provide the spouses, especially the wives, with opportunities to try out different lovers.

Rene had never had that opportunity.

She decided to swim awhile and then phone the Sonbergs, a fun-loving couple she and Jonathan had known for years, to invite them to dinner the next night. She glanced at the clock on the patio. She hadn't realized how late it had become and immediately went inside to make her phone call.

Arthur Sonberg, pianist and composer, winner of an Oscar for his music, had been unemployed when Jonathan was introduced to him many years ago. He played *Rhapsody in Blue* for Jonathan as an audition number. Jonathan hired him immediately and put him on his talent agency's payroll. Sybil, his wife, had been a professional organist in the days when the public had become fascinated with the wonders of electronic organ sounds. She frequently played commercial bookings.

Jonathan's instant confidence in Sonberg had been a timely factor in restoring Sonberg's hopes and had inspired him to dedicate himself to his career. The result was Sonberg's rapid advancement and an offer to take a major studio musical directorship; he became a prolific composer of music for top-rated television shows and motion pictures.

Rene dialed their number. It rang several times.

"Hello, Arthur. This is Rene." She was smiling.

"Why, hello, Rene. Are you in Los Angeles?"

"Yes, and that's why I'm calling you. Are you and Sybil available for dinner tomorrow? I'm staying at Ellen's house, and we could all have dinner here.

Arthur was pleased with the invitation, but rather hesitant. "Sybil hasn't been feeling well, but seeing you might make her feel better. Hold on just a minute, I'll call her."

141

In just a few seconds Sybil was on the phone. "Rene, I'd love to see you. I think the dinner would be good therapy. What time?"

"How about seven at Ellen's house?"

"Seven is fine, isn't it, Arthur? We'll be there." Then Arthur asked Rene if Ellen still lived in the same place. Rene assured him Ellen hadn't moved. The dinner was set, but she asked Arthur, whose piano recordings she had purchased from the first to the last, if he would play for her.

"I'll play my newest song. I've just finished it. See you tomorrow."

"Goodbye, Arthur. So glad you can come."

Her call completed, Rene went into the kitchen, opened a small can of tuna, toasted a piece of cracked wheat bread, and fixed herself a glass of instant tea.

Before leaving the kitchen, Rene wrote Ellen a note saying the Sonbergs would be coming to dinner on Thursday at seven. "I'll have plenty of time to plan the dinner, do the shopping, and have everything ready to serve by the time you and Anson get home and the Sonbergs arrive. Also, don't wait dinner for me tonight, as my late afternoon appointment with Dr. Spirrison may run into dinnertime. Don't wait up. I know where your key is. Take care."

Rene showered and dressed carefully. She didn't want to look overdressed for a business appointment, but she did want to be dressed appropriately in case Dr. Spirrison was late for his four forty-five appointment and wanted to make up for it by asking her out to dinner. Once dressed in her cocoa suit and beige blouse, she selected a gold necklace, inconspicuous matching gold earrings, and a gorgeous gold bracelet.

Rene left in plenty of time for her appointment at the *Chronicle*. She arrived early, parked a couple of blocks away and decided to look in on Little Tokyo and the New Otani Hotel. She remembered the area, but more particularly, she recalled visiting Olvera Street, where she and Jonathan had once walked along together and stopped for a Mexican lunch.

Howard Culbertson was an athletic club-type gentleman, about fifty years old. He looked and acted like a top executive, courteous and considerate. Ralph Lawton had already sent him Rene's resume, and he had given some thought to where he might send her.

"Actually, Mrs. Barron, if you were as you are now and you had been with us for ten or fifteen years, with your experience in journalism and business, I would guess you would have a very responsible management position in our organization." Then he smiled again. "You're almost too impressive a person for a normal job assignment. But let me send you to one of the most successful women in our company, and we'll see what she can come up with. How long will you be in Los Angeles?"

"I'll be returning to Washington at noon on Friday. Perhaps on my return trip to Los Angeles I could see the woman to whom you referred. That should be in about a month."

"The person I want you to see is Manitta Perkins, M-a-n-i-t-t-a. I'll send her your resume. But please do call me when you return, and I'll personally introduce you to Mrs. Perkins."

Rene stood up to leave. "Thank you very much. I'll phone Miss Sherpard for the appointment when I return."

Mr. Culbertson came around from behind his desk and walked Rene to the door of his office.

"Mrs. Barron, I'm happy to have met you, and I'll be expecting your call. Goodbye and good luck."

"Goodbye, Mr. Culbertson."

As she went through his outer office, Rene thanked Miss Shepard and said goodbye to her.

Miss Shepard replied, "Lots of luck, Mrs. Barron. So nice to have met you."

It was about a twenty-minute drive to the administration building of Southland University. Rene knew she would arrive almost an hour ahead of time but decided she could use the extra time to visit the registrar's office and the library to pick up the current university bulletin. She thought it would be important to be informed and up-to-date on any subject of discussion concerning the university.

She was generally familiar with Southland. Dr. Spirrison had spoken with her at the Carolina State seminar dinner about the breadth of programs offered by the school, so she had some basic information already. It wouldn't take her long to catch up on current problems and progress.

She went to the library first, browsed through university periodicals for a half hour, and walked over to the administration building. The registrar's office had assorted current bulletins, which she perused until four-forty. Then she went up to Dr. Spirrison's office.

Rene announced herself to the receptionist, and Dr. Spirrison's secretary came out to greet her, introducing herself as Miss Houghton. She explained that Dr. Spirrison might be as much as fifteen or twenty minutes late getting out of the meeting in the comptroller's office. She passed on to Rene his apologies and his request that she please wait for him.

At five o'clock, the receptionist and several other girls left for the day. Miss Houghton stopped on her way out and told Rene that she had just checked with Dr. Spirrison, and he would be arriving within ten minutes. She said he would be coming in through the reception office and would meet Rene there.

Rene was not surprised that Arnold Spirrison was going to be so late. She was definitely looking forward to this meeting with him.

Soon Spirrison came bustling in. He came over and shook her hand at length, then asked her to come into his office.

"Mrs. Barron, it's wonderful to see you again. No man should keep you waiting."

"I didn't mind, Dr. Spirrison, it gave me a chance to catch up on what's going on here at the university." She held up the bulletins she had been reading. "Besides, since I'm looking for a job, I'm glad to wait for some one who might be able to help me."

They entered his office, but Rene remained standing while Dr. Spirrison walked to the window and adjusted the blinds to cope with the late afternoon sun. When he turned around and saw Rene still standing he said, "Rene, please excuse me for not asking you to be seated."

He gestured to a chair in front and to the right of his desk. "Let's visit here for a while. Do you have a current vita with you?"

"Yes, I'll give you three copies, just in case you want to pass them along."

Dr. Spirrison leaned back and began to read the resume. He was probably no more than fifty years old. He appeared to be in very good shape. He was about six feet tall and weighed one hundred seventy-five pounds, more or less. He had plenty of brown hair, quite fashionably trimmed, and his voice was pleasant. But Rene thought he talked a little as though he were teaching a class or reporting to the faculty.

He looked up and across the desk.

"Rene—may I call you Rene? It's such a pretty name.

144

"I think I can work out a new position for you. It depends on whether you can wait for a few weeks or maybe longer. I'll need a little time to work things out. Are you applying anywhere else out here for a job?"

"Yes, I am, and on my return to Los Angeles, which will be in about three or four weeks, I have another appointment with the *Chronicle.*"

"Who is your contact at the *Chronicle,* if I may ask?"

"Howard Culbertson. He's a close personal friend of a friend of mine, a prominent corporate executive. I've already talked with Mr. Culbertson, and when I return, I'm to see a Mrs. Perkins."

"Well, Rene, you've got an influential contact in Howard Culbertson. He's also well informed. Our Graduate School of Business considers it quite a coup to have him conduct a guest lecture on our campus." He smiled at Rene.

"My husband has many friends in the corporate community. As his wife and as his associate in some of our professional and business activities, I've become acquainted with a number of very successful men and women." Rene leaned forward with interest. "But what kind of job do you have in mind for me?"

"Rene, it would help me with our trustees if you could supply me with personal and professional references from three or four leaders in the corporate community, because I'm going to have to create a special position for you. And if I undertake to do this, I hope you'll agree to give us a sort of first refusal on your job selection. I believe you could help this university, and I have confidence in your ability to make this a productive assignment."

"But," Rene asked quite directly, "just what is the special position you have in mind?"

As he began to talk, Rene pulled out her pad and pen. The position he was describing was rather multidimensional.

"Universities and various entities within the universities, such as the medical schools and the business schools, are always in need of money to hire better professors and to do more and better research. You know this.

"But they must also create a demand for their graduates. I believe these divisional needs are so disparate in their constituencies that we must have special directors, promotion directors, as it may be, for each of these influential subdivisions of the university.

145

"At any rate, the way I see it, a provost or a vice-chancellor or a senior vice-president, depending on the title and scope of the function, would oversee and coordinate the different directors of corporate development—a frequently applied euphemism for public relations, publicity, and fund-raising activities. And I want to add a director for the whole area of economic and business education generally, including the undergraduate business department and the graduate school of business.

"Increasingly, since more and more big corporations are hiring young people directly from the undergraduate schools, especially the business schools, we'll undertake an overlapping development program for the graduate and undergraduate business schools.

"How do you like that objective, Rene?"

Rene looked up from her note taking. "I believe it's realistic and maybe overdue. Of course, many universities have found it desirable to encourage their graduate schools to strive for such excellence that they may become too specialized and may become entities almost separate from the rest of the university. Your idea might help to add distinction to Southland."

Rene paused, thought a moment, and added, "Should you hire me, I believe it would be better for me to work directly with you first, to help you work out the details of the support plan for your program. Later, I could work in public relations."

Dr. Spirrison leaned back in his chair, folded his hands on the edge of his desk, and smiled appreciatively at Rene. He laughed and said, "Guess being smart helps make a woman pretty. However, too many women put the cart before the horse. Your experiences in academia could be very helpful to us.

"I want you to work here. Can you wait at least two months, maybe a little longer, before you join our organization?"

Rene smiled and hoped she didn't look too relieved. "Dr. Spirrison, I'll probably need two months before starting a full-time job. So the timing would be perfect for me, and I do believe my experience in this field qualifies me to contribute to your goals."

Spirrison stood up. "That's wonderful, Rene. Now, since I temporarily live alone out here, why don't you walk over to the Faculty Club with me and have a bottle of champagne in celebration of our getting together? Then, if you are free, we could have a quiet dinner at the club. But please come with Arnold, not with Dr. Spirrison."

All the pieces seemed to be falling into place for Rene.

"I'd love to," she said, smiling.

As they walked across the campus to the Faculty Club, Dr. Spirrison pointed out the various buildings and said they had two new buildings under construction. He also told her that they weren't very optimistic about their football team this year.

When they arrived at the Faculty Club, Rene was pleasantly surprised. The facility was more sumptuous than the one at Carolina State. As they stood a moment at the entrance she said, "Arnold, you haven't been here much more than two or three years, have you?"

"That's right. It was two years ago on July 1 that I took over this job. It's been an exciting and difficult challenge, but it's coming along. Enrollment and funding are slightly up, and that's good."

"You're quite young to be president of a first-class university, aren't you?"

Arnold smiled. "Thanks Rene, but I'm perhaps a little older than many of my peers. I've been in academic life almost thirty years!"

The waiter seated them in a rather private alcove, and Dr. Spirrison asked the waiter to bring a bottle of California champagne. Rene liked champagne because of the bubbly life it signified. It was celebration time, and they drank a toast to the new job. She now felt the situation and timing suitable to ask Arnold about his family.

"Oh, yes, I have a big family," he quickly responded. "We have a two-hundred-sixty-pound, six-foot-three-inch son, a former defensive tackle for Ohio State. He's now a happily married construction engineer in Houston. Then we have a smaller son, only two hundred and twenty pounds, who played wide receiver for Iowa. He's married and in the insurance business in Des Moines. We have a married daughter, a doctor's wife, who lives in Baltimore, which is also where my wife is a professor of molecular biology. She has an excellent assignment there. My wife lives and maintains our home in Baltimore, where the children and two new grandchildren can visit."

Rene was puzzled by the long-distance marriage. "Arnold, it sounds like both you and your wife have done well professionally and with your family, too. But isn't it hard to feel married or to enjoy marriage while being apart so much? How much time do you get to spend together?"

Arnold had been drinking his champagne. He didn't look up as he began to answer Rene's question. When he did, he didn't look at Rene.

"Well, I guess we're more separated than married. Since the children left home, and for the past six or eight years, I don't suppose we've spent more than two or three weeks a year together, and that includes Christmas. We might spend a day together every now and then, if we're in the other's neighborhood.

"But what about you? You must be planning to separate, if you're going to live in Los Angeles and your husband is going to remain in Washington." He paused. "Or is he planning to move to southern California?"

"Arnold, all I know at this moment is that I'll be moving to Los Angeles within the next few weeks, maybe sooner. I have an option on a rental apartment, which I may confirm next week. Our oldest daughter, Ellen, is a very busy lawyer with a distinguished law firm here. She's also pregnant and may need my help, if the baby is premature. The baby isn't due until sometime around September 1, but the doctor isn't convinced that Ellen will go that long."

Rene wondered what she should tell Arnold about Jonathan. She decided to be frank. "My husband, Jonathan, has been quite occupied with his Ethics foundation. He has just retired as active president.

"He believes it would be better for me to leave him, get a divorce, and remarry someone closer to my age who could share my more gregarious social life. Jonathan is twenty-three years my senior, and he says he doesn't wish to die and leave me with twenty or thirty years to live without him.

"He probably won't miss me much. He reads and studies so much one might think he's trying to get a high SAT score to enter heaven."

"Don't you think that's a little strange," Arnold interjected, "considering that he's apparently in good health? He could live to be ninety-five, and that's a long time from now."

"Jonathan is a strange man," Rene continued. "He looks at my future happiness as his ethical obligation.

"Now, I've probably given you more information than you really wanted."

Without waiting for Arnold to answer, Rene continued enthusiastically. "We have a very successful twenty-eight-year-old son, a creative genius in advertising, who is also a pianist, composer, journalist and scientist. Our youngest child is twenty-three and will soon have her MBA in finance. She'll join one of the big New York financial institutions as a financial consultant and broker in the very near future."

Arnold poured Rene more champagne, and the two of them quietly sipped their drinks.

Rene broke the uncertain silence.

"Arnold, tell me what you think the advantages and disadvantages of a separation are—as opposed to divorce."

"The advantage of separation? I don't think there is any advantage in separation or divorce. I suppose it depends on the situation, but either one is usually an unhappy development. And, either one is often a development and not a sudden panacea—like love in reverse.

"My wife and I separated, ostensibly, because each of us had separate and substantive careers to fulfill. I suppose we used that argument as a reasonable and acceptable justification to avoid facing the fact that, for years, we've really not been in love, nor have we been making love. But neither of us was ready to think of having another spouse, so we compromised. We simply stay apart and try to be helpful friends to one another."

"Well, it sounds workable," Rene said.

"I suppose in academia there may yet be, Lord only knows why, a certain opprobrium attached to divorce. It's ironic, because the prevelence of physical relationships between students and faculty is well known. Not just here," he added quickly, "but in Ivy League schools, the Southeastern Conference, Big Ten universities, all of them."

He laughed. "You can readily see the influence my sons have had on me. I named the schools by their football conferences!"

"Arnold, I'm reluctant to take the steps toward divorce. Can't you tell me something that's appealing about separation?"

He thought for a minute. "Well, in a way, aside from such professional consideration, there may be a few property and financial advantages. In our case, much of the money we've accumulated is in jointly owned commercial real estate that we want to leave undisturbed. But we've found no significant income tax advantages one way or the other. So the financial reasons are probably as specious as other reasons that we may be avoiding. It

149

would be consoling if we had more supportive religious reasons for not getting a divorce.

"Rene, what do you think about all this?"

"I think your views are helpful." She took a good drink of her champagne. "Right now, if I can persuade my husband to accept an indeterminate period of separation, I would prefer it.

"However, my hope is that a separation will lead us together again or will, at least, enable me to finally live my own life, which he's helped me so much to prepare for."

Rene added with a flash of insight and honesty, "I suppose I'm selfish. I want to be entirely on my own for the first time in my life, yet I want my husband to continue to be available to me. That's why I prefer separation to divorce. I would feel more secure with him as my friend and counselor.

"I was brought up a Catholic. Although I don't consider myself a Catholic or a member of any church now, I may be favoring separation over divorce because of my Catholic upbringing."

Rene and Arnold looked up and noticed the waiter watching them. They laughed and looked hurriedly at the menu. When Arnold nodded, the waiter came to take their order. He refilled both their champagne glasses and left, making notes on his order pad.

"Arnold, I think it's often been said that some spouses prefer separation because they can enjoy many lovers without making a commitment to any one of them in particular. Do you believe that's true? Men have been accused of enjoying a separate availability as lovers while using the marriage bond as an excuse to avoid obligation and commitment to any one lover. I think it's possible that the same observation could apply to many women today."

"Rene, you're describing my wife, and maybe me, too. My wife has had a series of lovers, mostly younger or older scientists who can identify with her friends. I have also taken advantage of my committed status. I feel absolutely free to have a lover."

"Perhaps you and I are more sociable and people-loving than our spouses; certainly that's so in my case," Rene said. "However, I live with a very perceptive, objective, and compassionate husband. I'm afraid that I'll not be able to sell him on separation. He says that long and distant separations between spouses reflect a weakness, a compromise, because neither spouse has the courage to confront the conflict.

"I truly believe that Jonathan's concern is for my future. He says that no man of eminence and substance would risk committing himself to a separated woman. He has always said that he would never make a woman his lover-friend if she were still someone else's wife, separated or not."

The champagne was gone, but the two were so intent on their conversation that neither one noticed.

"Your husband," Arnold said quietly, "sounds like a man of extremely varied interests with a lot of insight into personal and social situations. I'd like to meet him sometime. However, I'm not sure we would agree on all things, particularly about you." He smiled. "How could any man in his right mind, much less a man with the wisdom your husband is reported to have, ever want to cut any strings that tie you to him?"

"Arnold, thank you." She put her hand on his arm. "But one of the wonderful things about Jonathan is his concern for the welfare of others. And one of the worst things about him is his willingness to play God in trying to discern what is best for others. I would never leave him if he really wanted me to stay."

"Rene, let me hasten to say that I'm going to be counting the days until you can join us here at Southland. And I mean that both professionally and personally."

Their dinners arrived, and the remainder of their time together was spent in small, inconsequential talk about the Faculty Club food and the problems of getting and keeping a good chef. Eventually, Arnold asked Rene if she wanted a dessert.

"No, thank you, Arnold. But I would like coffee."

"I think I'll have coffee, too, instead of dessert." He motioned to the waiter. "It will save me more workouts in the gym."

Rene was impressed. "You look like you're in great shape. Do you exercise much?"

"Not as much as I should. What about you?"

"I'm a member of the same, 'Don't Exercise as Much as I Should Club.' But I have been playing racquetball lately."

"Well," Arnold said enthusiastically, "let's make a date. When you get out here, we'll play racquetball, if you promise not to beat me."

"I would never promise not to beat a man at anything," Rene said laughingly. Arnold laughed, too, and they both seemed happy about the prospect of a delightful association.

They strolled back to the reserved parking area near the administration building.

"I'm so glad you believe you can work something out for me," Rene said. "I would like to work on your projects for Southland. If you don't mind, as soon as I return to Los Angeles and get settled, I'll call you and check on your progress in developing the opportunity. Thank you for the lovely champagne and dinner."

"Rene," Arnold replied quite simply, "it's been a happy, stimulating evening for me. Please do call me as soon as you return. I want to keep you abreast of developments."

Rene unlocked her car and got in. "Goodnight, Arnold."

"Goodnight, Rene," he said as he shut her car door for her. As she backed her car out of the parking place and headed out of the parking lot, he longingly watched her drive away.

# 16

At the Lincolnshire Inn, Jonathan found his room to be quiet and his bed comfortable; nevertheless, he had a restless night filled with dreams. He rarely dreamed of sex or violence, but in his dreams something was frequently incomplete. Often he was not quite fully dressed, missing a tie or shoe, or he would just miss catching a plane. Sometimes the house he was in might be missing part of the roof. The dream situations always seemed to lack something to complete the picture. Did this persistent pattern of dreams reveal what his unconscious was holding back? He didn't take any theory of dreams seriously. Perhaps they portrayed another form of striving for perfection in real life and the feeling of falling short of that attainment.

But Jonathan was a realistic perfectionist. He recognized that perfectionism is a deterrent to progress, that there are many roads to Goshen, and seeking the perfect way may waste the day. His dreams seemed to confirm the futility of the concept of perfectibility, while affirming his human obligation to seek it.

A hot shower followed by a cold one usually served to wash out such abstractions. By eight-fifteen he had finished breakfast, checked out of the hotel, and was on his way to Wood Lake to close the sale on his last piece of farm property.

He drove west on Route 22 to Highway 14 and continued on that road to Wood Lake. Highway 14 was a curving, old-fashioned route that connected several northwest Chicago suburban communities, including Barrington, Palatine, Fox River Grove, and Wood Lake. It was not an attractive road, because it was narrow and was bordered by dinky signs. But it was, in a business way, memory lane for Jonathan.

During his last four years in Wood Lake, he and Rene had developed a successful real estate business. As he drove along Highway 14, he recalled how he had sold a particular business property here and there. One sale he recalled readily, because it had been a sort of white elephant property. It often happens that old-timers in the real estate business look at properties that have been for sale for a long time and just forget they are there. Shortly after Jonathan had opened his real estate business, he was driving past a long, irregular seven-acre piece of land with a rustic, abandoned lodge hall on the property, and he immediately thought of its possible "highest and best use." He visualized a long row of recreational vehicles and mobile homes displayed along hundreds of feet of frontage on Highway 14, where thousands of cars passed daily. He stopped and peered through a window of the old lodge hall. The natural wood finish of the walls and fixtures would provide a comfortable, relaxed atmosphere for casual sportspersons and lovers of outdoor activities.

He went to the head of the local lodge and asked how he would like to sell that unused financial burden. "Badly," the lodge chief replied. "How much money?" Jonathan asked. The chief said they had had it appraised and he would give him a copy of the appraisal.

The next day, Jonathan called on a fellow he knew who had long been in the recreational vehicle business. He didn't have a very big business, but it was the best in the area. Jonathan told the dealer he had been underestimating his market and that he should have several times the display he currently had. He advised him that if he wished to have one of the largest-volume recreational and mobile home businesses in northern Illinois, he should have the best location available for miles around. The fellow asked, "Where?" Jonathan told him. The man thought deeply for a minute, then said, "I've passed that place a thousand times and never thought of it at all as a place for me. But you're right as hell. Let's buy it."

On this June morning, as Jonathan drove past the line of expensive recreational vehicles displayed along Highway 14, he thought that more creative people should get into the real estate business. Maybe then more white elephant property would sell.

He wondered what his life would have been like today if he had remained in the real estate business after retiring from advertising. He would, very likely, have accumulated a sizeable fortune. But making a lot of money had never been his prime objective. His policy, his plan, was to make enough money to do the things he wished to do to achieve more of his human potential. Why he was like that puzzled him.

Having been the poorest kid in his hometown, he certainly understood the advantages and benefits of having money—or rather, the disadvantages of not having enough of it. However, he hadn't wanted to be a slave to money any more than he had wanted to be a slave to poverty. He knew something some of his friends had apparently failed to realize: that you are more likely to destroy your body and soul trying to stay rich and get richer than by just becoming rich in the first place and moving on to other, more meaningful things.

Making money, he thought, can be fun before you reach the point of making money for money's sake, the point at which you can catch the disease of greed. When greed takes command, you are no longer free. Greed feeds on greed. He was lucky enough to be able to make choices in regard to money, and he was also lucky enough to have established early in his life a value system that put human and humane priorities in first place. His human priorities were concerned with his own development, and his humane goals were concerned with his obligation to others.

But Jonathan believed in giving luck every chance he could to favor him. Four years before retiring from the advertising agency business in Chicago, he had placed a display advertisement on the first page of the business-financial section of a Thursday edition of the *Chicago Tribune*. He described in the ad exactly what he wanted to buy: a two-hundred- to four-hundred-acre working farm within fifty miles' commuting distance from downtown Chicago. He wanted to get back to the soil, have cows, grow crops. He knew that buying land within commuting distance of Chicago would also be a good investment. Furthermore, he was becoming too "citified," too neat. He believed that loading a manure spreader would soon correct that.

The ad stipulated that the owner's house must be a first-class modern residence with at least four bedrooms, plus a three-bedroom farm manager's house. He received several replies, but the one he favored and saved for last was a scribbled note on a postcard, giving the owner's name and phone number. Jonathan called Mr. Bridgman, the owner, and went out to see his farm the following Sunday morning.

The farm was situated on the city limits of Wood Lake, bordering the local country club golf course. It had a large two-story lannonstone house with four big bedrooms and a full basement. For the farm manager, there was a brick and frame two-story, three-bedroom house with a separate garage. The owner took Jonathan through the big house, and he walked from room to room without stopping and without commenting, even about the twenty-by-thirty-two-foot master bedroom. Then Mr. Bridgman led him outside and around the barns, equipment sheds, and, finally, through the big dairy barn. Some of the cattle were in the adjoining cow lot, and the others were across the road in the pasture. Altogether, there were about ninety to a hundred pure-bred Holstein cows, heifers, and calves.

Jonathan kept walking and looking. Eventually, Mr. Bridgman asked him into the house for a cup of coffee. Bridgman assumed that Jonathan was not really interested in buying and was like many other city people, not serious, just curious, about farming.

Jonathan accepted the invitation for coffee, and as soon as they sat down, he asked Mr. Bridgman what price he had been asking for the place. Bridgman, for the first time since Jonathan arrived, began to think that maybe this fellow was interested. He quickly replied that his asking price had been a little high, perhaps, but since Jonathan hadn't come to him through a real estate broker but directly through his own ad, the substantial commission he would have had to pay a real estate broker could be taken off the asking price.

"If I can make a quick sale," Mr. Bridgman said, "I'll include the thousands of dollars worth of equipment and all the cattle at no extra cost. That's a big bonus if you want to buy now."

Jonathan asked Mr. Bridgman what the problem was with the place, because Bridgman didn't seem to like it. Bridgman waited a moment and then said, "I had a very beautiful wife, a lovely woman, who was responsible for my getting into this cattle breeding business. I bought the place because of her. Five months ago she ran off with a newspaper farm editor."

Jonathan thought about what Mr. Bridgman had said and commented, "If I were in your place, I'd probably burn the damn place down. I was wondering why you had neglected all the shrubbery, fences, barn doors, and things.

"Name your lowest price for everything, and we'll not need to bother counting the cows or testing the tractors."

Mr. Bridgman named his price. Jonathan simply said, "I'll take it. If you have a sheet of paper, we can write out a brief note of agreement, and I'll give you a check now for twenty thousand dollars earnest money." The deal was made. Jonathan left with a purchase agreement signed and accepted.

So, after a thirty-minute stop at the place, he had acquired a close-in farm and an excellent investment property. This farm was especially valuable, because it was across the road from city sewer and water and bordered the town's only country club golf course. Jonathan was assured that the present farm manager had agreed to stay with the new owner for one year. He was a lucky man, and Mr. Bridgman was happy to sell the farm, because he hated the place.

Jonathan drove back to his Winnetka home, arriving late for brunch with guests. He explained to Rene and to the guests, who were old friends, that he would have been on time, but he'd stopped and bought a farm on the edge of Wood Lake, along with a herd of purebred Holstein cattle and a bunch of farm equipment, tractors, tools, and supplies. The guests were quite surprised. They simply couldn't visualize Jonathan as a farmer and a dairyman.

Rene had known that her husband was looking around for a farm and that he had run an ad in the paper. But she had also thought he wouldn't actually buy one for maybe a year or two— if then. She had been a city girl all her life. She had never even visited a farm, much less lived on one. However, she had always told Jonathan that she would be ready to go when and where he wanted to go. And she meant it. She believed in him, in his judgment.

From what Jonathan had told her of the joys of nature and farms, Rene thought farm life would be wonderful for the children. Jonathan knew that Ellen, Bruce, and Susan would be fascinated with the farm, but allowed that Ellen and Bruce might not want to leave their school. Ellen, then eight years old, was doing well in an excellent elementary school. Bruce, then six and a half, was certainly enjoying school—and his six-year-old girlfriend who lived in the next block.

But Rene and Jonathan guessed that the idea of living on a farm would take precedence over any reluctance to change schools, and it did. The family moved to the farm as soon as the school semester ended. In the meantime, Rene had visited the Wood Lake schools and had found them to be very good. The newest elementary school was within easy walking distance, actually bordering the pasture of their newly purchased farm.

## Love and Ethics

Fred Easley, the farm manager, proved to be a nice enough fellow, and Jonathan knew they would be able to work together until Fred was ready to go up to Wisconsin the following spring. Fred's delayed departure allowed plenty of time to bring in a new manager for the cattle and an assistant for the field crops.

Now, years after he had moved from the farm, Jonathan realized what an intensely full and happy life the entire family had shared there. Just living out in the country is good, but it doesn't compare with being a part of the daily operations of a working farm with animals and crops. The children had great experiences. One tough, challenging task for a couple of little youngsters was helping seventy to eight-five pound Holstein calves learn to drink their milk out of buckets. The Barron children learned a lot from working with the animals.

When Ellen was ten, she began to show her own special calf in cattle shows at county and state fairs. Her calf was the first one born as a result of Jonathan's selection of a specific bull's semen to be used with a particular cow. The calf won two championships and placed third in the International Show Competition. She continued showing her heifer until it had become a full-grown cow.

For some reason, the cows and heifers seemed to behave better for Ellen than for her father or Bruce. Jonathan thought his cows were among the first of their breed to be influenced by the new women's movement: they didn't like being led around by a man.

Ellen and Bruce joined a 4-H club, and Ellen won second place for showmanship in handling cattle in the show ring. Years later, when Ellen was sixteen, Jonathan defended her early admittance to college to a skeptical associate dean by pointing out the emotional strength required to get a 1700-pound heifer to cooperate in competition. Ellen's emotional qualifications complemented her intellectual ones.

Bruce's cattle often won prizes, too, but he had been disillusioned about cattle judges after the judge at a county fair, a prominent cattle expert, awarded the first prize, the Grand Championship, to a ten-year-old cow. At the awards ceremony the judge openly announced that the impressive black heifer shown by Bruce Barron should have been given the award, adding that the young heifer would have many other opportunities for championship awards because it was one of the finest young Holsteins he had seen. Bruce said nothing, but since it was one of the few times

158

when his animal had a chance to equal or surpass his sister's, he didn't like the explanation the judge gave.

Susan, the Barron's youngest child, enjoyed making friends with the cattle and knew most of them by name. She loved Ann, a large black cow whose stall was first, as one entered the milking aisle. Susan would go out and sit on top of the white board fence enclosing the cow lot. Cows would come over to be petted, and Susan would reach out to oblige them. She was not at all afraid of being accidentally pushed off her perch on the fence.

When Jonathan remembered how his children had loved and cared for their favorite cows, he thought of his cow, Rosie, that he had so loved as a child. He was glad that he had been able to duplicate for his own children the pleasant parts of his experience with animals.

The children had been given the opportunity to select their own middle names. Susan selected Ann, in honor of her friend, the big black cow in the first stall. Jonathan smiled as he thought it was a good thing his father hadn't done the same, or his middle name might have been Rosie.

All the children loved the opportunity to be alone on the farm, mostly sitting on fences or in trees. One time Bruce and Ellen got together and moved forty- to forty-five pound bales of hay in one of the big haylofts. They made little private rooms and then hid from Susan. Jonathan had cautioned them to be very careful about shifting bales. And to make sure none could fall on them, he showed them how to stack their den's roof so it wouldn't cave in on them.

Jonathan believed in families joining together, working together, in whatever goes on. But he didn't try to substitute palship and comradeship for the respect and admiration that was required in a parent's role.

The children did a lot of work on the farm, and their father was there to guide and to work with them. He remembered watching Ellen on a lawn tractor going full speed around the trees on the three-acre lawn, Susan painstakingly clipping around the trees, and Bruce doing most of the trimming with a small power mower. Jonathan took care of the rough spots.

The older children had heard the phrase "to cut the mustard." To them it meant "Do your job" or "Work hard." Little did they realize how hard and dull it was to actually cut mustard until one day they were given scissors and were sent out to cut an unusually large scattering of mustard blossoms, shooting up higher than the oats in one forty-acre field. Never again did they use or like to hear that saying.

Winters on the farm were fun, with the kids and Jonathan sliding down the snow-covered, high barn ramp, competing to see who could ride the sled the farthest. One snowy day in December when Susan was three and a half, Rene and Jonathan confirmed her suspicion that there was no Santa Claus. She looked very disappointed and said dejectedly, "Pretty soon, I guess you'll be telling me there's no Easter Bunny, either."

The snow could get deep, but the county kept the roads clear. Jonathan and the farm manager enjoyed competing in removing snow from the farmyard and driveway, using a frontend loader with a new tractor and plenty of horsepower. In late summer, Jonathan put all three children in the big, long bucket of the front loader and lifted them to the tops of apple trees. There, they grabbed the reddest and biggest apples that always seemed to be out of reach.

But all of this had happened a long time ago.

Jonathan enjoyed reminiscing about the farm. When he drove into Wood Lake this June afternoon, he turned off Highway 14 and went directly to his former home. The ten years, during the sixties, when the family had lived on this farm, had been enriching, absorbing, joyful years.

Where there had been acres and acres of soybeans and corn, there now stood scores and scores of medium-priced three and four-bedroom homes with manicured laws on both sides of wide, curbed streets. The big house had been rented, and the developer used the barns and sheds to store equipment, because they still had about eighty acres left to be developed. Across the road from the barn where Jonathan had had his cow pasture, there were now two-bedroom and three-bedroom condominiums in beautiful buildings surrounded by well-planned landscaping.

Jonathan sat in his car, parked on the street near the big barn and could not keep from crying. The totally wonderful memories of the farm—the prize-winning cattle, the county and state fairs, the marvelous dogs they had while living there (especially the border collies), the large vegetable garden, the patches of big raspberry bushes, the acres of sweet corn—all were so overwhelming.

There was the tennis court Jonathan had put in, and still there had been room left over for kicking footballs, batting baseballs, playing badminton, and playing croquet on the big front lawn. The children won scholarship awards and cattle show awards. Rene was a well-known community leader, and the Barron farm home in Wood Lake represented a great, wonderful way of life. They had been so very happy together.

Rene had taken to the farm life quite readily. Her main farm jobs were handling the budget and selecting attractive names to go with the correct prefixes for the purebred calves. Rene used to tell party guests that when her husband phoned from New York or some other place, he would first ask whether a particular highly classified cow had had a calf, and whether it was a heifer or a bull. Then he would ask about the children.

Jonathan had to admit that he made it difficult for Rene to keep a month-to-month budget, because he might go to New York State, Kansas, Pennsylvania, or elsewhere for a cattle auction and buy a high-priced cow or two. But he had fun at auctions. He watched the experts bid. Then he put his late bid in from the back of the audience. The interested expert buyers had been down front bidding and thought the bidder in the back must have come to the auction early, studied the animals, and was set on buying a particular one at any price. Subsequently, Jonathan got many animals at a favorable price because other bidders stopped bidding early. He bid on cows he had never even seen, simply taking his cues from the knowledgeable bidders down in front. He made money on every animal he ever bought at an auction, so Rene always managed to get her budget back in line.

In addition to her farm duties and maintaining a big home and garden (with help from everyone), Rene was active in various women's organizations. She received so many requests to handle public relations for this group or that group, Jonathan finally persuaded her to give them all up and enter some kind of business, where she would be working with men and women in and out of business. She decided to get her real estate broker's license and started working with a very knowledgeable old red-haired Irish real estate broker and builder. Rene enjoyed the real estate business. She liked doing business with customers from all over the Chicago area.

Jonathan encouraged Rene to run for a place on the college

board of trustees, an elective office, and she won. When he had first suggested to her that she run, Rene thought she wasn't sufficiently qualified. Jonathan told her she was smarter than any of the men on the board. She doubted that she could win, since she was relatively new in the area, but Jonathan bought outdoor billboards all over the area and put her pretty picture on them. She won easily, beating the old guard. Voters do like charisma.

When he retired from the advertising business, Jonathan planned to start a new type of one-stop, retail farm service center to include fertilizers, implements, feeds, and everything else the farmers needed. But, as he had always recommended to his clients, he researched the project and evaluated the market outlook. The evidence indicated too much short-run competition in fertilizers from oil companies, plus a changing farm market with fewer good small and medium-sized farms. He explained to his backer, one of the largest privately owned corporations in America, that the centers would not provide enough return on investment. He had spent his own money to research the venture and had then advised this big company, which was prepared to give him carte blanche purchasing authority and major stockholdings in the venture, not to proceed.

About that time Rene's real estate boss came to dinner at the Barron home and said that he and his wife wanted to move to Florida. He suggested that Jonathan buy his business. Jonathan listened to the real estate broker's argument, because he had been looking for something else to do, another business to master, so he bought the small real estate company. Rene was delighted. She and her husband would be working together in a business in which she had more experience than he—which was an important reason why he bought it.

Jonathan leased all the available billboards in the Wood Lake area and in nearby towns. He bought full-page advertisements, not to advertise specific properties, but to tell the public, his competitors, city and county officials, everyone, just exactly how his new company was going to do business. Within one year Jonathan and Rene had close to the highest volume of business in their area. He wondered where he had been all his life. Buyers began to respect his honesty and ability so much that they would buy a farm from him over the telephone. When Jonathan asked them if they wanted to see the farm, they said they wouldn't know if it was a good buy or not. But if he said it was, then they gave him the go-ahead to buy it for them. And Rene became so well informed about one fine residential subdivision in the Wood Lake area that any home owner in that subdivision who decided to sell would call only her to handle the property.

Why had he left the Wood Lake life? The immediate, pragmatic reasons for leaving that life were simple. First, two kids were going away to school and on to careers. The farm life could never again be what it had been. The second reason was that the land was too valuable to keep out of development, and the perfect buyer wanted to purchase the land at a very good price. Third, Jonathan, in selling the farm, was not willing to settle down. He felt an almost unseen hand leading him and Rene away to further expansion of their lives.

Jonathan could have sat in his car for hours, recalling streams of deeply rewarding, soul-satisfying, intensely joyful episodes from the ten years he and his family had spent on the farm. But it was time to stop reflecting, to go meet the lawyers and the buyers for the last piece of Illinois farm land he owned—the closing curtain for a beautiful drama.

The meeting was a case of satisfied purchasers meeting a satisfied seller. They checked the figures on the closing statement. Then buyer and seller placed their signatures on a series of papers, including the deed of conveyance. Jonathan received a cashier's check for the full balance due.

Carl Cochran, Jonathan's attorney, was in his usual good mood, as he should have been. He was a banker, lawyer, farmer, strong Notre Dame fan, and a non-ideological politician whose clients frequently alternated between one interest or its opposite. His talent lay in being a happy, considerate negotiator who gained the cooperation of potential plaintiffs and defendants and then brought in a meticulous law associate to work out the details of the verbal agreement he had achieved.

It's often the lawyer who isn't busy to whom partners or friends refer the little clients, especially clients who are not immediately qualified to pay high hourly rates. What happens, sometimes, is that little clients permit the not-very-busy, relatively low-hourly-rate lawyer to have a piece of the action, whether it's a real estate deal or a small manufacturing business he wants to start. That's why so many "dumb" lawyers wind up long-lived multimillionaires, while the high-rate billers wind up with a few hundred thousand or less, dead at sixty-three. Cochran didn't envy the famous big-city lawyers. He had plenty of time to play golf and coach a Little League team.

Cochran took Jonathan to the Wood Lake Country Club, where the Barrons had eaten frequently when they lived in Wood Lake. They felt literally close to the club, because their farm bordered the club's golf course. It was a beautiful club, with well-appointed interior areas, a large swimming pool built for family use, a well-designed and well-maintained golf course, and marvelous foods, drinks, and service. As Jonathan looked around, he thought what a hell of a good life they had had going for them in Wood Lake.

During luncheon he and Cochran discussed many of the business deals they had shared and reminisced about the town and old friends.

"Carl," Jonathan asked, "whatever happened to the two Wood Lake lawyers who were convicted along with a Chicago bank official? I don't recall what they had been stealing."

"Those two fellows served short sentences at a federal penitentiary resort up in Minnesota. They quickly got over the trauma, if any, of going to jail. One of them—you knew him, Bob Hillard—was always overworked having to do the bidding of his clients, who got out of going to jail.

"Well, Bob came back healthier and looked like he'd been living in Palm Springs. He was fully reinstated to practice, and now his business is bigger than ever. Clients feel that he can now recognize what's crooked, but that he'll be honest, because his jail sentence hurt his family, especially his children."

Jonathan questioned Carl just a little further. "The lawyer who masterminded the whole deal never did go to prison, did he?"

"No. He was so well connected they didn't dare go after him for fear of affecting too many others," Carl replied.

"Carl," Jonathan asked, "why do we call lawyers 'officers of the court'?"

"I really don't know, but I should. I think that in this state, on admission to the bar all lawyers are sworn in as 'officers of the court.' I don't know where the term originated, but I believe it had to do with lawyers having to have certificates of good character to practice law. Why do you ask?"

"The main reason," Jonathan answered critically, "is that it's hard for me to imagine any valid reasons why the courts of this country should be denigrated by having thousands of unethical and irresponsible lawyers being called 'officers of the court.' Recently a friend of mine, a law librarian, asked many lawyer friends the same question that I asked you. They didn't have any idea about the term's origins and seemed not to care."

"Jonathan, why do you take such an innocent practice so seriously? There are some lawyers of integrity and character."

Jonathan answered directly. "One thing that prompted my interest was the difficulty the American Bar Association seems to have had with a segment of its membership in its effort to strengthen the Association's code of ethics. The term 'officer of the court' was first used in legislation enacted in the reign of Henry IV. It provided for a fixed number of attorneys to be appointed by the judges. It further provided that attorneys should be 'examined by the justices, and that by their discretion, their names shall be put upon the roll, and that they be good, virtuous, and of good name, and be received and sworn well to serve in their offices."

"Carl, didn't one of our Supreme Court Justices recently complain about the incompetence of so many lawyers who practice in the courts?"

"Yes, I think it was the Chief Justice but I'm not sure," Carl replied rather disinterestedly.

"In many of the cases," Jonathan continued, "issues of misconduct and ability were of prime concern; and it was within these discussions that the courts referred repeatedly to the fact that the attorney is an 'officer of the court' and thereby is required to conduct himself and his practice in a prescribed manner. I wish someone of consequence in the law schools and among our leading judges would help to eliminate the use of this term except in reference to the group of persons who actually work as part of the court, or limit its use to lawyers with very high qualifications. I think calling lawyers generally 'officers of the court' has been outdated for centuries.

"The law schools, influential judges, and bar associations, especially the state bar groups, might also do a better job of informing every lawyer what it really means to be worthy of the title 'officer of the court.' "

Jonathan laughed and said, "Okay, Carl, see what a good martini does to me?"

"I pity the lawyer who hears your opinions on officers of the court if you have a bad martini," Carl said, shaking his head. "Let's have lunch."

They ordered lunch, and it was excellent. The service was so quick, Jonathan suspected Carl had signaled the waiter to rush before he had to listen to another law librarian's report.

"Jonathan, I see some of your old real estate friends over there waving at you."

Jonathan looked to his right and waved back. The conversation turned back to real estate. He complimented Carl on the efficient and precise way he handled real estate closings and then thanked him for the lunch, which went on Cochran's bill since Jonathan was no longer a club member.

As he and Carl walked out through the dining room, Jonathan stopped to shake hands with a few of the old-timers who could still get out to lunch. Then with a goodbye to Carl, who sent his regards to Rene, he was on his way to O'Hare Airport to catch his flight back to Washington.

# 17

Rene had enjoyed the dinner with Dr. Spirrison. Not only was she pleased with the description of the job he had in mind for her, but she liked the whole idea of working at Southland and living in California. As she drove back to Santa Monica, she was still mulling over the advantages of separation in lieu of divorce. She knew she would like to maintain contact with Jonathan—to have him in her life as a friend and counselor. After all, she had shared with him three-fifths of her entire life! She wasn't eager to cut the cords of that relationship.

By the time she got to Santa Monica, she was beginning to think of the Sonberg dinner. She really liked the Sonbergs and looked forward to the bonus joy of Arthur's beautiful music. When she arrived at Ellen's house, it was almost eleven o'clock, and the house was dark except for the porch light. She parked her car, found the house key, and slipped off to bed without awakening anyone.

Rene slept soundly and didn't get up until long after Ellen and Anson had gone, and she had the house to herself. After showering and dressing, she had a light breakfast, checked Ellen's food supply, and made a list of what she would need for the dinner that night, including chicken and broccoli for the chicken Monte Carlo. She decided to buy several bottles of good California champagne, because she wanted the dinner to be a festive affair.

Shopping served a double purpose for Rene: to buy the things needed for dinner and to allow her to be out doing something instead of thinking so damned much. Thinking about the meeting with Jonathan the next day was beginning to make her feel uncertain and tense. She welcomed something she could be positive about and active in doing, even if it was simply selecting one head of lettuce instead of another.

She drove to Golden's, spent an hour shopping, walked around the Pacific Palisades shopping area for a while, and went into a few of the small shops and boutiques. These heterogeneous shops had a pleasant ambience.

Yes, she was really beginning to love California.

It took her all afternoon to put away the groceries and prepare the dinner. She decided to make enough chicken Monte Carlo to leave some in the freezer for Ellen and Anson, so they would have a couple of dinners ready to heat and eat on another day.

When Ellen arrived home, followed shortly by Anson, they found everything ready and told Rene it was like coming home to a resort hotel. Rene had added to the welcome picture by wearing her soft green, clinging silk dress, the one with the modest but inviting slit up her left leg. When a woman has long legs like Rene's, slits up the side appear rather modest, but the purpose of such design and the idea conveyed is, "I am a woman, and I feel like a woman."

Rene more or less unconsciously wished to convey, to women and men alike, the feeling that this relaxed and handsome woman had already cleaned house, made dinner, and was now their charming hostess. When Arthur and Sybil Sonberg arrived, they were impressed, just as she had intended.

"Oh, Rene, how splendiferous you look," Sybil said as she greeted Rene with a hug. "And Ellen, you just radiate joy and beauty." Sybil kissed Ellen on the cheek and gave Anson a little touch-kiss with her greeting.

Arthur stared at Rene and finally declared, "I can't believe it, Rene. I first saw you over thirty years ago and as recently as two years ago, when Jonathan invited us to brunch, but never have I seen you look so stunning—just absolutely gorgeous."

"Thank you, my dear. You're doing quite well yourself. That's a beautiful jacket," Rene said as she kissed Arthur's cheek. "And, Sybil, I think it's this shade of green that makes me look less than half a century old." She turned around to show the dress. "Jonathan shopped all over Washington before he found it for me. He said he could see it on me, and he bought it. And I surely do like you in that mandarin silk dress, Sybil. I hope you feel even half as well as you look."

"Thanks, Rene, but I'd rather feel twice as good as I look!"

"Arthur, champagne will be served as soon as you park yourself at the piano and begin the 'Beguine.' "

Anson went with Rene to the kitchen, got the glasses off the top shelf, took two bottles of champagne out of the refrigerator, and opened them. He poured the champagne while Rene found napkins and a tray. Arthur played the Cole Porter request, while Rene and Anson passed the drinks around. Then he played one of his new songs, and Rene soon started to sing with him.

Arthur asked her how long she planned to stay in California.

"I'm going back to Washington tomorrow, Arthur, but I may be back soon to help Ellen, in case she needs a cook until the baby arrives."

"Will Jonathan be coming out?" Arthur asked. "I'd like him to hear my newest compositions."

"No, Arthur, I don't think he will. He and I will be discussing our plans this weekend. We may be giving up our apartment. In fact, I've taken an option on a rental apartment on Malcolm Avenue, just a few blocks from Westwood Village. When I come out here in the next few weeks, my plans, at the moment, are to stay here and help Ellen.

Arthur looked rather surprised, but it was Sybil who said, "Rene, does renting an apartment mean that you and Jonathan will live across the continent from one another? Are you planning separate lives?"

"Actually, Sybil, we're not sure. Right now, I'll be coming out to be with Ellen until her baby arrives."

Arthur and Sybil looked at each other, but Rene pretended not to notice. "Jonathan says he can't stand having me sitting around our apartment on the floor of the living room with people half or less than half my age, discussing a thirty-four-dollar balance in our journalism society's treasury. He offered to replenish our chapter's treasury if we would just hold our meetings elsewhere." Arthur and Sybil smiled at this last statement, but Rene was very serious.

Arthur left the piano to join the group and to get more champagne.

"It's funny, Arthur," Rene said matter-of-factly. "I don't want any other real love. I don't think Jonathan does, either, but I would like a separation for a few weeks or months, so I could live on my own, be self-sufficient, and be free to choose my own friends.

"I shouldn't have to feel guilty about associating with my friends," she said emphatically, "just because they may be younger and more happy-go-lucky."

She thought to herself, I've been faithful to Jonathan. Before

169

marrying, I was a virgin. Now, I think I'm entitled to enjoy lovers when I wish, although I don't believe I'll ever find a man to take his place in my life.

"Now, Rene," Arthur said softly, interrupting her thoughts, "you know Sybil and I love both you and Jonathan. We've watched you grow from a twenty-year-old girl, married to Jonathan, to a magnificent woman, successful in business and journalism. Jonathan was your greatest fan. It was his encouragement and support that helped you become what you are today. What do you mean by wanting to be self-sufficient?"

I ask myself the same question time after time, Rene thought.

But to Arthur she replied, "As you know, Jonathan and I have three of the smartest and most wonderful children anyone could possibly want. Each of them has lived on his or her own all over the country and half the world. I'm almost fifty-one, and I've never been on my own.

"I was twenty years old when I married. I had only lived in a sorority house away from home, and now I feel that for a while, at least, I want to be entirely on my own and make the little decisions, as well as the big ones.

"Do you realize that I've never gone out and bought my own car?"

Sybil laughed and said, "But, Rene, if your husband wants to save you the bother and buy you a car, that shows his caring and concern for you, not your inadequacy! What's so great about buying a car, anyhow? Since we've been married, I've had several cars, including my new Cadillac El Dorado, but I don't know whose idea it was to buy the car. What's more, it doesn't matter to me."

"Sybil," Rene laughed, "were you ever on the road with a band as a singer and instrumentalist?"

"Sure, Rene, but I was happy as hell when Arthur's earnings became so large I could 'play' at singing or composing at home. It isn't so great 'out there.'"

"But, Sybil," Rene pursued, "didn't it make you feel free to be on your own with the big band, traveling, and making the hotel, night club, and theater dates?"

"I'll tell you what it made me feel—tired. It simply isn't the glamorous, free-wheeling life you imagine it to be," Sybil said.

"I didn't get all that much of what I wanted in those days, but if I wanted to go with a lousy piano player, I did." She looked at

170

Arthur. "Until I met a good man, who happened to play the piano, my quiet husband here, but I do see what you mean, Rene."

Ellen and Anson had spent their cocktail time in the kitchen, partly because they wanted to spend a few quiet moments together and partly because they wanted to give Rene and her friends a chance to catch up on the events of their lives. Now Ellen came to the dining room door and said, "Mom, I think we'd better get dinner started. I'm starved."

She glanced at the empty champagne glasses and said, "We'll get another bottle of champagne, too."

Anson said, "I'll get the refills, Ellen, and you put the chicken in the oven."

As Anson made the rounds pouring champagne into everyone's glasses, the conversation seemed to lag.

"You've known Jonathan many years; do you really think he wants a divorce?" Rene asked Arthur, almost pleading for his opinion.

"Rene, I have no way of knowing what Jonathan wants. But considering how you apparently feel, a few months' separation might give him the time to work out his projects and give you that long-delayed opportunity to live on your own and do as you please," Arthur replied, trying to console Rene, as well as being honest.

"I shouldn't be talking about this," Rene said. "But you were kind enough to ask about my moving out here. Arthur, I think you're right about me, but Jonathan wants a divorce. I'm pretty sure of that. I don't know if he'll go along with a separation. He truly wants me to be free to marry again."

"Rene, it sounds like Jonathan has your best interest at heart," Sybil said. "I think he's right, if you'll be careful."

Arthur added, very seriously, "I think you're running a big risk. You're attractive, indeed, but you're also gregarious and tolerant. You'll have to be very selective out here. Unworthy, as well as worthy, men will be on your doorstep. May I suggest, from what I know of Hollywood and a lot of other places, that you learn to make friends first before you make lovers. Friends often become lovers, but seldom do lovers become friends."

"Oh, Arthur," Rene replied rather innocently, "there may be a few honorable men left who like older girls."

"You're right, Rene. There are plenty of men who need the

171

strength and wisdom of the older woman. But you're not just an older woman at fifty. You're a very pretty woman who can compete with women twenty-five years younger. But it may be the weak fellows that you'll probably have to fight off, like Sybil used to have to fight off those trumpet players in the band.

"The truth is, an awful lot of men in this town—especially some of the unemployed musicians and actors—would like to capture an attractive, smart woman of independent means."

Sybil said with a bright look in her eyes, "Rene, Arthur isn't kidding. I had real problems pushing them off. I was glad—really glad—when Arthur took charge. And I'm glad he's still in charge."

She laughed and moved over to pat Arthur on the back. "Rene," she said, "did you ever think that, despite all the 'new woman' junk, there are tens of millions of women in this country who go to work every day, making a living with or without a man? There's certainly nothing great about living alone, whether you're a man or a woman.

"What does a woman have to prove by living on her own? Millions of women have been doing that for hundreds of years and then some."

Rene didn't answer, so Sybil continued, "I think if you really want to try it on your own, do it. But you've been a businesswoman who could make good money ever since Jonathan's producer, dear old Freda, hired you. So, what's new? I ask women who think only they have awakened. Lots and lots of women have been making it on their own—and making men—since day one.

"What would you gain? It would be different if you had a lunk-head husband who didn't want you to work, who couldn't stand the competition. But Jonathan has inspired and helped you to become the outstanding woman you are now.

"And besides, there's one thing we all learn sooner or later, man or woman. There is no such thing as being self-sufficient. The only self-sufficient human I ever saw was dead!"

Sybil concluded with finality, "And having many lovers denies a woman's ability to be self-sufficient. More often, having lots of lovers indicates a woman's insecurity, uncertainty, and dependence. The same goes for a man. I've often said that when a man needs many women, he is incapable of having a successful relationship with one—no matter which one."

"Sybil," Arthur interjected, "you ought to teach a course on

172

modern womanhood. How did you get so on top of the current situation?"

"Don't forget, Arthur, you and I have both learned a lot in show business."

Rene got up and walked around nervously. "But, Sybil, Jonathan has been too much my mentor, my father, my husband, my god." She added softly, "And I need to be free. I like my friends. I've changed a lot since going back and getting my degree in journalism and working with young journalists.

"They're getting things out of life that I missed."

Rene wanted to drop the conversation. It had gone on long enough. "Shall we have dinner? I see we're all out of champagne."

Walking toward the kitchen, she asked, "Anson, shall I come in now and help?"

"In about five minutes, the chicken will be just right. And Ellen has put the salads out ready to be placed around. I have a pot of coffee made." Anson reported with pride.

Rene was still nervous, not her usual relaxed self. "Arthur, Sybil, let's share another bottle of champagne. Anson is busy. I'll pour." Rene poured the glasses full. She was drinking more than usual, drinking fast instead of sipping.

Arthur went back to the piano and told Rene there was something he wanted to say about Jonathan.

"What's that, Arthur?" Rene queried.

"You'll recall that as an artist in Chicago I was under contract to Jonathan for a long time. When I wanted to come to California, he tore up the contract and advised me to get an agent in Hollywood. Your husband is one of the finest men I have ever known.

"I was sorry when he disposed of his interests in the entertainment business. He knew good talent and good music. He still does. He's a very perceptive man. He was very loyal to the people with whom he worked."

Arthur raised his glass to Rene. "Rene, I wish you well."

Arthur played a melody on the piano, and Sybil and Rene were quiet, each perhaps lost in her own thoughts.

He turned and spoke solemnly. "Rene, my dear friend, you have long been the person Jonathan has cherished most. I do hope you will do nothing to tear down either his values or your own.

"Now, with that final word, I'll play you a portion of Jonathan's favorite piano number, Gershwin's 'Rhapsody in Blue.' I wish he were here to listen."

Arthur played with a special, glorious feeling, just as he had long ago, when he played the same music for his audition for Jonathan. Now, they applauded Arthur's spirited, almost spiritual presentation of Gershwin's monumental composition. With the last of the champagne, Rene raised her glass to toast their wonderful pianist.

Rene and the Sonbergs recalled the fun times they had had on Chicago television.

Arthur once asked Jonathan if he ever regretted having left the television programming business that he had pioneered. "Yes," he answered, "but doesn't the song say 'whatever will be will be'? There are always so many things to do, so many roads one can travel. Perhaps certain roads that one must travel."

The dinner was served in grand style by Anson, and the conversation at the table was as pleasant as the meal. The chicken Monte Carlo was superb. Rene's strawberry mold salad provided a taste surprise and a contrast to the chicken dish.

The dinner party ended with a little more music from Arthur and a lot of angel food cake and fresh coffee. The dessert Rene had prepared as a surprise for the Sonbergs was her own original favorite recipe for angel food cake. It had body to it, not just fluff.

After warmly saying goodnight to Arthur and Sybil, Rene told Ellen and Anson that her plane didn't leave until noon the next day. She said she was feeling so tired, she would probably sleep too late to have breakfast with either of them.

"No wonder you feel tired, Mom," Ellen said. "You shopped, cleaned house, cooked an incredibly good dinner, talked with old friends, and consumed lots of champagne."

Rene laughed. "Ellen, you and Anson were so kind and helpful with our guests. It's always a joy to be with the two of you. Goodbye now. I love you both, and soon I'll be saying that I love all three of you."

She hugged Anson. "Anson, even Jonathan was practically overcome with joy when Ellen appeared on the scene. You're both about to be introduced to the wonderment and joy of having a baby. Goodnight."

As Rene started down the hall, she called back over her shoulder, "And don't bother with the kitchen, Ellen. I'll have at least an hour to finish cleaning it up before I leave for the airport."

174

"Hope you have a good night's sleep, Mom. You've had a busy day."

Everyone had seemed pleased with the evening, although it was perhaps not as light and diverting as Rene might have wished. Before she drifted off to sleep, she fleetingly recalled that her younger daughter, Susan, had once told her that what is present time is only a suspension bridge connected to the past and future.

# 18

About the same time that Rene was in Ellen's kitchen in Santa Monica preparing dinner for the Sonbergs, Jonathan was taking a flight from Chicago to Washington National Airport. When he arrived he picked up his luggage, caught the shuttle bus to the satellite parking lot, picked up his car, and drove to his Watergate apartment.

Before unpacking, he went down to the reception desk to pick up the mail and the back copies of the *Washington Post* that had been saved for him. He occupied his evening skimming through the mail, the *Post,* and the magazines. He felt compelled to try to keep up with everything that was happening anywhere, feeling that this was one way he could share the various interests of his children as they made their different ways in the world.

Before going to bed, Jonathan went to the kitchen and made a list of groceries for the weekend. He would shop and clean house tomorrow in preparation for Rene's return and Bruce's visit. It was good to be home.

The next day, with the satisfaction of having caught up with all the mail, phone calls, house cleaning, and shopping, he was eager to go to the airport to meet Bruce at seven o'clock. Bruce was taking the shuttle plane from New York.

Arriving at National he parked in the short-term lot close to the terminal entrance and went in to meet his son. The shuttle was on time, and Bruce was among the first passengers to enter the terminal.

As he shook hands with his son, Jonathan said, "Glad you could come down this weekend, Bruce. I was just observing you as you came in, and I have to admit that you were quite right in buying the Gucci bag. It is so obviously expensive, it makes your old jeans look first class."

"Glad you noticed the effect, Dad. Since I'm a creative director, I need to wear something very casual like jeans. But, since I usually take the place of the account management people in making pre-

sentations, the Gucci bag is my passport to their department."
Bruce smiled at his father. Jonathan gestured toward the baggage
carousel, and Bruce shook his head. He traveled light on week-end
trips.

When they reached the car, Bruce asked, "Where are we going
now? To pick up Mother at Dulles?"

"Yes, her plane is scheduled to arrive at eight-fifteen," Jonathan
said as he opened the trunk and Bruce dropped his bag inside.

The two men were silent as Jonathan negotiated his way out of
the parking lot and through the fee gate. Once out on the parkway,
they resumed the catch-up-on-the-family conversation. "I phoned
Ellen a couple of days ago to see how she and the baby were getting
along," Bruce said. "She told me that Mother had an option to rent
an apartment out there."

"Why would Mother rent an apartment?" Bruce asked. "If Ellen
needs help, she could just stay with Ellen, couldn't she?"

"Well, that would work well until the baby comes. But after the
baby's arrival, your mother would lose her room there, and while
she would still be needed to help, she would also need a place of
her own where she could get a good night's rest. Babies don't seem
to know the difference between day and night when it comes to
being hungry or needing to be held."

Bruce nodded.

"I didn't know she had rented an apartment," Jonathan continued. "I did suggest to her a few months ago that she consider
a job in Los Angeles."

"The doctor seems to think the baby may be premature, and
then your mother would have to stay in Los Angeles regardless of
our plans."

"Yes, I know, Dad," Bruce said with concern. "I talked to Ellen
a couple of weeks ago. She seemed to be worried about the baby
being born too soon, but she did take some comfort in your prediction that it would arrive the first week in September."

Jonathan smiled. "I hope that I estimated the date correctly, for
both Ellen's and the baby's benefit. But I've asked Ellen to follow
her doctor's advice to the letter. I certainly don't want anybody to
depend on my predictions. Ellen will do everything the doctor tells
her."

"I think she is taking everything in stride," Bruce said, "but
she's always been a worrier."

For a few minutes both men seemed lost in thought.

Bruce asked his father, "What plans do you and Mother have regarding your futures?"

"We're still a little undecided. That's one of the reasons we're so pleased you're here for the weekend. You're not only one of our most caring but also one of our wisest counselors."

"I'm not sure that we've done any agency research on the marital choices for a husband and wife who respect and care for one another but who are traveling different roads at different levels.

"Speaking of predictions, Dad, didn't Susan start the rumor in Church City about five years ago that you and Mother were going to divorce?"

"Yes, in a way. I remember that your mother and I were surprised to hear from some of our friends that we planned to separate. Susan said she picked up the rumor at one of our cocktail parties. Rumors are titillating by-products of cocktail parties.

"I think, Bruce, that you and Ellen, as well as Mother and I, have always perceived Susan as being quite pragmatic and innately shrewd."

"Dad, Susan had to become an alert observer in order to survive when we were growing up. When I think of all the tricks Ellen and I played on that kid, I wonder how she can still like us. But she always managed to pull a few good ones on us, too.

"Those were great days on the farm. Susan had to remember a combination of passwords before we'd let her enter our castle in the barn that we built with bales of hay.

"And Susan certainly knows you well, Dad. When she was at Carolina State, she heard from some of her classmates that Mother was trying to be 'one of the students,' even though she was a well-known person in the community and the mother of children as old as her classmates, or older. Susan told me then that you would never be able to adjust to the level of Mother's Carolina State friends.

"It beats me why Mother tried to act twenty instead of forty-five. Maybe she was heading into an identity crisis. But I've met other older women in college who weren't too different from Mother."

"Well, Bruce, Rene has always liked to get along with everyone. That's a wonderful characteristic. But one must understand that getting along with everyone doesn't necessarily obligate a person to adopt or adapt to the standards of behavior and the values of those around them.

178

"Maybe I should be more gregarious," Jonathan added thoughtfully. "I know I should be more tolerant. However, sometimes when you earn the respect of people, rather than just being nice and acquiescent, the relationship is likely to develop into a worthwhile, lasting friendship. Being readily agreeable makes for more harmonious short-term relationships, but not necessarily long-term ones.

"But we must remember—*I* must remember—during our entire married life, your mother has tried and has succeeded in being what her children and husband needed. Now it's her turn, maybe a turn back to the person she was before our marriage."

Jonathan saw a need to concentrate a little more on the traffic, so he said to Bruce, "Let's talk about your work. How are things at the agency?"

"Well—one thing that may interest you, Dad, as a former television and advertising agency executive, is the announcement I received yesterday that one of my television commercials won the award as best of the year."

Jonathan smiled broadly. "That's wonderful. Which one?"

"It was the musical one we made for Kolor Corporation. I played the pre-release tape for you and Mother on my last visit. Remember?"

"Well, we share advertising experiences, but our agency never won an award for the best TV commercial. We did win the best radio commercial awards, though, when radio was the big medium.

"For a creative person as good as you are, Bruce, I guess winning a first-place national award just comes along with your everyday work. I'm very proud of you and your accomplishments."

Both father and son were smiling, and Jonathan asked, "What segments of the television commercial were you directly responsible for, the overall concept and production?"

"That's right, Dad. But I also wrote the copy and music, selected the performers, and supervised the direction. We hired a good film director, too."

"So, that's all you did, just everything. I suppose you made not only the television spot, but perhaps the beautiful girl who was featured as well? I recall that she was a gorgeous Irish brunette."

"As a matter of fact, Dad, the way she rewarded me made the national award seem quite secondary. That's why I didn't call you."

"I congratulate you for keeping your priorities in balance," Jonathan said to his son, smiling.

For a while, father and son were both quiet, probably thinking about the wife and mother they were soon to see, perhaps wondering how life would be with the core of the home about to be split.

The drive was easy and fast, thanks to the unimpeded Dulles access freeway. They arrived and parked in the short-term lot and were in the terminal at seven forty-five. They checked the arrival time of Rene's flight and found it was not due until 8:40, so they had plenty of time to eat something.

Jonathan and Bruce were at the designated gate to meet the shuttle bus from Rene's flight several minutes before the doors opened for the passengers to enter the terminal. Soon they saw Rene's light, strawberry blonde hair. She greeted them merrily and kissed her husband on his mouth and her son on his cheek. Then she hugged her son. She didn't hug Jonathan, because she knew he didn't like to engage in more than the minimum kissing in public. In private, and when in the mood, he was quite different.

Jonathan asked Rene for her baggage check, gave her his car keys, told her where the car was parked, and suggested she go on with Bruce to the car and hear Bruce's good news. He would wait and bring her luggage out. She hesitated, but Bruce gently took her by the arm, and they walked on together, talking away. Luckily, there was not delay with the baggage, and in a short time Jonathan joined them.

In the car Rene and Bruce continued their discussion, but Jonathan paid no attention until he had paid his parking charge and was on the Dulles access highway, headed for the Watergate.

Rene asked how his Chicago Ethics Inquiry Group board meeting had turned out and if the farm closing was satisfactory.

"The Ethics board accepted my resignation, effective at once," he replied unemotionally. "The meeting was pleasant and promising. I'll continue as a member of the board and of the executive committee, and I've also agreed to serve as president emeritus. That simply means I'll be available for consultation now and then.

"As to the farm sale closing, Carl Cochran had everything in order and gave me a cashier's check for the balance due. So we own no more farm land in Illinois."

Jonathan chanced the subject. "I hear you were lucky enough to find an apartment?"

"I found one that looks pretty good. It's near Westwood Village, not far from Ellen's place. I have a verbal option on it right now. That is, the landlord said he would hold it until I call him on Tuesday, after Ellen goes back to the doctor.

"But how did you know I found an apartment? Did you read my mind?"

"No, Bruce talked with Ellen, and she mentioned it. Did you have a chance to make any job calls?"

"Did you see the college president who addressed the Carolina State seminar that you attended? The man Dr. Otis spoke to so favorably about you?"

There was tension in Rene's voice when she answered. "Funny you would remember my mentioning him to you. Yes, I did see him—Dr. Spirrison, president of Southland University. He said that he wanted to create a new position in order to promote more effectively the undergraduate and graduate schools of business."

Jonathan seemed pleased. "Rene, that fellow is on the right track, and you could do that job. Exactly where do you stand with this president of Southland?"

"Oh, I feel optimistic. But before calling on him I had an interview with Howard Culbertson, a vice-president of the *Los Angeles Chronicle*. He's a friend of Ralph Lawton. He was very courteous and told me that when I returned to Los Angeles he would introduce me to a woman executive in personnel. But Dr. Spirrison specifically asked me not to take any other job until I checked with him."

"Well," Jonathan asked, "What did you tell him?"

Rene replied in a very soft voice. She knew her answer could well be the clinching argument to support their separation. "I promised him I wouldn't take any other job until I talked with him again.

"One good thing about the job he has in mind for me is that it won't be available for about two months. He asked if I could wait that long, and I assured him that I would probably need at least that long, because of Ellen's uncertain situation."

Jonathan said, with a slight sigh of relief, "Well, Rene, I would say you've had a very successful trip. Don't you think so, Bruce?"

He glanced into the rear view mirror to catch a glimpse of Bruce.

"Mother, it does sound like you had a good trip. And you can

181

contribute so much more to a university job because of your Carolina State experience," Bruce said.

"Rene," her husband said reassuringly, "I think everything will work out well for you."

"You do want me to go to Ellen's and to try living in California for a while, don't you?"

"Yes. I think Los Angeles would be a fine place for you to go. Ellen will welcome your help and your nearness, before and after the baby is born. And, as Bruce said, you can use your talents and contribute a great deal to Southland and to Dr. Spirrison's plans."

"I'm glad you both feel like that," Rene said, "because I think I'd like the Southland job."

"What does Jonathan mean," she wondered, "by my talents contributing to Dr. Spirrison's plans? If he means what I think he means, he shouldn't mind, because a college president fits his 'worthy-of-me' requirements. Actaully, he seems quite happy about my leaving. I wonder if he will go for just a separation and not insist on a divorce."

As they drove into the Watergate garage, Jonathan said, "Bruce, welcome to our apartment—maybe for the last time."

"One never knows, Dad. And, if you remained here, I doubt if I could come to see you very often."

"Bruce, what do you mean?" his mother asked quickly, as they got out of the car.

"I'll tell you when we get upstairs. It's really exciting news. It's something a real specialist in placing top advertising executives is cooking up for me. At least, he says he is. I didn't call him. He called me."

Rene and Jonathan were both eager to hear their son's news. Some good news would be welcome. After the car was parked in its allotted space and Rene's luggage unloaded, Bruce grabbed his bag, and they all headed for the elevator. While they were waiting for the doors to open, Bruce said, "All I'll tell you is that my office would be in Tokyo."

"Tokyo, Japan?" his mother exclaimed. "That's half way around the world from here. Would you live there all the time? Is there a big advertising agency there? And what will you do about speaking Japanese?

Bruce laughed at his mother's exclamations and questions and answered, "Yes, to all of the above."

Jonathan, never surprised, said calmly as they rode up in the elevator, "It's a good thing that you have such aptitude for languages, son. You'll probably land in Japan already speaking Japanese, if they give you a month's notice."

Jonathan had first visited Tokyo many years ago. He had come back thinking half the male population of Tokyo looked exactly like New York advertising agency account executives, with their Brooks Brothers' uniforms and standard attache cases. He remembered thinking, "Those guys are taking our lead, but they're working harder and more seriously than we are."

Rene was unable to comprehend the idea of her son working in Tokyo among all those Japanese. Jonathan accepted such a move as normal for an up-and-coming executive. He also thought that Japan was the best place for Bruce to go. He had recently read a very optimistic report about the enormous economic development outlook for the Pacific Rim countries.

"Oh, what pretty flowers," Rene said as she entered the apartment living room. "What a thoughtful welcome. I'll bet you got your friend at the Watergate flower shop to give you some of every kind they had. I like all the colors—red, pink, white, blue, orange. How festive!" She gave him a warm kiss. Maybe she, too, was thinking of the conditioning influence of pretty flowers.

"Bruce, why don't you and your mother put your clothes away, and I'll heat up some Sara Lee pecan coffeecake," Jonathan said. "I'll plug in the percolator—it's ready to go." He started into the kitchen. "Oh, and Bruce, come back in as soon as you can and tell your mother about your television commercial?"

Soon they were all together again, enjoying coffeecake and each other's company. Bruce reviewed his television commercial award news for his mother, who promptly said, "I told you it was good. And when you hummed the tune over the phone, before you brought the tape down, I said I liked it."

"Yes, I remember, Mother. You sure were right."

Bruce told them that one of the top job recruiters in the advertising and marketing field had called him for a luncheon appointment to find out whether he would be willing to change jobs and move to a big international advertising agency in Tokyo. The job would pay almost twice what he was presently making and would include a free apartment. In addition to his increased income, his company ranking and responsibilities would also be greater.

183

"And what did you tell him, Bruce?" his father asked.

"Well, Dad, I didn't tell him I wanted to talk it over with you first, but while I'm here, we can do that. I did tell him I would think it over. In any case, I couldn't leave my present job for at least three months, because I'm already committed to a whole series of television spots for two of our most important clients. And one of them absolutely insists that I supervise the production, since I wrote the copy and music.

"I like working for this agency in New York, so if I should go to Tokyo, I would want the transition caused by my leaving to be as easy for them as possible."

"Bruce," Jonathan said, "I know you've considered all aspects of the offer along with your obligations to your present, wonderful employer. However, the agency you would be joining in Tokyo is also a great company. I think that, since most large businesses are world businesses, sooner or later you'll need to know all the major international markets. Any you're just the right age to fill in the international requirements you'll need as you move way up in the advertising business—or in any transnational corporation or in our national government, for that matter."

"I'm glad to hear you say that, Dad, because those are the factors that I'm giving the most weight to in my considerations."

Rene was listening and thought this was a topic for Jonathan and Bruce. All the children placed a very high value on their father's opinion. He had earned their respect.

Rene finished eating her piece of coffee cake and was drinking her last sip of coffee, "It all sounds so wonderful—and strange. We'll talk more about it tomorrow. Let's go to bed. Okay with you, Jonathan?"

The truth was that Rene often felt a little left out when father and son talked about advertising and politics. She preferred to go to bed, where she could be a very knowledgeable participant.

"I just happened to be thinking the same thing," Jonathan replied. "Are you about ready for bed, Bruce? I've already put all new sheets on the bed and clean towels in your bathroom."

"That's fine, Dad. Thanks. See you folks around noon," Bruce said as he got up and walked toward his bedroom. "Good night, everyone."

"Good night, dear."

"Good night, Bruce."

184

Rene picked up the dishes and cups and saucers and rinsed them quickly. She put them in the dishwasher and switched off the light. Meanwhile, Jonathan turned off the hall and living room lights and headed for the bedroom.

As Bruce went to bed, he was thinking that the relationship of his father and mother must be different from that of almost any other married couple he could imagine. Here they were, having finally decided to separate, yet they were acting very normal and even hastening off to bed.

Of course, he knew they had been watching themselves grow apart over a period of years. He also knew they wanted to stay together, but they had become quite different people, especially his mother.

Bruce remembered that when he and Susan were both in school at Carolina State, and Ellen was away at law school and working, he had begun to notice changes in his mother. They often played bridge or poker with their parents. Starting five or six years ago, his mother had become very combative in the games. In poker, she would keep meeting the bets his dad would make, virtually without regard to whether she had a pair of twos or four of a kind. His dad was a good player, and she hated to see him win so often. In bridge, when he and his mother and dad would sometimes play three-handed, his mother would often outbid his dad for the dummy hand—once again with almost no regard to what was in her hand. She had seen her husband bid like that and pick up amazingly good dummy hands, but his dad could read the bids better than she, or else he was just plain lucky. Then she would often double-check to make sure someone hadn't reneged.

One thing Bruce readily admitted was that his dad's comments could often make a person feel diminished, but what he had to say was always constructive. Nevertheless, he knew that his dad could criticize his mother rather mildly, and she would react ten times more strongly than if anyone else had made the comment.

Actually, as Bruce saw the situation and as he had observed the changes—his father becoming increasingly depressed and his mother more independent—he thought neither of them could have avoided the changing pattern of their lives. The difference in age was only one thing. The real issue was that they were basically different people now; and after all these years, as he had told his dad, his mother was apparently going through a change of identity.

Bruce thought her identity crisis was probably caused by cultural changes and by her increasing need to try out her wings on her own.

Bruce had discussed the problem several times with his sisters, and all three children had very sympathetically agreed that separation would probably be best for both of their parents. So they chose to regard the situation as a logical progression of events, rather than as a loss. It probably helped that they were all away from home and starting new lives themselves.

Bruce was pleased that his dad remained ever thoughtful of his mother and his family, as evidenced by his cleaning the whole apartment thoroughly, doing the shopping, buying flowers, and remembering that his mother welcomed a brandy or a dessert before bedtime.

Bruce thought his mother had been very pleasant and nondefensive when his dad asked about her job prospects and Dr. Spirrison. He knew his mother wanted to live by herself, for the first time in her life, and she seemed to look forward to life in California. Of course, it would be special being with Ellen and her first grandchild.

"Imagine," Bruce said softly, "I'll soon be an uncle."

Sleepily summarizing his thoughts, Bruce saw his mother's strength and perseverance in becoming a very smart, sophisticated, and beautiful woman as a story in itself. He knew that she was caught between two lives, his dad's and others—the college crowd of students and professors, the alumni and journalism groupies, and those from her original cultural environment in Chicago. It seemed to Bruce that all those groups were acting like Japanese beetles, seizing upon the rose that was now in full bloom in their garden.

His dad, he saw, was torn between two choices: to divorce his wife, or to honor his wedding vows and the institution of marriage. His father, Bruce thought, was caught in an ethical dilemma, much like a lifeboat (which do you save?) situation. With that understanding of his father's position, Bruce let the whole matter rest. The Watergate apartment was quiet and dark as Bruce fell asleep.

# 19

Rene and Jonathan slept rather soundly. Rene got up an hour or so before her husband. She put on a cerise silk blouse and black velvet slacks. The day seemed rather cool for June. It was cloudy, and the balconies were wet.

"No pool today," she thought, as she went into the kitchen to prepare breakfast.

By the time Jonathan was dressed and ready, breakfast was on the table. Rene had already eaten and had also finished reading the paper.

As Jonathan came into the kitchen she said, "Good morning. Hope you had a restful night."

"It was a very recuperative night," he quickly replied, "and it's so nice to have breakfast waiting for me. Thank you." He kissed her lightly.

Jonathan was looking especially fresh in a light blue sports shirt and black slacks. As he picked up the paper, he asked, "Anything like an earthquake in the news this morning? Oh," he caught his own slip of the tongue, "I'm sorry to have said 'earthquake,' considering that you're going to live in California."

Rene smiled. "No, all is well except for a plane hijacking and a few million dollars missing, along with one of the vice-presidents."

Then she grew serious. "Jonathan, you seem to have approved my going to California. Shall we talk about when and how, before Bruce gets up? If we've already discussed our plans, then we can check with him for his opinion."

"If all other factors were half as good, maybe one-tenth as good, as our sexual compatibility, I wouldn't care where we lived as long as it was together. But we have long realized that other facets of our relationship aren't so beneficial to our brains and bodies. Also, I believe we have put off separation because of our mutual regard and respect for one another.

"Rene, I love you enough to choose loneliness and barrenness, so you can have a better chance for greater happiness than I can give you. God, I wish that I believed you could be as happy with me as without me, but, sadly, I don't, and if you're not happy, I won't be, either."

Both Rene and Jonathan were silent, apparently lost in thought. Within a moment or two, he continued, "Perhaps it has occurred to you, as it has to me, that what we call fate, for want of a better name, may have dictated our marriage. You had already broken off your engagement to the fellow from Notre Dame, and you were about to rent your own apartment. I had been dating a number of beautiful, worthwhile women, especially three who were quite pretty and intelligent, who seemed willing to give me all their love regardless of their careers.

"Yet, we met and married after only sixty days and ten dates with not one sexual contact. We were very different, but the forces of fate gave us no choice.

"Did fate know that we would create a wonderful home life and bring into this world three children of great character and accomplishment? When a wave removed your wedding ring and took it into the sea on the beach in Portugal, was that fate warning us? Ever since that singular omen, our separation has appeared inevitable."

Jonathan poured himself a cup of coffee and went back to sit at the table with Rene.

"I believe we've both struggled to stay together. Strange how we've been washed along in life by this fate, this destiny, that we can't hear or see and can only vaguely sense, as one would sense a change in the atmosphere long before the storm."

He sipped his coffee, waiting for her to say something. When she didn't, he asked, "Have any of these feelings, any of these thoughts, possessed you, too Rene?"

"Yes, Jonathan, terribly so!" Rene said with emotion. "What do you think fate has in store for you and for me? What shall we do now? Do you mind if I smoke over here?" she asked as she moved to the far end of the table.

"If you must, I suppose you must. I hate to see you smoke, more than the smoke bothers me. But let's do what we must do," he said in a very businesslike manner. "First, our lease expires August 1, and I recommend that you contact our very helpful friend, the managing director of Watergate, and ask him if it will be convenient for him if we vacate the apartment on July 31. That's only a month away. Although he previously told us we could extend our lease on a month-to-month basis, let's cooperate with him on timing the termination.

"If necessary, I could remain here until September 1," Jonathan added rather unenthusiastically.

Rene got up from the table and poured herself a fresh cup of coffee. She thought how much time she had spent in recent days thinking about the implications of separation, and how little time thinking about the mechanics of one. Jonathan, as usual, had obviously thought out an efficient plan for them to put into operation.

He continued talking as Rene came back to the table.

"Second, let's call at least two movers for estimates and see if they can make dates to move us between now and August 1. Your furniture could go to Los Angeles and remain in storage until your apartment is available. If you call today, you may find that your apartment would be available sooner than you requested. They may be open on Saturday."

He waited for Rene to answer, but she didn't.

"Third, within the hour, let's also call furniture appraisers, at least two. In the meantime, we can each select the furniture we want, decide what neither of us wants, and compromise on the items both want. The children certainly don't want any more furniture now, not in Tokyo, New York, or Los Angeles. And one thing we know is that neither of us will probably want to take the grand piano or the Baker dining room group—both are too large for any apartment either of us is likely to rent, and much too large for Ellen's home."

Rene remained silent. She appeared to be listening, but she wasn't looking at Jonathan. She was staring at her coffee cup.

"Fourth, due to your methodical and comprehensive bookkeeping, we can send all financial data to our accountants in Chicago and have them recommend valuations. We'll call today or Monday to ask appraisers to check our real estate. Are you in agreement so far, Rene?"

She said very softly, but confidently, "Yes, I'm in complete agreement. We've made a very good working business team. I'm sure we can expedite everything. You've always been the one to visualize the actions to be taken, and I have to compliment myself on having kept the accounts and list of assets up-to-date. So, I'm sure we can get things arranged easily."

Then she looked at him directly. "But you haven't mentioned a pretty important point." She was almost whispering. "Shall we just separate? That's what I'd like to do."

"What length of separation do you have in mind?"

"Whatever you would like. I think that we should leave the length indeterminate or, perhaps, make it for only six months." Her voice grew stronger. "I just want to get away on my own for a while. And I do want to go to Ellen's, as soon as she needs me."

Rene fingered her cup. "I hope for her sake and mine that I'll not be needed out there until the movers have cleared everything. I don't know how we can do all of this in one month."

Jonathan returned to the core of their problem. "Let's go back to the question of separation. It's satisfying to me to know that you prefer a separation, because a separation doesn't seem to be as final as a divorce. But I'm opposed to separation on principle. I've told you many times that you are a very pretty, competent, intelligent, and sexy woman. I think you should get married as soon as you can find an interesting, personable, pleasant man, one nearer your age than I am. The kind you need and deserve.

"But, Rene, I don't believe any man of substance, character, and intelligence is likely to want to propose marriage to a woman who is still married, however separated by a continent's width she may be from her husband."

He was standing by his convictions, and it sounded to Rene as if he were rejecting separation.

"By mutual agreement," he concluded, "a divorce can be readily obtained, possibly right here in the District of Columbia within six months, maybe less. I'll have to check."

"Jonathan," Rene said almost incredulously, "do you want a divorce? Do you want to get the divorce?"

"Rene, I don't think either of 'wants' a divorce, but I believe it's best for you, particularly, that we get a divorce," he answered, with a touch of resignation in his voice.

"Me? Why me, particularly, Jonathan?"

"Because you're still relatively young. You should be available for marriage, and you're not available if you're only separated."

"But what if we want to get back together?"

Jonathan smiled. "That would be easy. You could buy the license, and I could pay the parson. But even if you don't find a man you want to marry, you may prefer being an independent woman, being a *free* woman who can select a man for whatever the occasion."

Rene was not completely soothed. "I had hoped that we would only separate. But, if you prefer a divorce, I'll be agreeable." Her voice was getting softer and softer. "Do you wish to take care of the details of getting the divorce?"

"Yes. I think it might be quicker for me to get a divorce here in Washington. Of course, since I have no work commitment, I could even go to Reno." Then he stood up and looked at his wife.

"I don't know. Perhaps we should agree to separate on or before August 1. The sooner the better. I'll be the plaintiff for the uncontested divorce request."

"You mean, agree to separate on or before August 1? By then you will have determined where and how you will proceed to get a divorce?" This was all moving a little faster than Rene had anticipated. But it sounded easier than she had expected, because Jonathan seemed to have thought it through carefully.

"Yes, that's what I mean."

They were both quiet. He went over to the counter and poured another cup of coffee, and she just sat at the table and fingered her cup.

Eventually, she spoke. "Jonathan, will we need separate lawyers? Can we avoid bringing in lawyers? You and I can work out everything together, can't we?"

He answered her very forcefully.

"Divorce lawyers, in general, I find socially destructive. Divorce, itself, is not pleasing to me. I'm ashamed that we've come to divorce. I shall always consider it a personal shame and always feel that I didn't do enough."

He added with a sigh, "But there is no better choice. I couldn't foresee the radical changes that would occur in our lives. At least, that's the way I perceive the situation, and I admit that you may see it differently."

He waited for her to speak, but she didn't.

"I don't need a lawyer to represent me against you," he continued, "and I hope you don't want one to represent you against me. Among divorce lawyers there are more wreckers than builders. And you can be absolutely certain, however uncontested our divorce decree, if I bring in a lawyer and you bring in a lawyer, together they would find a way to make you an atheistic communist and me a born-again Christian, or vice versa, whichever they thought would require the most billable time."

Jonathan thought they needed a break in the seriousness of their conversation.

"Incidentally, Rene, do you know what they say the difference is between a communist and a Christian?"

Rene looked up, a little startled.

"No, I never really thought about it," she said.

"The Christian is asked to believe something he can't see, and the communist is asked not to believe anything he does see." Jonathan smiled.

So did Rene. "Now, who told you that?"

"Well, I think he was a Harvard theologian.

"But, Rene, let's get back to the divorce.

"Between our creative-director son, Bruce, and our journalist, you, and the ex-advertising man and currently retired philosopher, me, I think we can write a much more understandable agreement than a lawyer could. We know what we want, and the lawyer would just question whatever statements we made.

"Although we have a daughter and a son-in-law who are both lawyers, they, fortunately, don't handle divorce cases. I believe there are lawyers who handle virtually nothing but uncontested divorce cases. They charge little and don't try to convert non-combatants to combatants. I'll call a friend or two at the Domestic Relations Court and get a recommendation of a lawyer who expedites non-contested divorce cases.

"Does this meet with your approval?"

"Yes," Rene answered, "I don't want any arguing attorneys. We saw enough of them with real estate and zoning issues. But, we might get our accountants in Chicago to ask Jerry Costain, our tax lawyer, to double-check their recommendations on property settlement."

"That's a good idea. We want that tax factor to be correct. As you remember, John Boatman, who handles our account, is a lawyer as well as a C.P.A. They can make very accurate and impartial recommendations. They're two of the few people we know who like me as well as they do you. You're so good with accounting they forget you're a pretty woman."

192

"And you really want a divorce instead of a separation?" Rene asked again.

"Yes, my darling. I want to remove any obstacle to your future happiness, and I hope that future will include marriage for you to a fellow who can dance as well as that alumni director we used to know at Carolina State."

Rene quickly responded, "Me? Married again? Not for a while. I'd have to consider buying a license first if I married again, wouldn't I, Jonathan?"

"Yes," he replied, "and you'd make the right man a great wife and companion. I hope you'll decide to get married again in due time—that is, when you find a good man."

"What about you, Jonathan? Are you going to get married again?"

He smiled. "That question reminds me of the remark attributed to Groucho Marx, when he was asked if he wanted to join a country club. He was reported to have said he wouldn't want to be a member of any club that would take him as a member.

"In any case, if any woman of any age was willing to marry me, I'd consider her too insane for me to marry."

"And I'd have to be insane, myself, to marry again, at my age and in my abstract phase of life. I'm so spiritually isolated and depressed, I couldn't bring happiness to anyone."

"If I thought I could bring anyone happiness, I'd make it for you. That's what I want for you that I can't give you now. We're just not in sync, I guess."

Jonathan thought for a minute and said, "I've lived with two beautiful wives. I've had more than my share of luck with women. With any further effort the odds would be against me. I'd never be interested in marrying."

"Furthermore, Rene, I think you know I want to be alone again, just as I was in my youth. And I believe you wish to go back to your pre-marriage days. Perhaps we both need to return to the lives we lived before our marriage—to each his own. Apparently, the passage of time hasn't eradicated our earlier personalities."

Rene was skeptical. "Perhaps not. But, Jonathan, don't downplay yourself. At your age you look better and are more virile than men twenty or twenty-five, or even thirty years younger. And, if a woman ever went to bed with you, all her doubts would be removed."

"You're being awfully nice to me," Jonathan quipped, "now that you're leaving. Is this the time for you to ask how we divide the assets we have left?"

"I know you've always been fair to everyone," she replied confidently. "I'm sure you'll be fair to me, so I leave that to you."

"I've thought about it, and I do wish to be fair to you and to me, even though I'm much older and may not live all that long. I want you to have a good income whether you work or not. I want an adequate income, because I never want to have to ask anyone to 'accommodate' me."

"Considering my perfectionism, if I ever need a nurse for an extended period of time, it will cost me two or three times what she would charge a nice fellow."

He looked at Rene, expecting a reaction. She didn't respond, so he continued. "What I've considered is that you have contributed to our income and to my ability to work more effectively, because you managed the home so well. You also contributed to our business successes in TV, on the farm, and in real estate."

"On the other hand, you were only twenty when we married, and I was in midlife, with a good income and some assets to which you had had no opportunity to contribute.

"So, considering these facts, I thought it would be quite fair for you to take forty percent of everything and for me to take sixty percent. Over a period of time, I've given you a substantial amount of jewelry, which is yours alone and would not be considered in the joint assets for division. The income from forty percent of our present assets would enable you to live as we have lived and as I would live.

"What's your opinion of that recommendation, Rene?"

Rene nodded. "I think it's fair. Now we have to get to work and get the appraisals made and let the accountants make recommendations as to how the property should be divided; that is, who takes what."

"My guess is that the accountant will recommend that you receive as much as possible of your portion in cash. Then, since I bought the real estate and have been managing the commercial properties, I can continue with those. But let's leave such recommendations entirely to them.

"I hear our son showering, which means he'll be ready to eat breakfast in a half hour," Jonathan said. "I'll try to put in writing all the points we've discussed, in the form of a memorandum of agreement."

As he put his coffee cup on the counter, he turned and said, "Oh, incidentally, have you given thought to changing your name back to your maiden name or to your professional name, Terry Haley?"

"No, I'm pleased with my name." And then with remarkable firmness she said, "It's the same name that my children have."

Jonathan started across the kitchen. As he reached the door he said, "Just thought I'd ask.

"After I write the agreement, you can check it over and then see if Bruce has any suggestions. We can sign it with him as witness, as well as counselor."

Rene was up and moving aimlessly around the kitchen until she thought of something constructive to do. "While you do that, I'll run down to the drugstore, then check the desk for mail. I'll be back up in time to serve Bruce his breakfast."

"Shall we shake hands or kiss to seal our agreement?" she asked tentatively.

Jonathan remained in control. "Let's just shake hands and keep this an 'arm's length' agreement, as the lawyers and IRS would want. I've thought about a simple but basic agreement, so I'll write it out now and you can type it while Bruce is eating breakfast. However, when our business agreements are all signed, let's kiss and be friends."

By the time Rene returned to the apartment, Bruce had come in for breakfast, bright and vigorous—and hungry. His mother quickly prepared two scrambled eggs and two English muffins and placed on his plate five strips of bacon that she had cooked extra for him.

While drinking his orange juice, Bruce asked if his services as a consultant would be needed.

"No, Bruce," Rene replied, "I think your father and I have reached an agreement."

"Mother, are you agreeing to have a trial separation?"

"No, your father believes an immediate divorce would be best for both of us, especially for me. He thinks this is particularly important in the event I wish to get married again."

Both Rene and Bruce looked very sad.

"Mother, all of us kids will be sorry for both of you and ourselves, too, because you and Dad have provided us with a wonderful home, in every sense of that term.

"But we also understand that you and Dad have been developing into different people, with different interests and different friends.

"Each of us will wish the best for each of you. Since you're terminating your marriage on a friendly basis, I hope that you and Dad will remain friends."

Rene joined her son at the table.

"Bruce, I certainly hope we can, too. I'd like to feel free to call on your father for his advice."

"It's nice that you feel that way, Mother, but when you're divorced, I doubt that you'll wish to follow Dad's advice."

Rene was a little taken aback. She always went to Jonathan for advice.

"Why do you say that, Bruce?"

"Perhaps because I realize the different types of friends you and Dad now have. And seldom does Dad approve of your friends," Bruce added honestly. "But, I have to give him credit, Mother. He has tolerated them."

Rene changed the subject. "How's your breakfast?"

"Very good, thanks. I'll clear the table and put the dishes away."

Rene moved across the kitchen toward the door. "Your father has probably finished writing; I'll go type. We both want you to look at the agreement and make suggestions. We'll also want you to sign it as a witness."

Just then Jonathan returned from his desk with the agreement, all ready for typing. Rene took it and went to her own little bedroom office to type it up.

Jonathan helped Bruce clean up the breakfast things.

"Well, Bruce, what do you think of our getting a divorce now instead of having a trial separation?" he asked.

"In effect, Dad, you and Mother have been living a trial separation for the past four or five years. So I'm glad for both of you that you're finally going to live your separate lives separately."

"In a way I guess you're right, son. And I certainly hope you'll try to help her."

Bruce and Jonathan were finished with the clean-up chores but remained in the kitchen, engrossed in their conversation. "Her freewheeling, nice, happy friends cooperate to destroy this fine woman that is your mother—and I can't live with that!"

"The way I see it, too many of our loose-end crowds seem to feel better when they help to weaken the strong and good and beautiful, all of which describe your mother.

"It's sad, Bruce. But let's wish her luck. Perhaps moving to Los Angeles will introduce her to more challenging and uplifting friends, if she so wishes."

"Dad, what are you going to do now that Mother will be gone and you won't be working at the Ethics Group office?"

"Right now, Bruce, I would like to die." Jonathan paused. "But I guess it's my duty to you and Ellen and Susan, and to friends, seen and unseen, to try to keep on living. If I do, I'll try to make my life serve some purpose worthy of what I believe will be for me an increasingly difficult struggle to live. One cannot live a good life without having a good purpose," he concluded.

"Dad, as long as I live, I'll need you and want you," Bruce said quietly. "I'm sure I speak for Ellen and Susan, too. As we grow older, our challenges grow greater, and we'll seek your counsel with eagerness and increasing appreciation.

"You must live for us, for others, and for yourself. If you aren't here, who will I phone for advertising campaign ideas that help make me look good?" He smiled. "You'll never stop learning and thinking and contributing to others. That's been your life. As you've grown older, I think you've grown wiser."

"Thank you, Bruce. To illustrate that wisdom, I'll be calling on you for advice, too, from time to time."

Rene returned to the kitchen with typed papers in her hand. Jonathan looked at her.

"Here, Bruce, you take this original." And he took that one from Rene. "Mother has made two carbons. Let's all read it. Once this agreement is signed, we should consider ourselves separated, pending proceedings for obtaining the divorce."

"Jonathan, do you really want to make our separation effective instantly?" Rene asked incredulously.

"Rene, I know now that I'm going to miss your pragmatic questions." The tone of his voice was kind, but Rene felt an inordinate need to sit down. Bruce joined her at the table. Jonathan remained standing in the middle of the kitchen.

"Perhaps our agreement should simply stipulate a date on or before July 31, 1982. If our separation were effective instantly, I'd have to go search for a big puritanical bolster to place in the center of our bed to separate us. I wonder if those bed bolsters worked for the Puritans?"

"I don't think so, Jonathan," Rene responded quickly. "If they had worked, there wouldn't be such an incredible number of Mayflower descendants."

While Rene and Jonathan were talking, Bruce was reading the agreement before him. In some ways this whole situation seemed unbelievable to him. Yet, in other ways it seemed like the inevitable culmination of a long chain of events. He was certain that his sisters would feel the same way.

All three sat at the table and read to themselves.

DIVORCE AGREEMENT
between
Jonathan B. Barron
and
Rene H. Barron
dated June 26, 1982

1. Effective immediately, the parties to this Agreement mutually and freely, acting with the hope to improve the health and happiness of each and the other, agree to terminate their marriage by divorce and each will therefore go his or her separate way and maintain separate domicile wheresoever each may choose, according to his or her desire. It is further agreed that said separate domiciles shall be established on or before July 31, 1982.

2. It is further understood that both parties hereby agree that it would be mutually beneficial to immediately institute divorce proceedings in the District of Columbia. The divorce proceedings will be instituted without the slightest recrimination or hesitation by either party, subject to the property settlement outlined herein. Jonathan B. Barron has agreed to be the plaintiff because the law requires that one—the wife or hus-

band—must be the plaintiff. This action is taken without any primary responsibility resting on either husband or wife.

3.  A detailed listing of all personal and real properties belonging to Jonathan B. Barron, Jonathan B. Barron, Trustee, and Rene H. Barron, including Rene H. Barron's recent bequest from her deceased mother, but excluding her personal jewelry, will be itemized, evaluated, and totaled in a basic inventory to be prepared by August 1, 1982. Said inventory will be subject to clarification and advice of accountants and consultants on or before September 1, 1982. The total assets shall then be divided, effective September 1, 1982, on the basis that sixty percent (60%) of the total amount of assets will be delivered to and be owned by Jonathan B. Barron, and forty percent (40%) will be delivered to and be owned by Rene H. Barron.

4.  In order that a sound working evaluation of certain assets may be available, the parties herein shall consult with real estate and furniture appraisers. The present accounting firm of Sampson and Schwarzberger will handle all accounting needs. The expense of the accounting firm is to be divided equally between both parties. The persons employed to make the appraisals and evaluations of all the assets now jointly held will be subject to mutual approval. In the event there are variations in valuations determined by separate appraisers, such variations will be averaged and accepted as the correct amount by both parties to this agreement. If there is any further clarification needed beyond the above procedures, both parties agree to accept the recommendations of Sampson and Schwarzberger, whose Chicago office has long represented both parties to this agreement.

5.  During the period of joint occupancy of the present Watergate apartment premises, and during the period of this agreement, both parties to this agreement will strive to limit knowledge of this agreement and proposed separation to the immediate family. There will be professional and legal reasons to make the intent of this agreement known; however, both parties

should try to restrict this information, but will suffer no penalty if such restriction is not strictly maintained.

6. In reference to life insurance on Jonathan B. Barron, Rene H. Barron will remain the beneficiary and shall make the payments, if she deems such action beneficial. In reference to the life insurance on Rene H. Barron, Jonathan B. Barron will remain the beneficiary and shall make the payments if he deems such action beneficial.

7. The existing revocable trust in the name of Jonathan B. Barron, Trustee, dated January 4, 1969, and revised February 13, 1979, shall be revised on or before August 1, 1982, in order to reflect the terms of this agreement. Upon dissolution or revision of said trust, should new trusteeships be set up, Jonathan B. Barron and Rene H. Barron each may designate the beneficiaries of their choice.

8. Future contributions of financial aid to the children born of this marriage shall be made on the same ratio as set forth in the ratio of property distribution stated herein: namely, Jonathan B. Barron, sixty percent (60%); Rene H. Barron, forty percent (40%).

9. As a matter of record for anyone reading this agreement, such as accountants or any other advisers, the parties to this agreement wish any and all to understand that there are no factors of "other men" or "other women" or of the so-called alienation of affection considerations involved in this agreement to separate and to obtain, as soon as legally possible, a mutually uncontested divorce.

Signed June 26, 1982:

_____

Jonathan B. Barron

_____

Rene H. Barron

_____

Witnessed by:

_____

Bruce I. Barron


Eventually, Bruce broke the silence.

"Dad, Mother, I think the agreement is perfectly clear. It's a good thing an advertising man wrote it instead of a lawyer. I know the background for all that you've written. I've no suggestions, except to say I hope it brings happiness to each of you." Bruce's voice broke slightly. "I love you both."

Then he hugged his father and hugged and kissed his mother.

Without saying another word, Bruce took the agreement to his parents for them to sign. He signed as a witness, then went to the piano and began to play a medley of tunes he knew both parents liked—one for Dad, one for Mother, and one for all.

Jonathan interrupted the concert and asked, "Bruce, would you like a beer?"

"Yeah, I think I would, Dad."

Jonathan brought a beer to Bruce and placed it on a large coaster on the piano. Then he turned and asked Rene if she would like a champagne, wine, or a martini to drink.

"Jonathan, I feel like we just sold our farm and home for a fraction of what it was worth, losing virtually everything. I guess anything important I'll ever do will remind me of our days together on the farm and in the real estate business. Fortunately, we made a lasting success of that business.

"So let's have champagne," she said more cheerfully. "This is indeed a unique occasion—not one that calls for celebration, but for remembrance without recriminations."

While Jonathan got the champagne from the living room bar,

Bruce began to play a soft, dreamy little melody. He looked at his mother and asked, "Do you remember this song, Mother?"

"Yes, I certainly do—your very first published song, 'The Magic Sea.' How long has it been since you wrote that?"

"I think I was about sixteen. That would make it twelve years ago. That's a long time."

"Bruce, that is a long time, but your song is as pretty as ever. Please play it again." She sang a verse softly:

> "The world is full of make-believe
> And dreams of what will be,
> Come with me and I'll set you free
> To sail on a magic sea."

On the Tuesday following Bruce's weekend visit and the signing of the divorce agreement, Rene received two phone calls from Los Angeles. First, Ellen called to report that her doctor had just told her she was doing well but had said it might be desirable if her mother could come out within a week or ten days. Jonathan was not home, but Rene knew he would favor her going out to help as soon as Ellen wished. So she quickly assured Ellen that she would be there the next week.

Shortly after Ellen's call, Mr. Jordan, the owner of the apartment building where Rene planned to live, called and said the apartment manager had just advised him that a young couple sharing a two-bedroom unit were separating and wished to give up their apartment August 1. He told Rene that the apartment was about the same as the one she had looked at, but the location in the building was better. He was sure Rene would be pleased, and she could move in August 1 instead of September 1. Rene quickly assured Mr. Jordan that she would rent it and would immediately send him the first month's rent and a security deposit. Jordan seemed pleased and told Rene she could come in and sign the lease when she arrived in Los Angeles. As soon as Rene was off the phone, Jonathan returned, and she gave him the news.

"That'll work out fine, Rene. Within a week we can sort out and select the furniture and things. I just arranged with the Watergate manager to reserve the freight elevators for July 29 and 30. I suggest that you plan to go to Ellen's Wednesday of next week. In the meantime, we can confirm the selection of movers. Your furniture can now go directly to your apartment, and I'll put mine in temporary storage here. Why not call Ellen back and tell her you'll be there July 7 and that your apartment will be available August 1? She'll be happy to hear the good news."

Rene went to the phone, but before she picked it up she looked at Jonathan and said, "But going so soon will leave the moving chores and follow-up matters all in your hands. You did this before, when we were about to move into our new home in Church City. Now, here you are again, taking over the moving task so I can again go to a new job—but this time it's so different.

"I still don't understand you, Jonathan, after thirty years." She walked over and looked out the window facing the Kennedy Center and continued, "Sometimes I've thought you loved me, and other times I've thought I was just a protegee. I wonder if the conflict within you arises from the fact that I was never able to be the wife you needed, but I did become the protegee I think you've been very proud of."

"In a good marriage, Rene, each spouse should be the other's protegee," he replied. "Before we married, you asked why I wanted you. I said that I needed your discipline and perseverance. You've proved my early evaluation to be correct. You've been a very good partner in marriage. I was objective toward you as a protegee. But I know now that the reality of love between a husband and wife should be inescapably subjective first, and objective second."

"Well, I'll call Ellen," Rene said sadly. "Do you want to speak to her?"

"No, just wish her well for me."

The days that followed at the Watergate were filled with work, endless work, dividing up dishes and cookware and arranging the furniture in separate areas, one group for Los Angeles, the other for storage. The movers were able to give estimates before Rene left. She used one van line, and Jonathan used another. The furniture appraisers were selected and were busy listing each item and its appraised value. The arrangement of averaging prices had already been agreed upon by Rene and Jonathan. Each would purchase the pieces selected and pay the price into the general asset fund. The accountants understood how the Barrons wanted the assets divided.

All went well. There were no arguments or differences about the agreement they had signed. There were no disputes over choosing furniture pieces. The tax lawyer and the accountants thought the details of the agreement were clear and fair to both parties. Both Rene and Jonathan had enough self-respect, as well as respect for one another, to refuse to drag in a lot of adversarial arguments.

On Wednesday, July 7, Jonathan took Rene to Dulles Airport for the last time. They kissed goodbye, and each wished the other well. They would continue their contact by phone and by mail until all matters relating to the divorce agreement had been carried out to the full satisfaction of both. Each was beginning a new life alone.

Jonathan believed that Rene would play a part in a melodrama in which she would find a different and happy life. He sensed that he would play a part in a tragedy from which he might never escape.

# 20

The day after Rene left for California, Jonathan decided to return to the open spaces of the West, where he had traveled many years before. He had recently been to Boulder, Colorado, to visit two non-profit organizations that had contacted him when he founded the Ethics Inquiry Group. He liked Boulder. It belonged to the wide open prairies that joined it on the east and to the snow-capped Rocky Mountain ranges that formed its western front. In Boulder, a person could have the mountains and the plains, plus a distinctive local culture that had grown up around the University of Colorado, attracting people from all around the world.

Jonathan asked the movers to pack everything except books, clothing, and linens and to send him the necessary wardrobe containers and an assortment of boxes. Being involved in the preparation for moving was one way to stay busy until the actual moving dates. He had often commented to Rene that moving wasn't all bad, because people tended to accumulate too much junk, physical and mental—and a lot is discarded in the process of sorting and packing. In thinking about why people move, he philosophized that sometimes people move because they wish to grow; sometimes they grow and feel they must move.

On July 29 Rene's movers arrived on time and expressed satisfaction with the job Jonathan and the packers had done. Rene's things were labeled, sealed, and separated from his. The movers were on their way to California by early afternoon.

His movers were late and short-handed on July 30. He was impatient with them, especially with the two helpers they had picked up off the streets of Washington. One was fairly drunk, but kind and strong. The other was weak and lazy. However, with Jonathan lending a hand and some guidance for the drunk, everything was eventually loaded, and the van left the Watergate loading dock well before five o'clock.

## Love and Ethics

Jonathan called the management of the Watergate and thanked them for their cooperation and for the hospitality extended to him and Rene during the years the Watergate had been their home.

Before the movers had arrived that morning, Jonathan had packed enough clothes and personal items for a month or more and put them in his car. After the movers left, he looked around the apartment, made sure all the keys were left on the kitchen counter, walked through the apartment once again, and took an elevator down to the garage. He got into his car and drove north toward the Pennsylvania Turnpike, which he would take west to Interstate 70 and on to Boulder.

His drive toward Boulder was uneventful, until he crossed the Mississippi River via the Route 270 by-pass north of St. Louis and was continuing west on Interstate 70. Driving along at about fifty-five to sixty miles per hour, he began to notice a stream of big trucks passing him as though he were going only twenty-five. He checked all his gauges and hit the glass on his odometer, but everything seemed to be working. He didn't want to drive too slowly, so he speeded up to sixty-five and then to seventy miles per hour. The trucks still flew past. He ceased trying to keep up with the truckers and tried only to keep out of their way.

He wished citizens and their lawmakers would be more honest with themselves. In many areas, the fifty-five-mile-per-hour speed limit is generally impractical and should be increased to sixty-five miles per hour or seventy, especially in places like western Kansas and eastern Colorado. He felt foolish trying to go fifty-five miles per hour on an open, four-lane interstate highway, where there was no turn for thirty miles, and he could see almost that far ahead.

After passing Hane, Kansas, he was in an area he had traveled as a young man. He found the prairies peaceful and restorative. When he reached the vicinity of Oakley in the northwest corner of Kansas, it was about four in the afternoon. It was then that the Great Spirit of the Prairies began to welcome him back. Dark clouds formed along the horizon, making the white concrete grain elevators look like an endless collection of stark cathedrals, sixty to eighty feet high. Here, one could see the horizon in all directions. Fifteen to twenty-five miles away was a low, black umbrella of clouds. Here and there, lighter-toned fingers of rain began to poke themselves into the ground.

The rain missed Jonathan to the left, to the right, and ahead as he traveled along. The dark clouds were slashed by jagged, golden streaks of lightning, followed by great bursts of thunder. Between the clouds one could see patches of bright blue sky and sunshine.

He drove on through the dry path that seemed to open for him. As he turned west on Interstate 70, near Colby, a brilliant, towering rainbow appeared in the sky before him. It was like a giant archway beckoning him onward. The magnificent rainbow expanded to encompass the heavens, making room for a second, smaller, softer-toned rainbow to appear beneath it.

Jonathan experienced in his whole being the ecstasy of that moment. The great prairie was welcoming him back to his old home on the range. And what a spectacular welcome! Jonathan felt he belonged. As he drove on, still missing the spouts of rain that poured all around, he thought, "Here is where a man can be free and feel free, where he can be what he is."

He felt a oneness with nature. He felt at that moment as he had when Mindy first opened the door to a oneness with her—a door to the warmth and feeling of being as a human should be. He fantasized that he might find someone to enter that door with him again. He needed a miracle—a woman placed by fate and time where he and she could discover what each needed in another human being—an open soul, a mind that reaches out, a physical being that radiates tenderness.

He thought how strange and wonderful demonstrations of beauty made him feel: the prairie rainbows, a certain point in a symphony, a rose with morning dew, or a pretty woman slowly brushing her hair.

By the time he reached Goodland, Kansas, near the Colorado state line, he had driven out of the great circus tent of clouds and rainbows, but he was still feeling the tingle of that performance of the heavens. For the first time in years, he experienced an unalloyed joy in living. Pure beauty pervaded his mind and body, setting his soul free to roam. He wanted to stop driving so he could get out and walk around, so the blood could go back to his toes.

Burlington, the first town in Colorado as one drives west on Interstate 70, was only about a half hour's drive from Goodland; he stopped there at one of the chain motels. In Burlington this franchise was different, because the people were so relaxed and genuine. The town was too small for most tourists, so the bar and dining room were filled with natives.

After checking into his room, Jonathan surveyed the bar and restaurant and went for a walk in town. The implement dealer's place and the big garage and service station caught his attention. Two or three blocks away he found a pharmacy. He went in and purchased a popular brand of lip salve, made by a company he had founded many years ago. Every place he went would be likely to have something to bring back old memories.

He noticed that the implement dealer had on his lot tractors with about three times the horsepower of the ones he had used on his Illinois farm. Of course, he thought, if you're going to plant any crop in the plains region, you virtually have to do it big or not at all, and you need more powerful tractors for a few thousand acres than for a few hundred.

Returning to the motel, he went into the lounge for a leisurely martini and on into the restaurant where he was served an excellent outside cut of homegrown roast beef. Although he ate alone, dinner was enjoyable.

Back in his room, Jonathan lay in bed wondering where he would live the next few months, the next few years, or if he would live, or if he even wanted to live. Maybe Boulder would be the place, and maybe it wouldn't. He would look around and find a real estate agent with whom to spend a day or so.

Questions criss-crossed his mind. He leaned over and found a note pad and pen on the lamp table. He wrote:

> I only live to know
> What each tomorrow will teach
> I only live to know
> If love is beyond my reach.

After writing out his mood, he thought such lines might not make it in Nashville, unless someone played Santa Claus for him. But he felt more optimistic when he thought that the verse for country music often didn't really need to be verse, just feelings.

Jonathan was in no big hurry to get to Boulder, but he woke up early anyway. He checked out of the motel, decided to service his car and fill the gas tank before eating breakfast, and ate in the motel restaurant, since it was probably the best one available for miles. He left Burlington early enough to get to Boulder in the afternoon, with enough time to call a couple of real estate firms.

Jonathan thought that if he had been a city planner or an architect, he would never have done to such a beautiful place what had been done to Boulder. The planners and architects couldn't ruin the mountains or the prairie, but they had done little to capitalize on either. Everyone was so nice as he checked into his Boulder motel, though, that he forgot all about the collection of oddball buildings in the city.

At the motel he asked for a couple of references for real estate representatives and made an appointment with one for nine o'-clock the next morning at the motel. After making these arrangements, he drove around Boulder to get the feel of the community. Boulder had created the usual mall in what had been the original business center. Again, the best that he could say was that it was okay, but the people he met in the shops and in the mall were direct and cordial.

He walked around the campus of the University of Colorado, dropped in to talk with a wonderful old English professor, and visited the women's studies department. Everyone was friendly and hospitable. People in Boulder seemed to feel that such a beautiful area required them to be more beautiful, too.

In touring Boulder, Jonathan saw only two or three condominiums and apartment buildings that could be called high-rise structures. Someone had apparently figured out that high rises would obstruct the view. But Jonathan was used to a high-off-the-ground perspective, and he wondered what the real estate person would show him in the morning.

He returned to the hotel, changed his clothes, and went to one of the restaurants the boys at the motel desk had recommended. The restaurant really sold him. It was beautifully appointed and designed with taste and a high degree of pragmatism. The maitre d' was knowledgeable, discriminating, and accommodating. The martini was superb, and the food was comparable to the best anywhere. The service was good. And to his special delight, the diners looked interesting, especially some of the women.

After studying the diners, Jonathan concluded that a number of Denver-area oilmen patronized the Boulder restaurants, and a number of beautiful, well-dressed, well-mannered women patronized the oilmen. It seemed to Jonathan that pretty women admired entrepreneurial types, especially if they had struck it rich. He thought that that was appropriate because, when a woman is attractive and intelligent, she deserves a man with an innovative spirit. The most powerful aphrodisiac for a smart woman is a mature and secure man.

Jonathan liked his waitress. She was efficient, graceful, and pretty, with quite a lovely figure. And she seemed to understand him. He told her she had three brothers and one sister and that she had been born about September 28. Women who had younger brothers usually understood Jonathan. He guessed her sibling pattern correctly, but missed her birthday by two days. She was fascinated. He knew he could have arranged to see her the next day, but he didn't. He would have liked to make love to her, but he thought, why? For whose benefit? So he left the waitress talking to her friends about the "strange man" and returned to his motel room alone.

He sat in his room with his feet propped up on a table, looking at a pictureless picture. Hotel room pictures permitted one to see nothing. Maybe that's the way they should be. He thought about the waitress. He wished she were in his room just to hold him for a while and kiss him good night. Merely that would satisfy him this night. Then he thought about how he was with a woman. It was he who did the holding and kissing, not the other way around. But the thought occurred to him that maybe he now wanted a woman to change roles with him, or at least, to alternate. Often when a woman takes the initiative, that is, the *direct* rather than indirect initiative, she seems to hurry things along too much. Tenderness shouldn't be rushed—it should be allowed to blossom.

He remembered a line from an old song: "Sometimes I feel like a motherless child, a long way from home." He wasn't sure of the words, only the feeling.

He knew he didn't think he had ever really needed a mother. But never having had one, he couldn't know for sure. In a way, he was rather glad that he hadn't known one. If he had had a mother, could he tonight use the memory of her love as surcease from the pangs of wanting a kind and tender woman to hold him? He didn't know. It didn't matter.

# 21

The next morning Jonathan was up early and had a reasonably decent breakfast at a restaurant near the motel. Picking up a Denver paper and the ubiquitous *Wall Street Journal,* he returned to his room to await a call from the real estate agent who was to meet him at the motel.

Shortly before the nine o'clock appointment, someone knocked on his door.

"Probably the maid," he thought, as he interrupted his reading to open the door. To his surprise, it was the real estate agent, who had decided to come directly to his room, since it was on the first floor.

This wasn't just any real estate agent. She was a beautiful, tall, shapely woman of about thirty-five, who greeted him by introducing herself as Mrs. Lisa Bronson. Jonathan expressed only part of his pleasure in meeting Mrs. Bronson, and as she walked into the room, he asked her to be seated at the table where he had been reading.

He reviewed with her what he preferred in the way of a rental: two bedrooms and two baths in a high rise, if there were enough such places to warrant a look. He told her he preferred to rent but would buy if purchasing was the only way to get what he wanted.

Mrs. Bronson quietly explained that there were very few high-rise apartments or condominiums in Boulder, because of zoning restrictions. She thought that he might like to look at some new townhouse rentals and condominiums; several were available, located where the view of the mountains was excellent. In any event, she thought he should go with her to look at the apartments and townhouses she had selected to show him.

Jonathan readily agreed, knowing that he would like to go with her wherever she wanted to go, except to her home. He had already noted her wedding ring. He disciplined himself to keep his mind on apartments as best he could. After she stood up and he got a studied view of her own fascinating landscape, he knew that concentrating on real estate would not be easy.

Without delay, they went to look at apartments and condominiums or whatever Mrs. Bronson thought would interest an apparently finicky customer. They looked at one high-rise condominium, one of the very few and one of the best, although it had no inside parking. She asked him if he liked it, and he said, "No." Then she took him to a very pretty new development of two-bedroom condominiums on the west side of Boulder, higher up in the foothills. The location was excellent, but he asked her about the one nice-looking high rise he had seen as he was driving into Boulder. She told him there was a waiting list for the building. However, one of her friends worked there, and she said she would phone see if she could at least show him the place.

"That's fine, Mrs. Bronson. Why don't you make the phone call from the ritzy-looking restaurant we saw out near the mall an hour or so ago? Then we could have lunch there, and I'd be privileged to be seen with a woman just as beautiful—more so, as I look at her now—than any of the pretty women I saw at the excellent restaurant where I had dinner last night."

"Where was that?" she asked as they got into her car.

"Severino's, I believe."

"Let's go there," Mrs. Bronson said quickly.

Jonathan thought that pretty women who are modest and gracious still like to have a man appreciate their distinctiveness. He speculated that Mrs. Bronson instinctively wanted him to see her in the same setting in which he had enjoyed seeing those women the evening before.

It turned out that she also knew the maitre d' at Severino's. He greeted her ostentatiously and escorted them to an alcove table for two. Jonathan complimented Mrs. Bronson for her choice of restaurants and for obtaining such a nice, quiet table.

As he helped her with her chair, he observed questioningly, "You must sell a lot of real estate, if your customers bring you here to lunch so frequently."

"Yes, Mr. Barron," she replied, "I've been lucky in this business. Of course, I have the benefit of working for the best firm in Boulder." Then she changed the subject. "But I'm particularly glad you asked me to lunch. I think you're very uncertain about what you want. What brings you to Boulder?"

"Years ago, probably before you were born, I learned to love the open country. It was then that I first visited Boulder. Now, I return because I'm looking for beautiful scenery and a challenging environment."

"Do you want this apartment for yourself alone?"

"Yes, I do. Within the past month my wife and I have separated, and we're in the process of obtaining a divorce. I might add that the separation was a very cordial one and was made for her future, but possibly for my future, too. You see, I've become very much involved in the field of ethics. You may find a couple of my books in the university library."

"What is your main focus in ethics, Mr. Barron?"

"The pragmatic application of ethics to our everyday lives," he replied.

"That's very interesting. My first husband taught philosophy. He became so engrossed in the subject he forgot that I was around," she said with just a touch of regret.

"Yes, I can understand. Most husbands can't afford to pay too little attention to a pretty wife. Frankly," he added, "I was a little shocked when you came directly to my door this morning. I thought you might have been the maid. Then you walked in— stately, beautiful, wonderfully pleasing. My wife is the same— about your height, very attractive, and stately, just as you are. In fact, you're almost too lovely for me to be around at this stage of my recovery."

Mrs. Bronson smiled. "Thank you, Mr. Barron. But shouldn't we order now?"

Jonathan regrouped and said, "Oh, yes, I'm sorry! Would you care to join me in having a martini?"

"No, thank you, but I'll take a glass of wine. Their house wines here are very fine. While they bring the drinks, I'll call my aunt to find out if they can show us an apartment."

Lisa Bronson was gone only a few minutes. When she returned from making her call, she stopped for a moment to talk to their waitress.

As soon as she returned to the table, he asked, "What are the chances of an apartment being available at the new high rise?"

"Not very good, but my aunt says someone has just moved out of a one-bedroom apartment that has a balcony overlooking the mountains and miles and miles of the range, north and south.

213

She's on duty now, so we can go out and see it as soon as we finish lunch. Could you use a one-bedroom unit?"

"Possibly." Then he couldn't resist practicing his old mind-reading tricks. "Did you say you have one child?"

"No, I didn't say, but I do—a thirteen-year-old daughter from my first marriage."

"I get the impression from you that she's a well-liked young lady, plays piano and violin, and was probably born about the middle of June. Is that close?"

Mrs. Bronson blushed slightly as she slowly took a sip of wine. "I don't know what to say. Yes, you're more than close. She does take lessons in both piano and violin, and she was born June 14."

After she took another sip of wine she said, "Now, Mr. Barron, the reason I feel I'm almost blushing is that, with your uncanny perceptiveness, you might have been able to read in my mind that I liked you from the moment I saw you, but I felt you would know that's all it can be.

"And I'm sorry if I remind you of your wife," she said kindly. "I think she and I may have been lost by similar types of husbands."

Jonathan smiled and said, "Thank you. I believe you've mixed in a compliment for me."

He noticed the waitress coming toward their table with a tray of food and said, "By the way, did you anticipate my digressions and signal what the waitress is bringing for lunch?"

"Yes, as I went to the phone I ordered two reuben sandwiches —a specialty of the house. Incidentally, some of the waitresses here seem to remember you. Two or three worked the dinner shift when you were here last night. Why would they know you, if you haven't been in Boulder for years?"

"I haven't noticed that any of them seem to know me. They're probably looking at me adoring you." He laughed. "But it's possible that one of them may have heard from the waitress who served me last night that I guessed her birthdate or other things."

"How do you do things like that, Mr. Barron?" she asked, as she fingered her wine glass. "It does make people a little uncomfortable. You know that, don't you?"

"Yes, I know that, my dear Mrs. Bronson." Then he digressed again. "Your card says Lisa Bronson. I love the name Lisa." He brought himself back to the topic. "Of course, so many women are

asked only routine, expected, and often unwelcome questions by
men. So if a character comes along and notices their many other
human qualities, some women welcome the change, especially if
there's a touch of the mystical involved."

Since this was a not a lunch to be lingered over, Jonathan and
Lisa ate their sandwiches rather quickly. He said to the waitress as
she approached their table, "May I have our check, young lady? Do
you accept credit cards?"

"Yes, it's time for us to go. Thank you, Mr. Barron—Jonathan
—for the luncheon and pleasant conversation."

As they left the restaurant, Lisa said, "For dinner tonight I
recommend that you try the Cameron. It's not far from your
motel."

"Thank you, I will," he replied.

Lisa and Jonathan arrived at the high-rise apartment building on
time. It was easily the finest place he had seen in Boulder. He was
eager to see if an opening could be found for him. Lisa and her
friend talked in the office for a few minutes and then came out. Her
friend, Mrs. Christian, a dignified, buxom lady who looked like a
Sunday-school teacher, took them up to the top floor, the eighth
floor, Jonathan noted. Mrs. Christian told him they might possibly
let him take the only vacancy they had, a one-bedroom unit, because those on the waiting list preferred two bedrooms. "However," Mrs. Christian added, "the moment it's known that the
one-bedroom unit is available, it will be rented, so you'll have to
decide at once if you want it."

They arrived at the eighth floor and went to a corner apartment,
much to Jonathan's surprise, because corner units are seldom
smaller than two bedrooms. They entered the apartment. It was
very light and bright. The carpeting was a pleasing, soft green, and
the walls were off-white. He liked the kitchen and the bath.

He went out on the balcony alone. It was a clear, sunshiny day,
and he could see the snow-topped mountain range virtually everywhere he turned. The sky was very blue, in harmony with the high,
snow-covered mountains. He looked down from the balcony to the
swimming pool, with its concrete and tile borders. Suddenly, he
grabbed the iron railings and held on, then quickly went inside. He
was afraid he might jump, nature presented such an inviting pano-
rama.

Lisa asked him how he liked it. He told her it was a lovely

apartment, but he had better look for something larger. She seemed a bit surprised but said nothing. When they reached the reception desk, Jonathan thanked Mrs. Christian very much, expressed his appreciation for her special kindness, and congratulated her on the fine building and attractive apartments. But he was so glad to get back into the car with Lisa that he was not able to conceal the fact.

"Are you ill? What happened up there?" Lisa asked with concern.

"I'm sorry, Lisa. The apartment was beautiful. I would like a two-bedroom place, especially here in this building, but it would have to be no higher than the third floor."

Lisa looked at him sympathetically.

"I understand. And I feel sorrow with you in these days, being alone on that balcony, high up and seeing—almost touching—so much beauty."

She started the car. "Let's look for a place where you can see the mountains and touch the ground. Come to think of it, I know a broker who has just built a twenty-four unit, two-story apartment hosue farther out of town. You may like it, but as owner and broker he prefers that someone from his office show his apartments. I'll call him, and you can go see him in the morning. His name is Ed Harrell. When I phone you in the morning, I'll give you his number, and you can call him yourself and make arrangements to see what he has available. His apartments are all new, all two bedrooms. I believe they're the closest thing to what you want in town."

Jonathan was grateful. "I think you may be right, Lisa. Call Mr. Harrell, and I'll look forward to hearing from you in the morning. Thank you very much for spending time with me today. I wish that I'd been a more rewarding prospect. Would you consider accepting a two-hundred-dollar consulting fee?"

"Of course not, Jonathan. You know that we sell some, and we don't sell some. That's our business, and some that we don't sell we enjoy. One never knows—they may come back and buy. Thank you, though, for being so considerate."

She drove back to his motel, and before he could get out of the car Lisa said, "I hope it's all right if I kiss you goodbye."

Before he could answer she kissed him lightly, and he got out of the car. He waved to her as she drove away.

The next morning Lisa called Jonathan and gave him Ed Harrell's phone number, saying that Harrell was expecting a call from him. Nothing more was said, and Jonathan thanked her for calling Harrell. Lisa said she hoped he would find a place to live that he could enjoy.

Jonathan called, and Ed Harrell told him how to get to his office. Jonathan immediately went to meet him there. Harrell was a tall, lithe, interesting-looking man of about forty-five. Jonathan had checked on him after leaving Lisa the day before and he had found that he was a very reliable man, a bank director, and one of the most respected real estate brokers in the area. Mr. Harrell was cordial but seemed rather curious about why Jonathan was interested in living in Boulder.

One of Harrell's assistants took Jonathan to see the apartment, and he rented it, effective September 15. The building was brand-new, and the apartments were being finished off one at a time. The apartment he rented needed to have the appliances installed, the carpets laid, and the interior painted. He gave Harrell's office the usual security deposit.

After a brief lunch at Denny's, Jonathan took a tour of Boulder, going north to look at a new shopping center. Then he visited a social science research center and talked to a couple of their staff before returning to his motel room.

He phoned Ellen to get an update on her baby's progress toward the outside world. Ellen answered the phone, which was a sign she was doing all right. But she wasn't doing well enough. She now had to stay in bed on her back. The doctor was still sure the baby would be premature, but he had pushed back the predicted date of birth to August 15.

By this time Rene came to the phone and was surprised to hear that he was in Boulder. She said Ellen was so pleased to have her there. Rene reported that prospects for her university job looked very good. Jonathan told her she should be getting a phone call from the movers, because all her furniture had gone out on schedule. Rene said she had already received a call; the furniture was due in Los Angeles the following Monday, August 10. Rene also said she had looked at the new apartment her landlord had switched her to for early occupancy, and it was even nicer than the one she had originally agreed to take, at the same price.

With all well in Los Angeles, Jonathan lay down for a while.

217

After sleeping for an hour or so, he got up, took a shower, and shaved. He put on a summer-weight suit and went to the Cameron, the restaurant Lisa had recommended. It was only three or four blocks away, so he walked.

The Cameron was a rather elaborate place with a wide, curving stairway up to the cocktail lounge. A brunette Aphrodite greeted him, guided him to a very plush seat, took his drink order, and glided away. Jonathan wasn't exactly superstitious, but he had to wonder why, wherever he went in Boulder, he saw so many pretty women. And they were really pretty, he assured himself, not just seemingly attractive because he happened to be lonely. He also told himself that he really didn't want to be with a woman now—unless an unmarried Lisa Bronson came along.

It occurred to him that maybe it was the devil himself who staffed the Boulder restaurants. On the other hand, he entertained the idea that while the Lord didn't owe him any favors, maybe He was showing him some very good reasons to live. He settled his internal dispute by thinking that these pretty girls he saw were all so young—relatively. He decided he was going to fool fate if he found one who was smart and kind and had a yen for older men.

The truth was that he had been around pretty women all his life, but this Boulder scene was getting to be a little too much. He had to get his mind settled, because his body was becoming discontented.

Of course, he guessed something about this goddess who was serving as a waitress. She told him that she taught riding at a big stable between Boulder and Denver and that she was leaving the following week for Virginia. She was taking a job there as an assistant to a nationally known race horse trainer.

"There she goes," he thought, "that beautiful, obviously strong and determined young woman, a prototype of today's and tomorrow's combination person."

He drank his martini and went downstairs to the restaurant. He found it equally impressive. His waitress was young, pretty, and petite. She said she had only one semester to go to complete her MBA and she was eager for the fall semester to begin. She was divorced with no children.

Jonathan gave up. He made a date with her—just for a mid-afternoon get-acquainted tea, of all things. They agreed to meet at Marianne's Tea Shop in the mall at three the next afternoon.

# 22

Jonathan had no specific appointment or place to see or be until his afternoon tea date at three. One of the young men at the motel desk suggested that he drive up to the top of the Flagstaff Mountain, where he could get a good view of Boulder and the surrounding area. The altitude at Boulder was nearly fifty-four hundred feet. The desk clerk marked the route on Jonathan's Boulder-area map and said it was just a few miles from the motel.

He welcomed the idea of driving up the mountain. In a short time he was parked near the top at one of the lookout areas. He got out, walked around, and took one of the trails that led back among the trees. There, he found a big rock where he could sit alone and look down on Boulder and the endless prairies to the east. He remained on his big rock perch for a few minutes. Then he got up and walked around the mountaintop and returned to the rock.

Everything was so beautiful. But he was so alone.

In the presence of such majestic beauty, he found his aloneness devastating. Beauty is a magnet for the soul, but beyond a certain level of exposure and absorption, beauty must be shared. Having no one to share this beauty with made seeing and appreciating it painful. He felt that he had to run away from it.

After a while he began to feel better, thinking of the pretty girl he would be meeting for tea. He walked over to his car and drove down the mountain to his motel. He went to his room, read the papers, then walked a few blocks for an early, light lunch at a small restaurant. The hamburger was good and the family atmosphere thoroughly antithetical to romance.

He smiled one of his rare smiles, thinking how wonderful it used to be to take his kids to such a restaurant, and how sad that now, as a lone adult, other folks' kids seemed to be foreign annoyances.

Jonathan arrived early at Marianne's Tea Shop and obtained a small corner table. Soon his pretty waitress-divorcee on her way to an MBA came into the restaurant. She was greeted cordially by Marianne and escorted to Jonathan's table. He noted approvingly her well-tailored linen suit, worn with a moderate-toned rust blouse with an open mandarin collar. She had written her name on Jonathan's notebook during his dinner the previous evening.

As he rose and pulled the chair out for her he said, "Miss Woodward, I'm certainly glad you could join me."

"Oh, I'm glad to be here, too, Mr. Barron," she said as she situated herself. "The questions you asked while I was serving you last evening were different. So, I'm here partly because I'm curious about this man who asks his waitress serious questions like what she plans to do with her MBA when she gets it and what aspect of business fascinates her most.

"And, of course, you also rather interest me as a man. Frankly, I've had it with young men, at least for a while. I've found older men, certain older men, fascinating."

He said, with kindness, "Thank the Lord you think of me as a man and not just as an impertinent interrogator."

He turned his attention to the menu. "What kind of tea do you recommend? And what tea is your favorite?"

"I like the chamomile tea they serve here," Miss Woodward replied. "It's packaged in Boulder. Would you like to try it?"

She looked up. "But here's Marianne. She may look at you and recommend one of her special teas. Marianne, I'll take chamomile, and what do you recommend for Mr. Barron here?"

Marianne smiled cordially and said, "For this gentleman, Myra, we should serve a robust, full-bodied tea, a black Russian tea, not red Russian. We have just the right one."

Turning to Jonathan she said, "After your first cup, Mr. Barron, please let me know if you approve."

"Marianne, you read me well," he said. "I do like full-bodied, stimulating teas and things. Do you have some tasty, uncoated tea cakes?"

"Yes," Marianne offered, "your waitress will bring you an assortment. Enjoy your tea. I'm glad to see you again, Myra," she said as she walked away.

"Well," Jonathan said, "let me learn about you. Where were you born? Where did you go to high school and college? When did you marry, at twenty? How did you happen to come to Boulder? Where are your sisters now?"

Myra laughed. "Shall I answer all those questions with a simple yes or no? No, I shouldn't, because when you learn the answers to what you asked, maybe you'll have some suggestions for me.

"I was born in Amarillo, Texas, the queen city of the Texas Panhandle. I went to grade school and high school in Amarillo. Then I went to the University of North Carolina, because it was a good school and my aunt and uncle lived in nearby Durham. They had offered to pay my tuition and give me free room and board. They had no children of their own.

"During the last two years of college, I lived in a house in the country near Chapel Hill. My uncle had been transferred to Atlanta."

"And, yes, I did marry at twenty," she added wistfully. "In fact, my husband and I were one of two young married couples renting the house in the country. After graduating from UNC as an economics major, I worked as a secretary-receptionist in a doctor's office and helped send my husband through law school at UNC. But a year or so after he got a job in a Raleigh law firm, he gave me up. Didn't need my help any more, I guess.

"Actually, he wanted to marry a rich girl, a daughter of one of the firm's most important clients." Then, with more confidence, she said, "He was getting too weak and spineless for me, anyway. I knew I wanted to be around a stronger, more challenging man. We were married six and a half years—no children, of course."

Their tea arrived. After a brief taste Jonathan said, "What then? What did you do then?"

"Then, I wanted to get out of that 'old boy' Carolina culture, especially around Raleigh. I wanted to go back west. My husband borrowed the money to pay me off, or I should say, to reimburse me for sending him to law school—thirty-five thousand dollars and what furniture we had. I moved to Boulder, where I had friends, friends who had lived in Amarillo."

She brightened a bit. "Does that tell you more than you want to know, Mr. Barron? And is your tea full-bodied enough?"

"The tea is fine, Myra. But about your sisters, you have one older and one younger."

"Yes, my sisters—" She appeared startled. "My sisters? I don't remember telling you I had sisters."

Jonathan didn't reply.

"Anyway, my older sister is married happily to an Amarillo auto dealer, and my younger sister went to the University of Texas and is now a nurse in Waco. She has a doctor spotted, as soon as he gets a divorce." She added rather sadly, "I guess that's the way life is now. People go their own ways according to what pleases them in the short run—and never mind the long run."

"Tell me, Mr. Barron, are you married?"

"Well, yes and no, Myra. I'm in the process of getting a divorce, an ethical divorce I tell myself, after thirty years of marriage. My wife is twenty-three years younger than I. But more importantly, in recent years our interests have diverged. Our lives have become not one, but two different ones. She's had a successful career in business and journalism. From the day we were married, I encouraged her to achieve everything she could. She's a very attractive and intelligent woman."

As Jonathan drank his tea, he wondered how many times in the future he would have to explain his personal situation. The whole thing was so painful for him. "Because I may meet other strangers, I think I'll have my marital status resumé typed up and copied on white paper with black border. I'm so ashamed of being divorced, or feeling I had to get a divorce, that my explanation sounds like a recorded apology.

"But I'm sorry for the digression." He continued, "My wife has been provided with enough money so she won't need to work. But she prefers working and is being considered for an excellent job in a fine university in California. We have three quite successful children, two daughters and a son. My wife, or rather ex-wife, Rene, is now staying with our lawyer daughter for two or three weeks, pending the arrival of our first grandchild. However, she's already leased an apartment in the Westwood-UCLA area in Los Angeles. That's enough information for you, isn't it?"

"Yes, Mr. Barron, except I've been wondering what in the world kind of business you would be in. I've never met a businessman as sensitive as you appear to be."

"I've been in several businesses, including particularly the advertising agency business. However, I've been retired for years, working five to seven days a week developing a foundation for improving ethics, writing essays and speeches, and editing a couple of books in the field of ethics and political economics."

"How did you ever learn to read people so well, to know so much about them so quickly?"

"Oh, that's something one doesn't learn, Myra. I happen to love looking at and being with an intelligent, pretty woman. That's my excuse for ESP or whatever one wishes to call intuitive insight. Let me ask you why a pretty young woman—I believe you indicated you are about twenty-eight years old, maybe come November 9 . . ."

"November 6," Myra interjected.

". . . would spend time with a much older man, as I generously describe myself?"

"Speaking for this young woman, and I don't feel so young, I just happen to be rather intrigued by you. So much so, in fact, that I wonder if you'd object to my suggesting that I meet you at your motel tonight after I finish work at the restaurant, say about nine-thirty?"

"Would I object? No!" Jonathan said emphatically and enthusiastically. "How gracious and considerate and absolutely wonderful that you ask. I'll be honored, excited, and glorified by your presence. If I knew any other way to say 'Please do' more emphatically, I'd do so. Shall I wait at the entrance for you to drive up, or would you like to meet me in my room?"

"Why not wait for me at the motel entrance, and I'll pick you up and show you my Boulder home. It will only take me five minutes to get to your motel from the restaurant, and my apartment is fifteen minutes from the motel."

Myra glanced at her watch. "I'd better be going to work now. If I go in early, maybe the manager will let me off a few minutes early, if we're not really rushed."

The waitress placed the check on the table, and Jonathan left cash for the check and tip in order to save time. He kissed Myra goodbye very briefly and told her, "I'll be the man in the dark suit waiting at the motel entrance with a bottle of champagne in a white plastic bag of ice. I'll try to survive until you arrive."

And survive he did.

Myra drove up to the motel entrance at nine twenty-five, a gesture of timeliness much appreciated by Jonathan. She was driving a maroon Accord, a very sensible car for a young businesswoman who needed both good mileage and good taste. As she stopped, she reached over and opened the door for her guest, another proper gesture for man or woman. These indices of thoughtfulness increased his appreciation of this young lady.

"Congratulations, Myra," he said as he got into the car.

"Now what have I done to earn congratulations, Mr. Barron? Before you answer, for Pete's sake, you do have a first name, don't you?"

Jonathan closed the car door and said, "It's Jonathan, and the idea of a lovely young woman with a faint North Carolina accent calling me that and treating me as a welcome friend is very pleasing. I like it. Please say 'Jonathan' often."

Myra drove along quietly for a while. "I bought a townhouse condominium about a year ago, shortly after this area was developed," she said. "I think you'll like it."

As he looked out the window, what he was seeing looked familiar.

"It seems to me this is the beginning of the new section that the real estate agent recommended to me. In my opinion, Myra, you purchased at the right time and in the right location. Having been in the real estate business, among other things, my guess is that new sales in this area are already up fifteen or twenty percent in price since you purchased. It's the 'in' place, being out closer to the mountains."

Myra turned the car down a side street.

"I sure hope you're right. My condo unit is the one on the right at the far end of this block, just so you can get an idea of the neighborhood from what you can see by our modest street lights."

Myra touched her automatic garage door opener, and the light came on as the door opened, showing a clean, double garage with a two-step entrance to the apartment.

"Quite good, Myra," Jonathan remarked appreciatively as he got out of the car carrying the champagne bag carefully. They entered through a door which opened into a wide, short hallway serving as a buffer area to the side door of the kitchen. At the end of the hall, a door opened to a den with a fireplace, which adjoined a living room area more properly entered by the front door, which faced the yard and the mountains.

The den was cozily furnished, but not surfeited with pillows. The functionally necessary pillows were soft, in mellow tones of beige and green. The sofa fronting the small but well-proportioned fireplace was not bulky, but was long and wide enough, and the television console was positioned so that one could sit on the sofa and watch the television and the fireplace.

224

Myra, in effect, waved a wand of warm introduction to her home and told Jonathan she would like to show him the apartment as soon as they had their champagne. Then she came over to him, and he held her in his arms briefly while she said, "As they say in the movies, I'd like to slip into something more comfortable."

"I'll welcome your change into something more comfortable, but first let me tell you how much I like the combination you have on now. I noticed how becomingly you were dressed as you entered the tea room this afternoon. But you go ahead and I'll find champagne glasses, probably in the cabinet above the refrigerator."

Myra laughed and went upstairs to change. At the top of the stairs she called down, "Let's have a fire in the fireplace. It's cool enough tonight. All you need is a match. They're on the mantle."

Jonathan simply replied, "Wonderful."

He started the fire. It was well enclosed by a good mesh screen that did not obscure the glow of the flames. He found the champagne glasses and placed them in the freezer. Then he looked in a bottom cupboard, where he found a big green salad bowl into which he dumped the ice from his plastic bag. He opened the champagne, put it in the ice bowl, took a pretty green and white dish towel, and placed the champagne on a coffee table in front of the sofa. He searched for and found coasters, matching green leather ones, brought the cold glasses out, and watched Myra descend the stairs attired in a very hug-inducing outfit: light-blue velour slacks and a pale lavender silk blouse, which had a softly ruffled mandarin collar and buttons down the front that looked easy to handle.

Myra just stood on the bottom step, grinning at Jonathan's obvious delight with her. He walked over, picked her up, carried her over to the fireplace, and let her slide slowly to her feet. Myra noticed on her way to a standing position that this rather aloof man could not conceal his responsiveness, and they kissed warmly.

As Myra settled herself on the sofa, Jonathan moved a chair near the end of the sofa so he could just sit and look at her. She gestured to the sofa beside her.

"Yes," he acknowledged, "I'd like to be where I can hold you. But you look so enchantingly lovable, I want to caress you, to consume you with my eyes first. At the restaurant last night you were so efficient that I overlooked much of your beauty.

"But you're smart in presenting yourself that way in your work. In that class of restaurant, customers shouldn't be distracted by the pretty figures of the waitresses. That way you can also screen out the oafs."

There was a short period of silence while they tasted the champagne. Then he resumed the conversation.

"But, Lord, Myra, why did you let me in your door? I'm more than twice your age, and I'd gladly settle for that estimate. What does a smart, beautiful, and—now I know—luscious young woman see in an older man like me?"

Myra stood up and laughed as she poured a little more champagne for each of them. She walked over to him, put her champagne glass near his, sat in his lap, and began a confession-like statement.

"There can be lots of reasons why a young woman likes an older man. You've just illustrated one. The older man, especially the intelligent, really grown-up man, will admire the total woman. He doesn't just focus on any special part of her body. He caresses her from the tips of her toes to the top of her head. He adores the whole woman. Also a woman, young or old, is curious about a distinguished-looking, obviously different kind of man. Young women, especially, wonder what this man would be like in bed."

Jonathan was quiet. When Myra saw that he wasn't going to reply, she continued.

"Furthermore, a young person, any woman or man, learns so much from the experienced, successful older man."

He smiled. He tended to agree with her.

"The simplest and most prevalent reason a young girl goes out with an older man," Myra said, "is that he probably has much more money than young men, and he's proud to be seen spending it on her, taking her to all the nice restaurants and places. The older man treats a young woman like a princess. He appreciates her. I often overhear conversations of guests in the restaurant. One thing I've noticed is that the older man and younger woman always seem to have more stimulating conversations than young couples. They talk business, politics, travel—worthwhile subjects.

"Couple this with the fact that the older fellow will often be better in bed than the younger man, and you have about all the reasons a girl needs." Then she added, "If she isn't looking for a husband.

226

"That husband factor is important, because women can become spoiled by the money and attention we receive from older men and become too critical of young men. I know all these things, but I don't always act the way I should."

Myra wondered if she hadn't perhaps said too much. But he seemed to enjoy hearing why older men were so appealing. It was increasingly encouraging news to him.

After sipping some of her champagne and having her glass refreshed, she said, "If the older man is mature, he may be less self-conscious, less self-centered, and may express far more care and appreciation of the woman as a whole person. He's interested in what she's all about. He isn't so hung up on himself; he's over his growing pains in sex and business.

"Take sex, for instance, and please do." They both laughed. "It takes imagination and creativity, as well as sexual virility for a man to be a good lover." Jonathan was beginning to feel like he was on top of the world. He was feeling appreciated.

"Now," Myra continued, "this is a big reason I like *this* older man. You're an intriguing, sophisticated, sexy male. I don't care whether you're twenty or eighty, and you shouldn't either."

She kissed him softly, warmly, fully, deeply.

"Often, the older man can tantalize and satisfy a woman longer and better than most young men will, whether or not they can.

"Now, then, you seem to be relaxing and expanding all over. Perhaps you're getting warm. Let's take off this lovely necktie, and let's unbutton your shirt. Your belt seems a bit too tight, so let's unbuckle it. And we must loosen your pants, because something in there seems to need more room."

After a few minutes of lovemaking, Jonathan said, "Myra, you're wonderful. You're so young. How did you get so good?" He was playing for time, more time for her to keep doing what she was doing.

"I can't talk now," Myra mumbled. Jonathan was satisfied with her answer, and she was audibly getting satisfaction, too. She reminded him of Mindy.

In a little while Myra said, "Let's finish our champagne here and then go upstairs to bed. We can stay in front of the fireplace for a while."

He agreed.

An hour or so later, they went upstairs to her king-size bed.

"Such a big play yard for a one-hundred-twelve-pound person."

"All the better to eat you up!" she said, laughing.

He thought her the loveliest wolf who could ever have entered the little condo cottage.

"Jonathan," Myra said, running her hands and lips over his body, "I've been keeping a secret from you. Do you want to hear it?"

"What is it? Please don't tell me you're not really a divorcee and your ex-boxer husband is in the other bedroom."

"No! You nut," she said laughingly, "I would never keep a bad secret from you. But I thought you should know that I really don't go to bed with strange men as often as you might think. Of course, after our tea this afternoon, you weren't a strange man. Didn't you have just a touch of love for me, too?"

"I certainly did and do, but that's no secret, Myra. What's your secret?"

"Do you remember Mrs. Bronson?"

"Yes, and I will for a long time. Why?"

"I bought this condominium from Lisa. She's a close friend now. She said that I might see you at our restaurant, that you were new in town and making the rounds of the top eating places. She described you. In fact, she had you and me in mind when she recommended the Cameron. I saw you come in, and the hostess caught my signal and brought you to my table. Lisa told me that if I ever felt like really making love to a man, I should try to get you. She actually said it would be good therapy for both of us. She said you had recently separated from your wife and were under great stress for that and other reasons. So, what do you think about that for a secret?"

Jonathan was complimented but not caught off guard.

"I can tell you that Mrs. Bronson should know that I wanted a lovely woman. I loved her company, her presence, and wish I could have loved her body. Lord, how I wanted Lisa. She knew it and knew that neither she nor I would make love to another's spouse.

"Now, Myra, I'll tell you a secret—my secret. I was curious about you—such a pretty and smart young lady agreeing to the 'check-out' tea. So, I called a gentleman I had just met in Boulder who had also recommended your restaurant. I asked him if he had met you and what he knew about you. He said you were very well regarded by himself, the restaurant manager, and restaurant patrons who knew you.

"You see, Myra, I have an obligation to avoid danger, and a beautiful woman can make a man her slave. So our mutual secret —that each of us took the time to find out about the other— explains why we could make love so freely, so fully, and with such faith in one another.

"Thank God for all friends, and especially for understanding new friends. They helped us do our personal homework."

"Do you think we've done anything wrong in loving one another?" Myra asked. "Is sex, as we've had it, evil?"

"Myra," Jonathan replied in a protective manner, "there's absolutely nothing inherently wrong with sex. It is certainly not evil. And sex as we have had it, between two persons whose minds and bodies and souls could unite, where there were no uncrossable bridges of feelings, but regard and respect for one another, could only be restorative and beneficial—as well as fantastically enjoyable. Very importantly, there were no third parties, no innocent bystanders, for our actions to hurt. If we had loving spouses at home, our action tonight would have been unethical because we would have been harming others; we would have been stealing from others. The aspects of sex that are unethical are those that were long ago put forth in the Commandments pointedly rejecting adultery, covetousness, and lying. Dishonesty between lovers and spouses is the sin that begets sins."

Myra didn't seem to have anything to add at this point, so he continued, "There are two additional and compelling caveats on sexual relations. If sexual relations are to be beneficial and not deleterious, they must be accompanied by at least a modicum of beauty, possible only when there is mutual respect and regard. These are components of a type of love that's struggling to survive in our increasingly vulgarized society.

"Another, and very important, essential for non-destructive sexual relations is the presence of pride. A significant percentage of divorced men and women, especially recently divorced women, are literally afraid to risk 'falling into a love trap' again. They don't want any semblance of love with their sexual relations. Yet so many divorced singles, especially women in the general age group of thirty-five to fifty-five, seem to be compulsively sex hungry. They don't want sex and love, they don't care about having pride in their partnerships, and the mere mention of love, adoration, not even to hint at worship, will prompt them to say with intentional vulgarity, 'I don't want to be worshipped—I just want to be screwed.'

229

"Some of them, Myra, make it through this period of promiscuity and self-destructive spite, but often not soon enough. The scars show in their eyes, in their changing tastes, and in their increasing inability to choose a worthwhile partner. So I think that if you're not hurting others in your sexual relations, and if you're selective enough not to hurt yourself, you'll be able to give and receive ecstatic excitement—with no unconscious, inhibiting reservations."

Myra nodded in agreement and understanding.

"Visualize yourself, treat yourself, like a Mercedes-Benz convertible, not like a used pick-up truck," he concluded. "I think of a lovely woman as precious, in the true sense of the word. I want the woman to know that and to think of herself as precious."

"My God, Jonathan, you make me feel better all over." Then she said softly, "Let's make love again."

"My darling Myra, that's the most wonderful thing you could say to make me stop talking. With you I move, *am* moving, into another world, dreamy, totally joyful."

"Jonathan, would you feel the same way toward an older woman, say a woman of fifty or sixty?" she asked, snuggling into his arms.

"The answer is yes, but, unfortunately, the opportunity would be rare. Too many older women, although sexually very satisfying and satisfiable, resign themselves to the concept that men are all the same and thereby become too matter-of-fact about the sexual act, too pessimistic about finding or creating romance. In fact, they may lay aside kindness, tenderness, and beauty, and almost force the male to be quite prosaic in loving.

"A primary cause for this attitude about sex and romance on the part of older women is that by the time men are fifty-five, many are so covered with the dross of materialism that sensitivity to beauty and romance is hard to arouse. Their virility may be present, but not their sense of worship and appreciation of the total loveliness of a woman. Thank God there are exceptions, male and female. And, contrary to what many contemporary, assertive 'new' women think, charm, beauty, courtesy, consideration, and lots of sex appeal are all often found in women who have achieved great professional and business successes."

Once again Myra didn't respond, so Jonathan said, "I saw a lady just the other day in Washington. She's the president of a sizable

230

corporation, having been promoted from vice-president and general manager by a very demanding chief executive officer. The woman president must be between fifty-five and sixty. She looks forty. She's beautiful. She's lovely. As a man, I could adore and worship her just as much as I could a twenty-five-year-old, perfectly shaped model. Actually much more, because there would be so much more in the lady executive for me to reach for, to aspire to share.

"But what the hell. I'm an idiot not to answer you with just one word and kiss you endlessly. It's nice to think a little and make love last longer, though."

"I enjoy loving you so much," she purred. "But I enjoy listening to you, too. The main problem is that when you become the philosopher," and she smiled a little, "the evidence of your virility subsides. But I enjoy bringing you down to earth, or I should say up."

"Myra, sharing thoughts and sharing sex helps make sex so much more fun.

"Will you let me stay all night if we keep on doing what we're doing?"

"Yes, yes," Myra said, stroking him gently. "I'll drive you back to the motel when I leave for work at eleven."

"You're wonderful," Jonathan replied.

"You're amazing," Myra said.

# 23

When Jonathan awakened in Myra's bedroom the next morning, she was sitting on the edge of the bed, all dressed and looking as fresh and bright as a field of dew-covered daisies in the early morning sun. She had just awakened him with a kiss.

"You've been sleeping like a kid, honey—I hope your dreams were pleasant," Myra said.

He looked at her, wondering where he was. He wasn't asleep, but he hallucinated for a moment that he was in another world and an angel, his mother, was taking care of him. Then, as his mind cleared, he said, "Good morning, my dear angel. I must have slept very soundly. I didn't dream at all until I opened my eyes and saw you. I hope I didn't keep you from sleeping well."

"No, my darling Jonathan. I slept late, for me. It's nine-thirty, and your breakfast will be waiting for you as soon as you're ready for it. Sorry I don't have a toothbrush for you, but there's some mouthwash in the cabinet in my bathroom." She gestured to the left. "I put a razor with a new blade and some shaving cream and big towels out for you."

Jonathan reached out and touched her face with his fingers, took her hands and kissed them. "Yes, you are real. I'm glad I didn't dream, because no dream could have compared with you. But I'm not sure that you and this room are real. A shower should clear my head. I'll be down soon."

Jonathan came downstairs fifteen minutes later to a clean and orderly room with no champagne glasses or comforter. Myra came up to him and kissed him nicely, the kiss of a loving companion, to make his breakfast taste better.

"How lovely you are, Myra. And your home is so charming."

"Thank you, Jonathan." She motioned toward the table. "Drink your juice. Will toasted English muffins, pear preserves, and milk be enough, along with coffee?"

"Sure. The muffins and preserves will be a special treat. When do you leave for work?"

"We can take our time," she said as she glanced at the kitchen clock over the sink. "I don't leave until ten forty-five, and your motel is directly on the way."

Jonathan drank his orange juice. Myra served muffins for both of them, put the preserves and percolator of coffee on the table, and sat down, looking at him strangely.

"What are you thinking, Myra?"

"I hope I'm thinking about the same thing you are. It's a very happy thought that past times make sad. I wish you were as loving as you are and young enough to want to marry and bring up children. And that you loved me and I loved you. We could start a wonderful home together. Maybe you would be a professor or a real estate developer and I could use my MBA in a local company, close to home, a ten-minute drive."

Then she threw up her hands. "Oh, how silly."

"Myra, you've made me understand that life with you would capture all the richness of my past lives. In life and in song it's been said, 'What a difference a day makes'—one night of love, one day of knowing you. I've been totally in love with you for a day. I know it's a dream. But I want a young man for you, about your age, maybe a little older, so he'll have had more time to mature. I want him to love you totally, and marry you soon, and have a family with you—two boys and a girl.

"I think you'd be good at bringing up little boys. As old as I am, you can handle and mother me.

"But, I also think the best we can do now is promise to wish the best for one another and, maybe in a year or so, meet again. You're an apparition, Myra. That's the best way for me to believe I've known you so completely, loved you so ardently."

Myra smiled at Jonathan and then looked wistfully, yet confidently, across at him. "I've been thinking as you have. But I have something more to carry with me into the future, something you've illuminated for me. I have the challenge to be like the apparition you've seen. I'll try to live the kind of life you've envisioned for me, with a young man like you for me. I know what I'm looking for. And I'll find one—someone who can love me, adore me, and yet challenge me.

She handed him a piece of blue note paper. "Here's my local address and that of my parents, in case you ever want to find me. Will you write down your address and phone number for me?"

"You can always reach me at my Washington business address," he said as he wrote it down for her.

Jonathan folded her note and put it in his wallet.

"Myra, I'll write to you later. I have a feeling that I can't stay in Boulder. Will you tell Mrs. Bronson that I thank her very much for being so perceptive and so kind in speaking to you of me?"

Myra said she would be sure to tell Lisa. They finished breakfast and rinsed the dishes and put them in the dishwasher. It was time to leave, and neither one knew how to say goodbye. But, as man and woman, they reached for one another and kissed tenderly.

"That's our goodbye," she said. "I hope it's not final."

"You've stated the case for me, too, Myra. Except that I feel like getting on my knees and thanking you for giving me another reason why I should want to live."

"One more hope to be expressed. When you get your MBA in a few months, why not plan a vacation in London? Visit the London School and talk to some of their economics professors. Just look and learn. We'll stay a week in England. Have tea at the Savoy. All expenses paid from Boulder and back to Boulder. If you need help getting a good job in Washington or New York, I'll be at your command. No obligations of any kind."

Nothing more was said until she let him out of the car at the motel. They shook hands as they said goodbye, and Myra said with a smile, "I've never been to London—I'll need a guide, you know."

When Jonathan entered the motel, he checked to see if there were any messages and then went to his room to change suits. His ears seemed to be itching. He wet a washcloth with warm water and rubbed his ears, inside and out. There was a little blood on the washcloth. He checked with a new wet cloth, using part of the cloth for one ear and part for the other to see where the blood was coming from. Blood, not much, just a little, seemed to be coming from inside his ears, although there were no abrasions that he could see.

He went out to his car and drove west on Base Line Street to a big pharmacy. He asked the pharmacist to recommend a doctor. There was a doctor's office in the same building, so Jonathan went in and explained to the receptionist his unusual ailment. She told him the doctor had no appointments open but said that he could wait in the reception room and the doctor would try to see him between appointments. She gave him the customary data sheets to fill out, in the meantime.

Before long, the nurse came out and took him into the doctor's office. The doctor looked at the history sheet Jonathan had filled out and asked the nature of his present problem. He also asked about his previous ear trouble, two annoying periods of vertigo, which had caused about a fifteen percent permanent loss of hearing.

The doctor looked out his window and asked how long Jonathan had been in Boulder and if he had lived in a high-altitude area for any length of time.

He said that he hadn't and that he had been in Boulder for several days.

The doctor put the forms back into a folder and told Jonathan that the blood from his ears was the effect of the higher altitude, exacerbated by the fact that his ears were already impaired. He stated that Jonathan might become acclimatized to the area within six or eight months, but he couldn't be sure. Jonathan didn't think 5200 to 5400 feet was much of an altitude and asked the doctor if an abnormal amount of sexual activity, like three or four times in a twelve-hour period, could have induced this bleeding of the ears. The doctor said, "No," but he looked at his patient with some surprise.

Jonathan went to his car and sat quietly for a few minutes. What signal was fate giving him now? He thought the big rainbow demonstration given him as he drove through the prairies had been an omen of welcome to the West. Now he would have to go to lower altitudes, wherever that would be. He wondered if he should really leave Boulder or if he should wait to find out if he could adapt to the altitude.

He didn't like the idea of six months or more of bleeding and continued uncertainty. He could not hear well, but quite well enough, he thought. He would like to keep his hearing and everything else he had in good working order. He decided to leave Boulder at once. His first action was to go talk with Ed Harrell, the owner of the condominium he had just leased.

Harrell wasn't in when Jonathan arrived at his office, but he was expected back soon. In ten or fifteen minutes, Jonathan heard a motorcyclist drive up to the door. It was Harrell, who was almost as much a loner as Jonathan. The two men had had a pleasant meeting when Jonathan had leased the apartment, so he explained the situation about his ears as Harrell listened sympathetically. He asked the name of the doctor, and Jonathan gave him the doctor's name and address.

Ed Harrell called his secretary and told her to see the book-keeper about returning Jonathan's deposit. Jonathan told Harrell that his offer was kind and generous and said that if it was all right with him, he would like to pay the man in Harrell's office who had taken him out to show him the apartment. He also mentioned that Harrell's secretary had been kind enough to get him a set of keys. Therefore, he said, he would like to give each of them something to cover their time and their courtesy.

Harrell looked at Jonathan and said, "That's thoughtful of you, Mr. Barron, but it's not necessary. However, if you wish, would a hundred dollars for Mr. Seaton, our sales representative, and twenty dollars for my secretary be satisfactory to you?"

Jonathan said that that would be fine and thanked Harrell for his cooperation.

He returned to the motel and phoned his movers, telling them to keep his furniture in storage until further notice.

It was just one o'clock, so Jonathan went to the motel cashier, paid his bill, and advised the clerk that he would be out of his room in fifteen or twenty minutes. He packed his cases, put them in the car trunk, hung his suits inside the car, and headed for Denver.

On the way out of Boulder, he took a long look at the high rise where Lisa Bronson had taken him. His trip to Boulder had not been a disappointment, even though the altitude hadn't agreed with his ears. He liked Boulder. It did have its own life-style, but how could a place miss, with spectacular scenery, beautiful women, and wonderful food, all tied together with warm, western hospitality?

He headed for Denver and hoped the Brown Palace hotel was still like the Brown Palace he had known over the years, intimate and excellent. When he arrived there, he found a room available. Jonathan took in one case and his suits. He left the things in his room and went back downstairs to see if the Palace Arms Cafe was still open for lunch. The headwaiter greeted him with butler-like dignity and courtesy. All was as he'd expected—a good martini, fine food, attentive and proper service, and an interesting group of patrons.

After lunch he went out to walk blocks and blocks around downtown Denver. Checking up on things was a holdover from his old marketing and real estate days. He returned to the hotel, stopping at the newsstand to pick up a group of newsmagazines and newspapers.

After reading for a while, he began to think about the purpose of his life. Perhaps he should teach, as Mindy had suggested. Or, better than trying to be competent and patient enough to teach, he might plan and propose a course on purposeful living that others could execute.

But where should he present the plan? He decided it should not be offered to a big university, nor to one of the inbred, so-called better colleges. He felt the appropriate school should be part of a state university system located in an area where the culture is homogeneous and the values are still influenced by a heritage of decency and trust in one another. From a marketing-test standpoint, he thought the site of the college should be reasonably insulated, by geography as well as by social factors, from big-city overlap. Jonathan wished he had a map in front of him, but actually he didn't need one. He knew the country very well.

He thought of Pullman, Washington, but Washington State was really a rather large school and strong in the athletic department. Indiana had several possible schools, but there wasn't much distance between here and there in Indiana. Eastern schools were not, as a group, as free of multiple social forces as the test school should be. Because of his years of traveling the prairies from West Texas to Canada, Jonathan thought of Kearney, Nebraska, then moved down his mental map to western Kansas. He would be driving through that area the next day. But Kansas State University at Manhattan had grown to be too big and complex. Then he had a thought, a very good thought.

When he had driven through Hane a few days before, he had noticed a car with a Western Kansas State University sticker. An economics professor, who had called on him in Washington shortly after he had founded the Ethics Inquiry Group, taught at Western Kansas State. What was his name? He had published a book on ethics a year or two after his Washington visit and had sent Jonathan a copy. He was chairman of the economics department. Yes, Dr. Walter Weeks.

He would stop in Hane tomorrow and see if Dr. Weeks was still there. Hane was right on Interstate 70, out in the middle of the high plains country, about halfway between Kansas City and Denver. If he left Denver about nine in the morning, he might reach Hane before the professor left his office.

Now he would finish reading his *Journal,* watch the news, and skim through the magazines. By that time he would be ready to check out the rest of the Brown Palace cocktail and dining facilities, but he thought he would most likely wind up eating again at the Palace Arms. They would have excellent roast beef to go with their English decor and headwaiter. His evening was not a disappointment.

The next morning Jonathan left Denver and arrived in Hane, Kansas, about three forty-five. It took only one stop at a service station to get directions to Western Kansas State University, by far the largest enterprise in Hane. It's hard to hide a university with an enrollment of five or six thousand students in a town of fifteen thousand, Jonathan thought.

As he drove around the campus, he was amazed that all the buildings were so well maintained and the campus was so neat. There were no students to be seen, because it was between summer and fall semesters. He parked his car and asked the first person he saw, a pleasant-looking woman, in which building he could find the department of economics.

"Who are you looking for?" she asked.

"Professor Walter Weeks. I think he's the chairman of the economics department," Jonathan replied.

"Yes. I know Dr. Weeks. He doesn't teach any more. He was vice-president for academic affairs, but he retired last year. However, if you go into the building across the street on the corner, that's Orr Hall, and the administrative offices are located there. When I came out of the library a few minutes ago, I think I saw Dr. Weeks walk into the building with President Thompson. Go into Orr Hall and enter the first office on your left. The secretary in Admissions will check to see if Dr. Weeks is in the building."

"Thank you very much. And where is the library?" Jonathan asked.

"It's right here, Foreman Hall. I'm the assistant librarian."

"Well," Jonathan said as he motioned toward the library building, "from what I see, you have a rather impressive library. Do you offer the master's degree in library science?"

"Oh, yes. Library science is one of our stronger departments."

"Thanks again," he said. "Perhaps I'll get to visit your library soon."

He walked over to Orr Hall and asked the secretary in the Office of Admissions if she could tell him, by chance, if Dr. Weeks was in the building. She said he was with President Thompson. And if he would tell her who was calling, she was sure Dr. Weeks wouldn't mind telling her when he would be available.

"I'm Jonathan Barron of the Ethics Inquiry Group in Washington."

# 24

"This is a pleasant surprise, Mr. Barron," Dr. Weeks said as he walked briskly up to Jonathan and shook his hand. "What brings you to Hane?"

Dr. Weeks spoke as brightly and as sharply as he walked. He looked like a fifty-five-year-old welterweight boxer, still in fighting shape.

"I came by to see a fellow who wrote a book on business ethics and was kind enough to drop by our office in Washington to give us a copy. I was driving back from Boulder to Washington and thought I'd see if you were in town. I wanted to check out an idea with you on teaching ethics in social science. Is there any time in the next day or so that you'll be available?"

"Yes, let me talk with my friend and neighbor, George Thompson, the president of our university. He'll be glad to meet you. We've just finished our little business chat, so come on with me, Mr. Barron. That's Jonathan, isn't it? I'm Walter."

They walked down the hall through Dr. Thompson's reception room and into his office. Dr. Thompson, a tall, rancher-like man with a pleasing smile, had already moved from his desk toward the doorway to greet Jonathan.

"Dr. Thompson, this is Jonathan Barron, the founder of the Ethics Inquiry Group in Washington," Dr. Weeks said with a measure of pride. "He stopped by on his way back to Washington from Boulder."

"Glad to see you, Dr. Thompson," Jonathan said quickly, as he reached out to shake Thompson's extended hand. "It's kind of you and Walter to let me interrupt your meeting and walk in like this."

"Mr. Barron, one of the nice things about an isolated, small city and a small university is that one has time to catch up. We can do things a little more simply and quickly. We're glad to meet with distinguished guests when they come our way. I already feel as though I know you, because a corporate executive friend of mine sent me a copy of your book on ethics and economics. I liked what you said and placed the book in our library."

"George," Walter said, "Jonathan says he wants to get my opinion on an idea he has about teaching ethics in a department of sociology. I thought you might like to join us. We can't play our usual Friday afternoon golf. It's been raining too much today."

"Let's sit down over here at the table, Mr. Barron. I welcome a chance to talk about ethics, a subject that Walter and I have often discussed. I was his unsolicited consultant when he wrote his book on ethics. You know, I started out wanting to be a theologian but switched to biology in my third year of undergraduate work. If I remember correctly, you stated in your book that ethics has its roots in sociology, perhaps in biology, and is related to ecology in terms of making the best use of what we have. As a biologist with an early interest in theology, I heartily agree with what you said." He looked at his watch and then at his friend.

"Walter, it's getting along toward five o'clock. Why don't we take Jonathan to the club? He might like a beer."

Turning back to Jonathan, he said, "Our wives drove down to Greensburg to an art exhibit. They'll be back to have dinner with us at the club in an hour or so."

"Let's do that. Jonathan, you may be surprised at what a nice club and golf course we have. It's only about a five-minute drive. George, do you want to ask Dr. Littlejohn to join us, if he's still here?"

"Good idea. I'll phone his office now." As he dialed, he said to Jonathan, "Littlejohn is from my hometown of St. Francis. He's chairman of our sociology department."

He waited for the phone to be answered. "Oh, you're there, Karl. How would you like to join me and Walter and a guest at the club? We're leaving now. Okay, we'll see you there."

Dr. Thompson turned to Jonathan and said, "I've known Karl for many years. He's a little lost now because of his recent divorce. He'll meet us at the club.

"Why don't you take Jonathan with you, Walter? One of us can bring him back here to pick up his car after the meeting."

As an afterthought, he asked, "Jonathan, have you checked into your hotel yet?"

"No, but I have a reservation at the Hane Inn."

"In that case," Walter spoke up, "Why don't you follow me to the Hane Inn? It's on the way to the club. You can register and be sure you have your room, and I'll take you on to the club."

"That's good," George agreed. "I'll see you both in the club lounge in a few minutes."

Jonathan followed Walter to the Hane Inn, went in, quickly registered, and rejoined Walter. As they drove on to the club, Walter decided to detour a few blocks to show Jonathan what a beautiful, well-designed, well-maintained golf course the members of the Hane Country Club enjoyed.

They arrived at the club, an impressive brick ranch-style building with two extended wings enclosing a big swimming pool. George and Karl Littlejohn were waiting in the nicely westernized lounge, adjacent to a large dining area with windows overlooking the eighteenth hole.

"Quite a place," Jonathan thought.

George introduced him to Karl, a man of medium build with a better-than-medium stomach. He offset his lack of slender contour with a rather expensive brown thinly-woven alpaca jacket. He also wore a pipe. He greeted Jonathan happily, but with a look that indicated his mood could change quickly.

"Well, Jonathan, I usually have a beer, but you're welcome to order whatever you want, maybe a scotch or, more likely, a martini." George was right on target.

"You guessed right, George. A martini on the rocks, please."

Walter took a beer and Karl, a scotch and water. Jonathan continued, "I'm impressed with your club and the excellent golf course. But what was that well-kept open area that looked like a golf course I saw over near the university?"

Walter spoke up, "Oh, that's another golf course, owned by the university, but maintained by the city. It's a pretty good course. George and I play there frequently."

"And what population does Hane have, about fifteen thousand?"

"That's about right, Jonathan."

"With a lovely country club, two golf courses, and a first-class university, do you think you can keep this paradise a secret much longer?" Jonathan looked at all of them.

"Well, Jonathan, to be direct about it," George answered, "we're not overpromoting what we have. To the extent that it's possible for a state university, we're trying to limit our growth. We have about fifty-eight hundred students now. And I don't believe you noticed any big Hane Chamber of Commerce-type booster signs as you drove in. This town is a secret, in a way. We have lots of money here, much of it oil money. Over toward Russell, you'll notice many wells still pumping away."

The drinks arrived, and George said, "I'll quit bragging about Hane. You'll get plenty of that tomorrow if you take a tour with Walter. He's now the unofficial town-and-gown promotion director. He's supposed to be retired."

"But let's hear your comments about ethics and social science, Jonathan."

This was the opening Jonathan had been patiently anticipating.

"I've long been concerned about the so-called value-free teaching and value neutrality of our educational institutions. In my opinion, this value-free concept began to find acceptance in education following World War I. It was accelerated in the 1930s, particularly by those who were impressed by Max Weber, one of the patron saints of sociology. Then, a couple of professors at the University of Chicago further fostered the notion that value neutrality was one of the basic tenets that made the social sciences scientific.

"I think the Weberian argument has been a considerable handicap in the useful development of sociology. In my opinion, the concept of ethical neutrality is an absurdity, and one of the weakest arguments for ethical neutrality in the social sciences was made by Max Weber himself. There is no such animal as a value-free scientist, because there is no such thing as a value-free human being. Every human being has a set of values, whatever they may be, and every institution reflects its own values. I state this as a caveat to my course recommendations to you."

"But," Karl asked, "whose values would one use?" He took a puff on his pipe as if to indicate that the discussion was closed.

"In your asking such a logical question, Karl, I think you're helping me make a case for my recommendation, which I hope I'll get around to before this good martini delays me. We should use the values, the ethics, of those in our society who are *opposed* to murder, rape, stealing, vandalism, deceit, and dishonesty. One may say there are no absolutes, yet we absolutely know that an individual shouldn't walk down a street shooting his friends or anyone else, including children who happen to be in range. We absolutely know that an individual should not rape his neighbor's child.''

"Jonathan," George asked uncritically, "who knows what is right or wrong?"

"I think we all do most of the time, and nobody does all of the time. But if most people in our country didn't agree on most things that are right or wrong, we wouldn't be able to maintain order."

"Okay," George continued, "I like your commonsense answers. Now, what do you think of 'situation ethics,' a concept that began to flourish in the 1960's?"

"George, if all mankind assumed there was no God, we would have to invent a God in order to offset the indeterminacy and destructiveness of ethical relativism, the parent of 'situational ethics.' A society must have a core of absolutes in order to cohere and survive. The institution of religion, with its hierarchical structure, was devised not only to propagate the 'faith,' whichever and wherever such faith existed or exists, but also to provide sanctions for the absolutes, such as—but not limited to—the Ten Commandments.''

"I'll tell you, Jonathan," George said, shaking his head, "I'm going to have to pass that one along to my pastor for comment. He'll be surprised to hear that instead of God having created man, man may have created God."

"What is your definition of ethics?" Karl asked.

"I once asked a renowned professor of philosophy that question. He looked at me with patient condescension and replied, 'Mr. Barron, it would take me a year to give you that answer.' I felt like a dummy. I rushed to his university's bookstore and bought three of his books. After trying to read them, I concluded that that particular professor would need a week to tell a student how to get to the men's room—the first door on the right, as he went out of the office."

They all laughed, but mostly at President Thompson's quick remark, "We have at least one of those in every department."

"After hiring researchers to collect all the definitions of ethics they could find," Jonathan resumed, "our group selected the definition given by Dr. Albert Schweitzer. 'In a general sense,' Dr. Schweitzer said, 'ethics is the name we give to our concern for good behavior. We feel an obligation to consider not only our own personal well-being, but also that of others and of human society as a whole.'

"Dr. Schweitzer's definition supports the widely accepted belief that the Golden Rule is an ethical imperative. To me, ethics is simply our way of being human. If it were not so, mankind would not have survived. From a sociological standpoint, honesty and ethics are basic working social principles, not simply moral guidelines. That's why ethics should be taught, especially in sociology departments."

"Okay, Jonathan, you make a lot of sense," George said. "What do you recommend that we do about it here?"

Jonathan had done a lot of reviewing on his way to Hane, and he had a well-thought-out answer ready for his listeners.

"I would like to see a strong sociology department establish a course in ethics as an integral part of its curriculum. I would recommend, as a first step, a once-a-week, three-hour seminar-type class. If necessary, to avoid delays and academic hurdles, such a course could originally be a part of continuing education. I don't recommend a name, but to explain the concept, the course would be on Purposeful Living."

Dr. Thompson leaned back and took the last sip of his beer, while motioning for a refill. "How would you use the three-hour period?" he asked.

"The first of the three hours might consist of a lecture on the ethical aspects of a particular course already being taught in the sociology department, such as the sociology of urban communities, research methodology, marriage and the family, social services, or other subject areas. The basic theme of each week's session could be how honesty and ethics affect that particular aspect of sociology. The lecture would be given by the professor in each area. This means, of course, that the professors teaching their specialities would have to learn something about ethics. It would be good insurance to have one of your most qualified professors serve as permanent program chairman. But during a given semester, two or three nationally prominent professors, especially those with experience teaching ethics in the social sciences, should be included as lecturers."

"Jonathan, I can see where you're going, but I don't see how ethics and social research could be combined."

"In my opinion, gentlemen, it's in social and behavioral research that sociology has its best, if not only, claim to being a science. Many sociology departments give considerable attention to the problem of deceit and irresponsibility in the methodologies used by some sociologists in research. But apparently it's never occurred to department chairpersons that they might not have to spend so much time trying to correct ethical deficiencies in research if they themselves exhibited strong ethical leadership and took ethics seriously and pragmatically enough to teach it."

"Then, where do you go?" Karl asked.

"The middle hour," Jonathan continued, "would consist of carefully prepared questions relating to specific problems. This modified case study approach is useful but shouldn't be dominated by the presentation of ethical dilemmas. Often the word 'dilemma' encourages ambiguity, and we then use ambiguity to endorse situational ethics or no ethics at all, thus returning to the 'value-free' bugaboo.

"The remaining hour of the three-hour session would be devoted to a panel discussion period conducted by the permanent chairman. Everyone could participate. If such a course is included as part of the university's continuing education program, then the student participation should be more interesting because of the wider age range and the inclusion of those already working and raising families."

"Jonathan," President Thompson said thoughtfully, "from the description of the course you propose, I think I'd like to be the non-rotative teacher and seminar chairman. My doctorate is in biology, and my sense of the need for better ethics has been greatly enhanced by my work in science. Do you know if courses such as the one you've described are now being taught in any of the undergraduate colleges?"

"Congratulations on feeling the urge to teach again! Politics, endowments, grants, and administrative responsibilities, including that of being faculty umpire, must place heavy demands on the chief executive officers of universities. But it would be great for the student body, as well as for the president, to come together in the direct process of teaching and learning, one from the other.

"In answer to your question, I don't really know. I doubt that any social science departments are teaching a course such as I've described. Doubtless they have come up with effective single-hour courses given two and three times weekly. The University of Wisconsin-Whitewater has, I believe, done some developmental work in courses in ethics in social science. Professors Green and Salem of that university stated in an article on applied sociology something to the effect that 'if we are going to teach applied sociology we are going to have to start talking to our students about ethical practice, about right and wrong, good and bad—heretofore taboo topics in many, if not most, sociology classrooms.' Also, I've heard that the University of California-Davis is experimenting with ethics courses in their social science department. One of the exemplary courses in ethics taught in sociology is that of Dr. Donald Warwick at Harvard. However, in choosing from the normal curriculum of course alternatives, students may not flock to courses in ethics. That's sad, because as society becomes predominantly service-oriented, increasingly high-tech, and ever more interdependent, we must all be more ethical. We have to trust and depend on one another in order to survive in a complex world. If mankind is to survive, the great nations of the world must form a foundation of trust and cooperation.

"George, Dr. Warwick recommended in his monograph on 'The Teaching of Ethics in the Social Sciences' that all social science departments seek ways of introducing students to the ethical dimensions of their disciplines," Jonathan continued.

"Jonathan," Littlejohn said in an effort to keep the conversation social and not professional, "one of the reasons other than those stated by our friend Max Weber, that sociologists think in terms of value neutrality is that they borrow the concept from anthropologists, whose missions have been to observe and report, not evangelize."

"Karl, if I'm ever reincarnated, one of the lives I would like to live is that of an anthropologist. They have been great benefactors of mankind, except those who didn't honestly report what they had observed with 'ethical neutrality.' But we've learned from recent books by anthropologists that two different 'value-free' minds can look at the same South Sea island tribe and come up with entirely difference 'facts.' "

George Thompson was obviously considering carefully the points of the discussion. "Karl," he said, "let's have your summary remarks regarding the suggestions Jonathan has made."

"I'd like to ask Jonathan one more question. Don't you believe that ethics is the province of the philosophy department? It is at this university—and most others that I know of. Sociology doesn't want to invade philosophy's turf, and we wouldn't want them to come onto ours."

"Today, Karl, more and more graduate schools, especially in business and medicine, are teaching ethics. And those who have selected professors from philosophy to do so generally have not been pleased. They're beginning to use their own staff. It does seem that many philosophers and, to a surprising extent, sociologists, are apparently drawn compulsively into theoretical, involutional linguistic exercises in order to protect the jargon of their discipline and to keep other folks off their turf, as you've just pointed out."

Feeling an obligation to his own department, Karl said, "George, while I certainly do appreciate the views Jonathan has expressed—and I have a very high regard for the sociology departments he mentioned—there are three or four caveats I'll mention.

"First, there is a certain touchiness among academicians with regard to being given orders. They generally prefer to originate their own courses, although I'm confident our department would be open to suggestions.

"You know, there is within academia, and particularly in the field of social science, a wariness when it comes to what might be broadly called the subject of 'values.' As you say, Jonathan, Weber was one of the patron saints of sociology, and his value-neutral sociology had a great influence in this country. In the social sciences and in the humanities, we take the stance that is is our task to *de*scribe, rather than *pre*scribe. There is also concern among academicians about the meaning of words, and 'ethics' is high on the list of words for which they believe there is no widely accepted meaning.

"Notwithstanding all of these obstacles, I consider the course you suggest 'do-able' if we set our minds to it. We might even be able to give it a try about a year from this coming fall semester."

Jonathan was impressed and pleased with Karl's statement, and before George could comment he said, "Karl, you've pointed out the hurdles quite accurately, I believe. But I think all of us in this country, including academicians, are going to have to quit being neutral or tolerant or ambivalent toward things that our society believes are plain wrong, actions that serve to destroy society, any society."

At this point, Jonathan thought it was time to change the pace of their conversation. After a deliberate pause, he said, "And now, gentlemen, let me say that you've all been very hospitable and

248

generous with your time. And Karl, since you're the sociologist here, let me express special appreciation for your courtesy and understanding."

"Well, Jonathan, just for that nice remark, I'll take you back to the hotel, because I know George and Walter are waiting for their wives."

Walter beamed with satisfaction. He had been fearful that Karl and Jonathan might not be so considerate of each other's opinions. "Karl, that'd be great," he said, "because I think I saw our wives come in and head for the ladies' room. And, Jonathan, I'll call you in the morning if you'd like a tour of the university and community."

"I certainly would enjoy it. And as soon as you're ready, I'll be waiting at the hotel."

They all said their goodbyes, and Jonathan and Karl headed for Karl's car.

"I'll buy you a dinner if you'll lead me to a good steak house," Jonathan said.

"Jonathan, I know just the place."

# 25

The trip from Hane, Kansas, back to Washington was a blur of minor memories. The day he left Hane, Jonathan drove approximately eight hundred miles. He drove continuously and long, stopping for gas, a lunch of milk and a sandwich and three hundred and fifty miles later, for gas again, a cup of coffee, and some vanilla ice cream.

He was hurrying back to Washington where, ironically, no one awaited him. He didn't even have a home to go to, and his furniture was in storage. What would he do when he arrived in Washington? Where did he wish to live? He still wasn't sure he wanted to live anywhere.

Strange, he thought, that I feel compelled to carry a burden and fulfill a mission or quit living. But it is purpose that makes the future inviting to all humans.

His last night on the road was spent at a motel on a hilltop four or five hundred miles from Washington. Late in the afternoon the next day, he arrived in Washington and checked into a semi-residential hotel on New Hampshire Avenue. The next morning he decided to search for a condominium to lease or buy and to get his furniture out of storage. He thought he should at least have a "home" address for his mail.

During the next few days, he talked to two or three different real estate agents. One of them, a retired vice-president of a big corporation, showed Jonathan a two-bedroom condominium unit in the building where he himself lived. Jonathan liked the building and grounds, the excellence of the maintenance, and the simplicity of decor. He especially liked the apartment on the third floor with a long balcony overlooking trees, grass, and flowers. He leased the place with an option to buy at a predetermined price within six months.

After a couple of weeks of getting settled, Jonathan called a newspaper travel editor he knew and asked him to recommend a travel agency. At the travel agency he was referred to Mr. Robertson. Jonathan had seen travel agents before, but none quite like Mr. Robertson, a slender, six-foot-two, dignified gentleman, about sixty-three years old. He had sandy gray hair and patient gray eyes. Mr. Robertson greeted Jonathan in the manner of a visiting professor of comparative literature welcoming a graduate student in English to his class—very graciously and quietly consultative. He asked Jonathan where he currently lived.

Taking a seat on one of the pair of green leather chairs at Robertson's desk, Jonathan replied, "I've been living in the Watergate here in Washington for the past several years. But I've just moved across the river to McLean, Virginia."

Mr. Robertson leaned back in his chair and turned his pen end over end in his hands. "What trip have you in mind? And about how long do you plan to be gone?"

"I have no particular place in mind," Jonathan said quietly. "I just want to get lost for a month or so."

He wondered if the continental demeanor of Mr. Robertson indicated a forthcoming recommendation of a beach hotel at Dubrovnik, Yugoslavia, or possibly a new, English-operated hotel near Perth on the southwest coast of Australia. Either one, or anywhere for that matter, would have been fine with Jonathan.

Mr. Robertson asked pointedly, "Mr. Barron, are you planning this trip just for yourself? And when would you want to go?" He poised his pen over a multicolored note pad.

"I'll be going alone, and I could leave tomorrow or the next day," he answered.

Mr. Robertson put his pen down and looked across the office at some travel posters displayed on the far wall. He was thinking, like a travel doctor, about the special patient who had come to see him, who had a need to "get lost" for a month or so.

"It's the low point of the off-season in the Caribbean," he said, "but it could be very nice at certain hotels that would not be likely to have reservations readily available during regular seasons. I'm thinking of a small island, Virgin Biras, one of the British Virgin Islands. There is a fascinating hotel off by itself on its own bay, with wonderful beaches, very personal, efficient service, and food that one rarely finds of such variety and excellence. It's a Norwegian-owned inn, I think, called Somerset Creek, with small intimate individual cottages. At this time of year, it's a little warmer than

251

other months, but not unpleasant; temperatures range from about seventy-two degrees to the upper eighties. With waters on two sides of the promontory of land where the hotel is situated, there is usually a pleasant breeze. You might want one of the cottages located right on the beach. The one I occupied was so close to the water that, as the surf rolled in, the water sprinkled my bedroom windows. If you think you would like it, I'll phone them and make reservations. You would fly there via Miami and San Juan, Puerto Rico."

"Go ahead with all the arrangements," Jonathan said immediately, "and I'll come by after lunch and pick up the tickets. While I'm in the Caribbean, you might think of some other places that would be enjoyable. Since I plan to be in Los Angeles for Christmas, let's leave Australia and Yugoslavia until later."

Mr. Robertson looked at Jonathan and quickly replied, "I should have everything ready for you when you come by after lunch. I think you'll like the Somerset Creek Resort."

On his way to the British Virgin Islands, Jonathan stopped off in Miami, rented a car, and drove up to Boca Raton. He had previously checked out areas around Tallahassee, Gainesville, Sarasota, and Naples. Perhaps he might like Florida, if he accidentally found a spot that would not force him into spiritual leukemia. It occurred to him that if he lived near Florida Atlantic University, he might be able to work out a suitable research project there.

He checked into a motel for an overnight stay and called a number of friends in the area to say hello. Much to his surprise, the first thing they did was to express regret about his and Rene's separation. Apparently the first thing Rene had done when she arrived in California was to send a note to everyone on the family Christmas card list, so they would know about the upcoming divorce. Jonathan didn't care, but he wondered why Rene would think all their friends would care enough to justify instant notification. He could only speculate.

Maybe she felt that mutual friends would be more likely to sympathize with the separated wife. Maybe she was hoping there would be at least one friend who would prevail upon Jonathan to opt for separation over divorce. Or maybe she was heeding his advice that she marry again soon and was letting her friends know where to send prospects. Maybe she had previously been propositioned by some husbands she would now like to see, should they happen to visit California. He hoped this was not what she had in mind.

No matter, he thought. The quick notice to friends about the separation was a rather subjective response and maybe a little demeaning for such an outstanding woman. But then again, maybe it was her way of gaining strength and support for herself as she started a new life alone.

The next day he returned to Miami and flew to Puerto Rico. He elected to stay a day or so in San Juan and checked in at El Covento, the old hotel in "old" San Juan. There, the devil's agent for irritation caught up with him.

After placing his clothes in his room and changing his slacks, he walked up four or five steps at the end of the hallway to look at the patio area adjoining his room. Just as he started out to the patio, a brunette in a wrap-around, off-the-shoulder, coral-colored blouse and a white slit skirt walked down the steps from the patio into the hallway. Jonathan was a minute too late to have been on the patio alone with her, to draw her attention to the beauty of the ships in the harbor. Later, when he went for tortillas at Maria's, she was there with a handsome but tough-looking young man, obviously not her husband. The next morning at breakfast in the atrium cafe, she was sitting across the room. Later, when he was walking around El Morro, looking at the old fortifications, his dream brunette was entering one door as he was leaving. He would have preferred not to see such a beautiful woman at this stage of his readjustment to living alone again.

But some force always seems to make certain that a vulnerable man remains vulnerable. He felt that he was being assailed by annoying reminders of the delights of women. That brunette should have been dowdy and unnoticeable, but she had to be gorgeous and not alone, just to disturb his peace of mind.

To hell with pretty women, he thought, with a sour-grapes justification. A man can waste an awful lot of time with a woman.

The next day at two o'clock, he prepared to leave San Juan for Virgin Gorda, the third largest of the group of forty little islands constituting the British Virgin Islands. The plane was a Britton-Norman propeller aircraft with two Continental motors. Jonathan had ventured a guess that the engines were Lycoming.

When seven passengers congregated at the plane, most appeared surprised and a little uncertain. How could this little plane carry them with all their heavy, bulky luggage? The pilot probably wondered the same thing when he saw the luggage for two sets of honeymooners. But eventually, all the people and luggage were loaded, leaving enough room for the bright, wiry young pilot, who exuded so much personal assurance that all the passengers began to relax. It was a short trip, possibly only fifty minutes, more or less, and they flew low, maybe as low as one hundred fifty to two hundred feet above the water and well under any clouds. Jonathan could see schools of fish and dolphins.

Before they landed, Jonathan looked over and saw what he assumed was St. Thomas. He didn't want to disturb the quiet by asking the pilot, who was sitting within a few feet of everyone, what he was seeing. He just wanted to enjoy the view.

Shortly after landing, the luggage was unloaded, and Jonathan found that he was the only passenger for Somerset Creek. He hoped this didn't mean that he would be disappointed with the place. He got into a small four-wheel-drive bus with a pleasant native driver. They went about three hundred yards to a messy-looking garage with a fenced parking area. There, he and the driver loaded his luggage onto a four-wheel, Jeep-type bus, even smaller than the one he had just left, and headed somewhere. Jonathan didn't really care where.

The driver talked about his life and told him there were a thousand people or so on the whole island. A mile up the narrow road, they had to slow down because of a funeral procession. The driver said that half the native population was walking in this funeral procession behind a small pickup truck carrying a coffin.

"Who died?" Jonathan asked, as he watched the people trudging along behind the truck. "One of your most important citizens?"

"It was old Ben. Everybody knew old Ben," the driver replied. "He was ninety-four years old. Until the day he died, he cut weeds alongside the roads. That was his job for as long as I can remember. Everybody liked him. He was a good man and a hard worker all his life." Then he added rather sadly, "He was killed by a young hooligan." Jonathan wondered how many people in Washington or Paducah or Yakima would turn out for the funeral of an old weedcutter. He felt peaceful and was in no hurry to leave the funeral procession. But the procession eventually left him, as it turned into a little churchyard farther down the road.

Jonathan and the driver, Bob Winters, drove on for a few more miles to a bayside pier, about five feet wide and thirty feet long. There, he and Bob loaded the luggage into a small motorboat. Jonathan thanked Winters, said goodbye, and got into the motorboat. He soon found that his one-man crew certainly knew how to handle the boat, with its powerful outboard motor.

As they moved across the water away from the pier, he thought about how simple these people's lives appeared to be. He craved simple ways of living—the life of the jeep driver, the fellow in the motorboat, the weedcutter. These men were all doing useful work and at day's end knew what they had done. He remembered that when he was ten years old, he had cut weeds with a hand scythe along the roadway where his hand-pushed lawnmower couldn't do the job. That had been simple, rewarding work; he saw immediately the results of his efforts and easily measured how much he had accomplished at the end of a day. He seldom felt that way about the abstract work he had been engaged in for the past several years.

After circling around a couple of small islands, they came to the inlet of Somerset Creek and tied up to a fair-sized pier. A bellman was waiting to take the guest and his luggage directly to his cottage. Jonathan helped the bellman put the luggage into a motorized cart and off they went around the hill, on top of which the hotel offices, lounge, and restaurant were situated.

A row of cottages was located on the open-sea side of the hill. Jonathan's cottage was apparently the same one that Mr. Robertson, the travel agent, had occupied on his trip. It was quite pleasant, and so quiet; only the rhythm of the surf broke the silence. He unpacked, hung up all his clothes, washed up, and walked around the hill up to the hotel office. His reservation was in order, and the general clerk-assistant manager was hospitable. He said the manager would like to meet Jonathan at the seven o'clock cocktail hour. Apparently Mr. Robertson, the travel agent, had talked with him when he phoned to make the reservation.

Since seven o'clock was only forty minutes away, Jonathan talked with the not-very-busy bartender, ordered a martini, and walked outside to a large deck area overlooking the waters and hills. As he sat on the wide veranda of the hotel on top of the hill, the skies darkened and formed Rorschach-like figures above a bright pink curtain of sunset sky below them, like a Chinese tablecloth. Above the cloth of clouds, sitting around the table, were grotesque cloud figures. The cloud figures were very dark, but their softly attenuated edges let you know that they weren't going to do any harm, that they weren't villains, Jonathan thought. Their tops were crested with white clouds.

Two ships, a small three-masted sailing vessel, approximately forty-two feet long, and a sizable yacht, were anchored and silhouetted against a little mountain off an island at the end of the bay. The larger vessel had twinkling lights at the top of the foremast, mainmast, and mizzenmast.

As he looked to his left, he noticed the manager's house on the side of the nearest little mountain, glowing with many lights. Then all the lights went off at once, and the only thing he could see were the headlights of an automobile coming down the hillside road. The manager was leaving his home for his ceremonial rendezvous at the bar. Jonathan went inside, ordered another martini, and waited for him.

Mr. Strand, the manager, was a tall, well-built, once-blond, Norwegian man of about sixty. He had the charm and dignity of an old sea captain—a profession, it turned out, that had been his life. His wife, Inger, was an attractive, tall woman of rather good size. She was dressed flamboyantly, but beautifully, for the hotel dinner. Her gay mood and delightful manner went with her costume. Everyone seemed to enjoy making the manager and his wife the ceremonial king and queen of Somerset Creek.

Jonathan guessed that there were only about thirty or so guests, because of the season. The manager and his wife, Sven and Inge, as they wished to be called, introduced Jonathan to several of the guests, who were typically nice people, too nice to be as curious as Jonathan. Inge Strand was in charge of food service at the hotel, and Jonathan complimented her on her splendid selections and their excellent preparation. He thought back to his years in advertising, when he had had as clients two of the largest manufacturers of fine foods and frozen delicacies. That experience enabled him to appreciate readily the culinary achievements at Somerset Creek.

He spent the first couple of days at the island resort just walking around the area and along the beaches. Fishing was a local pastime. Although he had done some deep-sea fishing in his earlier years, he didn't care to do any now. He just wanted to be alone, and he knew that one shouldn't fish alone on ocean waters. It occurred to him that his next vacation excursion should include a small lake or stream for fishing by himself.

On the third day the manager, Sven Strand, came up to Jonathan as he was looking at a century plant that was in bloom. "That plant blooms once in its lifetime," Sven volunteered. "It takes eighteen years or more before a plant like this will bloom. Depends on the nourishment. The blooms yield the seed."

Jonathan empathized with the century plant. "How long do the blooms last, Sven?"

"Not long," the manager replied. "About three weeks. It is sad, because they bloom so rarely."

He gestured in the direction Jonathan was headed. "If you like, Mr. Barron, I'll hike along with you and show you some of the vegetation we have here."

"That would be wonderful. That's very kind of you, Sven. I'm Jonathan." As they walked on together, Jonathan reached out and touched a plant with bright red blossoms. "What are these prolific bloomers?"

"Those are frangipani, cultivated frangipani, a red jasmine. They bloom only once a year, but the flowers stay on for weeks. They stay in bloom so long that people sometimes think they bloom two or three times a year."

Sven turned to his left. "That tree you are near is called a pencil tree. They often grow fifty feet high."

As Jonathan walked with Sven, he wondered how this sea captain knew so much about vegetation. Sven answered Jonathan's thoughts by telling him how they could grow many things aboard the ship. "And in my youth, I helped my father in his nursery. He taught me a lot, and I inherited a love for flowers."

He stopped beside a singular-looking tree. "Note this tree. It's a wild nutmeg. There's lots of nutmeg in the Caribbean."

As they walked along, Sven called attention to whatever he thought was special. "Here's a Norfolk pine," he said as he rubbed his hands along the tree, as though calming a pet dog. Then he pointed out a species of hibiscus Jonathan had not seen before and plenty of bougainvillaea, West Indian almond trees, a gooseberry tree, a croton plant with large three-pronged leaves, and a tree Sven called a cotton tree. There were more different trees and plants than he had imagined possible on such a small island; each of them Sven introduced to Jonathan as a well-loved friend.

Sven is a fine man, a real man, Jonathan thought.

So many men in business or the professions, qualified in their specialities as Captain Strand had been, don't seem to think it macho to express love for and feel intimacy with a rose bush or a wild nutmeg tree. Admiring and absorbing beauty are really essential parts of being Man, not just being a man, he mused. As they circled back to the hotel, Jonathan expressed to Sven his deep appreciation for the tour and complimented him for retaining his sensitivity to beauty.

Jonathan preferred walking on the beaches and mountain paths to mingling with the guests, although he was politely cordial when he passed one out for a stroll. He didn't bother to play tennis, because he couldn't play well enough to interest strangers in politely challenging him. It didn't occur to him that there might be another guest who felt the same and who would make an appropriate partner for him. Often he would just sit on a rock at the edge of the water and feel and smell and hear the surf. The complex music of the surf helped him to shut out all other sounds—and he wished it could drown out other thoughts as well.

He didn't go into the water, though. Throughout his life he had swum very little. This week was no exception. As a four-year-old child, he had almost drowned in Catahoula Lake near his birthplace, and perhaps that was why he had never taken to water.

But he had two additional reasons for not liking to sit around swimming pools and popular beaches. He preferred privacy, which public beaches or club/condominium pools were seldom able to provide. He admired beauty in human form as well as in nature, but the mass of swim-suited humanity seldom lived up to his criteria for beauty. Often, those with the most bulging bodies wore the skimpiest swim-suits.

After a week of increasingly self-imposed solitude, enforced by so much beauty and no loved one with whom to share it, Jonathan thanked the managers and staff people and departed for Washington. He felt little better than when he had arrived, except for the residual enrichment from exposure to so many new plants and trees, and the added absorption of the music of the surf.

He arrived in Washington on Tuesday evening, September 1. The first thing he did after entering his apartment was to call Ellen. He should have called her earlier in the week to check on the progress her baby was making, but he took for granted that the baby would not be born before the first week of September, according to his prediction.

The phone rang only twice. Rene answered.

"Hello," she said.

"Hello, Rene, I just got back in town. How's Ellen?" Jonathan was never one to be indirect. "Is she in good condition? When is the baby's arrival expected, or has it arrived?"

"Ellen is fine," Rene hastened to say, "and the baby hasn't arrived, but it's expected within forty-eight hours. Isn't it exciting? I know you don't need any further assurance of your prescience, but it does appear now that your long-predicted birthdate will be proven correct."

She added with a sense of appreciation, "Even though you haven't been out here in California, Jonathan, you've comforted Ellen, in a way. It doesn't make sense to her, but she has faith in your prophecies, so she hasn't worried excessively about the baby's early arrival. She's really quite happy about everything.

"Here, just a minute. Hold the phone. She'll want to talk to you herself."

In a moment he heard Ellen's cheery voice.

"Hello, Dad. Glad you called. I do feel fine, and the doctor says I'm in good condition and will have a healthy baby in just a day or two, at most. Where are you, and what have you been doing?"

"Well, Ellen, I'm now in my new apartment in McLean, Virginia. You should have received a note with my new address and phone number on it by now," Jonathan said as he looked around at his familiar furniture in the new, not-so-familiar surroundings.

"Yes, Dad, I have. And I tried to call you a couple of days ago. Where were you?"

"I was trying to get lost in the British Virgin Islands at a very lovely resort hotel. My cottage was so close to the water that the surf sprayed the shutters on my bedroom windows. Someday you and Anson and your family should go there." He said softly, almost to himself, "It's too beautiful a place for one person to visit alone."

Not wanting to pull Ellen into a "feel-sorry-for-Dad-being-alone" mood, he said, "What's Mother's news? Has she moved into her new apartment yet?"

"Jonathan, I'm still on the phone," Rene interjected. "Yes, I moved in. Anson's mother came over and helped Ellen while I got settled. Everything arrived in good shape, and it's really a lovely apartment. I like being with Ellen, but I'm eager to go to my own new home, maybe even next week."

Without waiting for him to reply, she said, "So, you've been traveling? Will you be out here at Christmas to greet your first grandchild?"

Jonathan thought about Christmas. It seemed a long way off. But he said, "I'll try to do that, Rene. By that time, Ellen's daughter should be talking."

Rene didn't miss his new prediction.

"But how do you know it will be a daughter?"

"I don't know, Rene. That was just a spontaneous identification. Anyway, glad to know Ellen is fine and that you're all moved in. When do you start your new job?"

Rene hesitated and said a little reluctantly, "I don't definitely have a job or a starting time yet. But I've talked with the president of Southland University, and he says he still wants me. He believes the position he has in mind for me will be opening up by October 1. I certainly hope so, because the job he describes is just what I want."

Jonathan decided not to pursue Rene's occupational situation. Instead he said, "So, all is well in California. Call me as soon as the little wizard arrives. Tell me what she does when she greets you, Ellen." He added fondly, "I remember your first greeting to the outside world."

"I will, Dad. I'll call you as soon as I'm able. Goodbye."

"Goodbye, Jonathan."

"Goodbye," he said as he hung up the phone.

Before unpacking, he called Mr. Robertson at the travel agency and told him that Somerset Creek had been an excellent recommendation. Mr. Robertson was pleased and assured him that he could find other interesting and beautiful places for him to visit in the future.

Jonathan didn't say yes or no to the idea of further travel. He just thanked Mr. Robertson again and hung up. He certainly didn't plan to go to another depressingly beautiful place in the near future. He would do well to get to California for Christmas to see his new granddaughter.

Shortly thereafter, he went down to the desk to pick up his

accumulated mail and several magazines. It appeared that the post office was still doing its job.

It occurred to Jonathan that he should call Barbara Ballinger for a luncheon date. Barbara actually challenged him, which was a rare interpersonal occurrence for Jonathan.

# 26

Rene spent most of August at Ellen's, doing the necessary housework and usually getting everything ready for dinner so that when Anson arrived home from work, she could return to her apartment. During the evenings, she shopped for additional pieces of furniture or whatever she needed to complete her decorating and organizing. Her apartment was now a very attractive place, with pillows and pictures, rugs and vases, all arranged to create a warm and relaxing atmosphere.

She had another get-acquainted dinner with Dr. Spirirson, who said she had been a great deal of help to him in formulating the job description and determining how the niche for the new position would relate in rank and salary to the functions of other departments at the university. Rene welcomed the opportunity to help sketch out her own job. Her experiences at Carolina State were very applicable, and she was pleased that the professional qualifications for the new position at Southland actually coincided with her own. She truly believed she had been as objective as she could be.

She was also glad that her personal qualifications seemed to please Dr. Spirrison. Because they were both responsible professionals, she was sure that neither she nor Spirrison would confuse personal and professional requirements.

Rene thought that Arnold might like to see her new apartment and be her first dinner guest. The completeness of her newly established dwelling would indicate that she was prepared to stay for a long while. She thought this would be an important factor in the job plans. But because she wanted to arrange a very special dinner for him, she didn't feel free to do so until after Ellen had her baby.

Rene didn't have to wait long for Ellen. The twenty-four- to forty-eight-hour estimate Ellen had told her father about on Tuesday evening proved quite accurate. On Thursday morning at scven-thirty, Anson called Rene and said that he had taken Ellen to the hospital at about six forty-five and that Ellen was well into labor. The attending doctor estimated the baby's arrival for early afternoon. Anson told Rene he had called his mother, and she wanted Rene to meet her at the hospital around nine o'clock. Rene said she would be there and asked if Ellen seemed to be calm and doing all right.

"Ellen's happy as hell that the baby's finally decided to show up, and so am I," Anson said emphatically. Then he said quickly, "I'll be seeing you and Mom soon."

Rene knew he was eager to get back to Ellen, but she thought she should warn him about first-time grandmothers. "What a glorious day, Anson. When your mother and I arrive, be prepared for us to act like we're the ones having the baby, but without the labor. See you at nine."

Rene was happy for Ellen and Anson and was pleased that everything was going smoothly. She would need to keep her fingers crossed just a little longer.

Laura was born at 1:45 in the afternoon. She was a very active young lady of reasonable size—seven pounds—and was definitely a blonde, with a glistening over-tone of strawberry sheen, like her mother and Rene. Her facial features were perfect and were more clearly delineated than those of many new babies. The unanimous verdict of the parents and grandparents present was that she certainly didn't look like every other baby.

Everyone was ecstatic, especially Ellen, who had come through in fine shape. Anson called Jonathan and told him he now had a granddaughter named Laura, and that mother and daughter were doing fine. Jonathan was very pleased and, congratulating his son-in-law, asked him when he might speak to Ellen.

"I don't know exactly. Since Ellen didn't have any anesthetic, she'll probably be in her room within two or three hours. The hospital isn't crowded now, so she'll be alone in a double room. Will you be home this evening?" Anson asked.

"Yes, all evening."

"Good! Ellen will want to call you just as soon as she can. I can't say exactly, of course, but look for a call from her around eight or nine o'clock your time."

"Thanks so much, Anson, for giving me the wonderful news," Jonathan said warmly. "I'm very pleased, especially for you and

263

Ellen, and I'm relieved to hear that all went well. I suppose your mother and Rene are right there."

"Oh, yes, Mom and Dad and Rene have been here for hours. In fact, I've had quite a problem keeping them pacified. One would think a first grandchild is a bigger deal than a first child."

"I know what you mean, Anson. I'll be waiting for a call from Ellen when she's feeling up to it and when it's convenient for her. Goodbye."

"Goodbye."

As soon as Anson returned from calling Jonathan, Rene asked him what his father-in-law had to say and if he were excited. Anson told her that Jonathan was very calm, but very pleased, and added that he wouldn't really expect Jonathan to be too excited, since everything—time of birth and sex of the baby—had gone according to his predictions.

That information reminded Rene of the special qualities of her soon-to-be ex-husband. She appreciated all those characteristics of Jonathan and thought that even now, if she had to be left alone on a desert island with any one man of her choosing, she would prefer Jonathan, with all his talents and sagacity. She knew that she could depend on him to figure out a way to get food and build a house, even out of seashells and sand.

The label "ex-husband" rang in her ears. She knew she might just as well become accustomed to identifying Jonathan as her ex-husband, even though the final divorce decree was still a few months off. But the thought of him as her ex-husband was rather disquieting. She decided she would try not to use the term. She would simply call him Jonathan, from whom she would soon be divorced. And she wouldn't talk about him unless absolutely necessary.

It was so different for her to be completely on her own, to be free to see men who weren't so mentorish, who hadn't brought her up—although they might not be as exciting, even in making love, as Jonathan. Rene knew she could make a male mannequin respond if she really wanted to, and if she could satisfy Jonathan, almost any other man would be easy to master. With that feeling of confidence, she went to a pay phone near the hospital gift shop and called Dr. Spirrison.

"Hello," she said as soon as the phone was answered, "this is Rene Barron. Is Dr. Spirrison available?"

264

"Yes, he is, Mrs. Barron," the secretary replied. "He tried to reach you just a few minutes ago. Can you hold? He'll be with you as soon as he finishes another call."

While Rene was waiting, she put her mini-notebook back into a side zipper pocket on her purse. So Arnold had been trying to call her. She wondered if she and Arnold had been thinking the same thing.

Dr. Spirrison came on the line and greeted her warmly. "Hello, Rene, I called you earlier thinking that, if you were available Saturday for dinner, we might finish our discussion of your new position. It looks like October 1 will be okay."

Rene smiled to herself. This was looking like a day of extraordinarily good news.

"That's wonderful, Arnold. I think I can do a good job for you, and I'm eager to begin. But regarding dinner on Saturday—could I persuade you to come to my new apartment and be my very first dinner guest? I'll fix you a steak and vegetables Mornay. But first we can celebrate my new job and new home with champagne. I gave you my apartment address when we had dinner in Malibu. Do you still have it handy?"

"Yes, I do. What time will you start serving champagne?"

"How does six-thirty suit you?"

"I'll be there ringing apartment twenty-four at six-thirty." He paused and then said, "I'm looking forward to seeing you. Goodbye."

"I'm so glad you can come, Arnold. Goodbye."

As Rene hung up the phone and went back to wait for Ellen to be taken to her room, she felt a little guilty for not having told Arnold that she was a brand-new grandmother. But she thought discussing grandmotherhood wouldn't help promote the romantic mood she hoped she and Arnold were sharing. Of course, Arnold was already twice a grandfather, and she would tell him about Ellen's baby when she saw him. She didn't think being an acknowledged grandmother would change her own feelings, and she couldn't imagine that it would change the feelings of an older man, whether or not he were a grandfather. But just to be on the safe side, she wasn't going to put "grandmother" on her calling card, any kind of calling card.

Rene was looking forward to visiting Ellen. She rejoined Anson's parents, Esther and Charlie, happy to be sharing the joy of the new grandchild with them. It wasn't long until the new grandmothers were hugging and kissing Ellen and congratulating her on having such a beautiful and obviously precocious child.

The nurse soon suggested that the grandparents run along, because she wanted to bring the baby in for Ellen, and according to hospital rules, visitors were not allowed while the baby was with the mother. They were told they could come back to visit with Ellen after the baby was returned to the nursery. As they were leaving, the doctor came by to say that Ellen should plan to stay in the hospital until Sunday afternoon. He said that they could visit her daily if they wished but advised them to delay any extended visiting until mother and child were home.

Rene was delighted with her perfect granddaughter and was pleased that, after all the uncertainty, Ellen had come through in good shape.

She was also very happy about her conversation with Dr. Spirrison and his recommendation that she start her new job October 1. That was another uncertainty removed. When she thought about her upcoming Saturday dinner date, she was as excited as she had been before her first real date in high school; this was going to be her first real date as a free woman. Being separated and in the process of divorce, she believed she had every right to consider herself a free woman.

Rene decided she would prepare a lovely dinner, served with candlelight and crystal, for Arnold. Now she wished she hadn't suggested that Jonathan keep their Steuben collection. But she hoped no man invited to her apartment would be likely to notice the glassware for long.

As Rene drove her new car into her own apartment garage that afternoon, she felt really free. As she entered the intimate-looking apartment, she thought how it contrasted with any decorative plan Jonathan would have approved. For one thing, he would never have so many useless pillows lying around. He would consider them too bourgeois. He liked the finest of furnishings, but simple and uncluttered; he didn't even want family pictures hovering over him.

Yes, her life was now her own. But with the beginning of her new freedom came a touch of uncertainty, maybe a little fear, at being completely on her own after thirty years of guidance and support from Jonathan.

I must get over all that, Rene thought. Jonathan had a full life when he was a widower, with all his television shows, artist bookings, and glamorous advertising life. No one should object if I enjoy life, now that I'm on my own. After all, I have an attractive new apartment, a new car, and a new job.

In addition, Rene had an independent income and other, more personal, assets. She knew she was still pretty, because her husband had said so, and she knew she was a fantastic lover, because she had been able to please him. In fact, Jonathan had often said she couldn't really know how good a lover she had become, but now she was certainly going to find out. What she hadn't done at nineteen, she would do now. And she intended to do it much better than any nineteen- or twenty-nine- or thirty-nine-year-old woman ever thought of doing. She had read every how-to book she could find on making love. If Jonathan said she had become as good at sex as Mindy, she thought she must be very good indeed.

But Rene still lacked confidence. The first time could be a little awkward. And awkwardness was the last thing she wanted with Arnold. Because she had been celibate since leaving Jonathan, she thought that perhaps she should practice on someone less important in her life than Arnold Spirrison. Then she thought of her landlord. He was about her age, or a little younger. He had been very attentive and helpful. Only yesterday he'd left a note telling her he would come by her apartment Friday morning to explain the new thermostat that had been installed. He hadn't mentioned it, but she appreciated his having put new, beige-colored miniblinds in her bedroom. The more Rene thought about him, the more she concluded that he should be her first encounter as a free woman.

At about nine-thirty on Friday morning, she had finished her breakfast and was having coffee and reading the *Chronicle,* when the soft chime of her doorbell sounded. By purposeful chance, she was wearing a very low-cut satin lounging costume. In fact, there was no fastener on top until its two sides were brought together by a pretty waistband. She felt just right for a conquest and greeted her landlord with a youthful gaiety. The landlord, Dan Jordan, was dressed in sports clothes and looked quite happy himself.

"Come on in, Dan," Rene said as she opened the door and waved an arm to encompass the room. "I like my apartment better each day. Will you join me for coffee? I have some fresh, all ready to serve."

"Sure, Rene, I'd love a cup." He sat down at a small table in the living room. Dan couldn't keep his eyes off Rene's bosom, since both breasts were partially exposed every time she moved.

Rene noticed his preoccupation.

"You like my outfit? It's for coffee or cocktails."

"I sure do! I sure do!" Dan said as if he couldn't believe his eyes.

As Rene went into the adjoining kitchen to get another cup and pour the coffee, Dan got up, followed her, and stood gawking over her to get as full a glimpse as he could without touching anything.

Rene stopped pouring the coffee when the cup was only about half-full and asked laughingly, "Dan, are you sure you want coffee, or would you prefer milk?"

"Frankly," Dan laughed, "if your breasts weren't so pretty, I wouldn't be so spellbound. I'll take coffee now, but may I give you a welcoming kiss to Jordan Arms apartments?"

Rene put the coffee down and turned around as Dan put his arms around her and kissed her, a nice, welcoming kiss, then a warm, friendly kiss, then an open-mouth, hot kiss as he cupped one of her breasts with his left hand.

"What incredibly luscious nipples, Rene. I think I'll have milk instead of coffee," he said quickly, as he leaned over and kissed the breast he was holding.

Rene slowly turned back to the coffee and said, "Dan, you may need a strong cup of coffee to give you the strength to show me the thermostat."

Holding two cups of coffee, she said, "Let's go back to the table. But while we drink our coffee, I hope you'll be able to keep up your enthusiastic spirit until we go back to my bedroom to see the new blinds your carpenter installed for me. I certainly appreciate all the things you've done to make this such a nice apartment."

Dan sat down by the table, and Rene said very nonchalantly, "Here, let me make you more comfortable now, or you won't enjoy my fresh coffee."

She knelt in front of Dan and unzipped his pants. She was obviously pleased with what she saw, because she kissed it, but then got right up and calmly started drinking her coffee.

Dan was so excited he could scarcely lift his cup to his mouth.

"Ah, hell, Rene, let's go now." With that request, he got up and

268

went to Rene, kissed her, lifted her from the chair, and with one arm around her, guided her down the hall.

As soon as they were in the bedroom, she helped Dan undress and had the usual pleasant difficulty getting his shorts off over the obstruction she had raised. But neither one minded.

She pulled the bedspread back, and Dan gladly sat on the edge of the bed. He simply couldn't believe that this gorgeous woman was giving him something better than he had ever hoped to receive. They quickly stretched out on the bed, just in time. All in all, Rene's first conquest as a free woman seemed to be a big success. The truth was, it was too easy and too fast.

After they were up and dressed, Rene said, as she walked Dan back to the living room, "Dan, you were wonderful, but you know we can't, we mustn't, do this again."

"Yes, Rene. Lord, if I made love with you again, I'd never want to go home. But I wouldn't have missed your loving for anything. Right now, just the leftover feelings are making me tingle. No, I agree! Rene, I'll stay away for your good and mine. But I hope you'll have pleasant memories, too, when you think of your landlord, just as I will when I think of number twenty-four."

"Dan," Rene said jokingly, "you mean I'm the *twenty-fourth* tenant you've made love to in this building?"

"No! No! I mean your apartment number," he said, blushing.

"I know, silly. Now, shall we check the thermostat? My own has subsided from the boiling-over point."

"Mine will, too, when I get out of here," Dan said. "But let's take a look at the thermostat on the wall over there."

He gestured toward the doorway between the living room and the bedroom hall, and they both walked in that direction. The thermostat seemed to be working perfectly. Rene thanked him for being so thoughtful in getting her a new one. Dan went on about his proper landlord responsibilities, and Rene sat down for a little more coffee, marveling at how excited she could make a man. She knew Dan had been amazed and amazingly pleased.

Now she was glad, very glad, that Jonathan had inspired her to be good at everything she did. She knew he was probably not getting what he was accustomed to receiving from her. She knew that their intense sexual satisfaction with one another had kept them from separating at least two or three years before they had actually decided to live apart.

Rene thought about the deep conflict Jonathan must have felt, believing that they would both be better off separated, yet knowing he would have to give up the great joy and temporary release from depression her sexuality had brought him.

Although she hoped they could, she doubted that they would remain close friends, when so much of their togetherness had derived from intense lovemaking. Their external social interests were too different.

Rene felt exuberantly confident about the future. She knew now that Jonathan was right when he said older women should not only develop sexual artistry, but should also learn to enjoy sex intensely.

He also said young women and young men should develop more of the old romantic spirit in order to make sex glorious. But they probably just didn't know how.

Rene thought about her encounter with Dan. He was too easy. She would have to be slower and a little more careful with Arnold. She knew she could satisfy him more than any lover he had ever had, probably including any of the young graduate students. Rene felt that she was a woman who could share enough with him to satisfy this mature, intelligent man who had a choice of choices.

# 27

Rene smiled as she thought about how she had begun her day. Jonathan wouldn't like this expression, but she felt she had really "started it off with a bang." While the glow of satisfaction remained, she decided to go shopping. She was thinking about buying a hostess dress to wear for her dinner with Arnold.

Rene was feeling rather smug about her sexuality. She was even beginning to feel that she could prompt any man to want to possess her. She found that she loved the surprise effect of her unexpectedly surpassing talent. Dan had acted like he couldn't believe it.

She also found that she enjoyed making a man feel incredibly good and, because she enjoyed his pleasure, she found she experienced a great deal of satisfaction also. Then too, during lovemaking she was in total control of her man. Consequently, she was eagerly anticipating other conquests. Any man she would want would be smart enough to enjoy the game of who gets whom into bed, but Rene was looking forward to calling the plays. Now that she was accomplished in sexuality, enjoyed it, and was free, all on her own, she intended to make up for those lost virgin years before she had married Jonathan.

Rene had to give Jonathan credit. He had helped to fashion her into a distinctive and distinguished woman, to use his words, in accordance with his Old South desire to put women on pedestals. She was grateful to him for that. How patient he had been with her sexual education. But now Rene wanted to jump down from the pedestal he had placed her on into a big bed with a big man.

She went shopping but failed to find anything nearly as glamourous as the outfit she had worn that morning for Dan. She knew it wasn't the most appropriate morning wear, but her intention had been to give Dan the idea that she wanted him to have her very quickly. She bought a few other items, including a new perfume. After she returned to her apartment, however, she decided to use one of the fragrances Jonathan had once selected for her.

She searched through her jewelry and came up with an exquisite bluish-green cameo, a rare gem that had been mounted on the center of a delicate gold rectangular frame. It had been given to her by Jonathan's older sister. It was so petitely feminine, so Victorian in its modesty, it would be ideal to wear about halfway, or maybe two-thirds of the way, down the open blouse front of her satin "coffee" costume. Rene thought that the tantalizing association of her bosom with the old-fashioned, but very lovely, brooch might prove to be as quickly seductive with Arnold's more abstract intellectuality and sophistication as the completely open front had been with Dan.

The gorgeous, flowing satin costume was made to be worn when serving champagne. Jonathan had bought it for her to wear at a small New Year's Eve party they had given the year before they moved from Church City. For a moment she was back in their wonderful home, drinking a champagne toast in front of the huge fireplace. She felt sudden, unexpected tears as she pictured the scene and the New Year's kiss. "No," she said to herself, "he wanted me to go, and I'm gone."

With that thought of resolution, she decided to go to the hospital to see Ellen and her new granddaughter. She was proud of the new baby and was pleased to be a grandmother, but she wasn't going to flaunt it. There *are* grandmotherly grandmothers, but that description didn't fit her looks or her feelings.

Once in her car and on her way to see baby Laura, Rene began to think about contemporary grandparents from the standpoint of the grandchildren. She wondered whether current crops of grandchildren were losing out because grandparents were so busy with their own renewed and expanding lives that they had a good deal less traditional grandparenting time to spend with the new generation. She knew that grandparents were generally living longer and remaining active outside their homes longer than in earlier years. And she also knew that improved health care and the changing behavioral patterns of society combined to make it all right for older people to play, to participate in sports, games, and—yes—sex. What she didn't know was how the grandchildren would be affected and influenced by these changes.

Then she thought about her own grandparents and her parents as her children's grandparents. Yes, she said almost aloud, there definitely has been a change in how some older people perceive themselves. Why, look at Jonathan! He's never quit learning new things and entering new areas of personal and business activity.

It occurred to her that while she was growing up with Jonathan, he had remained a perpetual forty-year-old, mentally and physically, and she could certainly attest to his continued virility. Now that she was moving into her fifties, she felt she might at long last be able to be a partner for him. Rene thought to herself, another man like Jonathan who is also a socially compatible person would be hard, if not impossible, to find.

Rene realized that Jonathan had known for several years that she would enjoy living on her own, but she wasn't at all sure that he could take their separation without a deep sense of loss. She wondered how he was doing. She knew his priorities were for her happiness, not living just for himself, and for that he had made a considerable sacrifice. He had a sense of responsibility for other people as well to himself. Yet, he would never see framed in his mirror the person he wanted to be.

On the other hand, many older people she knew and liked refused to take responsibility for the world in which their grandchildren would live. They simply didn't think about life that deeply. They were probably still looking for the end of the rainbow and living from day to day. A lot of them were fascinated with being with people, lots of people, ordinary or otherwise. Perhaps that would be her life, Rene mused. Maybe most people just wanted to float along instead of making the effort to swim. She didn't know if that was bad or not. But she did know that many people lived that way, so it must be okay, at least for them.

Rene had been so absorbed in her thoughts that her arrival at the hospital was almost a surprise to her. She parked her car in the closest lot, after waiting for an attractive older woman in a bright red dress and a matching red compact car to pull out of a space. As she fairly flew up the entrance steps, Rene was aware of a new sense of energy and enthusiasm in her walk.

Ellen was happy to see her mother. Rene was delighted to find the baby visiting Ellen, but that didn't last long. The nurse soon entered and took Laura back to the nursery. Rene helped Ellen arrange her pillows and then pulled a chair up closer to Ellen's bed.

Ellen looked tired. She put her head back on the pillow and closed her eyes. Rene didn't say anything for a minute or two.

Then Ellen looked over and smiled a happy-new-mother smile.

"How is Anson surviving, now that he has the responsibility of fatherhood?" Rene asked.

"Oh, he's doing fine, Mom. But I'm not sure he realizes yet that Laura's going to live with us for a long time to come. I'm not sure I do either, for that matter. He acts like she's a doll that we have to return after Christmas." She laughed. "Wait until he's changed a couple of hundred diapers."

With a more serious tone in her voice, Ellen said, "I'm so happy that Anson is as happy as I am about Laura. Mother, don't you think she's a pretty baby?"

"Ellen, I thought you were about as pretty as a baby could be, and now I think the same about Laura. She may be like Anson, too, but she really looks exactly like you did. I need to find your baby pictures and show you."

"Speaking of pictures, Mom, why don't you come over next week and take some pictures that I can send to Dad? I don't think he'll come out to see Laura before Christmas. I'd take some, but you seem to come up with better shots than I do."

"I'll be glad to do that, because I'll want several for myself, especially with you and Anson holding Laura."

Rene thought Ellen looked wonderful, but she knew she needed to rest while the baby slept. So even though their visit had been short, she picked up her purse and got ready to leave. She told Ellen she would phone her on Saturday, and, if Ellen wished, she would bring over frozen vegetables Mornay and prepare dinner for them on Sunday. "Perhaps Anson's parents would like to come over, too," Rene suggested.

"Mom, I would like you to come over and help with dinner on my first day home, but wouldn't it be too much to have dinner for five—or six, I should say?"

"You're probably right, especially your first night home. Why don't I just drop by to see you about dinnertime—around six or seven. You'll probably be home from the hospital by three. I'll bring you the Mornay, and Anson can cook a steak for the two of you." As she walked toward the door, Rene said, "But I'll be talking with you before then.

"And by the way, you and the baby are looking great, Ellen. Do you feel as well as you look?"

274

"Pretty good, Mom. But I'm a little tired. I'll be talking to you," Ellen said sleepily.

Rene walked back and gave her daughter a kiss. She left feeling that all was right with her world.

The first thing Saturday morning, Rene checked her grocery needs and went shopping. She got all her vegetables and the steaks. At the liquor store, she bought several bottles of champagne and a couple of different brandies. She already had plenty of gin and vermouth. She had a notion that Arnold might bring her some roses, but she bought an assortment of brightly colored flowers to put on the stand between her dining alcove and the living room, just in case he didn't. Furthermore, if he was thoughtful enough to bring flowers, he would notice her own bouquet and perhaps feel that he had really surprised her by bringing roses. Anyway, better two vases than none. She decided that if Arnold should happen to bring her flowers, she would put them in the number one spot in the living room, where anyone in her sofa circle could see them.

She wanted to make a good impression on Arnold, personally and professionally. Efficiency at home implies efficiency anywhere. She wanted to demonstrate her efficiency in everything—business, cooking, entertaining, loving, and whatever it took to assure him that any job she was given would be done well. She even decided not to smoke, for fear the smell might bother him. She would wait and see. One additional thing was certain. She wanted the satisfying impression she could make in the bedroom to be a bonus to him.

Saturday evening finally arrived.

When Arnold called from the entrance phone, she pressed the door opener, and he started up in the elevator. She didn't wait for him to ring her door chimes but stood at her open door and greeted him as he came down the hallway. He looked handsome and impressive.

"Arnold, I'm so glad you're here. You look wonderful. Come on in." She noticed that he had a long white box under his left arm.

"Rene," Arnold said as he leaned over to respond to her hello kiss, "I brought something to compliment your beauty." And he handed her the box.

"Oh, did you bring me roses? How sweet! Thank you so much."

And she kissed him briefly. She closed the door and walked across the living room. Arnold followed and stood in the kitchen doorway watching her.

"Let me get a vase," Rene said. She "found" the vase she just happened to have handy. As she arranged the flowers, she wondered if they were a professional welcome or a personal gift, or both. She would just have to wait and see. Regardless of Arnold's intent, the dark red, long-stemmed roses were really something.

As she filled the vase with water, she said, "Arnold, they are just so beautiful, so lovely. They're the first roses I've received for my California home."

He moved out of the doorway as he smiled warmly at Rene, and she carried the vase back into the living room.

"Just look at them," Rene said, as she placed them on her Baker commode.

"They do look great, Rene. And that's the perfect spot for them. Let me look at your new apartment. This living room is certainly distinctively furnished and so invitingly decorated. I like that long, curved sofa. What do you have—two bedrooms?"

Rene was at her very best.

"Arnold, you must want to make sure that my living arrangements are comfortable so I'll do good work for you. Let me pour the champagne, and I'll show you a desk I believe you'll like."

Rene got the champagne glasses out of the refrigerator and handed the champagne to Arnold; he opened it with just the right "pop." He handed the bottle to her for the pouring. Then she handed him a glass and took hers.

"Welcome," they both started to say, but laughed at themselves and drank to one another.

"I'll show you my office, which could be used as a second bedroom." They walked down the hall and entered her office. "Here's the desk I like so much. Have you seen one of these Danish folding desks? Just look at the drawer space and writing area. Yet, it all folds into a beautiful teak cabinet."

"I've never seen a desk like that, Rene. How does it fold?"

She placed her champagne on an end table, removed several books and a yellow pad of paper, and demonstrated the desk. This was not the routine she had planned, but she felt complimented that Arnold was showing so much business interest in her, as though they were already working together.

276

After showing him the desk, Rene took Arnold to the large corner bedroom, her bedroom. Arnold glanced around and said, "This is really attractive. Where did you get that magnificent bedspread? It's the finest I've ever seen—not that I've seen many bedspreads, you know."

"Of course, Arnold, I know you don't have time to shop for bedspreads. But if you did, you wouldn't find one like this. I had it made for me in North Carolina at a big textile outlet store."

They moved quickly out of the bedroom into the hallway and back to the living room. Arnold seated himself on the sofa and put his champagne glass on the long coffee table. As soon as she saw that he was seated, Rene brought the champagne in a silver bucket of ice. She poured more for him and filled her own glass. Then she sat down on the curved end of the sofa so she could face him comfortably.

"How am I going to speed this up with him over there and me here?" she wondered. "But I like this comfortable, friendly relationship. Give the champagne time and let him talk. He seems to want an audience more than a woman right now."

Arnold sat back on the sofa looking perfectly at home, drinking his champagne by drafts, not sips. "Arnold, you look comfortable, and I'm glad, because if you had a faculty committee meeting it's going to take you a while to unwind. I don't believe the faculty at one university differs much from that at another. Let me take your jacket and hang it up," she said as she got up. "And don't worry about putting your feet on the coffee table. It has a tough coating on it."

Arnold liked her solicitous attention. He got up and removed his coat. As he gave it to her, he kissed her nicely and said, "Thank you." As Rene hung up his coat, he settled back down and said, "So you guessed I've been to a faculty committee meeting. I have, but I didn't know it showed."

"You know, Rene, faculties are the producers of a university's product. They sow the seeds of learning and nurture the garden of students, in whose minds and hearts the seeds hopefully fall." He sat back down. "But it's amazing how little faculties know about administration and organization and how to be constructively co-operative. Even in the business schools that I've observed here and elsewhere, organizational efficiency standards are often so low, it's fortunate that industry leaders are accustomed to making allow-

277

ances for academia. But as an administrator, I can't make every allowance the faculty seems to want."

Then he sighed. "I'll tell you, Rene, you and the roses over there and the pretty pin you're wearing and the champagne will soon remove faculty problems from my mind. Have you had any other ideas about the duties we could add to your position?"

"There is one duty that you can add now, Arnold. I must help you forget some of these daily pin pricks."

Arnold smiled. "I'd just like to forget some of the pricks on our faculty. But speaking of pins, your cameo reminds me of one my grandmother had. May I look at it?"

Rene acted as if she were having difficulty removing the brooch. As she unpinned it, she leaned over to hand it to Arnold. He was so distracted by her open blouse that his hand missed her hand, which held the pin. Rene pretended not to notice but moved alongside Arnold to let him examine the brooch.

"If he's intentionally using this 'grandmother pin' story to get me to remove it," she thought, "he's much more subtle than some men."

And that cleverness might have been true, because Arnold reminded her in a way of Jonathan, a pleasant reminder derived from Jonathan's habit of creativity. Of course, Jonathan would have had a grandmother's pin. But Arnold wouldn't make up a story either, she concluded.

Arnold appeared to be fascinated with the pin. It was almost exactly like one his mother-in-law had given his wife, he said. He hadn't seen his wife's pin for a long time. Instead of returning the pin to Rene to put on again, he placed it on the far end of the coffee table. Rene observed the careful placement of the pin, which was now out of her reach.

"Arnold's pretty clever," she thought. "If I reach over and pick up the pin and put it back on to fasten my blouse together, he may conclude that I've said no. But if I pay no attention to his careful placement of the pin, I may literally be making it hard for him without having to commit myself. Guess that leaves the balls in his court," she said to herself, with a touch of glee.

She found Arnold very interesting, aside from the fact that he was a potential sexual prospect. She carefully brought the conversation back to business to see if he would remain stuck on business while he was looking at her rather open blouse.

"Arnold, I studied your quarterly newsletter for the MBA program. I think it does the job, but I believe you and I both know it needs improvement."

"It sure does," Arnold agreed.

"Well," Rene continued, "in addition to improving both the graphics and the content of the quarterly, have you given any thought to the possibility of creating an internal newsletter that could be distributed to the junior and senior undergraduate economics and business administration majors, and to the students in the graduate school?"

Arnold was nodding and sipping his champagne. He was listening to her professionally. Rene decided to continue with her idea.

"You know, Arnold, some of the best prospects for your MBA program may already be here in an undergraduate program that might lead them to get their MBA somewhere else instead of staying here. It could give undergraduate business-oriented students something in common with graduate business students, serving to increase their loyalty and preference for Southland.

"An internal news bulletin should be brief and inexpensive and should be published monthly. I believe there might be a half-dozen schools already doing something like this. If you approve, I could check into their experience."

Arnold put his glass on the table in front of him.

"I think that proposal would be very good for Southland right now. It could not only do the things you mentioned, but it would give us another showcase for both faculty and students. Let's have a meeting and discuss it after October 1."

Then Arnold smiled warmly and said as he reached for her glass, "I'll put your champagne right where I would very much like you to be."

He placed her glass next to his and stood to welcome his now totally non-business friend to her seat, almost in his lap. It wasn't long until that was exactly where she was sitting, after a long, deeply satisfying, and not very businesslike kiss. Rene could feel that Arnold was rising to the occasion.

"Rene, let's move toward the corner of the curve in the couch so I can hold you in my arms and you can put your feet up and stretch out. I've endured not holding you as long as I can.

"You're a very appealing woman and bright as hell," he said almost breathlessly. "I'm as honored as I am excited."

279

Rene smiled and nestled down in his arms.

"I'm so pleased that you're pleased. Shall we finish up the champagne?"

Arnold answered by pouring the last of the bottle and filling both glasses. There was a moment of comfortable silence between them.

"Are you getting hungry, Arnold?" Rene asked. "I have dinner already cooked except for broiling the steaks."

"Rene," Arnold said softly, "I'll answer that with the lyrics of a country music ballad—I'm only hungry for you." With that, he kissed her intensely, slowly caressing her body as far as he could reach while holding her in his arm. And when he had reached as far as he could, his hand came slowly back to hold her breast.

Just as the other men had told her, Arnold commented very softly, "Your nipples are perfect, irresistibly enticing."

Rene responded casually to Arnold's teasing compliment and soft, warm touch, "You know, from what I've been feeling, I think I should make you more comfortable, too."

She slid her hands down and unzipped his pants. Rene handled him gently. Dignified as he was, he couldn't refrain from exclaiming, "Oh, God, Rene, you can't be real."

Rene took one more sip of champagne. For some time thereafter, they were both speechless.

Eventually that evening, Rene and Arnold, two hungry friends and lovers, sat down to enjoy their medium broiled steaks, cooked the way both preferred, and lots of Rene's vegetables Mornay. For dessert, there were fresh strawberries and cream.

Having experienced a completely satisfying emotional and physical release, Rene and Arnold were relaxed and happy at dinner as they discussed a wide spectrum of topics and shared interests.

With the coffee, Rene brought up a question that had been on her mind the day she and Arnold had made the dinner date, the day Laura was born.

"Arnold," she asked, "over the years that you've been separated, have you ever gone to bed with a grandmother?"

"Now, that's a question out of the blue," Arnold laughingly replied, knowing Rene wouldn't ask it just to be asking. "I can't say that I have, and that's a real confession.

"My wife and I have two grandchildren. But since we've become grandparents, we've not had sex together. It's rather strange that you would ask. But it was a good way to learn more about my relations with my faraway wife."

"That's not why I asked the question, Arnold," Rene said almost shyly, "although I appreciate your feeling free to tell me. What I want you to know is that now you can no longer say that you've never made love with a grandmother. On Thursday afternoon, my daughter gave birth to my extraordinarily beautiful granddaughter."

Arnold rose from his chair, went over to Rene, and kissed her. "If I ever meet a woman so gloriously beautiful and sexually satisfying again—if there could be another, which I doubt—the first thing I'd say to her would be, 'I hope you're a grandmother.'

"Rene, that's terrific. Congratulations for being a new grandmother—and for being as you are. Now we have something else in common!"

He kissed her gently and returned to his chair and coffee.

Rene smiled and said, "Thank you, fellow grandparent."

Arnold sat quietly for a few moments and then seemed to awaken from deep thought. "Rene, I realize you've been separated for only a short time, but may I ask if you think you'll get married again?"

Rene beamed at Arnold's having quietly developed the gumption to ask her the question at this particular time. With an obvious lack of seriousness, she replied, "Oh, I don't know, Arnold. It's too soon to tell. Why? Did you have a prospect for me?"

"No, Rene. You should have someone less burdened with things than I am. I was just thinking what a shame it would be if you didn't marry again." Arnold seemed a little self-conscious about prying into her personal life.

But Rene kept the conversation light. "Well, I guess that takes you off my prospect list," she said, with an ostentatious sigh of sadness. "No, Arnold, I don't plan to marry for a good while, no matter who I meet. I want to live on my own for a time. I've been on stage for so long as Jonathan Barron's wife that I just want to enjoy, even savor, being in the balcony. That's why I wish Jonathan had been willing to agree to a separation. I could have been comfortable in the balcony or standing in the wings and remained married to him."

Despite Rene's attempt at levity, the conversation had become serious. She found that she had no choice but to continue.

"But he wants me to marry again as soon as I can find someone he describes as worthy of me. Apparently he doesn't believe I can maintain my high standards unless I marry a man of consequence, and I'm not speaking of economic standards.

"Jonathan thinks I deserve a man intelligent enough, he says, to appreciate the totality of my personhood, as well as my womanhood. Of course, he believes the man should be successful enough in his business or profession that I could be proud of him. He doesn't mean a rich man. He thinks many rich men are so committed to money they couldn't appreciate my sexuality."

"Seriously, Rene," Arnold said, "in the hope that we can get together once in a while, I very selfishly want you to remain free. But objectively, I agree with your husband. I hope you find the man of consequence whose mood is a happy one to match yours."

"Now that I know what you and my husband, two distinguished men, want for me," Rene responded rather briskly, "please don't hesitate to aid in the selection process.

"In the meantime, Arnold, I may only want to be the mistress of a 'man of consequence.' I've had all the responsibility of being a wife that I want for a while. I even asked my husband to just let me be his mistress," and her voice trailed off to barely a whisper, "but he turned me down. He said I would wither away as a mistress."

"I know you're half kidding, Rene; no one would turn you down on that offer." And then Arnold mercifully changed the subject. "The next time the two big football powers in this town, UCLA and USC, meet at the Coliseum, perhaps you'd consider accompanying some of my football friends and me to the game. That's only a few weeks away. We'll follow up on that either at the office, or maybe you'll let me take you out to dinner. Although, wherever we go, we'll not get a dinner as good as the one you prepared."

By this time it was after eleven and time for Arnold to leave. He seemed a little reluctant.

"Rene, when I go home, I'm sure I'll feel more alone than I have for many years."

"Thank you, Arnold. I've enjoyed being with you, too."

Rene got Arnold's jacket for him and held it as he put it on. He held her and kissed her gently.

"Good night, Rene, my darling."

"Good night, Arnold, my Prince Charming, who brought me such lovely roses."

They both laughed at themselves, as Arnold turned and walked down the hall to the elevator.

# 28

Jonathan was tempted to go out to see his new granddaughter, but he thought it best to wait until Christmas. He was sure he would be kept up to date through phone conversations and pictures of the series of firsts performed by Laura. He knew that one of the countless joys of having babies around is the opportunity to note the infinite number of developments that occur in their rapid growth.

Thinking of baby Laura triggered thoughts about his own children and their childhoods. Jonathan found that parents learn a lot about themselves by looking at their children. And while he had never underestimated his children's capacity to learn, he was aware that some parents often did. He had observed that the more mature the parents, especially the males, the more they understood the wonderment of a child. And so often, Jonathan thought, men have to be forty or older to fully appreciate a woman, especially a woman who knows she can do so many tasks well, inside or outside the home.

The problems posed for women by the challenge to be attentive, nurturing mothers and to be accomplished in whatever profession or business they choose are difficult indeed, even with understanding and fully sharing spouses. He hoped that new parents would keep in mind that, as the high points in the quakes of social faulting subside, women will still be women and men will still be men. He believed that the equality of their separateness would be enhanced by the mutual understanding of their common human needs. But, he thought, more wives and husbands would have to realize that separateness must not be synonymous with selfishness. Ellen, Anson, and Laura were all involved in cultural groundbreaking. He wished them well.

Anyway, Jonathan knew that he had learned a great deal from his own children. On occasion, he had found them just looking at him when he said or did something out of character. Their stares had quickly revealed to him that they were asking themselves, "How can a grown-up act that way?" He figured that parents would do well to pay attention to such messages from their children and sometimes reprimand themselves, not the child. Children, after all, are often just trying to put two and two together—trying to find consistencies in what the parents said or did yesterday and what they say or do today.

Jonathan understood his children rather well, and he never considered time spent with them as merely playtime or parental-duty time. To be sure, he also had fun with them, and they had fun with him.

As they grew up, continued their schooling, and entered business and the professions, Jonathan had continued to check things out with them, as he had with his and Rene's problem of separation. The children had also continued to consult him. He believed that accepting his children as separate persons, right from childhood, had enabled him to achieve a greater feeling of oneness with them. In other words, he and Rene hadn't considered their children merely appendages of the parents.

Recalling a Biblical admonition, he didn't fear to approach life with the simplicity of a child, joining the wisdom of one concluding a journey with the innate wisdom and faith of one beginning a journey. This attitude toward life kept him in a continuous learning cycle, a process that kept him always current, ageless in outlook. There was no communication gap between Jonathan and his children. He hoped that there would be none between him and his grandchildren. He would be ready to learn from Laura.

Thinking of Ellen and Anson and the beginning of their family life prompted him to reflect upon the increasingly prevalent notion, followed more slowly in practice, that husband and wife should share responsibility in and out of the home. He didn't think that this should carry with it the assumption that authority is equally shared. Children often determine for themselves which parent is the chief authority, and they look more to that parent for direction. In the beginning, it is likely to be the parent from whom the child receives the most nurturing, but as they grow, children may turn to the one who really brings home the bacon. It's a complicated process, but it's not so complicated if parents join together and agree on matters.

Jonathan thought about himself and Rene as parents. They had discussed decisions with their children almost from the time the children could understand and express their understanding. In any event, he felt that children should not be confused by contradictory directions. He and Rene had avoided that kind of parenting. They had provided their children with guiding lights that didn't waver, or go on and off. The idea of separate and different instructions for children, he thought, as he recalled the news headlines, may be as confusing and destructive of children's stability as the disparate voices of a Congress and a President are to friend and foe alike.

"At any rate," he said to himself, "it's unfair to the child for the mother and father to look at one another and ask, 'Which one of us should correct Junior this time?' " He hoped, in fact he was certain, that Ellen and Anson would avoid that trap.

Thinking about his children and realizing that he hadn't seen her for some time, Jonathan decided to call Susan and invite her to come down from New York to visit him the following weekend, Friday the tenth, if she were not otherwise committed. Susan, at almost twenty-four, would always be the youngest, of course, but neither Rene nor Jonathan, nor her older siblings, really considered her "the kid" anymore.

He phoned Susan that very evening, and she gladly accepted his week-end invitation. She said she would take the train down Saturday morning so she could get in an extra three hours of studying. He could pick her up at the Washington Union station at twelve-thirty.

Susan greeted him with a smile, as she walked quickly through the station lobby to their customary meeting spot. She had on a banker's gray, well-tailored suit and medium heels, her red hair swept up, but not too tightly.

"Hello, young lady. I'm glad you deserted your boyfriends to visit with me."

"Nothing special, Daddy. I just figured you could afford to take me to a more expensive restaurant for dinner tonight." She grinned mischievously and kissed him on the cheek.

Susan was Jonathan's first guest in his new apartment. She was delighted with its long balcony and with the trees so close she could almost touch them. It was very different from her Village-area apartment in Manhattan. Jonathan had the extra bedroom all ready for her, including a lovely flowering plant.

286

When she saw the plant, Susan hugged him and said, "Daddy, you're always so thoughtful."

"Just want to make you feel at home."

"Daddy, if you're talking about the home we had on our Illinois farm or the one you built in North Carolina, then, yes, I feel at home. If you're thinking about my little Manhattan place, I'm lost here."

Jonathan started back down the hall. "Why don't you put your stuff away and come in and have a beer? I bought a fresh six-pack just for you. I think I'll forego a martini and join you."

Susan began unpacking, and he headed for the kitchen. He took a couple of beers from the refrigerator, poured them into tall crystal glasses (he thought beer deserved to be dressed up once in a while), and placed them on the long coffee table in front of two coral and ebony chairs in the living room.

Susan joined him, kicked her shoes off, and put her feet on the table. With a sigh of satisfaction, she looked at the pretty glass of beer for a moment before taking the first drink.

"So, how are your graduate courses progressing?" he asked.

"I'm doing fine, Daddy. I like school very much, and I like my classmates, too. Some of them are really smart—good competition. I even like most of the professors. And I do love New York. My apartment is small, but I was lucky to get it, with Bruce's help."

"Well, Susan, all of the things you like add up to happiness and success. You're lucky, even though you're working hard to get more than your MBA. You've been lucky in having so many things going for you. But isn't there one thing that really bugs you? Just one thing that isn't going perfectly?"

"Well, let me think about it, Daddy." She took a drink of her beer and pondered. "Come to think of it, I've got two things that have been bothering me, one professional and one personal."

"Tell me about them."

"I have two classmates working on their Ph.D.'s, and one professor in a course I'm taking in mathematical theory, who think I'm smart. At lunch in the cafeteria, they'll corner me and try to convert me to some of their Marxist concepts. They talk about the disparities in economic life-styles among some of their friends, especially in minority groups. They blame the disparities on our profit system. What can I say to them without wasting time?"

"Very simple, Susan. Tell them that where there's no profit,

287

there's no freedom. But remember, the reverse doesn't always hold true."

"Is it that simple, Dad?"

"Yes, Susan. Just ask them to think of a single exception among world societies."

"That sounds neat, Daddy. And in my instant replay survey, I think it's right. But what do I say when they talk about the great differences between the rich and the poor?"

"Just point out to them that critics of the profit system should understand it would be difficult to have a rich country without some people getting rich. But I won't deny that there's a desperate need to improve our ethics. We also urgently need an increase in competition in our country at all levels of business and the professions."

Jonathan took a slow drink of beer and asked Susan about her personal problem. She smiled a little shyly and said, "I wasn't going to tell you about it, but up until last week there was a dire unavailability of eligible men who weren't afraid to be committed to a decent relationship, a long-term friendship, or marriage. That bugged me."

"Oh? And what happened last week to change this?"

Susan began enthusiastically, "For the first time, in all my years and with all my dates, I met a man who interests me very much and who seems to be just as interested in me. Of course," she added hesitantly, "we've only had two dates, but the possibilities look inviting."

"How old is this lucky young man that you regard so highly, so far?"

"He's twenty-two, a little younger than I am, but he's so intelligent and mature, it doesn't matter who's older or younger."

"Susan, the way you speak, I would guess he's got the hell beat out of those musician friends of yours, especially that guitar player you knew in Chicago."

"Oh, Daddy," she said laughingly, curling her legs under her in the chair, "those friends were okay, but Harlan is something. His name is Harlan Harrison. He went back to his home in the Midwest this week-end. Ask me about him three months from now. In the meantime, I have to really bear down on my studies. We have frequent exams. I want to make good for myself and for you and Mom. I don't want Bruce and Ellen to get too far ahead of me, either."

"A couple of days ago, Susan, I had lunch with a career counselor for professional men and women. Interestingly, she started out counseling women, but now she has more men than women clients. This surprised her, but after working with many young men and some not so young, she understands their feelings of insecurity and uncertainty."

Susan nodded and toyed with her glass.

"That doesn't surprise me, Daddy. I have any number of male friends, just friends, nothing more. They're so committed to money and getting ahead that they don't have the time or interest for home or love. They're concerned only with their own individual success and seem to have no concern for real human values. Their future social roles, having a wife and family and a decent place to live, don't seem to be important to them.

"A girl friend and I visited the apartment of two young men a couple of weeks ago. Both have MBA's, both are two years into their jobs and making good money, but the apartment they live in has little or no furniture. Their beds are pallets on the floor, and the curtains are newspapers pasted on the windows. We couldn't believe they lived there. Incredibly, they'd been living like that for over a year. They never learned to take pride in their home. They're nothing but transients, with transient, adaptable values. They perceive their identities only in their job environments. They seem to lack respect for everything else, including themselves. We checked them off our list, but quick."

"How sad," her father replied. "Many young men and women have grown up in homes where things beautiful and spiritual were knocked out by the idea of money and getting ahead. Nor could they learn to appreciate human values in our value-free educational institutions, and least likely in MBA courses.

"We've reached many schools, including graduate schools of business, with our ethics publications, and there's been an increase in the teaching of ethics in universities in the past half-dozen years."

"But, Dad, would a knowledge of ethics have inspired the fellows we saw to clean their rooms?"

"Oddly enough, yes, Susan. A sense of ethics and a sense of order and self-respect do go together."

"Daddy, I don't believe we've passed out of the youth culture of the sixties and seventies yet. So many young men simply don't want to grow up. They want to get rich, but they still want to be kids as long as they can. They don't seem to have very high ideals or high personal standards. But maybe it's understandable that they should live for money and for now, considering the violence all over the world."

"Yes, there are reasons for being irresponsible and selfish. But there have *always* been reasons for man to use uncertainty of the future to excuse himself for being less than he knows he could be."

Susan nodded, and Jonathan continued.

"Some of my friends worry about not having a deep religious faith. Maybe they should worry. But some of them might take a cue from the practitioners of the positive mental attitude philosophy —those success-oriented salespersons who usually tie their motivating force to a religion, to God. The funny thing is that the plan works for so many. Perhaps you should go ahead and have faith in the future, the long-term future that demands a foundation of ethical values. You have everything to win and nothing to lose, but having faith in the future shouldn't lessen our feeling of obligation to do all we can to help make sure that we'll have a future.

"Anyway, what else is new? Why do you and your girl friends want to make it so big in business?"

Susan smiled. "Oh, that's easy to answer. We're also among those who want to earn a good income and be free, be on our own. Furthermore, Daddy, work is still the most recognized and valued form of activity in our culture. The measurement of strength, independence, and security has changed most noticeably as this concept is applied to us women."

She finished her beer and noticed that her father's glass was almost empty, too. "Shall we have another beer? I'll get them."

She picked up the glasses and disappeared into the kitchen. It wasn't long before she was back with the beers. Jonathan actually didn't care to drink another one, but as long as Susan was willing to talk, he wanted to listen.

"The female career counselor I talked with," he said, "commented that in several business and professional organizations she counseled, she observed that the female workers, especially those above the rank and file employees, were actually more hard-driving and ambitious than their male counterparts. Considering the pervasive bureaucratization of work, even in the professions is there a place for the entrepreneurial, individualistic young person, much like yourself, to get ahead?"

290

Susan's voice was emphatic. "I think the answer is yes, if you keep your objectives clearly in mind, short-term and long-term, with a form of personal management by objective. But you must be prepared to work much harder, study more, and know more than those around you. Some may interpret this dedicated approach as antisocial and alienating in the group. They act like that in the classroom toward the superior students. I believe you should go out of your way to help others. Learn to cooperate.

"When one of my girl friends, who got her MBA last semester, was taking tests and being interviewed for jobs, she learned the hard, frustrating way: don't come on too strong; don't think your MBA over-qualifies you for any job less than vice-president; don't try to place your opinion ahead of what the company knows are facts; and, if you're really intelligent and qualified, be smart enough to sell yourself first, or you'll never have a chance to know if you really are smart.

"I guess the truth is, corporations need very few arrogant mavericks. Yeah, she learned a lot about what not to do in getting a job. And what she learned is helping me develop my own thinking. I'll know what not to do when I get my big job opportunity. I won't be sycophantic on the one hand, or domineering on the other.

"I am surprised, however, that the professions still aren't opening up to women and minorities as fast as I had hoped. A woman should study the individual corporate situation before taking a job where the vestiges of tokenism still exist."

Jonathan smiled. "Susan, many times a young person seeking a good job will learn more from job interviews than from going back for a doctoral degree. Sometimes a graduate student gets so wrapped up in studies, he or she may become very self-centered, subjective, and dogmatic, especially when quoting right from the book. You're not like that, are you?"

"No, Dad," she said, leaning forward as if to share a secret with him, "partly because you've had more patience with me than I've had with myself."

Father and daughter were quiet for a minute, lost in their own thoughts, or perhaps just enjoying being together. Jonathan broke the silence.

"Susan, have you learned from any of your research courses and discussions if a married woman is as good a worker as a single woman?"

Susan looked a little surprised. She thought a minute and then said, "I haven't seen any research data on that, but I'm sure there must be some. I haven't known enough women in the work force in my Chicago job or in New York to answer that question from my own experience. But my guess is that the married women are often better performers, because single women are so busy worrying about their current personal situations with men. I think the married women at the company where I worked in Chicago were more productive workers than the single women.

"An outstanding advantage that many of the older married women have is that they had a better fundamental education, in the 'basics' that we talk about today. They also seem to have a greater sense of responsibility, a higher respect for the work ethic. They don't try to substitute sex and new MBA degrees for the old values."

Susan added what she considered to be an important factor in her perspective. "Please keep in mind that I was probably the youngest person on the staff in Chicago. I suppose if I'd been thirty years old and there was no man on my horizon, I would've been worrying, too. But some of the married women are concerned about another matter. The younger women are getting better educational credentials than many of the older women have, especially those thirty-five to forty or older. So I guess the quality of a woman's professional performance depends more on the individual rather than on whether she's married or single."

Susan looked up from her beer and fully expected her father to interject something into the conversation. She wondered if he was thinking about her mother. She knew she was. But when he didn't say anything, she decided to relate their conversation to Rene.

"Please don't consider this comment a criticism of Mom, but we younger women experienced our adolescence when we were adolescents. Some of the older women, married or not, try to act younger than the youngest of us. A forty-five-year-old woman acting like a twenty-two-year-old doesn't play in the Peoria's of the business world. Older women who go back to college after a twenty-five-year absence shouldn't try to be part of the younger scene, especially the married women. For the so-called reentry women, a degree or advanced degree often means divorce. Maybe Mom's attempt to be a pal with my college peers at Carolina State brought this home to me—and maybe to you.

292

"Of course," Susan added, "Mom's business experiences were so strong that her identity problem didn't affect her job. Yet, she always declined top administrative roles."

Jonathan wanted to steer the conversation away from Rene, but he knew there was some truth in what Susan was saying. Nevertheless, he didn't think that he wanted the conversation to continue along this line.

"Susan, I know what you're saying. And I certainly should. But when you're forty-five, you'll be rich and retired and running for the United States Senate."

Susan gave him a look of mock horror. "I hope not, Daddy. I want to enjoy life more than that."

Jonathan smiled at his daughter. She was a delight to watch in action.

"Let's go back to this young man you met last week. You seemed to like him as a possible prospect. If he's a year younger than you are and you already act five or ten years older than you are, wouldn't you probably be too strong a woman for him?"

"We scarcely know each other yet, but he does seem stronger, more mature, and more secure than men I've dated who are thirty-five and forty years of age. I know I want a strong man, and he certainly seemed to like the fact that I'm strong enough and smart enough to interest him. I think a man shows maturity and strength and brains if he can enjoy a woman's company without going to bed with her."

Now it was Jonathan's turn to feign horror. "I'll have to keep that thought in mind, Susan."

"Daddy, do you think you'll get married again? I know you've campaigned to get Mom married again. I'd like to see you both marry again, even to each other. But you and Mom have become such different people, I wouldn't advise that, at least not now."

"Susan, you know I'll not marry again. At my age and with my perfectionistic demands, any woman who would marry me would be too insane for me to marry. This doesn't mean I wouldn't go to bed with a desirous and desirable woman. The old saying about New York City is applicable. I like to visit but wouldn't want to live there."

As Susan uncurled her legs and put her feet on the table in front of her again, she said, "Now, if you're so bad, why do so many women, even very much younger friends who've met you, think you're a fascinating man?"

"Such women, Susan, are only curious *about* me, not curious *for* me. Let's talk about the possible, not the ridiculous."

"Don't be too sure. You might be selling yourself short. You remember how the phone calls came in when you were a guest on three or four television talk shows. I think there are so few strong, secure, wise, and independent men in this world today that many women would rather just talk with you than go to bed with an uncertain man less than half your age."

Jonathan smiled lovingly at Susan. "You're quite partial to my years, and I thank you. However, I've never had a preponderance of platonic friends among women, and I'm too old to change my ways now."

Looking at the beer glasses in front of them, he said, "Our beer's all gone. Now let's go over to Clyde's for dinner or supper, or even a Reuben sandwich."

The weekend went particularly well. Jonathan enjoyed his visit with Susan. He found her a very stimulating person. With her several years' experience in advertising, plus her undergraduate degrees in journalism and philosophy, topped by her MBA in finance, she certainly had the foundation for growth and success. But her real success, as she had indicated in her comments about women with whom she had worked, would depend primarily on her basic work-ethic values, her self-discipline, and her willingness to sacrifice to achieve her goals. She admitted to setting her own personal management by objective targets.

All their children had learned to love learning at a very early age. They had learned to work hard simply by doing hard work around the house, in the yard, and on the farm. All of them had chosen to go to summer school or to work at outside jobs during their high school and college years. Through the years, they directed their goals at personal and professional fulfillment, not at making money. But they soon found that their hard work, ambition, and accumulated qualifications inevitably resulted in making money. And far better than he, Jonathan thought, his children found it easy to work and to cooperate with all kinds of people.

In the beginning, and as they grew up, he and Rene had tried to set exemplary patterns, guidelines for living, for the children. Now he believed the lives of their children represented challenges for him and Rene. He hoped that they could meet the continuing expectations of their children. He was acutely conscious of this obligation to himself and to them. He thought that parents too often relaxed their own standards and quit growing enough to keep in step with their children's advancements.

In reference to their divorce, he and Rene understood that the children loved each parent equally. The children had made this fact plain. However, Jonathan had asked them to give a little extra portion of love and attention to their mother during the transition period of separation and divorce. Whatever his own future, he believed that Rene would need more guidance and love from the children than he. This, he quickly admitted to himself, wasn't quite working out that way now. Rene seemed to be taking their separation far more easily than he knew he was.

# 29

The Monday following Susan's week-end visit, George Gregson called Jonathan to ask if he could come into the Ethics Inquiry office Tuesday and Wednesday to answer a number of letters that had been directed to him personally. Gregson also wanted him to attend a Wednesday luncheon meeting with two business school professors to discuss a proposed research project on the relationship of ethics to productivity. Jonathan had expected some duties such as these to be carried over, and he readily agreed to Gregson's request.

While he was at the Ethics office, one of Barbara Ballinger's friends came in to pick up some booklets that Barbara had told her might be useful in the volunteer organization she was developing. Her visit reminded Jonathan that he had mentioned to Barbara at a Washington awards dinner several months ago that she should join him and Fred Osborne for lunch some day. He thought that this might be a good time to arrange that luncheon.

He called, but Barbara was out of her office. He left a message, and she called him back within an hour.

"Jonathan," Barbara said, "I hope you're feeling all right. I heard that you and Rene finally decided to separate. I hate divorces, especially when there are two fine people involved. Anyway, I wish both of you well."

"Thank you very much, Barbara," Jonathan replied rather perfunctorily. "Rene and I separated as friends, and we have a continuing high regard for one another. What I called you about was to find out when you could go to lunch with me and Fred Osborne."

"Let's keep that in mind, Jonathan, but now that you're back, I wonder if you'll be available Wednesday for lunch with me and a sorority sister, Katherine Browne, who is vice-president for public affairs of City National Bank in Chicago. Her bank has decided to develop a code of ethics, and I know you can help her."

Barbara quickly added, "Incidentally, the two of you have something else in common—you're both separated and divorced after long marriages."

Jonathan reached for his pocket calendar and saw the Wednesday lunch date he had just written down. "Barbara, that sounds wonderful, but I already have an obligation for lunch Wednesday."

"Are you by any chance free today? If you are, I suggest we meet at the International Club at twelve-fifteen. I'll make the reservations."

"That's fine, Barbara. I'll be looking forward to seeing you and meeting your friend. Let me discuss her project in general over lunch, and later she can come to the Ethics office and talk with George Gregson, the executive director. He has a lot of material on how to set up codes of ethics."

"I knew I could count on you to be a good resource and friend. Thank you."

Jonathan thought she might be ready to hang up, so he brought the conversation around to her busy life. "Barbara, how are you doing? You sound as perky as ever."

"Oh, I'm going all the time. It'll be very good for Katherine to talk with you, and I always enjoy listening. Goodbye, Jonathan."

"Goodbye, Barbara."

Jonathan hastened through his paper work and divided the correspondence that had been accumulating, according to need and urgency. He spoke briefly with the secretary about Gregson's plans for the rest of the week, as he wanted to be able to tell Katherine Browne exactly when she could call on George for the suggested pamphlets he had in mind for her. By now, he was on his way out of the office. He could walk to the International Club in ten minutes.

Arriving a little early for his luncheon appointment, he checked his lightweight topcoat at the checkroom at the ground floor entrance and walked up the wide, curving staircase to the second-floor reception area and dining rooms. He liked to sit in the corner of the lounge where he could see people come up the stairs, some rushing because they were late for their appointments, others strolling up with friends and greeting just about everyone in case they should know them. Many lobbyists, lawyers, politicians, and public relations people frequented the International Club, which was conveniently located at Eighteenth and K Streets.

297

Soon he saw Barbara and her friend walking slowly up the stairs, talking animatedly. They were both attractive and attractively dressed, Barbara in a light brown dress with gold accessories, and Mrs. Browne in a navy blue suit and light-blue blouse. Mrs. Browne was as attractive a brunette as Barbara was a blonde. She was a little taller than Barbara, about five feet eight, and perhaps not as slender, which was just right.

Jonathan rose, greeted them at the top of the stairs, and was introduced to Mrs. Browne, with the emphasis on Katherine.

As they walked over to the main dining room, he asked her, "Did Barbara have so much vivacity when she was a Delta Gamma at Michigan?"

"No, Mr. Barron, but she had a good start on it," Katherine replied with a smile.

As soon as Barbara gave her name to the maitre d' for the reservation, she quickly said to Jonathan, "I remember having told you I attended the University of Michigan, but I don't recall having mentioned my sorority." She turned to Katherine and said, "You see, Katherine, I warned you about his guessing games."

Jonathan, unusually relaxed for some reason—maybe because of the presence of two mature and appealing women—smiled and said, "Barbara, I simply made a biased observation. When I was in college, I dated several DG's, and from what I observed, their whole house was filled with intelligent, attractive girls, all generally dressed tastefully. So I just figured, as Sherlock Holmes might have, that two obviously smart, well-dressed, pretty women were clearly representative of the Delta Gamma tradition as I knew it. Nothing mysterious about that, don't you agree, Katherine?"

As he turned to Barbara's friend he said, "I call you Katherine, because I've just been memory visiting your sorority."

At this point they were being seated at a nice corner table, and both women seemed to be quite relaxed, probably also memory-visiting their days at Michigan together.

"Whatever the reasons you figured we were Delta Gamma, it's pleasing to receive such complimentary attention," Katherine said to Jonathan.

She had not expected an ethicist, as Barbara had described Jonathan, to be so sensitive. She now felt free in a personal, friendly way to discuss any problems relating to her ethics code assignment.

298

Barbara and Katherine each ordered a glass of white wine, and Jonathan requested his usual martini on the rocks with no fruit. They drank a toast to Katherine's new ethics project, and he asked whether her bank was creating a new code of ethics or updating an old one.

"We've had a brief statement of principles, but that statement has long been out of print, which, in effect, means we're starting our code from scratch. We want a comprehensive code of conduct that we plan to promote to every bank employee, starting with the chairman and chief executive officer," Katherine stated rather firmly.

"That's exactly where an effective code must begin," Jonathan interjected, "with the full support of the chairman; and I would go a step further. It should be discussed in detail and approved by the entire board of directors, with each director signing the agreement to give the code not only full support, but full sanction. The sanction and publicized support of the board should be clearly stated. Dismissal for code violations and prosecution, if any laws are violated, should be affirmed. Board members should be subject to sanctions, just like anybody else. After all, a little dishonesty at the top produces a lot of dishonesty at the bottom."

"Well, we hadn't thought of that procedure, but I'm sure we can get the support of all our directors. I'll need to make a point of mentioning that at the next meeting with my boss," Katherine replied, as she made a reminder note in her little gold-trimmed notebook.

"But in reference to our discussion here, Katherine," Jonathan continued, "let me comment only on the idea of a code and its nature. Our Ethics Group office has a complete booklet on how to establish a workable code of ethics. You should visit the Ethics office and talk with Mr. Gregson. He's in New York right now, but he'll be back in Washington later this week."

Their drinks arrived, and Jonathan continued to explain some of Gregson's activities. "Incidentally, one of the meetings he'll have in New York will be with a committee on ethics that one of the large New York banks has created to update its code, with special attention focused on how to implement its provisions. You may wish to set up such a committee at your bank.

"Gregson can give you a great deal of information, including case studies conducted by one of the big New York banks regarding specific ethical problems that they've confronted. That bank has authorized our distribution of the material. Incidentally, who initiated your bank's interest in having a code of ethics?"

Before Katherine could reply, the waiter handed them menus, and Barbara suggested that they order.

"As to who initiated the ethics project I'm working on, I don't really know, Jonathan. I was assigned the task by my boss, the bank's senior executive vice-president. I'll admit that our public affairs office routed to him a number of articles and speeches on ethics by top corporate executives. In fact, we sent him a copy of a speech you made to a major trade association. In your speech, you banged the corporate leaders pretty hard about their glossing over internal management's conflict of interests that reflected upon the integrity of the whole institution.

"There's also been so much attention given to the great changes in the financial community. It is, to say the least, in a state of transition, but no one seems to know toward what. Changes in the laws, the tremendous effect of increasing technology, and other pressures are causing a revolution in the industry. I think our people saw that any move that would help to improve individual responsibility and respect for the company as a whole would be a pragmatic one, indeed."

Jonathan was supportive in his response.

"I think the reasons you've just indicated are very compelling, and I do hope you'll upgrade your project to a number-one priority. The results will show up in increased efficiency, better profits, and fewer outrageous gambles. I think what's baffled the public most has been the unbelievable risk-taking, not only on dubious loans, but on buying even more dubious loans.

"Long ago I tried to get banking groups to lead the way in setting up stringent codes of ethics. The honest ones didn't think they needed stringent, enforceable codes, and the dishonest ones knew good codes could be troublesome. The current demand for codes of ethics by most corporations and banks, especially in recent months, reflects the diminishing reputation and credibility of financial institutions. Banks and other financial institutions, especially some insurance companies, will need to watch themselves more closely. Money centers, notably banks, are built on public trust and can't survive without it. But you already know this."

"Well, yes and no," Katherine said a little hesitantly. "I think a

300

lot of us in banking are aware of the picture you describe, but not enough of us are recognizing the dangers. I think we still have too many bank officers who knowingly make high-risk loans for high-risk profits, while recognizing that their productivity for the bank in the short run will enable them to move on to another institution before the other shoe falls."

Katherine was really diving into her project, Jonathan thought, as he observed her almost pounding her beautiful, but strong, hands on the table. He wondered if he would ever cease to enjoy looking at a pretty woman. He hoped he would continue to admire women as intelligent and competent human beings, but as long as he was the man he knew himself to be, he hoped he would keep on enjoying them because they also happened to be lovely women.

Katherine had been thinking and said with confident finality, "I'm beginning to understand that my responsibility to develop a strong code of ethics and see it through to adoption and enforcement is going to be one of the greatest contributions I can make to our bank. I'll call Mr. Gregson's office today and ask his secretary to call me as soon as he's available."

"How's your martini, Jonathan?" Barbara asked, thinking that he and Katherine might want a respite from their discussion of codes.

"Oh, I have a little left. Since you and Katherine have some wine left, I'll skip another drink. But thank you, Barbara."

He looked up and across the dining room. "I think our waiter is coming with our food.

"Katherine, where did you live in Chicago, or do you live in the suburban area?"

"Up until four or five years ago, we lived in Barrington, but with the children grown and away, and with both my then-husband and myself working, we moved into a condominium off Lake Shore Drive."

"I used to live on Chicago's Near North Side and liked it very much," Jonathan said. "You probably walk over to the Lake Michigan beach, up to North Avenue, into Lincoln Park to Division Street, and back down to your apartment."

"Yes, I do. That's exactly where I walk. Did you used to take that tour?" Katherine asked enthusiastically.

"Many years ago, Katherine." And he got off that track quickly.

Barbara had been listening, but now she returned to their previous discussion by asking, "What do you see as the difference between morality and ethics, Jonathan? I wanted to ask you that question when you spoke to our religious foundation, but you got too many other questions."

"My darling Barbara, I appreciate your compliment in asking the question, but surely you don't want to hear more about a subject that has me somewhat locked in."

Barbara returned Jonathan's smile with a great deal of interest and acceptance. "Yes, I do. You must remember that I have a strong commitment to the ecumenical efforts of our religious foundation, and I not only need to hear views on morality and ethics, but I enjoy the discussion. More people should become concerned about the moral character of our society rather than being afraid to discuss the subject, which is worse than being indifferent."

"Go ahead, Jonathan!" Katherine urged. "You don't get two women to ask you to talk seriously very often, do you?"

"No, as a matter of fact I don't, and I appreciate the two I've captured. At another time I hope we'll be listening to music and watching the sunset—but back to earth.

"The terms morality and ethics, as you know, are often used interchangeably. Philosophers like to talk about morality because the term permits them more indeterminacy in their thinking. Theologians prefer morality because the term, in their usage, places more responsibility on God. Or rather, in their view, it relieves them of some of their responsibilities.

"But in our society, what is moral or immoral usually relates to religious guidelines. Ethical standards, though common to all major religions, need not be related to any transcendental or religious source. However, there's no conflict between being ethical and being religious, except that being ethical is more difficult and not as culturally acceptable as being religious.

"One whose good conduct is solely dependent on religion may feel that his or her god is compassionate and that sins will be forgiven, maybe every Sunday. But one who depends on high ethical standards finds it more difficult to be forgiving of his own misconduct—he has to live with his conscience all day, every day. He can't depend on the solace of Sunday for the sins of Saturday. Fortunate is the person, however, who has both ethical and religious guidelines."

"That's a view, Jonathan, that both philosophers and clergy

might question," said Barbara. "Yet, I remember what you said to our religious convention. 'Faith is the beginning of religion, and ethics is the implementation of faith.' There was a lot of agreement with that statement, especially among Christians who've been told that 'faith without works is dead.' "

"Of course, my patient friends," Jonathan responded warmly, "I should have answered simply by saying that *morality* is concerned more with *self* and *ethics* is concerned with *others.*

"Not long ago we conducted a random sample of interviews with people in different localities, of different ethnic groups, and with various economic backgrounds. It was interesting that morality and immorality were associated primarily with sex. Ethics was associated primarily with honesty and dishonesty."

"Jonathan," Barbara continued, "I don't know if I agree or disagree with what you found. It does make sense, and apparently your research revealed slants on the subject that you probably wouldn't get in college or church.

"What do you think, Katherine? You seem lost in thoughts of some kind."

"I'm inclined to agree with Jonathan's observations. But what bothers me is that I think he should have been a teacher or preacher," Katherine observed with a mischievous smile. "It seems strange to hear an entrepreneurial businessman speak as he does on such an esoteric subject. Many people are really afraid to be forthright and honest.

"Jonathan, you seem to have done research on many things. Have you researched women? You'd need a large number of samples, I guess. But then, that wouldn't have bothered you too much, would it?" Katherine inquired mischievously.

"Barbara, this friend of yours reads me pretty well for what I hope is just the first of a series of meetings. What easy question would you ask me about women?"

"How does ethics relate to women?" Katherine asked very casually.

"So, you surprise me by asking a question still within the field of our discussion. I have to be serious yet?" Jonathan said lightly. "Let me answer specifically and as a challenge. If equity, fairness, and justice are to be achieved for women in the workplace, we must considerably improve our overall standards in business ethics, particularly in the ethics of big business and big government. It is hypocrisy in the workplace that women have found so frustrating in their efforts to get fair treatment, to get equal pay for equal work. Further, women have been locked into so many job classifications where pay has historically been low. There must be an interchange of jobs—women into men's and men into women's. This has been happening, but not as rapidly nor as broadly as it should."

"Too bad, Jonathan, this audience is already converted," Katherine said, "but we like to hear the gospel of equality anytime."

"Thank you Sister Katherine and Sister Barbara," he said, recognizing their spirit of the ethical gospel.

"We should understand that the more ethical American business becomes, the better it is for all workers, not just for women workers," he continued. "Treating others as equals, regardless of color, creed, sex, or age is the fundamental first stage of acting ethically. Good ethics contributes to pride, to order, to efficiency, to self-respect; and all these factors contribute to productivity and profits. Treating others as *equals* is the beginning of both morality and ethics. It's the Golden Rule at work.

"Another example of the Golden Rule at work is women giving consideration to male co-workers, those below and above them. A man's self esteem, whether he's young or old, should be handled with great care by a woman. This applies in the workplace or in bed. It's a vestige of our culture. Of course, men as well as women should remember that *reciprocity* is implicit in the Golden Rule."

Barbara had indicated to the waiter that they were ready for coffee, and he brought it immediately. It tasted good to Jonathan. He needed it. He was quite pleased with these two women. They had intelligence and attractiveness, but also a great deal of character. He knew that Barbara was a very capable and highly regarded woman, and he liked her very much. But he was also very impressed with Katherine, without regard to the fact that they had both moved from marriage to being single.

As they began to drink their coffee, Barbara asked Jonathan another serious question. He welcomed the questions, but he would like to have just sat there drinking his coffee, looking at and listening to them.

"Jonathan, you just said that treating others as equals is the beginning of morality and ethics, that it's the Golden Rule at work. Is the Golden Rule an ethical or a moral injunction?"

"Barbara, you're a darling woman, but you feed me some of the damndest questions, and they tempt me to try answers.

"The Golden Rule is both a moral and an ethical imperative. Within the concept of the Golden Rule, not only does ethics join morality, but it's where many great religions share a common foundation. This is easy to understand, because there would be no mankind had humans not cooperated, and shared, and applied a basic measure of the Golden Rule precept to their struggles for survival.

"Throughout history some very profound thinkers who made it to the top—Jesus, Mohammed, Buddha—placed a lot of emphasis on what, in today's world, may seem like an impractical 'do-gooder' platform. The Golden Rule, as the world refers to it, is the name given to a saying by Jesus of Nazareth as recorded in the Sermon on the Mount. Jesus said, 'All things, therefore whatsoever you would that men should do to you, do also to them.' This admonition was cited as the 'Golden Law' for the first time in 1674 A.D. The Christians have used the positive form of the rule, while the Jews have cited the negative form, as stated by Tobit around 200 B.C. 'What is hateful unto thee do not unto thy fellow.' The realistic Confucius was once asked, 'Is there one word which may serve as a rule of practice for all one's life?' He answered, 'Is not reciprocity such a word? That you do not like if done to yourself, do not do to others.' Incidentally, we had a graduate divinity student research the Golden Rule for us, so I have almost a book on the history of the Golden Rule."

Katherine smiled and looked at Barbara, who was staring at Jonathan. Then Katherine said jokingly, "How does that grab you, my dear sorority sister?"

Barbara laughed aloud and said, "I guess I asked for it."

"Okay, you paradoxical princesses," Jonathan returned, "because of my obsession I've given you a surfeit of ethics. The next time I see you, and I hope you'll allow it to be soon, let's talk about fun things: sex, sports, and politics."

Barbara looked surprised. Katherine simply said, "If we do, I hope you can deliver in those areas as well as you have in ethics."

Barbara and Jonathan both laughed, and Katherine joined in. They rose and left the dining room. While Jonathan had been declaiming, Barbara had signed the check. When she invited someone to lunch, man or woman, she considered it her right and duty to pay the check. Jonathan accepted her hospitality and thanked her.

Before saying goodbye, Jonathan asked Katherine for her business card. "Yes, you should have it," she said, as she pulled a card from its file in her purse. Quickly, she wrote her home phone number on the back of the card and said as she gave it to Jonathan, "Be sure to call me when you come to Chicago."

"I'll come to Chicago just to call you," Jonathan replied quietly. "Beautiful brunettes born around October 12 or 13 can be incredibly interesting."

Katherine looked surprised, but pleased. "It's October 13."

Barbara and Katherine went to the garage next door to pick up their car, and Jonathan walked back to the Ethics office, knowing he would now have to be in Chicago very soon.

# 30

During the months after Rene left for California and Jonathan returned from Colorado, he seldom needed to go to the Ethics office. He spent quite a bit of his time researching and writing a textbook on everyday ethics for use in high schools. Feeling compelled to continue learning, he read extensively in fields of particular interest to him—politics, economics, sociology, philosophy, medical science—along with new books he heard about or saw on his frequent trips to the bookstores.

It was about time for his annual physical check-up. Interestingly, his doctor's report was inquiring as well as informative. "What do you do to keep in such good shape for a man your age? I have many men come in here who are twenty or twenty-five years younger than you are, but they aren't in nearly such good shape."

"Well, doctor, I exercise my brain. Keeping my mind active helps to keep my body moving," was Jonathan's explanation.

His doctor hesitated and then said, "I guess you're right, but I'll tell you, it's a lot easier to get some of my patients to jog their bodies than to jog their brains."

Jonathan decided he should keep his appearance as contemporary as his mind. So he went on a rampage of getting rid of suits, shoes, shirts, and ties that he seldom wore. He was now beginning to take frequent trips to his old hometown of Chicago. He had many friends there, but it was his new friend, Katherine Browne, who was making Chicago more inviting. Jonathan had been quite taken with Katherine at the luncheon with Barbara and had been even more pleased when she wrote her home phone number on the back of her business card. Later that afternoon he had noticed that under her home phone, she had written, "In case your plane arrives in Chicago after banking hours."

Katherine was the nearest to a composite of what Jonathan liked in a human female that he had seen in years. She was even smarter than Rene and much more ambitious and humorous. She had a good measure of Mindy's spontaneous, delightfully loving characteristics. And Katherine's statuesquely beautiful figure reminded him of Lisa Bronson. Jonathan wondered why such an impressive, desirable woman would want to spend time with him. When he asked, she answered, "That's something for me to decide," in the tone of a big bank president, which she was on her way to becoming.

Katherine Browne had divorced her husband three or four years before Jonathan and Rene had separated and divorced. She was fifty-two and had two grown, married daughters, each with two young children. One daughter lived in Denver with her oil executive husband and the other daughter in Hartford with her insurance executive husband. Katherine's husband was a very successful North Shore automobile dealer, owning three major dealerships. Although he had tried living in the Lake Shore Drive condominium with Katherine, he soon decided that her friends were at once too dull and too bright for him, and he wanted to move back to the suburbs, with horses, dogs, and his twenty-eight-year-old secretary. This arrangement pleased Katherine, as well as her husband. Katherine wanted a real career, and she didn't want any part of the horsy set. She had money, a beautiful Lake Shore condominium, and ambition. Jonathan could fit into her plans, and Jonathan approved enthusiastically.

He and Katherine were partners in her ambitions, as well as being friends and lovers. Neither of them seemed to want to marry again. Jonathan once asked Katherine, "Why don't you go with a fellow your own age?" They were having dinner at the International Club in the Drake at the time, and Katherine replied without hesitation, "Well, my dear, I'll tell you exactly why. I've tried men my age. They're not as well-informed as you, can't help me in business any more than you can—if as much—and in bed, on a scale of one to ten you're the only one who ranked above eight. In fact, I've not only tried men half *your* age but also a couple half *my* age. The young ones rated less than five. They seemed to need to go to bed with a mother." "Now, Katherine," Jonathan replied, smiling, "you know that in the process of making love one doesn't think 'This guy rates a six' or 'This girl rates a seven.' "

"You're right, Jonathan. But in retrospect, I think if more lovers would rate their partners in advance, the next time they might not want to settle for a five or six. The challenge for men, as well as for women, should be to think about who they plan to go to bed with before they get to the bedroom. If they do, they'll probably greatly reduce their number of lovers—leaving only the very few who could earn an eight, with maybe *no* tens. A woman should always leave a ten-rated man as part of her dreams—he may become a reality at any given moment."

Jonathan listened. Then he said, "I'm so happy, my darling Katherine, that you and I have in our minds and bodies automatic, built-in, electronic rating devices—installed by that most experienced technician, nature."

Katherine laughed. "Can you imagine how silly this conversation sounds to the eavesdropper at the next table? But one of the many reasons I enjoy being with you is that we can talk stupidly about serious things and seriously about stupid things. Now, I wish we weren't too dignified to kiss these thoughts away." She waved him a kiss.

This was how Katherine and Jonathan were with one another. They found fun and value in almost any observation. For example, on one of his early visits to Chicago, she invited him to use one of the bedrooms in her condominium. "Why not?" Katherine explained. "The money you'd pay for a nice room in a high-priced hotel you can use to take me to dinner." Thus, she indirectly indicated that she believed in sharing, where sharing was appropriate.

In the context of that conversation, Katherine also said, "Jonathan, I don't know how much money you have, and I don't care. You don't know how much I have, and I'm sure you don't care. I say this because I do want our relationship to be a sharing one, as with good friends. The best place for each of us to try to give more than we receive is in bed—in that way we both come out big winners."

"Oh, God, Katherine," Jonathan laughed. "You've figured everything out so well that when you become head of your own bank, you'll have established such a reputation for fairness that investors and borrowers alike will want to come to you for objective advice."

In Chicago, Katherine and Jonathan dinner-dated. They found more good restaurants in Chicago than either could remember finding in any other city, with the possible exception of Washington. They sometimes weekended in New York for theater-dating. Neither Jonathan nor Katherine even thought of placing any restrictions on the other. They both knew each was so hard to please that only the one could regularly satisfy the other. Of course, Jonathan lived in Washington and Katherine in Chicago. They worked out a tentative schedule of dates, including their occasional week-ends in New York. Jonathan wasn't sure he could resist if she wanted him to move someday to the city of her choice.

He knew that Katherine wanted to become president of a big bank, preferably the one in which she was now vice-president. He supported her ambitions. He collected all the data in the financial field that came in from his lawyer friends, his financial consultant friends, and his many old business associates in Chicago. One of his Chicago friends of long standing was on the board of Katherine's bank, and another of his personal friends was one of her bank's most influential customers.

To foster Katherine's career, Jonathan was even willing to attend the Chicago Lyric Opera, accepting an invitation to opening night that in earlier years he had turned down.

Jonathan was still well known in Chicago, and not being active in business or competitive with any possible bank clients, he was the perfectly "proper" date for Katherine to be with in public. She knew that Jonathan considered her, if not his final protegee, at least his ultimate project.

Jonathan couldn't refrain from reminding Katherine that by the time she had achieved her professional goals, she would still be less than sixty, would still be young enough to marry "right" and keep on going. Katherine laughed at this notion of Jonathan's. She had in Jonathan the man she wanted, but she realized that despite his still-dark hair, fast mind, fast walk, and lasting virility, his life couldn't go on forever as it was now. She didn't believe she would ever marry again.

Jonathan accepted Katherine's program—a philosophy that was rather reminiscent of Rene's—enjoying each day to the fullest. But Katherine kept her tomorrows in mind, planned them, and placed no limits on them.

As for Jonathan, he was a little bewildered, which was a new feeling for him. When he thought of having had a life with Mindy, though so very short, and a life with Rene, and now in only an occasional but very total way a life with Katherine—well, he had no explanation for such a crescendo of blessings. He thought that maybe even he should start going to church, any church, in order to have someone or something to give thanks to. After living without Mindy, then without Rene, his moments with Katherine absolutely confirmed for him that not sharing life, even in part, with a woman was not for him—not ever. True, he and Katherine were not married, were not living together, and each was free. Yet the few days a month they were together burned so intensely that the glow remained throughout the times between. Ethics and doing good deeds had brought him and Katherine together. We generally meet the people we are prepared to meet. And good begets good, no matter the reason. Meeting Katherine taught Jonathan how wrong he had been in losing hope.

So Chicago became Jonathan's other hometown. Well, he thought, he had always supported the Cubs, Bears, and White Sox. Now, as he walked along Michigan Avenue, he created new realities, a new garden of beautiful memories to join those he still carefully nurtured.

Over the Halloween weekend, he called Ellen and asked how she, Anson, and the baby were doing.

"All's well with Laura," Ellen reported. "She's growing about an inch a day. She's healthy, and so am I."

Jonathan asked the inevitable question for the young mother of today. "When do you plan to go back to work?"

"Well, Dad, I thought I'd stay home with Laura until after the first of the year," Ellen replied. "In the meantime, we're evaluating a day-care center where they take only a very few children and, in the case of babies, they have one person assigned to no more than three. I don't believe the center we're considering will take more than three children of Laura's age at any one time. But no matter how good the care is, it's going to be hard for me to leave her."

Jonathan was concerned about both mother and baby. "Of course, in earlier days it was easier to get a very competent live-in nurse," he said, "as we did for you and Bruce and Susan. I wish you'd consider an arrangement like that, but you probably don't have room even if you could find and afford a good person.

"If I can be of help, please let me know," was about all Jonathan could say to such a competent daughter.

"Rest assured, Dad—Anson and I have everything in hand, and we'll take great care of Laura. But thanks for offering."

"When are you coming out to see her?" Ellen asked. "She's adorable, just like you used to think I was."

"Right now, I think I'll come to Los Angeles about December twenty-second, and I'll plan to stay through the Christmas holidays. Your mother offered to meet me when I come out, but tell her I still like her too much to have her driven crazy in the Christmas traffic at Los Angeles Airport. It would be bad enough at three o'clock in the morning in mid-July. I'll rent a car and drive directly to the Bel Air Sands. Will you call them and make reservations for me?"

"Sure thing, Dad. I'll make your hotel reservation. We don't have any plans for the holidays. We're saving them for you, and we're looking forward to your visit."

"Thank you, Ellen. I'm looking forward to it, too. I'll be talking to you again soon, and I'll see you on the twenty-second. Goodbye."

"Goodbye, Dad."

Because of the time he spent with Katherine in Chicago and New York, November and December passed rapidly. Jonathan's relationship with Katherine was intensely personal and yet effectively professional. They said very little to their families about one another. They didn't feel they had a "secret" romance, but they did want to keep their special partnership to themselves. As for the holidays, they both thought this time should be reserved for their respective families and old friends. For Jonathan and Katherine, a phone conversation could provide an interim ecstasy that might require intimate contact for most men and women—how often it is, he thought, that romance seems to be such a wonderful and unique possession.

Before he knew it, Jonathan was on a plane to Los Angeles for Christmas at Ellen's. It was about four o'clock in the afternoon when he checked into Room 410 in the wing of the Bel Air Sands hotel that was up on a hill. The room faced south, overlooking western Los Angeles, and he could see the endless rows of high-rise office buildings and apartments strung along Wilshire Boulevard to Santa Monica. He liked the view. To him, it represented the best of Los Angeles and the best from his years in southern California.

All of southern California held many memories for him, stretching over so many years. He had lived there with Mindy during the first two years of their marriage. He and Rene had spent their honeymoon night there, in the Town House on Wilshire. And there were the days before either marriage, when he was a student at UCLA and when he had worked for the Santa Monica newspaper, living in a cottage near the beach.

Jonathan unpacked, put on shorts, and walked down one flight of stairs and across a grassy lawn to the swimming pool. It was such a pretty place and a pretty day. There was no smog.

After an hour of relaxing, he went back to his room, showered, shaved, and dressed for his dinner at Ellen's. He wanted to look the best he could for Rene. He knew Ellen would invite her.

On the way to Ellen's house, he stopped at Golden's big supermarket. He was still a food marketing man and enjoyed checking to see what various product brands were doing, what their shelf or freezer space was. He had been a pioneer in frozen food merchandising when refrigeration had been quite different from what it was now. The array of frozen food products and the variety of fruits, vegetables, and countless new products utterly fascinated him. He inspected the store thoroughly before going to the meat department for the steaks he would purchase for dinner.

He arrived at Ellen's about seven. Rene was already there. In fact, she opened the door for him, and they kissed briefly but warmly. Ellen came up the hall with Laura in her arms and immediately wanted her father to hold her baby, which he did, just as he remembered having held Ellen. He hadn't held a three- or four-month-old baby for twenty-three years or more, so he didn't feel very confident.

But Laura was happy to see him. She looked like a duplicate of Ellen at that age—blonde and bright-eyed. And she seemed to feel perfectly at home with her grandfather. As he walked around the room to the big windows and past the pictures on the wall she seemed to say, "I've had this trip before."

Rene took Laura from Jonathan's arms, and as they both looked at the baby, Rene's eyes reflected for a moment what Jonathan had felt when he first held Laura: once this was to be ours together, and now she is ours separately. Neither one said a word.

When Ellen took Laura to feed her, Jonathan asked Rene if she wanted a martini.

"I would, especially if you'll make them."

"Gladly," he responded and went into the kitchen. Because they would both be driving later, he mixed only one apiece.

Rene seemed to be rather skittish and ill at ease—perhaps fear-ing that her ex-husband might be reading her mental diary, which he probably was, as he looked at her and listened to the inflections in her voice as she spoke with him. He was aware that the martini would probably stimulate her sense of self-sufficiency and independence. Perhaps that was needed. But Jonathan was sympathetic to Rene's position. He wished that he could have remained available to her as a friend and adviser without impinging on her new separateness and independence, her sense of being totally on her own.

They drank a toast to one another for happy holidays and their new granddaughter. In the intimacy of the home environment, Jonathan didn't feel at ease with Rene and wished that Anson, probably delayed in holiday traffic, would get home soon.

Rene spoke up with eagerness and said, "Jonathan, I want to show you my new car. We can take our drinks with us."

"Yes, I do want to see it, Rene. What's special about it?"

The walked outside to look at Rene's new import, a brand and body style still in limited supply. It was parked in the wide driveway to Ellen's garage. Rene took Jonathan on a slow tour around the car.

"How do you like it?" she asked. "Do you approve? Would you like to drive it?"

"Honey," he replied with kindness, "I think you made a very good choice. I like your car, particularly this model and the maroon color. Let's take our drinks inside, and you get your keys. You can take me for a ride around a few blocks, okay?"

That idea pleased Rene, and when she returned to the car she asked, "Sure you don't want to drive?"

"I'm sure," he replied, "because it's your car, and I want to learn more about it."

So Rene sat in the driver's seat, a place and a role she had seldom taken during her marriage to Jonathan. Through the years there had never been any problem about her driving, which was excellent. It was simply that Jonathan had been accepted as head of the family and chief chauffeur.

Rene backed out of the driveway and drove toward the ocean front, only four or five blocks away. Nothing was said, giving Jonathan an opportunity to listen to the motor and to observe how nicely the car handled.

"Do you realize that this is the first car I ever bought on my own?'' Rene said. "It was such a good buy. I bought it from a San Diego dealer, a friend of Bill Bowen's, your old broadcast protegee. He called the dealer for me."

Jonathan thought he might be picking up a hidden message. "That was fine of Bill. Did you have dinner with him?"

"Yes, I did. He wanted to show me his big home, where he lives alone. He still admires you very much. His five-hour daily radio program has the highest rating in town. He says he owes it all to you and your late-night phone call to him when he was working in Denver so many years ago."

"Bill was always selling," Jonathan thought, smiling.

"We just had dinner—that was all," Rene continued. "He seemed pleased that I went to his auto-dealer friend."

"Well, for a first-time car buyer," Jonathan commented supportively, "you took the most important first step—going to a dealer who has been well recommended by someone you trust. But it never occurred to me, Rene, that you would give a damn about buying a car 'on your own,' as you say."

He motioned with his hand. "Look, let's park here for a few minutes. It's a good view of the ocean, and I also want to look at what I'm riding in again."

Rene parked, and they got out and looked down from the palisades to a beautiful stretch of beach. The surf could be heard over the traffic on the highway below. They were both silent. When they simultaneously turned to go, Jonathan reached for the keys and opened the car door for her to ride in her usual seat. He went around to the other side of the car and slid in behind the wheel. Then he carefully looked over the dashboard instruments, started the car, and slowly turned to go up to the corner and return to Ellen's house.

Rene couldn't wait. "How do you like it? Drives very nicely, doesn't it?" She looked at Jonathan for his confirmation of her own beliefs about her new car. His confirmation would also be an affirmation that she could make wise decisions without asking him for advice.

"Rene, it handles very well, The driver feels like a part of the car. Overall, it performs well," he said as he picked up a little speed. "Congratulations. I hope you keep on making good selections."

Jonathan parked in Ellen's driveway. Before getting out of the car, he said rather apologetically, "Honey, I used to go out and just bird-dog the best values and most attractive cars and then go get you to look them over. I believe you felt free to either approve or suggest another car or model. But you always appeared to be pleased with the cars I recommended, especially that marvelous gold sports car you had."

Rene looked at him, and for a moment she was quiet. Then she said probingly, "Jonathan, you do understand, don't you? Purchasing this car was a first for me. And you're right in saying that I was always happy with the cars you recommended. I never expect to have a car better or prettier than the gold sports coupe you found for me."

They sat together in silence. It seemed like a very long time before either of them made a move to get out of the car. Rene was first to reach for the door handle. She had seen Anson's car coming down the street. They greeted Anson and walked into the house with him. Both Rene and Jonathan picked up their drinks, symbolically assuring one another the conversation would be light and happy.

As he drank his martini, he decided again that he had done the best thing for Rene by getting a divorce and encouraging her to marry again. As painful as the divorce was for him, he believed he had acted in Rene's best interest and perhaps in his. He knew he was under less stress than he had been. The doctor had confirmed that. His blood pressure was down, and he no longer found himself gritting his teeth, as he had taken to doing the last two or three years of their marriage.

Rene tugged gently at his arm and said, "Come on and join the family." Anson was holding Laura, who was awake now. He was gently swinging her about, and Laura loved it.

The evening at Ellen's was pleasant. The baby was always the focus of attention when she wasn't asleep. There was lively conversation about the respective jobs of Ellen, Anson, and Rene. They liked to keep one another up to date, and Jonathan listened so he could keep abreast of their thinking and experiences.

When they were leaving, Rene asked Jonathan if he would like to see her apartment. He told her that he would come by tomorrow after she returned from work and asked if she might like to go to dinner with him at one of her favorite restaurants. She readily agreed.

316

Back in his room at the hotel, he thought about Rene, and he also thought about Katherine. Both Rene and Katherine were wonderful women. He wished that Rene had been a little more ambitious, more eager to grow as much as she could. Then she might not have had time for the crowd who tempted her to join them and just live day by day. That we all must do, Jonathan agreed, but we should also "take thought for tomorrow." He didn't call Katherine, because they had decided not to phone one another until after the holidays, but he had sent her a large basket of roses, arranged to look as if they had just been gathered from the garden.

# 31

At six-thirty the following evening, Jonathan drove up to Rene's apartment building on Malcolm Avenue. He was familiar with the area from his early days in Los Angeles. It was a good area in which to live. Her building was modern, well-maintained, and not very large. He used the outside phone buttons to ring her apartment. She immediately buzzed the door open, and he took the elevator to the second floor and walked down the long hall to her apartment, a corner unit facing the street. Rene was standing in the doorway, ready to greet him. She offered no kiss, and Jonathan did not seek one.

As he entered the apartment, he admired the careful placement of her Baker commode. She had prepared martinis, and he followed her into the kitchen, where she poured one for him. After a quick glance at the kitchen and her new extension dining table, they returned to the living room. She showed him her office, where he was surprised to see the sofa bed covered with about a dozen pillows. He withheld comment and followed her into the large, comfortable bedroom.

When they returned to the living room, she asked him what he thought of her apartment.

"I think it's very spacious and quite well done, except for one thing," Jonathan replied, "the frightening number of casual pillows around. Whose idea was that?"

Rene was caught off guard, and her voice reflected it. "A friend of Ellen's is a retired decorator. She offered to help me furnish and decorate the place. Don't you like the pillows?"

"Rene, I like pillows, but when a woman piles them up on sofas and in corners, it indicates how conscious she may be of sex, or the lack thereof. Lots of pillows are in the current decorator's repertoire, but they don't know why. You certainly don't need any vicarious sexual consolation, do you?"

Rene smiled and shook her head.

"I didn't think you did—that is, unless you've changed a great deal. So I'd get rid of at least half the damn pillows. They don't do you justice!"

Rene got up and went to the door of her office. She looked at the pillows, some ruffled and some plain, all piled up on the sofa bed. As she turned around in the doorway, she said to Jonathan, "It's strange that you have that reaction. I never thought about it. You may be right. The decorator was an older woman and perhaps is living more with sexual memories.

"Funny!" she said rather pensively.

As she came back into the living room, she was thinking about the pillows and Jonathan's observation. "But you notice everything, and everything seems to reveal something to you. Normal people don't go around looking under rugs.

"How do you like my martini?" she asked.

"Lord, Rene, the martini is superb and could be dangerously tempting."

"Well, I don't know about that. A very handsome professor came over to take me to dinner last week, and I was attracted to him. But the martinis didn't tempt him to rise to the opportunity."

"Where did you sit?" he asked curiously and casually.

"I sat right where I am now."

"And where did he sit?"

"Just where you are."

"Well, Rene, you may already be taking on more lovers than you should, but I can offer some suggestions. Never, never have a curved sofa in your main living area where you're most likely to sit for cocktails," Jonathan said, as he put his arm up on the back of the sofa and turned to face her.

"Have a straight, wide sofa, where the man and woman can sit alongside one another, like the beautiful, big sofa in our Church City home.

"You know, Rene, so many men and women in this age of free-wheeling love have forgotten how to be romantic. But then, perhaps some never knew how to begin with.

"At any rate, first sit next to the man. Don't sit in the corner of the sofa, where one of you would have to make an overt move to reach out to touch the other.

"And second, touch one another's hands often. So many men and women forget how sensitive hands are. A gentle placing of

319

one's hand on the other's hand, while sitting together on a big sofa, can lead to so much more. The touch of someone else's hand is very gentle and very proper—and very effective. Old or young, male or female—we're all subject to the romantic suggestion that 'just the touch of your hand on mine' can bring people together. This is true whether they be friends or lovers."

Once again the past came to his mind.

"When we were married, Rene, we often touched hands."

Rene didn't respond, so after a few moments' reflection Jonathan continued.

"Touching and holding hands, even for a moment or two, can convey regard and warmth. If the other person pulls back quickly, as if he or she has touched a cake of ice or a hot stove, it may reveal that the person so reacting is an all-or-nothing type of lover, fearful that he or she will let go too quickly—which is to say he or she would likely be a lousy lover in bed. So, for you, try the hand contact and you may save yourself an unrewarding sexual liaison.

"And last but not least, something should be said about kissing. Once you get to the kissing stage, a sophisticated lady like you should let the first be a gentle, soft kiss. Repeated soft, tender kisses help lovers absorb one another spiritually. When a woman, especially the woman, follows up the first kiss with a wide-open mouth, a so-called French kiss, as if she's ready to consume the man, a man often backs away.

"On the other hand, if the man quickly responds with the digging-in type of kiss, then the woman should know that he expects her to follow up by following down to where such a kiss is more satisfying to him."

Once again silence filled the room, and Jonathan wondered if this conversation would end here. But Rene continued it, even though he was prepared to change the subject.

"Jonathan, what if the man goes into the full-mouth kiss in instant response to the woman's soft kiss?" Rene inquired.

Jonathan had a ready answer. "If the man instantly responds like that, then the woman should figure he will be looking for his own quick sexual satisfaction and is also likely to be a disappointment in bed.

"You see, Rene, the problem is that so many young women and young older women think every man wants instant gratification. They see these hot kisses that are so commonplace in soap

320

operas and in movies nowadays, even movies rated PG. People who see this frothy action figure that's the 'in' way to show how sexy they are, how much they want to make love. In the soap operas and movies, right after they show the lovers devouring one another with such kisses, they seem invariably to turn off the light or switch to another scene, confirming what the viewer was thinking had to happen. Such treatment says making quick love is the expected follow-up to the wide-open-mouth, tongue-twisting kiss.

"Enough said?" he asked abruptly.

"Too much said, Jonathan. I've been that eager with you, but you were my husband. However, in case I'm ever carried along on a crest of martinis, I'll remember what you've just said."

Rene looked at Jonathan's nearly empty glass and poured him another martini. She freshened hers and went to get more ice. Jonathan seemed lost in thought.

As Rene returned from the kitchen, he said, "Well, maybe I should make one last suggestion. If a woman has invited a man to her apartment for cocktails and she knows she'd like to make love with him if developments encourage it, she should be sure that the drapes and curtains in her bedroom have already been arranged to ensure privacy. She shouldn't have to slow the action in order to pull the curtains."

He smiled and said, almost to himself, "I was just remembering the days when efficiency or studio apartments often had the pull-down, wall-type beds. By the time the bed was pulled down, the woman had sometimes changed her mind—a sad situation for an eager man."

Rene smiled too. "Jonathan, you didn't have that kind of bed in your apartment, did you?" she teased.

"No! But before I married you, one of the more mature girls I dated had a damn wall-bed."

"Knowing you, I'm sure the delay didn't affect your readiness," Rene said knowingly.

Jonathan nodded but chose not to respond with any kind of comeback. He knew they were getting on sensitive ground for Rene.

She never liked to think about how many girls Jonathan had had before marrying her. She didn't really care, but she had never ceased to wonder why he hadn't tried to seduce her. If she had known then what she knew now, she was sure she would have appeared more available.

She grinned and thought, "If Jonathan had known me then as I am now, he certainly would have tried and succeeded. I know now I was too reserved as a young woman, and for the first few years as his wife. But he never complained and was always patient and tender with me."

Now her problem was to get rid of the barriers of her reserve without losing her dignity. Interestingly enough, Jonathan was giving her some very practical suggestions on how to do just that.

Jonathan spotted her grin and asked, "What are you smiling about?"

"Oh, about the range of your philosophy and the knowledge that you've always loved doing research before voicing firm opinions. You've just given me some pretty good advice about intimate relationships."

"Well, Rene, the point I was making is the advantage of having all things ready to go when it's countdown time.

"Incidentally, I have just one final little suggestion. To seduce a man without, as you said, demeaning yourself, always reach for his hand before you reach for his zipper."

Both he and Rene laughed and reached for their martinis. They knew that this touch of levity meant their instructional session was over.

"Now then, our very good cocktails here are finished. Where are we going to dinner?" Jonathan asked.

As Rene took their glasses to the kitchen she said, "There's a good restaurant on San Vicente near Santa Monica Boulevard. Let's go there—and let's go in my car."

"That's fine, Rene. You know the way better than I do."

The restaurant on San Vicente was one Rene had frequented often, and she seemed comfortable in it. After they were seated, she said casually, "We often come here."

"We?" Jonathan asked. "Who is 'we'?"

"One of my boyfriends and I," she said. "Do you mind if I smoke, Jonathan?"

Under normal circumstances, she would not have tainted their dinner with a cigarette, because she knew how much he disliked her smoking. But for some reason, she was aware that she was going to need something to fortify her.

322

"Go ahead and smoke if you have to," he said matter-of-factly.

Rene lit her cigarette and immediately blew a smoke ring, which she did well. Jonathan remembered that she had started making smoke rings at Carolina State, and he wondered if there was any symbolism in her learning to make them so well.

"What's he like?" he asked tersely. "Tall and dark with a Madrid accent?" He remembered Rene's obvious interest in a handsome man she had seen in a cafe in Madrid long ago.

"Oh, he's an ordinary fellow, nice looking—not tall, dark, or foreign. But he does pay so much attention to me. That's what I like about him."

"He does! Then he must be married and trying to compensate for not paying enough attention to his wife," Jonathan retaliated.

"Actually, he *is* married! But I don't mind, because I don't really want to mix love with loving." She added rather thoughtfully, "Unmarried men seem to want to fall in love if you go to bed with them."

Jonathan just sat there and looked at Rene. She looked at her cigarette, avoiding eye contact with him.

"That's a rather sad state of mind, Rene. *You* may prefer it this way, but do you think his children would think it fine and dandy that their father has a mistress, even if she doesn't wish to fall in love with their daddy?

"And what if you were in an auto accident with a married man? What would his wife and children and our children feel and say when they read it in the newspapers, heard it on the radio, or maybe even saw it on the evening news?"

Rene was taken aback. "I really don't think about the marital status of my lovers," she said defensively.

"Well, you should!" Jonathan said emphatically. "Obviously you already have many lovers. Are you trying to make up for the men you missed when you were young and single?"

Rene was ready with a sharp retort. "I still have a way to go to catch up with you, Jonathan. I remember on one of your television shows when three out of four models on the show had memories of your apartment."

"That may be true, Rene, yet only one in ten ever got into my bed. Furthermore, I was a widower, and they were all single women. There were no third parties and innocent bystanders to be hurt. Did you ever think of that?"

They fell silent as the waiter appraoched their table.

Jonathan looked up and said, "Here's our waiter. Have you looked at the menu?"

"No, but I know what I want."

She turned to the waiter and said, "I'll have the petite filet mignon, medium, and a mixed green salad."

"And you, sir?" the waiter asked Jonathan.

"I'll have your chopped sirloin, well done, and some Tabasco —also an order of sliced tomatoes.

"Rene, you may remember Sallie in Church City. You liked her."

Rene nodded.

"Do you also recall that she had long ago reentered college for an advanced degree? It was then that she adopted the amoral, vulgar, free mores of some of her young friends. You knew she was going with a married man."

Once again Rene nodded, but this time she smiled slightly.

"For reasons I don't understand," he continued, "you thought that was romantic. At any rate, as you may recall, she left her husband. Well, I talked with her just the other day.

"She had moved to Cleveland to be near her married lover. She reported that her lover's wife had tried to commit suicide. The attempt the woman made on her own life failed, but she was hospitalized. A few months later, she died naturally, probably out of despair. Through all of that, Sallie never stopped seeing the man."

He waited for Rene to say something, but when she didn't, he hoped he had started her thinking about her own situation.

"Since Sallie's lover's wife was dead, they planned to marry. But suddenly her lover, for whom she had left a husband and three children, for whose wife she cared nothing, died of a massive heart attack."

That brought Rene around, and she said with great feeling, "Oh, poor Sallie! Poor Ed! I hadn't heard about this. I did hear from Sallie that she and Ed were going to honeymoon in southern California, and they planned to call me. My God!"

Rene reached for another cigarette.

Jonathan continued as if he had not been interrupted.

"I asked Sallie how her life was going. Sallie said her life was a disaster."

324

"I haven't heard from Sallie for weeks," Rene said. "Are you going to see her if she comes to Washington?"

"Rene, if she wants my advice, I'll give it to her. But if she wants me to make love to her, I won't. She is unacceptable to me."

Rene frowned. "But, Jonathan, why be so judgmental? I don't like to pass judgment on my friends, and she was our friend."

"Rene, what if you had a cocktail party in your apartment for fifteen or twenty couples—all friends? The party ended, and the guests went on their way. The next day you heard a news broadcast stating that one of the gentlest and finest girls at your party had been found raped and strangled to death. A man who also attended your party was arrested and charged with the rape and murder. They were *both* your friends. Can you say that you wouldn't be judgmental of your friend who allegedly raped and murdered your other friend?"

"No," Rene said seriously. "I would be judgmental in that case. I'll admit there are times when one must be judgmental. But there are other times when one need not be. Why are you so critical of me? I haven't killed anyone."

"No, Rene, my dear, you haven't, and I'm sure you would never want to, not even when you get very angry with me. I'm sure Sallie couldn't possibly have killed any one, either. Yet she may have contributed to the death of her lover's wife—and to his own death, as a consequence of his great stress."

"Jonathan, I would never want to hurt anyone. I also don't want to be in love with anyone, if I can help it. I don't even want to be in love with you any more, but I'll always respect you."

They both sat quietly, not moving. Rene took out another cigarette, lit it, and looked away from Jonathan. He stared at the table, but he could see her in many scenes from the past. He could also see her in scenes from a possible future, and he was very concerned. He still cared very much for her.

He remarked, as though to a ghost, "It's not unusual for divorcees and many other single women, especially successful businesswomen, to want sex without love. They fear the bondage of love, and many have suffered greatly when these bonds of love were broken. All of us, men and women, suffer when many, many years of interdependence have been cast aside. So the divorcee tells herself that married men protect her from the entrapment of

325

love and allow her to have both sex and freedom at the same time.

"But when stealing an evening of pleasure injures innocent bystanders, the whole thing is wrong!"

He didn't give Rene a chance to say anything. He wanted to make very clear to her his adamant position.

"As attractive as you are, Rene, and as sexual as you have become, for God's sake, for your own sake, for the sake of others, please be selective! Being a married man's mistress is still 'back-street,' degrading, and cheap. You have higher standards than that. I know it. Why destroy them?"

His voice dropped, as did his eyes, as he uttered this last sentence.

Rene waited a moment to make sure Jonathan was finished, then said, "You speak as if I'm doing something terribly wrong in going to bed with a married man. I'm single, separated, free, and soon to have a final divorce decree. Talk to the married men. They do the wrong!"

"My God, Rene, surely you can't believe what you're saying. Remember, it takes two to tango."

"Jonathan, can't you approve of a simple sexual liaison between a man and a woman?"

"Yes, with the clear qualification that others aren't hurt, but their not knowing about it doesn't remove the hurt.

"You wouldn't steal another person's car or money. And certainly you shouldn't steal another person's husband. Because if you did, you'd be stealing love and happiness from children you never see."

Jonathan couldn't believe that Rene could be a thief of anything. He expected her to have lovers, but not someone else's husband.

As a clinching argument, he added, "Rene, imagine all the lovers you've ever had assembled in one room. Would you then have to go hide from yourself?"

"Jonathan," Rene said as she put out her cigarette, "I'll break off my relationship with this man the next time I see him."

"Can't you just tell him no over the phone? Why have any more contact with him? As long as one can say yes or no, one has tremendous power."

Rene thought a moment and then said, "I guess I could do that, but we've been good friends."

326

"Friends!" Jonathan said, sickened with disgust.

Just then the waiter arrived with their dinners.

"Our dinner is here. Let's try to eat it," Jonathan said.

No other words were spoken until they ordered coffee.

"I do hope you'll get married someday," Jonathan said quietly. "If I hadn't hoped that, I wouldn't have opted for divorce. If you don't want to mix love with loving, then mix pride with loving, pride in yourself and in your partner. I tell you what I often told our daughters: 'Treat yourself like a Mercedes-Benz convertible, not like a used pick-up truck. Think of yourself as precious.' "

Rene became very defensive, which Jonathan knew was a crutch to keep herself from crying.

"Do you realize that if I lived by your standards, I'd practically be celibate and be rid of most men? I like making love. You taught me to enjoy lovemaking and to be good at it—which I am. And now, do you expect me to throw all that out the window? Now it's selectivity that I'm supposed to learn. Just where do you suggest I go to meet these unattached, elite, prospective husbands?

"Furthermore, are *you* only going with the elite? What about those girls you went with when you had all the TV shows?"

"They were all pretty, smart, and single. I was single. Being elite doesn't mean being rich or snobbish. If you can come up with men of the same quality as the girls I dated, and the one I married— you—then pick any one of them for a bedmate or a husband. Men can't afford to be promiscuous any more than women can."

As they drank their coffee, both Rene and Jonathan spoke more normally. They had passed the peak of their basic disagreement. Jonathan even noticed a note of resignation in Rene's voice. They were now looking for solutions, a way out.

"Go to church. A high-society church is a good place to look for a good man."

"Church!" Rene exclaimed, taken completely off guard. Fortunately, the people at the adjoining tables had gone, so no one turned to stare.

"Yes. Go the the Episcopal church. There must be a large, ritzy one in this rich Westwood area," Jonathan replied.

"Why Episcopal?" Rene asked incredulously. "I used to be a Catholic, not an Episcopalian. Why not Methodist or Presbyterian or whatever?"

Then, feeling less tense, Rene asked him, "Would you care to share a piece of fresh lemon pie with me? They make it just like I used to. It's really good. Maybe a little dessert would be good for us."

He smiled with fond remembrance. "If it tastes like the pie you made, then let's get a piece. The waiter has been looking at us for the last ten minutes, but now I don't see him. I'll go find him."

Jonathan went over to another waiter and asked him to tell their waiter to bring one piece of fresh lemon pie for the lady and two fresh cups of coffee. "After all," he said to himself, "what if I can't go to sleep tonight? I probably won't anyway, so I might as well have another cup of coffee."

His waiter came out of the kitchen and signaled that he had gotten the message.

When Jonathan returned to the table and sat down, Rene said, "You're still as impatient as ever."

"You know, Rene, if I were alone, I really wouldn't be so impatient about service and things. But along the way, I had a lovely wife and three kids, and I got into the habit of trying to do for them whatever I could, even things like hastening an order for fresh lemon pie."

"Thank you, Jonathan. I guess I was confusing attentiveness with impatience. I appreciate all you've tried to do for me and the children. But I'd like it better if you could just quit giving me a dose of medicine with all the nice things you do."

"I want my patients to stay healthy," he replied. "The worst thing about my medicine is that I have to take it, too."

He waved a hand in the air, as if to clear away their light conversation, and resumed his sermon. "You were asking me why you should go to the Episcopal church. Well, the Episcopal church would make you, an ex-Catholic, feel right at home. But then, the Episcopal church would make a Methodist or a Presbyterian feel at home. As an ex-Baptist myself, I don't think many Baptists, except the old Northern Baptists, would feel so much at home with Episcopalians. You see, the Episcopalians are pretty close to being neutral. No other religion seems to feel competitive with them. People like bankers, advertising agency executives, lawyers, doctors, dentists, and other service-oriented professionals can be Episcopalian, and none of their clients will object."

Rene smiled at Jonathan across the table. "You do talk about serious things in funny ways sometimes. I think I used to be such a devout audience for you that you developed a lot of these ideas just to keep me absorbed."

Jonathan smiled, too. "Thank you, honey, for still indulging me a little, but I have an additional suggestion for you. Look for a dentist."

This time Rene laughed aloud. "A dentist?"

"Yes, a dentist," he returned. "They certainly used to like you. Don't you remember, when you were young, how every dentist you went to or took the kids to made a pass at you? In fact, there were certain dentists you yourself were quite pleased with.

"In those days, you were young and pretty and faithful. You're still pretty and don't need to be faithful, except to yourself. I don't believe you took on any dentists, but you did tell me about them in jest. Dentists can be quite sexy."

The waiter arrived with the coffees and the piece of very tasty-looking fresh lemon pie, which he put in front of Rene. She asked Jonathan to try it first to see that it was as good as she had said. He took his coffee spoon and cut a piece of the pie off the end.

"When you say food is good, I always know it will live up to my expectations. This is marvelous pie. Are you sure you don't come over and make it for them? I've been so busy talking, in case you didn't notice, I forgot to tell you how good my chopped sirloin was. Your filet looked just right, too."

"I'm glad you like the food here," Rene said, looking pleased. She tactfully refrained from saying, "We like it here."

"Tell me why dentists are often sexy. Are you joking or serious? But come to think of it," she added, "I believe you could be serious. Just about every dentist I've gone to has, more or less, propositioned me. They all seem to have been interesting men, too."

"Rene, I am serious. In contrast to doctors of medicine, dentists see a lot of women patients who come to them just for cosmetic purposes. They are often divorcees and are very often around their sexiest time of life—thirty to fifty-five. And I mean sexiest from the standpoint of wanting sex, not getting enough sex, and knowing what men like in sex."

Rene nodded and smiled knowingly.

"So a woman gets into the dentist's chair, and pretty soon she's stretched out horizontally. The dentist is standing over his patient in a power position, looking down on that horizontal female body.

Soon he's leaning over her, sometimes leaning on her chest, while checking her teeth. His eyes and face are often very close to her face. The proximity is such that he could virtually stick out his tongue and touch her mouth.

"You know, there's a lot of sensuality about the mouth. The tongue is an arousing organ."

Rene nodded again.

"Furthermore," he continued, "as the woman is stretched out in the dentist's chair and he's working and moving around, her elbow may accidentally touch his crotch. If he's been leaning on her chest, or if she's just damn pretty, she might find that her elbow has hit something hard, whether intended or not.

"Now, with that scenario, is it any wonder that dentists are often considered quite sexy fellows?" he concluded matter-of-factly. "Yes, Rene, the ideal mate for you is a successful Episcopalian dentist."

Rene looked at him in bewilderment and said, "That's one of the oddest stories I've ever heard you tell. But the funny thing is, I've had that exact experience with a dentist—in fact, two of them."

"And I can guess who—the young fellow, about thirty-five, in Wood Lake and the phenomenally successful dentist in Chicago who used to play tennis so much," Jonathan responded.

Rene looked surprised. "Yes! How did you guess?"

"Simple, my dear Watson. You always looked happier than a person is supposed to look after visiting a dentist."

"Oh, Jonathan," Rene said with feigned coyness, "I wish I could take some of your notions seriously. However, there is something in what you say, even when it sounds crazy. I've learned that over the years. Maybe I'll drop in at an Episcopal church someday. And —I'll watch my dentists more closely."

When the waiter brought the check, Jonathan handed him the charge card. He returned quickly, and Jonathan added up the amount to include the tip. They walked slowly out of the restaurant and took the elevator down a flight to where they had parked the car. After they had driven out of the garage, Rene thanked Jonathan for the dinner.

"Rene," he asked with real curiosity, "do you pay your share of the dinner checks when you go out with men? With your salary and the good return on your investments, you probably have a much higher income than the majority of your dates."

"I do offer to pay occasionally," she replied.

Jonathan continued as if he hadn't heard what she had said. "With all their independence and freedom, with no restrictions, I think women of comparable or higher incomes than their dates should pay their share. What do you think?"

"Well, I just don't make a big deal of it. Besides, most men seem to want to pay."

Jonathan didn't turn his head to look at Rene. He knew he was about to administer another dose of medicine to her.

"That sort of puts you in the position of exchanging sex for the price of dining at a classy restaurant, doesn't it? Of course, depending on where you go, a dinner for two could easily cost a hundred dollars, maybe two-hundred dollars including tips. But if you're going to make love for a hundred dollars, why not make love for five hundred, or better, a thousand? You're that good in bed."

Rene was aghast. "Don't you ever let up? That's not a very nice way to talk to me. Women have been in the habit of letting men pay. Furthermore, I enjoy having sex, and the price of dinner has nothing to do with that."

Jonathan knew he had picked a bad time and place to talk about such personal matters with Rene. She was driving very carefully, because she knew she was getting very angry. He decided to say no more than she wanted to hear. But if she kept talking, he would, too.

Rene knew that Jonathan had made a point that she should have thought more about than she had. She knew that two of her lovers didn't have nearly the income she did. Even her married friend wasn't rich, but she felt he should pay, because she had to admit to herself that she was his mistress.

She was not ready to end the conversation, as doing so now would leave her in a very vulnerable position with her own thoughts. "Why don't you just let me live my own life, Jonathan?" she asked.

"If you didn't have children whom you should care about, and I think you do, then your question would be fair. I'm in favor of allowing any woman to be a whore if she wants to be, or has to be, in order to eat or to feed her family. But you don't need to act like one. And I'm sure most women who have to be would rather have a choice. You're a woman of independent means, an educated woman with a high-class job and three wonderful children."

Rene was silent, and they drove several blocks without saying a word. As she turned the corner of the block on which she lived, she slowed almost to a stop and said very softly, "I feel that you rejected me by getting the divorce." She continued almost pleadingly, "Why don't you just let me live on my own for a while, have a few men, and then come back to you and be a better wife because I've had the experience I missed—experiences that you and my three children had plenty of when you all lived on your own?"

She stopped the car in front of her apartment building before she got to the driveway. Turning to him, she said, "I just wanted to be free for a little while. But you rushed the divorce. I suppose your ego and pride wouldn't stand for your separated wife to be having fun with other men."

Jonathan replied that he was indeed sorry for all the pain that their divorce was causing. "Rene, I feel like saying yes to all of the above. I really was concerned that you would be promiscuous, as you have been. I didn't want my legal wife sleeping around with virtually anybody. I thought if you had a divorce, you would at least try seriously to find a decent, able man and marry him. He didn't need to be rich or eminent, just a man who could appreciate you and enjoy your friends and the things you like. I hadn't been doing that for you. You were suffering, and so was I. We did the best we could to try to live together. But you're not doing the best you can to try to make a good life for yourself, a life that you and all your family can be proud of and want for you."

"Jonathan, I want to ask you something that's been puzzling me. Did you suggest that I go back to my maiden name or my TV name because you believed you might have reason to be ashamed of me?"

"Yes, I would have preferred that you do what you're doing under another name, for my benefit—and our children's. I'm ashamed of myself for being unable to do and be all the things that you seem to want. But I couldn't go back and arrange a different early life for you or for myself. You were a victim, in a way, of cultural changes. I've been a victim, too."

Rene came right back at him. "The children are much more understanding and forgiving than you are."

332

"Rene, you are their only mother," Jonathan said very softly and carefully.

She didn't respond, but he could see tears welling up in her eyes.

She took her foot off the accelerator and said in a whisper, "We're home. Let's not talk about personal matters any more. Can't we just be friends? Do you have to criticize my morals?"

"Rene, none of your lovers will tell you the truth or try to get you to think things through. They'll tell you funny stories and make love to you. They'll tell you what they think will please you and reward them."

He paused. "And when a pretty woman says to a man, 'Let's just be good friends,' the statement can often be roughly translated to mean, 'I wish to receive, but not to give.' "

As Rene parked her car in her garage, she said, "I'm almost sick. I feel a little weak. Please, just take me up to my door and go on. I suppose we'll see each other at Ellen's tomorrow.

"Yes, we will, and Rene, I'll try to keep all my displeasing thoughts to myself. I do want you to be healthy and happy."

She turned and looked at him. "Thank you. But I think you've made me very unhappy tonight. On the whole, though, I believe that I'm happier than you are with our divorced lives."

"You're right, Rene. I've missed you very much. I'm deeply ashamed that I didn't have the power to make our lives such that we need never have parted. You always had such faith in my ability to do everything.

"But maybe we've done the right thing," he said with growing confidence. "Maybe after a while each of us will again achieve the kind of happiness we once shared, except that this achievement will be independent of each other."

Jonathan had held Rene's arm while he was talking and walking her to her apartment door.

"Good night," she said as she turned the key in her door lock. "Sleep well."

"Good night, Rene."

# 32

Jonathan had a pleasant Christmas at Ellen's home. He and Rene were cordial, in keeping with the holiday scene. And Anson's parents were there. His mother dashed about, trying to help Ellen, while his father nursed a beer and tried to stay out of the traffic pattern. Rene and Jonathan finally got a phone call through to Bruce in Tokyo. Susan hadn't come out from New York, as she would have been able to stay only two days because of difficult exams coming up in her finance course.

Rene and Jonathan enjoyed the extended family group gathered at Ellen's home and were amused by the baby, who was a far greater attraction than the Christmas tree this year. Laura received so many gifts for her future use that Ellen almost had to catalog them.

Rene gave Jonathan a gray, cashmere pullover sweater. He gave Rene a very distinctive gold mesh ring. She thought it was beautiful but said she couldn't wear it, because it would rub against her fingers and cause irritation. She explained that years ago she had had a ring that did the same thing. Furthermore, she said that she had just purchased a new ring as a present to herself and that Ellen had approved her selection. It was a smooth gold ring with a scroll design that extended about an inch up to her first knuckle and a quarter-inch back toward her hand.

Jonathan invited Rene to join him outside on the entrance porch. He acted as if he needed to examine the ring more closely in daylight, but he also wanted to speak to her privately.

"Did Ellen actually recommend this ring for you, Rene?" he asked pointedly.

"Yes, she did. You can ask her," Rene said defensively. "Why do you ask?"

"Well," Jonathan said rather sadly, "the ring looks like an inexpensive piece of costume jewelry. To anyone who notices, and one can hardly miss it, it makes a certain statement about the wearer.

It says, 'Look at me! I am strong. I am self-sufficient. I am approachable—not selective, not distinctive or dignified.' "

"But, Jonathan," Rene protested, "my friends tell me I'm already too dignified. I don't want to be dignified. Even if I could wear the ring you gave me—and it is a rare and exquisite ring—it would represent a me I don't want to be any more."

"Rene," Jonathan began again, "I understand what you mean. I agree that you're entitled to be what you want to be. You want to be a pal to your co-workers and just a woman to your lovers. Knowing that to be the case, I carefully selected a ring to remind you of your recent impressive stature. I guess you might as well complete the metamorphosis, but please get rid of a ring that sends an aggressive, androgynous signal. Let's hope it's just a phase you're going through.

"Incidentally, did any of your lovers give you a Christmas present, such as a beautiful bouquet of long-stemmed roses, or a piece of fine jewelry, perhaps?"

"No, Jonathan," Rene answered tersely, "only you, my former lover." Saying that, she went back inside.

The remainder of the day, they talked casually but said very little to each other. They did not kiss goodbye when Jonathan left to go to his hotel. When Rene returned to him the beautiful ring he had given her, Jonathan noticed she had removed her newly purchased ornamental ring.

"Maybe your current friends will like your ring better than the plainer one I purchased for you," he said.

He hastened away so Rene wouldn't see him cry for her.

Earlier, before he gave her the ring and while they were all sharing good Christmas feelings, she had asked him if he might not like to have an apartment in southern California. Jonathan had said, "No," but later he asked Ellen to be sure her mother understood that if she ever really needed him, he would be there for her.

As soon as he was in his hotel room, he cried. He did not go out to dinner.

It took him a long time to get to sleep Christmas night, and he slept late the following morning. After a solitary brunch, he went back to visit with Ellen, Anson, and Laura. He played with the baby, watched a football game with Anson, and talked politics with Ellen.

As their visit was drawing to a close, Ellen and her father were watching Laura moving back and forth in her automatic swing. She inquired of him, "What will you be doing in the near future, Dad? I know you can't take a full week's vacation from your retirement without getting itchy to do something that we never expect."

"Ellen, honey, I really don't know what I expect to be doing," he said solemnly. "I don't wish to bury my mind and soul in an unproductive, diminishing retirement." Then in a livelier tone of voice, he shared his latest brainstorm. "But I did have an idea on the way out to Los Angeles—an utterly impractical notion about a low-cost but high-value movie—a satirical musical comedy.

"You may not recall, but one or two of my Palm Springs friends and I once helped finance a Broadway play."

"Yes, Dad, I remember."

"Well, my friends have plenty of money, and having tax-exempt bond coupons clipped for you isn't as much fun as being in show business. They may want something more 'in' than cattle, real estate, or off-shore tax shelters. I'll let you know what the prospects are in a month or two.

"I'll drive over to Palm Springs tomorrow, stay there a day or two, and fly on to Washington.

"I've enjoyed my visit, Ellen, but I think it's time I call it a day and return to my hotel.

"Let me tell Anson goodbye, and then I want to hold Laura one more time before I go."

Jonathan got up and went to the living room, where Anson was reading the sports page. He met Ellen and Laura in the hall by the front door. After kissing them both, he went to his car and waved to all three members of this new family as they stood at the front entrance. Ellen and Anson both helped Laura wave goodbye to him.

He drove slowly away from Ellen's house up to Sunset Boulevard and east to the Bel Air Sands hotel. Everything along the way was so Christmasy. It seemed to him that southern Californians needed double doses of decorations to make up for their lack of snow—or to convince themselves it was the holiday season. He bet it was cold and Christmasy in Chicago.

He could look back and see in all the season's symbols the Christmas trees he had had in Winnetka with Mindy and the trees with Rene and the children, especially the big trees they had had while living on the farm at Wood Lake. Yes, he supposed that he had had his share of merry Christmases. But surely, he thought, one should not live just for Christmases past.

In Jonathan's case, he appreciated those trees of love and happiness because, until he married Mindy, he had never had a Christmas tree, except as a child working as a janitor in the First Baptist Church in Cotton Creek, Arkansas. In the church he had helped put the popcorn balls and strings of popcorn on the real holly tree that the farm members brought in from the lowlands of the Little Missouri River. At the time, he had felt that he was sharing his Christmas tree with the preacher and the members of the congregation.

On his first Christmas with Mindy, he had had his very own home, his very own Christmas tree, with a loved one to share it. Jonathan thought that there is no need to have a Christmas tree without a loved one to share it. But how narrow and selfish he must be to need a loving woman, his special lover, to feel the joy of Christmas. Lord, he must grow up to be the mature man he had always wanted to be; so far, he hadn't reached that point. Now he must enjoy Christmas because of all the happiness it might bring to others and in gratitude for the happy Christmases he had known.

As he turned off Sunset into the hotel driveway, he stopped for a moment to look at the hotel entrance shimmering with holiday lights and flowers. At the top of the hill, he parked his car, then went to his room, changed into a dark suit and bow tie, and went down to the main lobby. Overcoming the pain of Christmas present, he brought forth the joys of Christmases past and went into the delightfully decorated dining room. He wondered if Katherine would be having even a few seconds of thoughts about him.

"Just one, Mr. Barron?" the maitre d' asked, with condolence in his voice.

"Yes, Edward. I thought I'd come down and enjoy having dinner at your place tonight."

He gave Edward a twenty-dollar bill and said, "Merry Christmas and a bottle of champagne for you."

"Thank you, Mr. Barron, and Merry Christmas to you."

The next morning, Sunday, Jonathan ate breakfast in his room. He sat facing the windows so he could look out over the broad expanse of the western half of Los Angeles. He ate slowly. There was no reason for him to zip through breakfast, but he was always leaning toward the next move. He picked up the Sunday *Times* and made a conscious effort to read slowly, while taking an occasional sip of coffee.

"After all," he said aloud, "it's a Christmas vacation time."

Through his marriages to Mindy and Rene, his early tendency toward isolation had been weakened. But he knew that he might always be susceptible to a beautiful rose, a lovely song, a view of a distant valley in early spring, or the Shenandoah mountains in late fall. There was within him a divine discontent that would forever keep him reaching out for another soul, another mind, and another body with whom to share beauty. He knew he must awaken to the same reality that he preached to others: "Do not try to drive out the darkness; instead, turn on the light." Somewhere, from someone, he must get a strong light to illumine the darkness of his isolation. Could it be Katherine?

Now it occurred to him that if he possessed the same faith and feelings of some of his religious friends, he could "take his troubles to the Lord in prayer." Maybe he should, but he couldn't.

Jonathan knew that one could substitute a commitment to a cause or to a mission for the warm exultation of individual love. He thought that perhaps he had paid too great a price throughout his life for his almost obsessive devotion to promoting better ethics and greater honesty to help maintain freedom in America. Rene had felt the loss of his time and attention, not to another woman, but to an abstraction that had sapped the strength of his mind and his body. Historically, however, more wives have lost their husbands to greed than to good. He thought that money is often a man's most demanding mistress. But whatever the reason, the loss of love is tragic, very tragic.

Jonathan was still uncertain about his final role in life. Fate kept dealing him new hands, apparently with the expectation that he continue to play the game.

He wondered if he had been searching all his life for the mother he had never known. Or was he, like Dante in the *Divine Comedy*, searching for a Beatrice, the angel of incomparable beauty and all-encompassing love and understanding? Indeed, like Dante, he had come through hell, but he was still in purgatory. He doubted that he would ever enter paradise as Dante had done in his great epic, unless a Beatrice came to fetch him. Maybe Katherine would be an earthly Beatrice for him.

Yes, he knew he was not going to enter paradise without being fetched or kicked out of purgatory. In the *Divine Comedy,* Dante had Virgil to guide him through hell to paradise, where Beatrice, the super-angel, could advise and console him. The poets understand what dreams are made of, he thought.

Jonathan understood very well the glory and beauty of love. It was love that gave Dante inspiration and strength and guidance. It is love that makes a home a paradise on earth.

He directed his thoughts toward his future and the best use of his time. Until Katherine appeared, he had virtually eliminated any social life. But Katherine must live her own life. She would be busy for a long time. Perhaps he should undertake and finance the long-postponed research projects he thought were so obviously needed, projects that probably no one else would do.

And he wanted to continue to learn as fast and as much as he could. Further, he liked to think, but not for too long without acting.

He stopped hallucinating over his coffee, went in from the balcony, packed his suitcase, checked out of the Bel Air Sands, and left for Palm Springs. As he drove along the freeway, he knew he would not, could not, stop dreaming about women and work. When an individual quits dreaming, he quits growing and becomes decadent.

The drive to Palm Springs was pleasant but dull. When he had taken this drive so many years ago in a Nash or a Studebaker—he couldn't recall which—the highway had been only two lanes, and the orange groves had been closer to the roadway. The towns had been small and off by themselves.

When he had first arrived in Palm Springs many years ago, he stayed at the Desert Inn and dined at the original Doll's House restaurant. Now, you could take Phoenix and Tucson and mix them together, throw in four or five El Dorado clubs, and find yourself in today's Palm Springs, Palm Desert, Rancho Mirage, or any other place in the desert. To Jonathan, they had all become one.

He thought that if people keep begetting people and money keeps begetting money, one might as well settle for a modest one-and-a-half-million-dollar condominium in Palm Springs. It seemed to him that if one has been conditioned over a lifetime to accept the system and to retire eventually as a chief executive officer, one might adjust well to golf, spas, gin rummy, swimming pools, tennis, and classy restaurants.

Jonathan had not felt comfortable in Palm Springs since the 1950's. When he came into town this time, he elected to stay at an excellent standard chain hotel, totally unreminiscent of Palm Spring's adolescent days when there had been a lot of wide-open space between the Desert Inn and Cathedral City. One of his favorite small hotels hadn't changed much, except to improve the food and exponentially increase prices. He didn't want to go where he and Rene had stopped during their honeymoon.

After he checked into his hotel, he called a couple of his friends, both former clients of his advertising agency. He made an appointment with Roger Thornton for breakfast at the El Dorado Club at nine-thirty and with Sam Berkovitz for lunch at his condominium in Rancho Mirage. Jonathan drove around the area to see what he could remember. He hadn't been in Palm Springs for ten years, and he had missed half the desert's growth. After parking his car at his hotel, he walked a few blocks around the old downtown area, looking for a certain small hotel where long ago he had fulfilled a mission for a friend.

He had been asked by an ex-husband to visit his divorced wife to try to persuade her to return to him. His friend's former wife was an attractive, intelligent businesswoman, one of the early "new" women. She had simply outgrown her husband, who was quite successful but dull.

What Jonathan remembered most about this five-foot-seven, very shapely (although a little heavier than she wanted to be), properly coiffeured blonde was that she didn't give him a chance to argue her former husband's case. All through dinner, she teased and enticed him with her impish smile, until he yielded to her delicate command to spend the night with her at the small hotel where she lived temporarily.

He had been a widower, and she was already divorced. They had high regard for one another, having been business friends for a long time. Jonathan figured that he couldn't report to her ex-husband that she wouldn't talk to him, and if she wouldn't listen without loving, he couldn't be accused of betraying his friend. He stayed with her for one wonderful week. And he did persuade her to return to her ex-husband, but she left him again after two or three months and subsequently married a doctor in San Diego.

Jonathan was never quite sure if he had really persuaded her to go back to her husband for a trial get-together, or if perhaps living with him for a week had convinced her that her ex-husband wasn't so bad after all.

He saw that her small hotel had now been converted into offices. When he returned to his room, he took with him some pleasant memories.

At nine-thirty the next morning, Monday, Roger Thornton met Jonathan at the El Dorado Club gate and escorted him to the club restaurant. Thornton had told Jonathan the evening before that Estelle, his wife, wouldn't be joining them, as she hadn't been feeling well.

As they walked into the dining room, Jonathan said, "Roger, I do appreciate your seeing me. Why aren't you out playing golf with Ron?"

"I've never been much for golf, and living here hasn't converted me. I do play once or twice a month, though, and Ron keeps after me to play more. Ron is out playing now."

There was a break in the conversation as they walked across the room to be seated at a table by a picture window. It was a beautiful, sunny, Palm Springs morning.

"Even though Ron is out playing now," Roger said, "he'll play another round this afternoon. You see, he's found a gold mine among his neighbors. Ron considers one over par a very bad round for him. So to make his game interesting, he picks up winnings of a few hundred dollars a day."

Jonathan looked out the window as a couple in their late sixties walked by with tennis racquets in their hands. He turned back to Roger and said, "What do you do out here, Roger? You look tanned and in great shape and as slender as I've seen you in twenty years. How long have you been retired? A couple of years?"

"Oh, I've been out here for—yes, a couple of years. Ron knows my weakness for making quick bargain purchases, and he found a good buy for me. On that basis, I bought a home and then had to come out and live in it. We sold our big place near the Halton Country Club, where you used to visit us when we were in Chicago, but we have since purchased a smaller home west of Chicago, in the Oak Brook area."

Roger picked up the menu but didn't open it. "As for what I do out here, Jonathan, I guess it's not too different from what I would do in Chicago. I work! I serve on several corporate boards. But what keeps me really busy is that I'm chairman of the finance committee on three of the boards. Starting about April 1, I'll spend most of my time in the Midwest.

"What are you doing now? I read a news item every now and then about your Ethics organization, but I understand that you've retired and are now president emeritus of the group."

Jonathan nodded, then explained, "The Ethics Group is going right along. The young man who joined shortly after its founding is now the executive director and is doing well.

"Now, I have an idea about producing a relatively low-cost movie that I wanted to check out with you. You may recall that Sam Berkovitz and I helped out on a Broadway show several years ago when his company was sponsoring television specials placed through our agency."

"I remember," Roger replied. "Your timing may be right again. Sam is thinking about getting into show business or cable television now. He enjoys promotions and communications. What kind of idea do you have in mind? Do you want to dramatize ethics? Ethics will probably always be of overriding interest to you. I'm glad somebody is promoting honesty, because most of us in business have been too busy promoting our own products and services.

"When I come in here for breakfast, they automatically bring me fresh orange juice, scrambled eggs, bacon, English muffins, an assortment of Danish rolls, and a pot of coffee. How would that suit you?"

Jonathan closed the menu and said, "Just right, Roger, but add a glass of milk and coffee later."

Roger turned to the woman who seemed to be his personal waitress and said, "Helen, please bring Mr. Barron the same as you bring me. He'll have a glass of milk with his breakfast and coffee later."

When the waitress had gone, Jonathan said, "Roger, as I recall, you did your undergraduate work at the University of Illinois and got your law degree at Michigan. Along the way, did you ever read Dante's *Divine Comedy?*"

Roger thought a long moment and then said, "I vaguely remember reading Dante's *Inferno* as part of an English course at Illinois. The professor reviewed the whole *Divine Comedy;* the *Inferno,* the

342

*Purgatorio,* and the *Paradiso.* Beyond that, all I recall about Dante is that he made a trip through hell and purgatory and into paradise or heaven."

Jonathan smiled. "That's about as much as I recalled, Roger, until I bought John Ciardi's superb translation of the *Divine Comedy.* And the reason I bought it was to try to figure out a way to teach values in a highly palatable, sugar-coated form.

"You see, I'm still afraid that the lack of value orientation throughout our society, with the increasing disregard for honesty, the lack of individual responsibility to and for others, and the acceptance of corruption in all areas of society, plus the institutionalization of gangsterism, will inexorably destroy freedom in this country.

"I'd like to use entertainment channels to convey the message. The central point of the *Divine Comedy* was to show the sanctions of hell and the power and pull of love."

"That sounds interesting, but how would you approach it? I mean, just what do you have in mind?"

"I'd like to get a good screenplay writer to take Dante's *Divine Comedy* and make it into a farcical, bitingly satirical, musical comedy, calling it *Dante's Masquerade.*

"The short-range goal would be to create an exciting, melodramatic spectacle, with the bad guys being kicked down to hell and the good guys being greeted by St. Peter, acting as if he were the manager of a high-priced English hotel welcoming an eminent Arab sheik.

"By making it farcical, we could make it funnier—and at less cost —while exaggerating our message. The primary aim would be entertainment, but the after-effects would be fire and brimstone for the evil and paradise for the good.

"I'll learn who's who in terms of getting a good writer to develop the concept and then take the script where the best agent I can get suggests. One agent has already recommended a writer."

Roger was listening intently. "Jonathan, that sounds interesting and workable."

"I think it is both, Roger, and it could be very effective if properly done. I came to see you because I figured that you and Sam Berkovitz and Leonard Towson and maybe some others would be bored with ordinary investments and might like to make money, have fun, and do a service to the nation, too. Do you think that when the story treatment and budget are developed, I could get you and Sam to help me organize a cadre of 'angels'?"

"I imagine that Sam would be interested, and I certainly am. How much would you guess the cost would be?"

"Well, I don't know! My first task would be to do the preliminaries. If we did those well, and if the marketing aspects looked good and timely, we might get one of the companies to finance it. Anyway, I'll pay for the preliminaries myself and see how the thing looks.

"Right now, I just wanted you and Sam to know that I'm working on a fun project that could yield a lot of social benefits—and make a good profit."

Their breakfast arrived, along with Jonathan's milk. Everything looked delicious.

"Jonathan," Roger said, "I was brought in as chairman of the finance committee of one large corporation because the bankers told the board of directors they would agree to keep the company afloat if they got me to be the man responsible for the money in the company, to be the final authority as finance committee chairman. The directors agreed, and I took the assignment. The bankers cooperated, and the company avoided bankruptcy. I mention this, because those who put in their money have to have faith in the one looking after that money. Others that both you and I know have faith in you. You never entered a business venture without seeing it through. So, when you get your screenplay, market analysis, and production and distribution details together, just make up a presentation like your ad agency used to do for our product promotion campaigns. Knowing Sam, I'm sure he'll want it simple, but you've known him longer than I have. Anyway, when you're ready, I'll be ready."

"Thank you, Roger. I appreciate your confidence, and I'm happy that you're interested in the movie. I can't tell you how long it will be before I know something more definite, but when I do, I'll let you and Sam know immediately."

While they had been talking, the waitress had filled their coffee cups for the second time, and they were again empty. Roger signed the check, and both men stood up and walked across the room and out into the sunshine.

As they shook hands, Jonathan said, "Thanks, Roger. Lots of

luck on all your finance committees. And say hello to Estelle for me."

"I always enjoy seeing you, Jonathan. Goodbye."

Jonathan pulled out of the parking lot and was on his way. It wasn't long before he was parking his car and looking around at the lush condominiums in Sam Berkovitz's Rancho Mirage neighborhood. Jonathan got out and gazed at all the money standing around in the form of lovely buildings and beautiful, bright, grassy, green, open areas punctuated by pools of water here and there.

"Jonathan," Sam called out to him, "What are you standing there looking at? If you're considering buying a condo, I have an extra one that my daughter, Ellie, doesn't need any more. You know, she's married again and lives back in Connecticut."

Jonathan looked over at his old friend, as Sam walked toward him with his hand outstretched.

"No, Sam, I didn't know Ellie had remarried, but if the price is right and if the rental income, interest, and depreciation deductions yield about a hundred percent return on equity, I might be in the market for a condominium. How are you, Sam? You guys out here sure keep your suntans and stomachs in good shape."

Sam smiled a broad, warm smile and said, as he put his arm around Jonathan's shoulders, "Come on in. I just got back from nine holes of golf and a good swim. I'm having a little martini. Would you like one?" Then he laughed and said, "Of course you would. Still like it on the rocks?"

Jonathan nodded. "Sure thing, Sam. Where's Martha?" He thought eleven-thirty not too early for a martini in Palm Springs.

"Oh, she went to some kind of charity program meeting to see where she can spend some of her time and money next year."

By this time they were inside Sam's home, and Sam walked directly over to the bar. With what seemed like only one move, he had the martini pitcher and matching glass in hand. He poured the glass half full and put in two pieces of ice.

"Here it is, Jonathan. That's the way you like it, isn't it? Dry with no fruit?"

Jonathan took the glass, tasted his martini, and remarked, "Sam, in case you run out of ideas and ventures when you go back to the city, you could tend bar at any one of the Chicago clubs."

Sam joined him in front of the living room window, which looked out on manicured lawns and clear, sparkling pools.

"What brings you to southern California? Your daughter and new granddaughter? Rene sent us pictures of Ellen, Anson, and Laura. The kid looks just like her mother."

Jonathan nodded. "I spent Christmas with Ellen's family, and Rene was there, too."

"And how is that gorgeous woman? I understand that your separation has been very friendly. Martha has talked to Rene a couple of times."

"She's doing fine," Jonathan said noncommitally. "She loves her job at the university and is very happy about her first grandchild. How many grandchildren do you have now?"

"We have a third one—born about a year ago. The other two, from Ellie's first marriage, are in their teens already."

Sam put his martini on the coffee table and settled back comfortably. Jonathan joined him on the couch.

"You said you had an idea you wanted to talk about. What's up?"

"It's just a germ of an idea now, Sam. I think I'll explore making a low-budget, farcical, satirical, musical comedy."

Just then a woman dressed in a sky-blue uniform appeared in the doorway to the dining room. "Just a moment, Jonathan," Sam said. "Erlene, here, wants to know what she can get you for lunch. She's going to make a Reuben sandwich for me."

"That sounds good. I'll have a Reuben, too, please," Jonathan replied.

Sam turned his attention back to Jonathan and his idea. "Now, what is this crazy idea you have about a movie?"

Jonathan laughed. "Sam, it is a little crazy, but only a little. Are you familiar with Dante's *Divine Comedy?*"

Sam shook his head. "No. But when Ellie came home from Sarah Lawrence one time, she was writing an English report on Dante's something or other. When I asked her what it was about, she said, 'Hell, purgatory, and paradise.' How could anyone get a musical comedy out of heaven and hell?"

"It wouldn't be easy, Sam. But as an old marketing man, you must admit there are a lot of people who would like to know more about their future homes, especially about hell, which I'd guess is growing like Palm Springs."

346

Both men smiled, and Jonathan continued. "Dante, an Italian poet, wrote an epic poem around the year 1300 A.D. It told the story of his passage through hell, where he saw some of his former friends, and into purgatory, where he spent most of his time on his way to paradise. It's a morality message which tells about great sins and loves, especially Dante's love for Beatrice, who was doubtless prettier than Elizabeth Taylor in her prime."

Sam noticed that Jonathan's glass was empty, so he got up and poured him another martini.

"Sam, millions of kids have read or have become familiar with Dante's *Divine Comedy* in high school and college classrooms. I want to get a writer and make a rambunctious, farcical, highly melodramatic musical comedy to be called *Dante's Masquerade*. I want a movie that the audience can applaud when they see their favorite 'bad' guys pushed into hell. The music could range from the worst of rock, which is hell to listen to, to the best of Beethoven. Even if most people wouldn't know Dante from a jackrabbit, everyone has heard of heaven and hell.

"As a marketing man, I know that people want to see or do something to get pet hatreds out of their systems or share an impossible romance with someone like Dante, who keeps searching for his unutterably beautiful Beatrice."

Without any change in the intent look on his face, Sam said, "Jonathan, how the hell can his Beatrice be so beautiful if she doesn't have a pair of pretty udders?"

"Bad joke," Jonathan said, laughing.

"I know," Sam said, laughing too. "I just enjoy thinking about those things."

"Some say Dante actually did know a physically appealing Beatrice who was, unfortunately for him, already someone else's wife. But back to my movie idea.

"I saw Roger Thornton this morning and told him I was going to see you and no one else at this time. Roger suggested that, when I have the comedy put into writing and all the production concepts and budget developed, I prepare a presentation like our agency used to prepare for him and especially for you. He thought perhaps a few of our friends out here might like to have a piece of a successful movie, as much as or more than they'd like a piece of mineral exploration.

"What do you think, Sam? You and I both used to think we

should have been in show business, and I guess we were when we bought all those television specials years ago."

Sam asked the inevitable question. "How much money does it take to do something like this?"

"I don't know yet, Sam. It depends on how good a story and treatment concept could be developed. I plan to pay for a preliminary estimate.

"But having worked for years with clients like you and Roger, any movie plan I come up with will be about a fourth of what the industry would consider normal cost. Right now, I'm just exploring, and I thought I would tease you with a show business deal. We can't do much worse than you and I did with our Broadway play years ago, can we? And you got me into that one."

Sam smiled rather painfully and nodded.

"Jonathan, some of your craziest notions have paid off, and this is a crazy notion for us at our ages—a farcical musical comedy. It should be fun, though. I'd like it! Maybe there would be lots of chorus girls?"

Erlene arrived with their lunch, and Sam motioned her toward the patio doors. As he and Jonathan went outside to enjoy the beautiful day and their lunch, Sam said, "When you're ready, let's look at it. If Roger okays the deal, we'll all come in. I remember when you helped our company become big time."

# 33

On Wednesday, January 6, Rene read in her morning paper that Dr. Arnold Spirrison had resigned as president of Southland University. He had accepted a position as chairman of one of the newly appointed commissions to study the status of undergraduate education in the United States. Apparently his leaving had been under discussion for a few weeks, because a new Southland president, whose name she hadn't heard before, was announced simultaneously by the chairman of the Southland board of trustees.

This news came as an unpleasant surprise to Rene. Arnold hadn't told her a thing about changing jobs. Since she also worked at Southland, he really shouldn't have told her, and she knew that. Nevertheless, he was her number one lover, and she wished he had at least given her a hint.

Rene had been wondering why Arnold hadn't called for the past few days. He had told her that his wife was coming out for the holidays, so possibly that was the explanation. As for his leaving town, she didn't want him to leave, and she certainly didn't want him to go without telling her about it. He wasn't her only lover, but he was the one with whom she felt she could share mind and body.

She hadn't seen Arnold since the night before Jonathan had arrived for Christmas, but she had expected to see him again on Saturday. Now she didn't know what to think. Rene hurriedly finished the paper and breakfast. She was eager to get to her office and find out about Arnold. She knew Elroy Benton, her immediate superior, would tell her what he knew.

Interestingly enough, neither Benton nor any of Rene's associates in the office knew any more than they had read in the paper. They were all surprised to hear that Dr. Spirrison was leaving and were even more surprised that his resignation was effective January 1, which meant that he had already vacated his position. Rene wondered if he had also left town—without even saying goodbye.

She had previously scheduled an interview with Bob Manning, chairman of the economics and business management department, at nine-thirty, so she got her material ready and walked the two blocks to his office.

Dr. Manning was on the faculty board's executive committee. If he didn't volunteer information about Spirrison's resignation, she thought she would discreetly inquire.

She didn't have to wait. As soon as she sat down to talk with Dr. Manning, a very genial and suave gentleman, he asked if she had heard about it.

"Only what I read in this morning's paper, Dr. Manning. It's not only surprising, but it seems so sudden. Had Dr. Spirrison planned this move for a long time?" Rene asked. "Rene," he said, "as most of us knew, Dr. Spirrison's wife was not able to move out to Los Angeles to be with her husband because of her own professional commitments. She's a full professor of biology at James Carlton University back east. One of the trustees reported to me at the December 1 meeting that the chairman and one other very influential trustee had raised the question of whether the university might not be better served if the president had a normal family life and maintained a home. Then, he could entertain faculty leaders and their spouses and be host to prominent businessmen and others who help the university in substantial ways.

"As a faculty man," he added as an aside to the main thrust of his information, "I understand the politics of a university bureaucracy. Contacts are important.

"Although none of the trustees questioned Dr. Spirrison's leadership and ability, they believed that another president could readily be obtained who might be as good an administrator as President Spirrison and who would also be in a social situation that is more advantageous to the university. If he were a real bachelor, that would be okay, but having a wife precludes having a hostess.

"The reason his job was filled so quickly is that one of the directors had long had in mind a candidate for the job, even before Dr. Spirrison was appointed."

Rene wondered how long Arnold had been aware of the board's dissatisfaction with his personal life. No wonder he had appeared to be under a great deal of stress when he first arrived for their evenings together.

"The trustees didn't criticize him for having dinner with a number of women. They could understand a man's need for female companionship. But some of the Southland's most influential supporters are also the most conservative—publicly, that is."

Rene nodded numbly. She wished she were anywhere but in Dr. Manning's office at that moment.

Dr. Manning was pacing up and down at this point, as if he were delivering a lecture to a class of note-taking students. He seemed oblivious to the fact that he had only one listener.

"As for the faculty committees," he continued, "since I'm on one of them, I can honestly say no university president could ever please all of them."

Dr. Manning smiled at Rene, and she tried to smile back. "That's the story, Rene. But don't print any of that in your *Public Affairs Newsletter,*" he laughingly cautioned her.

Rene said weakly, "I am sorry Dr. Spirrison left Southland. He's one of the most creative, innovative university leaders I've ever met."

Manning agreed. "Yes, he is a good man and a very likable person. However, you're not here to discuss our departing president."

Dr. Manning regrouped some papers on his desk, took some off his chair, and sat down. "Let's discuss what we can do to enhance the prestige of our economics department." He laughed. "And if we solve that problem, in these days, you and I could make a fortune as consultants to all the other universities."

The meeting with Dr. Manning produced some points to be developed, and Rene returned to her office to put in her usual day of hard work. She loved helping departmental professors get the recognition so many of them deserved.

But she found it difficult to concentrate. She couldn't get Arnold out of her mind. As she drove home, she wondered when Arnold would call her. She tried not to ask herself *if* he would call. She told herself that Arnold had known that Jonathan was arriving for the holidays, as was his wife. That she had not heard from him was understandable.

At her apartment, Rene picked up her mail, including a number of late Christmas cards. She prepared herself a martini and set out a small steak to broil later. Because she sent out a large number of Christmas and birthday cards, she received a lot of personal mail.

Rene loved people, so her mail-reading time, along with her martini, was a very restful, pacifying, and rewarding time for her. This evening she flipped through the stack to see who was sending her greetings. Suddenly, she stopped to look more closely at a hand-addressed letter on Dr. Spirrison's personal stationery. He had never written to her before.

She quickly opened the envelope and read the letter inside.

My dearest Rene,

When you receive this note you will doubtless already know that I have left the university. Actually, I think the trustees are correct in appointing a man-and-wife team to the president's position. It is good politics, internally and externally.

One of the most influential trustees is a close personal friend and a big contributor to political campaigns. He had heard of this opening in Washington and had talked to me about it. We both knew that a majority of the trustees might use my being an active bachelor as an excuse to get me out, because some of the more conservative faculty members thought I was making too many changes.

I did not call you, because my wife came in on Christmas Day and stayed until I had to leave for Washington. She waited to go back with me. She went on to her home in Baltimore.

I am writing to you because I want you to have my Washington address—602 New Hampshire Avenue, N. W., Washington, D. C. 20040. I expect to be at the above address, and I shall phone you and give you my Washington phone number as soon as I get one.

I do this hoping that, if you are ever in Washington, you will let me know. Also, I can assure you that when I am again in Los Angeles, which is not likely for a few months, I hope you will not mind my calling you. Needless to say, I shall miss seeing you and working with you.

I want you to know that all your co-workers and the executive staff of Southland have been very impressed with you as a person and with your considerable professional ability. My leaving as president will not affect the plans and positions we have in place. I hope you will agree to take on more responsibility when promotions are offered to you. One is in the works now.

When I see Wonderwoman on television, I am reminded of

what a wonderful combination-woman you are, personally and professionally. I am glad I have known you. Blessings to you, and may the right man come along and help make this New Year a happy one for you.

> With loving regard,
> Arnold

Rene noticed that the letter had been mailed December 31. "What a nice letter," she thought. "Arnold has been so kind. I hope we can see each other soon. Maybe I could go to New York and visit Susan, and he could meet me there. I don't think living close to his wife will change their personal situation."

She placed Arnold's letter apart from the others and continued to read the mail and sip her martini. The phone rang.

Maybe it's Arnold, she thought.

"Hello."

"Hello, Mrs. Barron? This is Gregory Edmondson. Arnold Spirrison introduced us at the post-game cocktail party—the USC-UCLA game. I hope you remember me."

Gregory Edmondson was one of Southland's trustees and the president of the big Barker-Bemis National Bank. Rene had seen him since the party on several occasions at the university.

"Yes, I certainly do remember you, Mr. Edmondson. Are you calling me in reference to Arnold's resignation?"

"No, Mrs. Barron. I saw the story in the paper and wondered if your job at Southland would be affected in any way by Arnold's departure. He was so proud that he was able to open up a suitable position for you, and as the months passed, he seemed more and more pleased by how well you handled your work. It was that kind of recommendation that made me wonder if you would consider a position outside the university."

He rushed right along and didn't give Rene a chance to say a word. "Before you answer, may I ask if we could meet for dinner next Tuesday and discuss what I have in mind for you?"

"That's possible, Mr. Edmondson. But in fairness to you, I must tell you that I don't have to support myself, and I do want to be happy professionally. That's why I've enjoyed working at Southland. I may have told you at the cocktail party following the game that I had previously been associated with a university before coming to Southland. I like working in an academic environment."

353

"I see," he replied a little dejectedly.

"However, since you've complimented me by your interest, I'll be glad to hear what you have in mind."

Mr. Edmondson sounded relieved. "Oh, good, Mrs. Barron. As I recall, you said you lived in the Westwood area. I have a condominium in the Century Plaza Center. Possibly we could eat at the Century Plaza Hotel. It has a couple of good dining rooms. Let's just meet in the hotel's main lobby at seven-thirty Tuesday evening."

Rene jotted a memorandum to herself on the calendar date book on her desk. But she knew she wouldn't forget this one. As she turned the pages to that day's date, she said, "That's fine. Tuesday, seven-thirty, lobby, Century Plaza Hotel."

"I'm looking forward to talking with you, Mrs. Barron, even if I can't persuade you to leave Southland. Good night."

"Good night."

When Rene entered the spacious lobby of the Century Plaza hotel on Tuesday evening, Gregory Edmondson was standing a few feet away, watching for her. She was pleased that he was there and waiting eagerly.

Edmondson suggested they sit in the rather elaborate cocktail lounge and have a drink before going into the restaurant. Rene was surprised to find Edmondson even more handsome than she had remembered. He was well over six feet tall and broad-shouldered, with a strong Nordic face and clear blue eyes. Only a touch of gray showed on the sideburns of his curly, brownish-blond hair.

He was very gracious. "This may sound like a cliché, Mrs. Barron, but I remembered how attractive you were, yet you're even more stunning than my memory of you."

Rene smiled. "Thank you. Please call me Rene."

"And I'd like to be Greg to you," he said as he took her by the arm. "Now, what would you like to drink?"

"I'll take a glass of white wine. I'm sure the Plaza house wine will be good." Rene decided she would refrain from smoking until she could determine how Greg felt about cigarettes.

"Since I'm with a beautiful woman, Rene, I believe I'll have a double scotch on the rocks with water on the side." As the waiter walked away, Greg added, "Waiter, make that J & B, please."

"Greg," Rene said attentively, "please tell me about your business and the job you had in mind for me. I recall that Arnold said you were a distinguished banker and a member of the Southland board of trustees.''

Greg nodded. "I'm in the banking business, but not as distinguished as my friend Arnold might have indicated. And today, when one says he's in the banking business, that can mean almost anything, considering the increasing ramifications of the finance business. I have a friend who's president of an advertising agency and another friend who's a corporate lawyer. I think we could all exchange jobs and never know we had switched companies.''

Their drinks arrived, and Greg continued, "But about the job. We have a marketing department at Barker-Bemis with a staff of twenty-eight to thirty. The job that we'll be filling in about six weeks is that of associate director for public affairs. We have a woman in that position now who has decided to resign and stay home for a couple of years, despite her professional excellence. Her first baby is due in about four months. Part of her job responsibility is to handle press relations, edit the bank's internal newsletter, and help executives prepare speeches. Now that we're losing a fine employee to motherhood, some of my peers don't want to hire another woman to replace the one leaving.

"It's a demanding job, Rene, but I remember you said you had obtained your degree in journalism and you had also done some newspaper work," he said persuasively.

"That's right. I'm surprised that you remember our conversation. There was so much going on around us." Then Rene smiled warmly. "That was an exciting post-game party, wasn't it?"

"Yes, indeed," he acknowledged. "Arnold is a great concept man when it comes to parties. If he had had a wife here with him, Southland would have refused to let him go and would probably have raised his salary. Much of a college president's job is ceremonial and promotional.

"My wife stays at our small ranch in Hidden Valley. So Monday through Friday, I live like a bachelor. I drive in on Monday morning, which usually takes about two hours on Ventura Freeway, and go back Friday evenings about four o'clock. You see, I used to manage the Ventura office, and I could live at home. My wife didn't want to move into Los Angeles, because one of our children is still in high school with one more year to go. Furthermore, my wife has three Arabian horses."

With a rather childlike look on his face, he said, "I think if she

355

had to choose between the horses and me, I might lose." And then he laughed.

The logistics of his marital relationship did not miss their mark. Rene was getting an increasingly welcome message. "How many children do you have, Greg?" she asked, in pursuit of the Edmondson file. She was thinking that Greg was very handsome. In fact, he reminded her of a blonde Jonathan Barron, but one who was happy and loved people.

"We have three children," Greg responded. "Two boys and a girl. Our daughter is the youngest. One boy is in his senior year at Stanford, and the older boy is in law school at the University of Michigan."

He looked casually around the room and back to Rene. "What about you, Rene? Arnold told me you've been separated for a few months and your divorce decree is about due. You have a married daughter living out here, I understand."

Rene couldn't quite decide whether to be pleased or not. "Well, it appears that Arnold must have given you my resumé."

Greg laughed, hoping to ease the consternation he saw on Rene's face. "Actually, Rene, he did. But Arnold was only trying to help you in case you decided on your own to leave Southland."

Rene relaxed. "Our oldest daughter is living here. She's a lawyer. I have a son, who is an advertising executive. Our youngest daughter, who is getting her MBA in finance, is at New York University. But I think we can forgive her, because as you say, the finance field is changing." Rene smiled and sipped her wine.

"That sounds like a wonderful family, Rene. And from my experience, I think there's hope for your banker daughter. You see, you should go into banking so you and your young daughter will have shared interests. You might decide there are some challenging people in banking."

Greg noticed that Rene's wineglass was almost empty and asked if she wanted another. She declined, and Greg signaled the waiter that they wouldn't need him again.

"About your job opening, Greg, it would be a fine position for me and might even pay more, but I love the academic environment. They need my type of person there, pragmatic when it comes to business administration, yet appreciative of the faculty's needs and moods."

Greg didn't comment on what she said. Instead, he changed the subject to Jonathan. "Rene, may I ask what was, or is, your husband's business?"

"My husband, soon to be my ex-husband, has done many things. His primary business, I suppose, was the advertising agency business, where he was as successful as he wanted or needed to be to get his diploma, as he so often said.

"But he also founded a real estate company and a pharmaceutical company. He was in television production, too, and even raised purebred cattle for a while. He did many things well, and I think he could have done just about anything he wanted to do.

"In recent years he's given all his time, some of his money, and much of his mind and soul to the creation of a foundation that promotes honesty and ethics, the Ethics Inquiry Group in Washington, D. C. You may have heard of it."

Greg nodded.

"The last task became such an obsession with him that I felt I was invisible to him. Also, he couldn't seem to tolerate most of my friends, especially those in academia.

"Jonathan was and is a great man who seems to hate the fact that he is human, as Erich Fromm once told him."

Rene stopped rather abruptly. Here she was, out with a very attractive man, and she was talking about her ex-husband. She didn't want to do this, particularly with a married man she already thought she would enjoy seeing often.

She added what she hoped would close the discussion. "You see, I've had a very challenging man, and I'm afraid I won't be up to having another marriage, at least not immediately. The one I had placed great demands on my emotional and psychological energies."

Greg looked down at what was left in his glass and appeared to be contemplating the remaining scotch rather sadly. Lest he think she was reluctant to be involved with men in her ex-wife life, Rene said, "Of course, I don't mind being challenged in my work—or in having fun."

She wanted Greg's reaction and was relieved when he appeared to be relieved. They both laughed as if they were sharing an unspoken secret.

Rene reached across and put her hand on Greg's arm.

"Shall we go to dinner, Greg?"

When they were seated, the waiter asked if he could bring them a cocktail. Greg looked at Rene, and she said, "Greg, now that business talk is over, I think I'll switch to my favorite drink, a very dry martini on the rocks."

"Make that two," Greg said to the waiter.

He also asked the waiter to bring the menu so they would be ready to order when the drinks were served.

Their dinner conversation covered a full circle of subjects, personal and business. When they were having their after-dinner coffee, Greg said, "Rene, I would really enjoy having dinner with you again next Tuesday. We could meet here at seven and then go to some other place, perhaps. Will you have dinner with me then?"

"I'd love to," Rene said, smiling, "but let's have dinner at my apartment. I love to cook, and I'll prepare a gourmet meal for you. I have an excellent recipe for pepper steak. You have to go out for lunch and dinner so often during the week, you might like a home-cooked meal.

"I'll give you my address now. It's on Malcolm Avenue, just north of Santa Monica Boulevard. Since you live in the area, it will be quick and easy for you to find."

She wrote her apartment number and street address on the back of her business card and gave it to Greg.

"Rene, my dear, you do flatter me. I'll certainly look forward to seven o'clock on Tuesday. I know your street, and it will be easy to find your apartment. I'll bring the champagne for your gourmet cooking. I wish it were Tuesday now."

Rene laughed. Greg was so delightful and such a handsome man, at least six feet two, muscular, and lean. His eyes weren't as piercing as Jonathan's, and she felt very comfortable when he looked at her.

"If Tuesday is going to arrive any sooner, I guess we'd better leave," Rene said.

Outside the hotel, they shook hands, and Rene kissed Greg good night with a little peck on his cheek. He walked her to her car and kissed her, not as lightly, before walking back to his apartment.

It took Rene just a few minutes to drive home. She didn't try to think while driving. She was satisfied simply to collect her feelings. She would think when she reached her apartment.

She drove into her apartment garage and used her key to open the back door entrance. Her apartment on the second floor was up a single flight of stairs. She usually used the back entrance, because the garage door opened into the hallway onto the stairs. She liked the private entrance, and it was handy for carrying the groceries up.

As soon as she entered the apartment, she headed for her bedroom, undressed, and slipped into the lovely aquamarine robe Jonathan had purchased for her. She returned to the living room and lit a cigarette, something she had been wanting to do for some time.

Rene thought about Jonathan, because Greg was the first man she had met who reminded her of him. Greg, however, was not as austere, searching, and tense as Jonathan had become in recent years.

She was glad that Greg was married. If he were not, she thought, they might fall in love. And she was aware that she was truly afraid to fall in love. She wanted to be completely free for a while. For how long, she didn't know or really care.

If Greg was as sexually satisfying to her as she now believed he would be, as she visualized his muscular, slender body in her big bed with her, maybe she could be his unpaid mistress, his part-time, non-exclusive mistress. She imagined how wonderful it would be to make love to Greg twice a week during his in-town Monday-through-Thursday-night stay. Maybe they could get in an extra night, in addition to the two regular ones on Tuesdays and Thursdays, depending on his and her business commitments. That would leave him free for his weekends at home. She thought that she had wanted him ever since she met him at the USC-UCLA game party but dismissed the idea as a passing fancy.

She even fantasized that what she could do for Greg in bed might make him a better lover for his wife. She might be doing his wife a favor by sending her husband home every weekend happy and primed. She remembered telling Jonathan many times that she wanted him to have pretty secretaries, because he always came home in a happy mood. She didn't think she was rationalizing her desire for a sexual adventure with Greg. She believed she was entitled to it.

She thought briefly about her age. She had forgotten, for the moment, that she was fifty-one on December 6. Jonathan hadn't forgotten, though. He'd sent her two dozen gorgeous roses.

Rene thought about possible meetings with Greg and what they would do to her already full social life. If Greg wasn't going to be in town Friday through Sunday, she would be able to date other men on the weekends, but only Greg on a regular basis.

She finished her cigarette and wondered for a minute or two whether Arnold, once he knew he wasn't going to be available, had actually prompted Greg to call her. Maybe he had recommended her to Greg for more than business reasons. Greg hadn't seemed too disappointed that she wasn't interested in his job opening. Maybe there really wasn't a job. Whoever or whatever had sent Greg to her, she anticipated him now in a way that caused her to be very thankful.

# 34

After their dinner date on Tuesday, January 12, Rene and Greg Edmondson began to spend every Tuesday and Thursday evening together. Greg usually left his office and went directly to his Century Plaza apartment, arriving home between five and five-thirty. Rene usually arrived at her apartment about six. Their arrangement was for Greg to phone her at six and to go right over to her place, five minutes or less from his apartment. If she wasn't home by six, she called him as soon as she got home. They were always very eager to be together as soon as possible.

When Greg arrived, they sat on the big sofa and started their martinis and sexual play. They often turned on the six-thirty TV news, and by the time the news was over they had finished their martinis and were more than ready to get into bed together. Rene was fascinated with Greg's pleasant humor and strong, lithe body. Greg might be tense and bothered by business problems when he arrived at Rene's place, but when the martini and Rene started working on him simultaneously, ecstasy took over.

Within the first month, it became apparent to both Rene and Greg that they were no longer playing mistress and lover. They were falling in love. They couldn't prevent it, unless they stopped seeing one another.

Rene continued to see other lovers, usually a different one each weekend, but sometimes there was a repeat with one she really enjoyed. She occasionally entertained a visiting lover from North Carolina, New York, Washington, or Chicago. Some of them had coveted her while she was still with Jonathan. They arranged to fly out on the weekends to make love to her, ostensibly going early to prepare for their Monday morning business meetings in Los Angeles.

But now Rene wasn't making love with these men for the satisfaction of conquest, for the joy of sex, or for the thrill of seeing how much she could excite any of them. Now her weekend lovers were diversions, attempts on her part to avoid becoming Greg's, totally and exclusively. She was the prime example of one making more love, but liking it less.

The events that followed fit a common pattern. When lovers who shouldn't be lovers can't stop loving one another, external events often intervene to bring about a crisis.

On Thursday, June 17, about five months after their first love-making session at Rene's apartment, Greg and Rene both came home before six o'clock, had their martinis and ardent foreplay, forgot about the news, and rushed to bed. At about eight o'clock, they got up, showered, and dressed for dinner. They were intensely happy with the satisfaction they were giving each other. As they walked down the back stairs to get into Rene's car, they were confronted by a woman Rene had never seen before.

As soon as Greg said, "Helen, Helen, please don't! Think of the children!" Rene realized it was Greg's wife who was standing there calmly, holding a pistol which was pointed directly at them.

"I should kill you both, especially you, Mrs. Barron, you thieving bitch," Helen Edmondson said quietly, disdainfully.

Rene replied, as if she were in a semi-comatose state, "Helen, please kill *me*, but keep Greg for yourself."

"Be careful, Rene," Greg warned. "Helen is an expert with a gun."

"Mrs. Barron, I wouldn't honor you with death. I'll just give each of you a reminder of me for the next time you want to make dirty love."

Thereupon, she shot Rene in the left foot and her husband in his left foot, also. She put her pistol back into her purse, walked about fifteen steps to the curb where her car was parked, got in, and drove off.

During the whole episode, Rene was oblivious to everything but the gun. When the shots were fired, she felt the sting of the bullet and saw Greg drop to a sitting position, trying to get his shoe off. Rene got hold of herself. She ran upstairs, feeling her shoe becoming soggy with blood. She called the police emergency number, gave her name and address, and requested an ambulance for two shooting victims. Grabbing a stack of clean dish towels, she rushed back to Greg. He had taken off his shoe and sock, and she tied a towel around his bleeding foot. Then she sat on the bottom step, removed her own shoe, and wrapped her injured foot with towels.

Rene had responded quickly to the emergency situation, but while she was doing so, the whole scene seemed so unreal she thought she must be hallucinating. Surely there was no one taking flash pictures! Yet, as she and Greg consoled one another, each apologizing to the other and both taking the blame, they agreed that there had been a man taking pictures from the moment they had come to their senses after the shooting.

A small crowd began to gather. The police arrived, followed by the ambulance. They told the police that the woman who had shot them had driven away immediately after the shooting. The ambulance door closed, and within five minutes they were in the UCLA Medical Center emergency room.

As soon as Rene had called the police, the dispatcher had contacted a patrol car and reported a shooting, which made it a high-priority call. The ambulance had been summoned from the 1090 Veteran Avenue station, arriving within five minutes.

In the meantime, the patrol car officer was advised that the person who shot Mrs. Barron and Mr. Edmondson, a Mrs. Helen Edmondson, had gone directly to the West Los Angeles Police Station, where she was arrested and booked for attempted murder. She called her attorney, who came to the station immediately. He told the police that charges probably wouldn't be pressed and asked them to cooperate in keeping all reporters away from his client.

After being checked in the emergency room, Rene was admitted to the hospital, and her physician, whom she had met through Ellen's doctor, was notified. Greg requested that an ambulance take him to a private hospital, and this was quickly done.

After making the call to her own doctor, a general practitioner, Dr. Gilbert Sukman, Rene decided she would call Ellen. It was only about nine-fifteen. The nurse said that she would make the call to Ellen and ask her to come to the hospital.

When the phone rang at Ellen's house, she was just putting the last of the dinner dishes into the dishwasher. She answered it on the first ring.

"Hello."

"Hello. Are you Ellen Folsom?" the nurse asked quietly.

"Yes, this is Mrs. Folsom," Ellen replied.

"I'm Mrs. Bethard, a nurse at the UCLA Medical Center. Your mother has had a very minor injury, but she wanted to know if you could come over and see her now. It's not serious at all, Mrs. Folsom, so take your time if you can come over. She's in room 308A. Just come to the third floor desk."

Ellen was so surprised that she didn't think to ask what had happened to her mother. "Thank you," she said mechanically. "Please tell my mother I'll be right over."

She explained the call to Anson, who said she should go right away and take her time, because Laura would be asleep for hours. "But call me as soon as you can, will you?"

Ellen arrived at the hospital within thirty minutes. On the way to the hospital, she kept wondering and worrying about what had happened. She guessed that her mother had had a car accident around Westwood and that she had probably been looking for a particular restaurant or store. She wondered if Rene had been alone or with the married man she had persisted in seeing, despite her solemn promise to Jonathan at Christmas that she wouldn't date married men. She would soon know. In any event, the nurse had said it was a minor injury.

When Ellen walked into the hospital room, Rene started to cry, saying over and over, "I'm so sorry. I'm so sorry."

Ellen quickly turned to the nurse and asked, "What was the accident? Where is Mom hurt?"

The nurse gave Rene a glass of water and then answered Ellen. "She has a minor injury in the left foot. Her doctor's been told of the injury and was advised not to come in until tomorrow morning. The doctor who attended her when she was brought into the emergency room said she should be here only three or four days.

"I'll go now, but you shouldn't stay more than a half hour, because she needs to sleep. Her foot may bother her, so she's been given a mild sedative."

Ellen was looking for the nurse to Rene, still wondering exactly what was going on. "Mom, what happened to your foot? Were you in a car accident?"

"No, Ellen," Rene said with a residue of sniffles, "I was shot in the foot by Greg's wife. I told you about him.

"She shot Greg in the foot, too. He went to another hospital.

"I'm so sorry about the whole affair, sorry for Greg and for you and the other children, although they're so far away. And I should say I'm sorry for Mrs. Edmondson and her children, too. I don't know why I've been what I've been. Maybe I've wanted to punish Jonathan, to taunt him."

Ellen patted her mother's hand very gently. "Now, Mom, you mustn't get too bothered. Just get well. You've been a wonderful mother, and we love you. And I'll bet Dad would join us in forgiving you, although he would probably just not make a big deal of doing so. May I tell him that you're in the hospital for a few days? He wouldn't forgive me if I didn't."

Rene started to cry again and looked down at the sheets. "No, please don't tell him."

"Mom, as a lawyer, I must ask you if you want me to get another attorney and bring any action against Mrs. Edmondson?"

Rene looked up at Ellen for the first time. "No, Ellen, none at all. I'll be all right soon. At least, that's what they tell me.

"I asked her to kill me, but she said I wasn't worth killing."

At this point, Rene tried not to cry, but the tears began again. Ellen handed her mother another tissue and waited.

Finally, she began to talk and told Ellen about the man who had been taking pictures. "Who do you suppose he was?" Rene asked. "Could he have been a newspaper reporter? If so, why was he there right at the time of the shooting? You don't suppose Mrs. Edmondson prompted him to be there, do you?

"I know your father would never stoop to having a detective trail me. I don't think he cares that much about me."

Ellen put her arms around her mother to console her.

"No, Mom, you know Dad isn't like that. He wouldn't hire a detective. However mad he may make you or us kids, he's always spoken to help us, not to hurt us."

Ellen went back to the chair she had been sitting in, and Rene put her head back on the pillow. She closed her eyes and sighed a great, long sigh. Both women were quiet. Ellen waited for her mother to rest a minute, thinking she might want to talk some more. But Rene was truly exhausted, and the sedative was beginning to take effect.

"I'd better be going now," Ellen said very quietly. She put her purse on the end of the bed and once again put her arms around her mother. She leaned over and gently kissed her flushed cheeks. Then she straightened up and took her mother's hand in her own. Rene opened her eyes.

"Thank you for coming over. You might want to call your father. He'd expect you to. Good night, darling."

"Good night Mom."

As soon as Ellen was downstairs, she called Anson and told him that her mother would be all right in three or four days and that she would tell him more as soon as she got home.

"What really happened to Rene?" Anson asked Ellen when she entered the house.

Before answering, Ellen dropped weakly onto the couch.

"Apparently, Mrs. Edmondson, the wife of the banker Mom has been seeing, shot her in the foot—and also shot her husband in the foot. The injuries seem to be minor, and Mom should be out of the hospital in three or four days."

"Shot! My God, Ellen! Is that all you know?" Anson knew there must be much more if a shooting had taken place.

"Yes, I'm afraid so. Mom had been given a sedative, and the nurse told me not to stay long. I'll see her again tomorrow. Maybe I'll see if I can go to the office at noon and stop and see Mom on the way. Remind me to take her my little stereophonic radio so she can listen to it if she wants to."

"What about your father? Are you going to call him? Did you ask Rene about calling him?" Anson seemed to be very concerned about what Jonathan would say or do.

He looked at his watch and said, "It's time for the eleven o'clock news. Let's turn it on. Maybe we'll hear something about the shooting."

Anson turned on the TV just in time to hear the newscaster say, "In Westwood tonight, at the entrance to an apartment house at 1659 Malcolm Avenue, Gregory Edmondson, president of Barker-Bemis Bank, was shot in the left foot by his wife, Helen Edmondson. Also shot in the left foot by Mrs. Edmondson was Mrs. Rene Barron, Associate Director of Public Affairs at Southland University. They were confronted by Mrs. Edmondson as they were leaving Mrs. Barron's apartment building at eight-thirty tonight. Both shooting victims have been hospitalized. Mrs. Edmondson was arrested and booked at the West Los Angeles Police Station for attempted murder. That's all we have on the story at this time." Along with the commentary, the TV news showed separate pictures of Rene and Edmondson and the newspaper photo showing them being placed in the ambulance.

Anson turned the news off and said, "This could be very harmful to Rene. I wish your dad would stop his prophesying, unless it's just for good things."

"I'm going to call him," Ellen said, tears filling her eyes. "I can't keep something like this from him." She went to the phone and dialed her father's number.

When Jonathan answered his phone, it was 2:10 in the morning. He could feel, as well as hear, the anxiety in his daughter's voice.

"Daddy, I don't want to alarm you, because it's not serious, but Mom was in an accident, and she's in the hospital at the UCLA Medical Center. She didn't ask me to call you, but the way she talked, I think she'd like to see you. Can you come out?" Ellen asked rather uncertainly.

"How serious was the accident? Is your mother's life in any danger?" Jonathan wasn't concerned with how Rene's accident had happened but only with the fact that he wanted to go to her if he could help. He would learn the details later.

"No, no, Daddy, she's not seriously injured, but she'll be in the hospital for several days. An ambulance brought her to the emergency room about nine o'clock. The hospital nurse called me about nine-thirty or so, at Mom's request. I was there about ten. Anson stayed with Laura. I'm back home now, because Mom had to go to sleep. The nurse told me she should rest and not talk much. Can you come out, maybe tomorrow?"

"Yes, Ellen," Jonathan replied quickly. "I'll try to leave here by noon and arrive there by three or four o'clock, your time. I'll rent a car and check into the Bel Air. Please reserve a room for me. Then I'll come to your house and talk with you before I see Rene. In the meantime, please send her a dozen and a half long-stemmed roses, yellow and red, if they're available. Just have the card read, 'Good health, fast recovery! Jonathan.' "

He could hear the relief in Ellen's voice.

"Thank you, Daddy."

"Okay, Ellen, my visiting nurse," he said affectionately. "Take care of Mother. I'll see you tomorrow, or rather, tonight."

"Goodbye, Daddy."

"Goodbye."

Jonathan hung up the phone and reached for the phone book. He had been asleep. Now, how could he put his mind at rest, get some more sleep, and get up early enough to make a noon plane?

First, he'd call for reservations. This he did and he reserved a seat on a plane leaving Dulles Airport at twelve thirty, arriving in Los Angeles at three fifteen, Pacific time. That would allow him time to drive to his hotel, sign in, change his clothes, and be at Ellen's house in time for dinner.

He thought about Rene.

She was lucky she hadn't been hurt badly, if she was in a car accident. Apparently, if the accident had occurred about eight or nine o'clock, she wasn't returning on the freeway from her office. So an accident around Westwood might not be as destructive.

But the news story—yes, in all probability there would be a news story, especially if she was with a prominent married man. He knew she hadn't stopped seeing married men, much to his consternation.

But Jonathan determined that he would just have to wait and see what had happened and why. Tomorrow would come soon enough. Now he would have milk and crackers and go to bed.

The plane arrived in Los Angeles a few minutes ahead of schedule. Before picking up his baggage and rental car, he called Ellen at her office. She reported that her mother was doing fine and asked him to have dinner at their house at seven-thirty. He said he would and offered to pick up some Chinese dinners at a restaurant in Pacific Palisades.

Ellen said that would be great. Jonathan thought he would enjoy dinner more if he knew Ellen didn't have to take time to cook it, time away from the baby. Laura was in a very good day-care facility but still wasn't with her mother enough, her grandfather thought. Ellen felt the same way, but she and Anson were happy and relieved that Laura did seem to be thriving in the small but experienced day-care center they had so carefully chosen.

By the time his baggage was ready to be picked up, Jonathan had rented a car, and he quickly took the rental-car bus to the parking lot. Surprisingly, there were no delays, and he was soon on the San Diego Freeway, going north.

Before he got to the Santa Monica Freeway outlet, he decided to take it over to Santa Monica and pick up a copy of the *Santa Monica Evening Star*. He bought the paper from a stand right outside the newspaper's office and resisted looking at it until he had arrived at the Bel Air and had checked in.

When he got to his room, he closed the door quickly and opened the paper. The three-column picture in the center at the top of the front page told the story. The picture showed a woman lying on one ambulance cot and a man on another. Both were being placed in an ambulance. The caption under the picture read:

> Gregory Edmondson, president of the Barker-
> Bemis Bank, and Rene Barron, Associate
> Director of Public Affairs at Southland
> University, being taken to the UCLA Medical
> Center after suffering gunshot wounds.

The story went on to give the details of the shooting. Jonathan read no further. He went down to the hotel newsstand to see if the *Los Angeles Globe-Gazette* had the story.

It did, with the same picture, only larger. Mr. Edmondson was an important banker and civic leader, and Southland was a well-known university. This was not an ordinary domestic shooting. It was news.

"Well," Jonathan thought, "as a journalist, Rene should be pleased with the press coverage."

But he thought that as a mother and a highly regarded professional woman, she could hardly like the picture or the story. She probably didn't like herself very much, either.

He recalled having asked her at Christmastime how she would feel if she were in an automobile accident late at night while riding with another woman's husband. She hadn't answered. Now she probably knew all too well how she would feel. Maybe something like this shooting had to happen to awaken her to her responsibility to others and to herself.

When the *Chronicle* came out at 6:00 P.M. with its pre-date edition, it didn't carry the photo but had instead a much longer story about the whole episode. A *Chronicle* reporter had contacted the chairman of the Board of Trustees of Southland University, asking him to comment on the story that one of their trustees, Mr. Edmondson, had been having an extended and serious affair with one of the university's executive-level female employees. The chairman had no comment, except to state that he had already received resignations from Mr. Edmondson and Mrs. Barron. He said that the resignations had not been requested but were being accepted, effective immediately.

Jonathan checked the TV stations and found that a reporter for a local TV news program had caught Mrs. Edmondson as she was being released from her overnight stay in the West Los Angeles jail. Mrs. Edmondson was accompanied by her attorney, Morris Leibowitz, who advised his client that she could talk with the reporter if she wished to do so.

"But first, I want you to know that Mrs. Edmondson has been released from all charges, as neither Mrs. Barron nor Mr. Edmondson wishes to press any charges. I've been informed that the District Attorney has declined to pursue the case because no one was seriously injured, and it was simply a domestic dispute. Now, your questions to Mrs. Edmondson," Leibowitz said, concluding his brief statement.

"Mrs. Edmondson, why did you shoot Rene Barron and your husband instead of taking them into court?" the reporter asked.

"Why go to court? I didn't want a divorce, and my husband had told me he didn't either."

"Will you now seek a divorce?"

"No," Mrs. Edmondson quickly stated.

"Did you ever confront Mrs. Barron about her affair with Mr. Edmondson?"

"I tried to contact Mrs. Barron. Twice, I left messages on her telephone answering machine, but she didn't reply. When I phoned her office, her secretary always said she was unavailable."

"Didn't you talk to your husband about Mrs. Barron?"

"Of course I did. I learned of their regular Tuesday and Thursday trysts the middle of May. I said nothing to him for a couple of weeks, hoping it was just a brief encounter. However, he continued to see Mrs. Barron, and when I confronted him with my full knowledge of the affair, he promised he wouldn't see her any more."

"What prompted you to carry out the shooting in such a careful manner?"

"I deliberately fired a single shot from a .22 caliber pistol into Mrs. Barron's left foot and a single shot into Greg's left foot. And I hasten to tell you that I'd previously checked with an expert on gunshot wounds who assured me that such a shot would do no permanent damage, would likely require only a couple of days in the hospital, and would leave no scar. You know, lots of people shoot *themselves* in the foot."

Attorney Leibowitz motioned to the reporter that the interview was over.

370

"Just one more brief question, sir, please?" The reporter paused, then asked Mrs. Edmondson, "How did you know the dating habits, the timing of Mr. Edmondson's meetings with Mrs. Barron?"

Mrs. Edmondson terminated the interview with her response. "I'll not name the person, but someone in that neighborhood kept me informed."

Jonathan turned the TV off. He thought to himself that Rene and Edmondson were lucky that the person who shot them had been so cool and collected, or they could have been seriously or fatally injured. He picked up the *Chronicle* to read the newspaper reporter's rather extensive interview with Mrs. Edmondson. He noted at the end of the article that the *Chronicle* reporter was a professor of psychology at Southland University. That could explain, he thought, why the *Chronicle* was first to know about Rene's and Edmondson's resignations.

In her interview with the *Chronicle* writer, Mrs. Edmondson stated, "The divorcees and single professional women in this country who don't want marriage are choosing to ravage homes, hurting wives and children, by seeking sex with married men. They want to have sex without the risk of falling in love with an unmarried man. The idea of illicit lovemaking seems to give them the 'romance' they think makes sex more exciting—the 'soap opera' type of romance."

"Mrs. Edmondson," the interviewer asked, "now that you mention soap operas, do you think that TV and movies have helped to put a social stamp of approval on such affairs?"

"Yes," she replied, "and many current novels do the same. Also, much of the horrible music, especially the rock videos, which would degrade a hyena, not just humans."

"I believe you were at one time a social worker," the interviewer continued. "Does your long interest in that area cause you to feel so strongly about these changes in our culture?"

"Of course it does. Anyone who has dealt with the results of abandonment and divorce—broken families and deprived children —would be deeply concerned about social and economic changes that weaken family life."

"One more question, Mrs. Edmondson. What do you think of the husbands, the married men, who have these affairs with single women? You know, I've had single women tell me that criticism of

371

extramarital affairs should be directed at the married participant, not at the single person."

"Whether the person is married or single, adultery is adultery," Mrs. Edmondson replied.

"Thank you, Mrs. Edmondson, for your comments."

Jonathan put the *Chronicle* aside and sat thinking for a long while. He wondered if Rene really wanted to see him. Ellen may have wanted him to talk with Rene in order to make her mother feel that all wasn't lost and possibly to help her avoid severe psychological consequences.

Rene had been a proud woman. Would she accept this event simply as part of her new freedom and as proof of her new role as an independent woman? Or would she contrast her present status with the thirty years she had lived as Mrs. Jonathan Barron, a respected wife, mother, and businesswoman?

He broke his reverie with a glance at his watch. It was time to go to Ellen's for dinner. He would see what she had to say.

While Jonathan was on his way out to Ellen's, Rene was lying in her bed at the hospital. She had finished eating dinner and had asked the nurse to leave the bed raised, in a position comparable to that of a poolside lounge chair. It had been only a little less than a year since she had joined her group of Watergate neighbors at the pool, she thought. Those days were so long past in her life. What had happened?

She was now a new woman in fact—her former self had undergone a drastic change. She had heard of mid-life identity crises, but her changes were more like those of the woman in *The Three Faces of Eve.*

"Just look at what's happened to me since I saw Jonathan at Christmas and promised him I wouldn't go with married men any more," she thought. "I wanted to please him. Until the very end of our marriage, until our separation seemed inevitable, I was faithful and kept my promises.

"But Jonathan had no right to judge my behavior after our separation. Or had he?"

She was the only natural mother his children would ever have. They were his children, too. He had not asked her not to have lovers. He had only asked her to be selective and not to have married lovers. He wanted to protect his children and her. He had warned her, specifically warned her, about the consequences of being in an accident with a married man and the effect of the possible publicity. No wonder he had suggested that she change her name back to Hamilton, her maiden name, or to Haley, the name she had used on TV.

She wondered what Jonathan would say or do. He couldn't think much worse of her than he had at Christmas. At one time, even up until Christmas, she had thought a separation would help them both and had thought they might get back together; but for some reason she didn't understand, she had felt at that time the horrible compulsion to taunt him with her freedom and to show him that she could do without him.

Most of the men she met wanted to make love to her. They were fun and never criticized her. They just made love and went on their way, without caring about her or what she did. That was the way she wanted it. Or maybe she didn't. She was very confused.

Now she didn't even have a job and friends at work to see and talk to. She had called her secretary the first thing, at nine o'clock that morning, to tell her boss that she would have to resign. She had simply said, "I know he'll understand, Mrs. Barron."

Even her secretary hadn't expressed sympathy.

Then she gazed at the roses that had arrived before dinner was served. They were so beautiful, with such soft petals. Jonathan always did things right. And whenever she had told him that, he had always said, "That's because I care for you."

Rene hoped he still cared for her. She wanted to see him if he didn't hurt her too deeply with his insightful, cutting truths.

"Why do I sometimes feel that Jonathan's words wound me?" she wondered. "Maybe it's because as his 'daughter' I've wanted to please him, but as his wife, I don't think he had a right to 'bring me up.'

"He should know that I realize what I'm doing, but I don't know that it's bad—or maybe I do. I don't know what has changed me." She whispered to herself, "Whatever happens to me in the future, I'll never be seen as the same by my friends, nor by my children, however forgiving they may be."

She hoped Greg was in good shape and that his career would not be sidetracked.

"There I go again," she said. "I've been a dutiful, faithful wife, with children. Why am I not concerned now about what I've done to Greg's wife and children? Oh, Lord," she said aloud, almost screaming, "why am I not as concerned now about my own children and my own friends as I surely should be? Have I become so selfish and alienated that I can't care about others?"

She turned her face into the pillow. She wanted to talk to Jonathan. Maybe he *could* help her. She would call Ellen as soon as Ellen came home to ask what he had said about the incident. She hated to think of it as a shooting. A shooting! She couldn't believe that this sordid series of events was what her life had become.

Her one ray of consolation was that perhaps Jonathan was on his way to Los Angeles.

Rene dropped off to sleep, a restless sleep with dreams in which snakes were coming after her. The dream woke her, and she thought fleetingly, "Snakes, snakes—how appropriate." Then she dozed off again.

But she didn't have to call Ellen. The phone rang, and it was her daughter on the other end.

"Hello, Mom. How are you coming along?"

"I don't know, Ellen," Rene said rather flatly. "I'm so sorry about everything. I hope you'll help me."

"Of course I will, Mom. Everything is all over. There should be no more newspaper stories after the one in the *Chronicle*."

Rene became more alert. "Did the *Chronicle* have a story? I'll ask the nurse to get a copy for me. I wonder if your father has read these stories."

"Mom," Ellen said very quickly, "you can ask Dad yourself. I just talked to him. He arrived in Los Angeles this afternoon. He wants to see you. I hope you'll be glad to see him."

Rene was relieved and yet a bit apprehensive. "Did he seem very upset and angry?"

"Not at all, Mom," Ellen said reassuringly. "He was only concerned about your condition and that you would be completely well in a day or two. Do you want to see him? He could see you in the morning, I'm sure."

"Ellen, I'm not sure that I want to see your father, but I know I need to see him. I'm uncertain about who I am and what I've become. Yes, Ellen, I want to see him. He might be able to help me—if he doesn't hate me."

Rene began to cry again.

Ellen tried to calm her mother. "Now, Mom, just hang in there.

I'm going to see Dad in a little while, and I'll talk with him. I'm sure you'll see him in the morning. Goodbye."

When Jonathan arrived at Ellen's a short time later, he had Chinese dinners for everyone and a kiss for Laura. He had a reasonably relaxed dinner with Ellen and Anson and a noisy one with Laura. Her grandfather thought she was every bit as demanding and ornery as her mother had been, and also every bit as delightful. As soon as the dishes were put away and Laura was asleep, Ellen reluctantly began to talk about her mother. They moved over to the living room circle. Anson was quiet. Ellen initiated the conversation.

"Dad, have you seen the pictures and articles in the newspapers about Mom?"

"Yes, I've seen them. Also a TV interview with Mrs. Edmondson," Jonathan said noncommittally.

"Well, Dad, what do you think?"

"Briefly, I think she's lucky that Edmondson had a controlled wife—relatively controlled, that is—or your mother would have been shot dead."

"Dad," Ellen almost pleaded, "Please don't be too hard on Mom. She has suffered and will continue to suffer for some time to come. Please, just try to help her."

He responded matter-of-factly. "Ellen, I didn't say anything hard or harsh about your mother. I made a practical observation. Under the circumstances, I'm glad she's alive and not dead or seriously hurt."

"Of course, Dad," Ellen said apologetically. "I know that Mom has created problems for lots of people, especially for herself. What do you think about the shooting and its effect on everyone?"

"Ellen, I'm concerned first about the innocent bystanders, you and Bruce and Susan. Have you called them? If so, what did they say?"

"Yes, I called them," Ellen said dejectedly, "but neither one had much to say. They weren't terribly surprised. At least, they didn't act like they were. They wanted to know about Mom's condition, and I assured them that she would be out of the hospital within a few days, as good as new."

"What, specifically, did Bruce say, Ellen?" Jonathan asked.

"Well, he said he was pleased to hear that she would be all right, but he said he was afraid she would never be as good as new. I didn't ask him what he meant."

"And Susan?" Jonathan asked.

"Susan didn't seem surprised or alarmed. Apparently, she had been feeling for some time that Mom was running a great risk in going around with married men. One of her married lovers even tried to date Susan. I don't know if Bruce told you, but when he was here in February he really read Mom the riot act."

Jonathan asked one last question. "Did you tell Bruce and Susan about Mother's good press coverage?"

"Yes, I did, but they had nothing to say. They believe it's her problem and that she'll have to work it out herself. That's the way I feel, too."

"Yet, Ellen, you were concerned enough to call me with the expectation, undoubtedly, that I might be able to help her. Wouldn't you have been disappointed if I had simply said, 'It's her problem.' I warned her. There's nothing for me to do. Let her work it out herself?'" His voice was firm and tinged with reprimand.

Anson spoke up for Ellen. "Jonathan, Ellen thought she was doing the best thing for you and for her mother by calling you. So please don't be too hard on her. As you know, she and I have been close to Rene out here. And Rene has been very helpful to us. We didn't feel it was our business to try to run her life."

"Anson, that's an understandable feeling. Adult children have so many problems of their own that what bothers their parents is often a secondary matter to them. Take it from me, that is a very unwise and, I think, unjustifiable attitude.

"I know I shall never outlive the deep regret that I feel for having made the same selfish assumptions about my father. He suffered a great deal. He lost his very much loved and totally devoted wife when I was born. Then he lost all his meager possessions in a giant flood. He had to sell his dearest possession, his violin, in order to get the money to move his family out of the bayous, away from the swamp and the floods, so we might have at least a small chance to live better lives.

"I am much less the man I would feel myself to be had I asked my father over the years what I might do for him. I know he would have told me to go on and go to school and achieve whatever I could. But I also know that I would have made him happier by asking him.

"I never had a mother, but I believe adult children should be very concerned about the lives of their parents, and be especially concerned about the happiness or unhappiness of divorced parents. They suffer, as do their children—much more if the children are already grown. Grown children should create an objective, supportive relationship with their parents."

For a long time it was silent in Ellen and Anson's living room. They were all lost in thought. Ellen broke the silence.

"What can we do for Mom now, Dad?" she asked.

"Your mother has no job now," Jonathan said sympathetically. "She'll need your encouragement to look forward to a productive future. But don't offer encouragement and help on an 'I know it's not my business' basis.

"And don't implicitly condone what she's done and what has happened. If you do, she won't have the faith in your support that she'll need.

"She knows she's done wrong. She's paid a heavy penalty. She's lost standing with her friends. She's lost her job. She may have lost enough self-respect to be unable to function constructively. I've been the only one of our close-knit family to consistently condemn her dating behavior. Therefore, I believe she'll look to me now for help, and I'll give it to her, with as much understanding and care as possible."

Ellen looked relieved.

"Ellen," Jonathan asked, "haven't you been somewhat indifferent to your mother's actions?"

Ellen recoiled and was almost tearful as she said, "Certainly not, Dad! Surely you don't think I haven't worried and worried about Mom. Of course, I know now I should have been more firm with her. But she was my friend, as well as my mother, and I didn't feel that I should interfere with her personal life."

"I appreciate your feelings, Ellen. But *because* your mother is your friend, you must help her when she needs guidance. I know you love her and that you're the oldest and closest child to her. But, you know, parents often need to look to their oldest child for advice. And you, more than many, are highly qualified to help your mother.

"My advice would be simple and straightforward. Don't be hesitant because she's your mother. Take the initiative because she *is* your mother."

"Dad, please don't be too stern with Mom."

"No, Ellen, I expect your mother will be surprised and pleased at how considerate I'll be and should be. I say that because she's already paid a heavy price. No need for me to condemn her further for her conduct. The first big payment has already come due. I must help her get out from under this burden.

"I'll encourage her to use the strength and self-discipline she used for so many years when she lived with me. I'll suggest new business and professional opportunities for her. She should continue to work. She needs the support structure that useful work provides.

"And I don't criticize her for wanting sex. So do I, but I value my self-respect above sex for its own sake. I've never condemned sex when there was mutual regard and when the circumstances indicated a mutually beneficial and enjoyable experience.

"But I do condemn adultery, as most civilizations always have. I condemn stealing, which adultery is. I condemn adultery or any other actions that harm innocent bystanders, especially when they are mothers and children.

"Anyway, I'll talk with her, constructively and in a far happier mood than I've shown here tonight. Your mother will be pleased to see me and will be glad I came out. What time do you think I should be there?"

Ellen said sadly, "I would think about nine-thirty or ten, after her breakfast. Oh," Ellen said, jumping up, "I hear Laura."

As she went to attend to the baby's needs, she said, "Please call me after you talk with Mom."

"Tell Laura good night for me, Ellen. I'll talk to you tomorrow," Jonathan said as Ellen disappeared down the hall to the baby's room.

He turned to Anson, who had been sitting very quietly, listening to all that was said. "Anson, you don't inject yourself very much into Ellen's family life. Do you have any questions for me?"

"Jonathan, I listen. I like Rene very much. That doesn't mean I approve of the last affair, or any of them, for that matter. But lots of men and women do as she's done." Anson stared unseeingly at the coffee table as he talked.

"Yes, Anson, and some of them get shot in the head or the heart, not just in the foot." Then Jonathan said in a kind voice, "I do understand your position. You've been a good friend to Rene. But

378

sometimes a good friend must say what should be said and not just what the person wants to hear.

"One of the great sins that we all may commit unknowingly is the sin of remaining silent and doing nothing. Silence can be misinterpreted as approval. And one of the synonyms for remaining silent is selfishness. I say this to you, Anson, because someday you may wish to advise your client, Rene, not to do something. Let me encourage you to feel free to advise me, as well as your mother-in-law. You've tried not to be an interfering son-in-law, but don't hold back your views too much."

He stood up and put out his hand. Anson stood up and shook his hand.

"Well," Jonathan said, "I'd better be going so you can go see Laura before she falls asleep. Good night."

Anson followed him to the front door. "Good night, Jonathan," he said. "Thanks for coming by. Good luck tomorrow."

It was about nine o'clock when Jonathan returned to his room. It would be eleven in Chicago, but he thought Katherine would still be awake, so he called.

"Hello, Jonathan. I'm so glad you called. I tried to reach you earlier this evening, but your secretarial service said you were in California. When I heard this, I thought something might have happened to one of your family."

"Katherine, Rene was in an accident, not serious, but she's in the hospital. Ellen called me at 2:10 this morning, and I arrived in time to have dinner with her and Anson. I deeply appreciate your concern."

"When are you returning? I'd really love to see you. Perhaps you could return to Washington via Chicago?" Katherine asked.

"Will you be available early next week?"

"I'll be busy Monday evening but expect to be free Tuesday or Wednesday evening."

"I'll be in Chicago Tuesday in time for dinner. May I come directly to your place?" Jonathan asked.

"That would be wonderful," Katherine replied enthusiastically. "See you soon."

"Goodbye, darling. Thank you for so much." Jonathan placed the phone down softly.

# 35

On Saturday morning, Rene was pleasantly anticipating seeing Jonathan. She told the nurse that he would be arriving about nine-thirty or ten and asked that he be sent right to her room. Leaning back comfortably against the pillows, she had finished reading the newspaper when Jonathan entered the room.

He went directly to the bed, leaned over, and kissed her gently. "Hello, how are you feeling?" he asked.

Rene looked at Jonathan. He was smiling. "I'm so glad to see you," she said happily. "I appreciate your kiss and your smile even more than the lovely roses." She touched the roses on her night stand. "Look at them! Aren't they gorgeous?"

As she looked at the large vase filled with red and yellow roses, her eyes became misty. She looked at him again and commented, "I don't know how you manage to stay so youthful. You look as young as you did when we were on the farm."

"Honey, are your eyes still okay? I'm not sure you can see the extra furrow in my forehead." He sat down in the chair beside her bed and said, "Say, did your Dr. Sukman come to see you yesterday? What's his report?"

"Yes, he came in and examined my foot and said I could leave the hospital Monday. He also said there was every indication that I'd have no permanent impairment of the foot, no limp, and not even a noticeable scar. I'm pleased, because for a few hours I didn't know if I would have a foot left; or at least, I thought I might have to use a cane." Rene looked a little puzzled as she said sadly, "And you know, I didn't mind the idea of having to use a cane. It sort of occurred to me that I needed a constant reminder.

"The doctor said the woman who shot us most have known exactly where to shoot. He made it very clear that I was lucky, because if the shot had been in the ankle area, I probably would have had a limp."

"Well, that's a relief," Jonathan said. "I'm certainly glad you'll be able to walk normally. And I don't think that you'll need a cane to remind you of this incident."

"No, Jonathan. I'll never forget it. That I know."

She paused, looking puzzled again for a moment. "I've been thinking, and now I remember hearing about Mrs. Edmondson before! She was the woman in the dream you told me about before we left the Watergate. You said the place was on a street bordered with tall palm trees—like in Beverly Hills. You said a man and woman had come out of an apartment house or hotel, and the doorman waved for a cab, but instead a woman in blue jeans and a checkered shirt rode up on an Arabian horse. She pulled out a pistol and yelled at the man and woman to dance, while she shot at their feet. After a few shots she rode away, and two ambulances came and took the man and woman away. Now I remember very clearly that you said they had towels wrapped around their feet. Jonathan! You saw in your dream something that happened to me. It was too much like Greg and me. You never knew, of course, but Mrs. Edmondson raises Arabian horses. Am I crazy, or did you tell me you dreamed something like this?

"I remember very well your saying you didn't make anything out of dreams, but what do you say now?"

"Rene, I do remember that dream. It does sound crazy, in view of what's happened. But I don't believe anyone knows much about dreams. While some write books on dreams, the problem is that the views of the experts wash out each other's expertise. So I don't see much in dreams, and I'm glad I don't."

"But, Jonathan, what about the dream you told me? You can't dismiss it just like that, can you?" Rene insisted.

"Rene, there are many things scientists learn almost daily about the incomprehensibility of the infinitely complex brain—the infinitely complex human. For all I know, the unconscious may commune with the totality that is nature. Perhaps the unconscious sometimes expresses itself in dreams because the conscious mind, the rational brain, man's neo-cortex or whatever, may not be able to interpret the signals from the unconscious. I certainly don't know. My advice to you and to myself is simply to allow for what may appear to be strange phenomena."

Jonathan noticed the "No Smoking" sign above her bed beside the oxygen outlet and asked, "How are you doing with the no smoking rule around here?"

"Well, not too good and not too bad. Since I'm not using oxygen, I asked the doctor if I could have a cigarette. He said, 'Absolutely not! No smoking allowed.' Then he asked, 'Are you much of a smoker?' I said, 'About average.'

"He looked at me and asked, 'Do you know what "average" is for a regular smoker?'

"I admitted I didn't know but told him that I probably smoke about a pack a day, maybe more. But I don't smoke all of any one cigarette.

"He wasn't satisfied with my answer and asked, 'How long has it been since you had a thorough check-up, Mrs. Barron?'

"I told him, 'Maybe a year or two.' And now he wants to give me a thorough check-up before he sends me home. I had a little cough when I came into the hospital, and he didn't like the sound of it. The tests will all begin on Monday."

"Well, that's probably a good idea," Jonathan said. "After all, you're already here, so you might as well take advantage of the opportunity. And you don't have to go to work."

"That's true. Dr. Sukman had the same reproachful tone in his voice that you had when I started smoking again when I began work at Carolina State."

"Do just the men who are concerned about your health and welfare remind you of me? Am I that bad?" he asked jokingly.

"Oh, no," she answered convincingly. "Maybe the reason I'm in this hospital now is that my friend Greg reminded me of you, more than any other man I've dated. Greg has brownish-blond hair, and yours is darker, but it's always had a little brown in it." She was looking at Jonathan.

"Greg was so sensitive and such a wonderful lover, so sure of himself, yet very considerate—like you are, unless you're scolding me," Rene said.

Jonathan took both her hands in his and held them. "Well, I guess I got my role as lover and teacher too mixed up. But I'm glad you do remember me."

She looked away from him and closed her eyes. "How could I ever forget you?" she said softly. "Do you realize that as old as I am now, and even as old as I feel I am, I've still spent more than half my entire life with you?"

She removed only her left hand from his right hand, squeezing his left hand to explain that her move was just for comfort. There was a moment of silence between them.

"So, which lover sent you the bunch of pink roses?" Jonathan asked. He emphasized the word "bunch," so no one would compare them with his roses.

"Here, look at this," Rene said as she handed him a note from the little table next to her bed. "The flowers arrived just before you did," she continued, "and I've just read the note. I don't quite know what to make of it.

"Read the note and tell me what you think."

He read the note half aloud.

Dear Mrs. Barron,

Please accept this bouquet of roses, along with my apology. I live in your neighborhood, and Thursday evening, as I was walking my dog after dinner, I heard what sounded like gunshots. I walked across the street to see what was going on. I stayed a short distance away until the police car and ambulance arrived. Then I walked up to your apartment garage. I always carry my camera, and I shot several pictures. I watched you hop around wrapping towels on your friend's foot before wrapping your own. After I saw the picture in the paper, I wished that I had not photographed this wonderful woman. I'm sorry if the picture hurt you. I shall never give any more of my pictures to any news media. May I come by the hospital and introduce myself? If you will be so kind as to call my office, I'll be right over. I will stay for just a few minutes. I want to apologize personally, and I think I'd like to meet you. I am a widower.

Very sincerely,
Gerald Clawson

P. S. I'll bring the other pictures that I took at the scene and give them to you.

Rene looked at Jonathan. "Does it make sense to you? Should I call him? I would like to see the other pictures he took. He could do no harm to me here in the hospital. I would tell him he could come here to see me, but he has to leave his camera at home. What do you think?"

Jonathan was looking at the letterhead.

Gerald Clawson, D. D. S.

"I'm thinking, honey," he said as he walked slowly around the room, looking at the flowers again. "My roses are a lot prettier than his."

He didn't expect a reply. He was just observing and thinking. He took the note and read it again. Then he grinned, which surprised Rene. He sat down again in the chair beside her bed.

"Rene, do you have a regular dentist here yet?"

She looked surprised. "No—but I went to Ellen's dentist once to have a filling checked. Why?"

Jonathan smiled again. "Dr. Clawson might be a good dentist. If he feels so sorry about taking the pictures for the papers, maybe he'll give you a fair price. But what's funny to me is that the person who happened to be walking his dog and happened along at just the right moment to take the pictures is apparently a practicing dentist."

"Why is that funny?" Rene hadn't expected her ex-husband to be so relaxed, considering the circumstances of his visit.

He said half to himself and half to Rene, "I wonder if Dr. Clawson, the dentist, is also an Episcopalian."

Suddenly, the light dawned for Rene. "Jonathan," she exclaimed, "now I know what's making you grin! When you were here at Christmas, you were preaching that the ideal man for me would be a rich, sexy Episcopalian dentist. You gave me all those reasons, funny reasons. But you didn't say he'd be an amateur photographer. Furthermore, I'll bet he's married."

She paused a moment and said, "On second thought, I'll bet he isn't, because his dog and camera take the place of the wife he doesn't have."

"His note said he was a widower," Jonathan reminded her.

"So it did. I'll call Dr. Clawson and talk to him while I'm here in a neutral setting. What do you think?"

He smiled once again. "Sure. Always give fate a helping hand. Call him after I leave. In the meantime, what did you think about the article in the *Chronicle* and the pictures and stories in the other papers? I heard a television news commentator talking about what Mrs. Edmondson had said. I compliment you as a public relations expert. You got wonderful press coverage. But I thought you'd decided not to date another married man. What changed your mind?"

"Jonathan, as I told you, he was the first man I've met who was as attractive to me as you were. He was very interesting, and he was so nice to me. Often when I looked at him, I wished you had been more relaxed and friendly.''

She put her hand up between Jonathan and herself, as if to stop him from speaking. "You don't have to scold me. I'm not going to take a chance any more. I think I'll be celibate. I thought about that when I talked with you at Christmas. I wouldn't be here now if I'd put that thought into action.

"But then, I would have missed having Greg," she said quietly. "There aren't any more Gregs, married or single, so I think I'll just close up shop for a long time.

"I hope the force you call fate won't punish me any more. I don't know what changed my life so much—or what changed me.''

"Rene, you realize, I hope, that you've paid only a modest price for your adventures with Edmondson. You're lucky to be alive, because there was at least one other married man, and, I understand, two more that you didn't tell me about. By telling me that part of Edmondson's appeal was that he reminded you of me, you've tried to prevent me from scolding you. But you've had so many lovers. All of them couldn't have reminded you of me, unless it's just that we all happen to be men.''

Rene looked down at the bed and said very sadly, "You really taught me and inspired me to be sexual. And I wish now that you'd said yes when I just wanted to stay home and be *your* mistress.''

"No intelligent, proud man wants a mistress, certainly not one dumb enough just to stay home and do nothing else," Jonathan said firmly. "You owed it to yourself to use your brains and professional experience. We should have moved to Australia to get away from your groupie friends. They're the ones who really alienated you, along with the already archaic 'new woman' novels and denigrating sexual freedom 'survey' reports on women by women to confuse women—and to sell books.

"But that day is gone. I have my more or less restrictive life, and you have doubtless had lots of satisfaction in being on your own —if being on your own means taking on uncounted lovers. I must say, I think that going from one lover to another is about the only satisfaction some women get out of being 'free'—that is, the only countable and measurable satisfaction.''

Rene didn't look up, and she didn't try to comment.

"If I weren't so selective," he continued, "I might find that

385

having many women would serve as an antidote to my lingering loneliness. But you know, Rene, I've found that making love without love makes one even lonelier.

"Think about it.

"Remember how Louise Saxton covered practically every man in Church City, including some of the clergy, and she became lonelier and lonelier?"

Rene looked up this time and nodded rather weakly.

Jonathan stood up and walked to the foot of the bed. He put his hands on the tray that was resting there and said, "Well, she came to see me in Washington just recently. I told her that I could only give her advice. She's still pretty, and I deserve a medal for saying no to her invitation to bed."

"Yes, I remember Louise," Rene said. "I'm surprised you could resist taking her to bed. The men in Church City seemed to think she was great. What did you advise her?"

"Something I rarely do. I suggested that she had never had enough tenderness and love at home—little or none from her father—that she had tried to get it just through sex with her lovers, and it hadn't worked. I asked her about her women friends. One she named was successful and smart. I told her to go visit her. She did, and she stayed."

"I'm sorry for Louise," Rene said sadly, "but maybe she isn't so lonely now. What shall I do, Jonathan? The friends I still have will now have reason to be rather cool to me. Many of my old friends dropped me after I moved out here. It's strange. They were friendly for a while. I think a few of my friends will stay with me, but I know that I've lost something they admired." She paused. "I think the children will stay with me."

Jonathan quickly interrupted her and said, "Of course the children will stay with you. They love you. They'll be very supportive."

"Ellen has been so wonderful to me. And Anson, too." Her voice drifted off. Jonathan waited for her to think about what she really wanted to say.

She surprised him by making an unusually objective statement. She spoke aloud, but more to herself than to him. "I don't think you and the children realize the tremendous pressure I was under, trying to live up to your expectations. These pressures were especially great because I have revered and admired you so much. And they've had their repercussions and have caused overreactions that may appear to be retrogressive. That retrogression, Jonathan, may have created within me some masochistic tendencies.

"Once I was out on my own, I felt compelled to deviate from the standards you had set for me. And once I had begun to deviate and make my own decisions, the momentum moved me on. Although you gave me a lot of love and care, I still felt that I was your 'project,' not free to be me.

"Furthermore, during the last two or three years, I had become seemingly invisible to you. You were so distant and distracted. I wish you'd compromised and agreed on our separating for a while. But you *closed the door* on me. After I got out here, I began to feel that you had rejected me just because I'm me. I became bitter and angry at you and at myself."

After a few moments of silence, she began again. "I've been thinking, soul-searching, since the moment I faced Mrs. Edmondson's gun. Like a flash in the sky I saw myself, and I didn't like what I saw. That's why I asked Mrs. Edmondson to kill me. I don't really understand it, but maybe you do.

"You were often depressed and suicidal because of your obsession with ethics and your concerns about me and my future. You saw things I didn't. Yet, you seem to have overcome the idea of self-destruction and deep depression. You look better now than you have for years.

"Over the phone last Christmas, when you asked if I would make love to Ralph, one of our long-time friends, I was angry. I told you I would if he asked me. You said, 'In spite of the fact that you're supposed to be a good friend of his wife's?' Later, in ending the conversation, I asked you if you would be my friend. I remember you said, 'No'—just like that. Then you hung up.

"I ask you now. Will you be my friend?"

Rene reached out for Jonathan's hand. He took her hand and held it.

"Yes, Rene, I will be your friend. But you're going to have to wade through, struggle through, this experience pretty much alone. You'll have blood in your shoes for a long time.

"Why don't you buy yourself a nice condominium in Santa Monica, near Ellen? Take your time and decorate it carefully for the woman you now want to become. That task will be fun for you, and as soon as you have it decorated and have moved in, start writing short stories and feature stories. You have expertise in feature stories, especially in the medical and scientific areas. Better yet, try your hand at a novel. Lord, you've had an incredibly wide range of experience, and you're a professional writer, though new to fiction.''

"Jonathan, thank you so much.''

She took her hand out of his, clasped both her hands in front of her, and lay quietly, smiling at him.

"I'll buy myself a condominium. I really should have done that anyway, for the tax advantages. I'd like to decorate it myself, all by myself, because I'll have the time now. I might be very lonely, being out of a job.

"You know, I enjoyed my job. Now it's gone, and at my age I don't expect another such opportunity. I wonder what promotion they had in mind for me. Dr. Spirrison said his leaving Southland wouldn't affect my job, and he understood I was going to be promoted.'' Her voice broke. "Oh, Jonathan, all that is gone now.''

She regrouped her thoughts and sounded a little more optimistic. "But I will move. And you know, it's just come to me. I think I know who told Mrs. Edmondson about Greg and me.''

Rene seemed relieved by this new thought, but a little angry, too.

"Yes, Rene,'' Jonathan said, "I think I know who told on you, too. It was your landlord. In my dream, your landlord was the doorman who waved to the woman on the horse. He was laughing, because he was punishing you and your lover. And when I came up to look at your apartment last Christmas, he was lurking around in the hall outside your door. He asked, 'Where's Rene?' as if it were his business to know. When I told him who I was, he acted rather frightened and sheepish.

"I think you've had a very jealous landlord. You must have paid him off for saving the nice apartment for you, and you must have paid him in a memorable way.''

Rene nodded and started to cry. But Jonathan didn't pause.

"Yes,'' he said firmly, "I think you should move as soon as you can buy your condo and furnish it. That will be in two or three months, probably. You have a lease, but he won't dare to try either to break it or to hold you to it. He's had sex with you and has told on you because you wouldn't accept him again. No doubt he'll be afraid not to honor your lease requests, so just treat him considerately as one should a good landlord. He can rent your apartment instantly, probably for more than he charged you."

"You make me feel so cheap. You know so much, and what you don't know seems to appear before you as on a screen. I made love to him once, partly because he had done so much for my apartment and partly because he was the first one after I left you. I wanted to see if I was as good at sex as you said I was. I needed a practice session. He almost climbed the walls and walked on the ceiling. He gave me too much sexual assurance, I suppose. It was fun seeing a man get so excited. I was in complete control of him."

Rene thought about what she was saying. "Jonathan, I'm sorry. Here I am, talking like a nymphomaniac. Today it all looks so juvenile, so cheap, so stupid."

She turned on her side. He said nothing, but lowered the bed so she could stretch out. She was exhausted, emotionally and physically.

"Jonathan, will you come back again and talk to me about real estate and condominiums?" she asked softly. "I hope you'll forgive me someday for being so sexually loose and indiscriminate. Promiscuous, yes, but not really indiscriminate. My lovers have all been pretty successful men and intelligent enough to appreciate what I gave them. But do you know that even before I was shot and publicized as a mistress and fired from my job, some of your friends wouldn't even talk to me on the phone?"

Then she whispered, "Didn't we have fun when we worked together as a team in the real estate business? Those were happy days."

Jonathan had never seen Rene in such a sad, nostalgic mood. She had made it a practice to live from day to day. Now she was thinking of the past and of the future.

"Yes, honey," Jonathan said in ready agreement, "we did enjoy being partners around the clock when we were in the real estate business. And we succeeded."

He smiled and stood up to leave. "You know, I think I'll come out and stay around a while. Ellen may have told you that I'd like to get a good writer for a farcical, satirical, musical comedy based on Dante's *Divine Comedy* and call it *Dante's Masquerade.* But forget that for the moment.

"Sure, I'd like to see you again. How about my calling you tomorrow and seeing you on Monday? Ellen and Anson and

Anson's parents will want to see you tomorrow. And after you've slept a while and had lunch, you might want to call your photographer, Dr. Clawson, and thank him for the flowers and note. You might be interested in his views of the shooting scene. But I'd advise that you let *him* talk and that you not discuss much about yourself or Edmondson.

"Call me if you wish—at the Bel Air Sands. I do want to come back when the bandages are off your foot. I want to see it. You may recall that I used to like to hold and massage your feet after you'd been walking around showing real estate properties all day."

By this time, Jonathan was at the door to Rene's hospital room. "Goodbye. I'll call before coming to see you, because you might not feel like seeing me for a while."

"Thank you again, Jonathan. I am tired. I guess being shot anywhere takes something out of you."

When Jonathan returned to the hotel, he called Ellen. He assured her that his meeting with her mother had been cordial and that Rene seemed to be glad he had come out to see her.

"How do you think she'll get along, Dad?" Ellen wanted to be reassured.

"She's doing well mentally and physically. The doctor has confirmed that she will have no permanent impairment of her foot, but he wants her to have a complete physical check-up before she leaves the hospital. Your mother does look tired. She needs rest. And she might as well get the check-up out of the way while she's still in the hospital. She hasn't had one for a couple of years.

"But you'll be seeing her soon. If you and Anson have time, please give me a ring, and I'll come out and get better acquainted with Laura."

"We'll make time, Daddy. How long will you be staying?"

"Only for a couple of days this time. I'm going to try to see a good agent or two about an idea I've had. Unfortunately, those agents from whom I used to buy talent are either retired or dead."

"Goodbye, Dad. I'm so glad your meeting with Mom went well. I'll call you tomorrow evening."

"Goodbye, Ellen."

# 36

Rene was very tired after Jonathan left. She thought he had been quite calm and considerate, in view of the circumstances that had prompted his visit. She was not unmindful of the shame that her actions had brought to him, to the children, and especially to herself. There was no doubt that she had let her family and her friends down.

She had been tense and weary ever since Mrs. Edmondson had confronted her with the gun. The publicity only added to her discomfort. The medication she was taking, her concern about whether her foot would ever really heal properly, her shame—all these things contributed to her almost unbearable depression.

Jonathan's visit was very helpful. She thought he must still care a great deal for her, despite the fact that now his friends would know that the wife he had been proud of for so long had become another man's mistress. She knew that some people would call her a whore.

Rene wondered what lay ahead of her, wondered if she would be able to start over again at fifty-one with no job and few friends, virtually locked out of the academic environment she had learned to love. She wondered if she would still be able to make a good life for herself. Jonathan seemed to think that she could.

No one had phoned except her California relatives: Ellen, Anson, and his parents. And, of course, Jonathan had come to see her and had sent her flowers as soon as he could.

Greg hadn't called, and he shouldn't have. Still, it hurt to know that in all probability she would never see him again. She certainly would never call him. She knew now that their love relationship, however joyful it had been, should never have happened in the first place. When she thought about it, she knew that the price they were both paying for that relationship was high, terribly high. Their personal and professional lives had been severely damaged.

"Oh, God," she thought, "why couldn't Jonathan and I have

remained married?" They had gone over that a thousand times together, and for a while even she had believed that a divorce was right for them. Now she felt that for all her maturity and intelligence, she had behaved like an errant child, the very role she had resented as Jonathan's wife. Self-condemnation can be a very cruel form of punishment, and no one could have judged Rene more harshly than she was judging herself at this time.

She lay in bed, almost weeping, and finally drifted into a restless sleep. In what seemed like only a few minutes, she was awakened for a lunch she didn't want. But the nurse had happy news, too. Ellen and Anson were coming over to see her at three o'clock.

She began to study the lovely roses Jonathan had sent her. Their fragrance seemed to penetrate her whole being. Picking up the small radio Ellen had brought when she first visited her in the hospital, she tuned in a piano concerto—Liszt. She loved Liszt. The pianist sounded like Arthur Sonberg, who had often played Liszt for Jonathan.

She turned away from Jonathan's roses and turned off the radio. Such beauty and poignant memories were too painful. She wondered if all the joys of the past would now just haunt her, rather than console her.

What was it Jonathan used to say? "The quickest way to conquer a crisis is to take action."

What could she do now?

Rene looked thoughtfully at the pink roses Dr. Clawson had sent her with his note of apology for photographing the shooting scene. She wondered if he were some kind of nut, walking around his neighborhood taking pictures. She wondered, too, if he might be an Episcopalian, as Jonathan's scenario called for. Rene was restless and decided to call the dentist. She dialed his home number, which was also on the business card that had come with his note and flowers. Since it was Saturday afternoon, she felt that his home was the appropriate place to try first.

The phone rang several times, and a pleasant baritone voice said, "This is Dr. Clawson speaking."

"Hello, Dr. Clawson," Rene said with a lilting bit of surprise in her voice. For some reason, she hadn't really expected an answer. "This is Rene Barron."

She felt odd, identifying herself to one who knew she had been shot as an illicit lover. But he had been at the scene, so in a way he knew her. She got hold of herself instantly.

"Well, how kind of you to call, Mrs. Barron," Dr. Clawson said warmly. "I hope you're feeling better and recovering rapidly."

"Yes, Dr. Clawson, I'm feeling fairly well, considering. I called to thank you for the pretty pink roses and for your kind note."

"I'm glad you liked the roses, Mrs. Barron, and I do hope you're going to let me drop by for a few minutes to introduce myself. I want to apologize personally for taking the pictures. I've been taking pictures a lot in the past three or four years, and many of them have appeared in the local papers. Once in a while, they're even picked up by scores of papers, including papers in New York, Washington, and Chicago."

Rene listened—Washington, Chicago. Had her pictures reached everyone she knew in those places?

"Oh, God." She fairly shuddered at the thought.

"Hello?" Dr. Clawson wanted to make sure she was still on the line. "Well, I've been proud of my hobby until I got to thinking about the sorrow my photo may have caused you."

"Dr. Clawson," Rene answered as normally as she could, "I'm sure you meant no harm to me. You were just doing your job, as any good journalist would." Rene thought that that was a good, impersonal comment.

"Oh, it's so kind of you to say that, Mrs. Barron. I've always wanted to be a journalist, but I followed my father into dentistry. If you want the other photos I made, I'll be glad to bring them to you, along with the negatives. It would make me feel better to give them to you personally. When can you have visitors?"

"On a restricted basis, I can have visitors now. My daughter and son-in-law are coming up this afternoon. If you want to come tomorrow about one-thirty, I think I'll feel well enough to see you for a little while."

"That will be a good hour for me to come," Dr. Clawson replied eagerly, "because I can leave church, have a cup of coffee, and be there at one-thirty."

Rene's curiosity was piqued, and she couldn't resist checking out Jonathan's guess, or perception, or whatever it was. "Dr. Clawson, do you mind telling me if you're an Episcopalian?"

"Why, yes, Mrs. Barron, as a matter of fact I am. I'm a vestryman at St. Matthew's Episcopal Church in West Los Angeles. Why? Are you an Episcopalian?"

"No, not at this time, Dr. Clawson. I used to be a Catholic."

"So was I!" he said.

"Well, just come to the third-floor desk tomorrow, and the nurse will bring you to my room. And please don't forget to bring all your pictures."

"I'll bring them all. And I do look forward to meeting you. Thank you very much for calling."

"Goodbye, Doctor," Rene said with a smile, and with relief. She didn't want him to think that her curiosity extended beyond the pictures.

As soon as she hung up, she said aloud, "Damn that Jonathan. How does he do it?

"I wish Clawson had been a Southern Baptist, like Jonathan was once," she muttered. "That would have contradicted some of Jonathan's perceptiveness. I'll have to ask Ellen and Anson about this business of his being right on target so much of the time. When I was living with him, I just assumed he would know things without my telling him. I wonder if that fact kept me faithful in our marriage. Regardless of Clawson's being a dentist and an Episcopalian, I am curious about the other pictures he made."

About ten minutes before three, Ellen and Anson came in and greeted Rene cheerily. She was very glad to see them.

"Look what I brought you, Mom, in case you aren't eating enough," Ellen said, handing Rene a two-pound box of her favorite chocolates.

"You really shouldn't have, Ellen, and I shouldn't indulge, either. But these chocolates are just what I want. Thank you." She pulled Ellen over and kissed her forehead. "And thank you, too, Anson," she said, smiling at him.

"Mom, you look very well. What have you been up to?" Ellen asked eagerly.

"You two won't believe it, but I've been talking to a man I've never met, and he's coming up to see me tomorrow. Guess who?"

"The dentist, Dr. Clawson, who sent you the flowers and made the pictures of the shooting," Ellen answered quickly. "Dad talked to us about it and said he figured you'd call him. He favored your doing so. What did Clawson sound like?" Ellen wasn't going to let her mother get by with anything for a while, at least.

394

"He sounded like an ordinary man, I guess. He seemed to be courteous and straightforward. I don't know, and I really don't care, so long as he brings the pictures and the negatives and doesn't bore me. He's coming up tomorrow, Sunday, at one-thirty. I just want the pictures, not a date or more pink roses." Rene was making sure Ellen knew that she was being cautious.

"Ellen," Rene said, "I want to ask you something. Do you really think your father had some psychic awareness that I would meet an Episcopalian dentist? You know, that's what he insinuated would happen when he was here at Christmas. He said I should find a dentist and go to church to do it—an Episcopal church, at that. Dr. Clawson is not only a dentist, but he's also an Episcopalian. In fact, he's a vestryman in the church. That's like a deacon.

"The whole thing really puzzles me. Your father always seems to know about strange coincidences."

"Mom, you should keep in mind that Dad was educated as a social scientist and psychologist. He's studied people and environments so much for so long. He's also an expert at demographics. He knows the probabilities. He's been almost everywhere. So he just adds the proverbial two plus two and guesses statistically.

"Don't be guided by his seemingly psychic abilities. After all, he isn't a hundred percent correct all the time. But I would suggest that you listen to his horse sense, based on experience."

Rene was skeptical. "Now, Ellen, is that how your father guessed the date of Laura's birth, fifteen months before she was born? And even told you that she would be a girl?"

"No," Ellen said, a bit flustered, "he just knew about what my timetable would be, because he knows me so well."

Rene asked a question that had been hounding her. "Do you suppose he advised the divorce because he knows me so well? Did he know that I wouldn't handle my freedom well?"

"Oh, no, Mom! If he'd known enough about what would happen to you, I'll bet you and he would never have separated. He just tried to play God once too often."

Her mother sighed. "I don't know. I really don't know."

For a few moments, the two women were quiet. Anson stood by the window, looking out, respectful of the silence. When Ellen saw that Rene wasn't going to pursue their conversation, she changed the subject.

"Okay, Mom, I hope the dentist surprises you and turns out to be a very interesting, nice fellow when he brings the pictures tomorrow. His note says he's a widower. So why not see him? Dad said he enjoyed seeing you and thought you were responding to events very well. Of course, he didn't approve of your actions, I'm sure."

Ellen had been sitting in one of the two chairs beside her mother's bed, but now she got up and walked around the room. Rene opened the box of candy and held it out for her and Anson to take some.

"Ellen, your father seems to have changed so much in the past few months, and all for the better. He isn't nearly so depressed. He looks wonderful, and he's a lot more understanding. I know he's not approving, but at least he's not as cuttingly condemning of me as he has been in the past, especially when he left me at Christmas. Yesterday we got along all right and talked about the possibility of my buying a condominium, an idea that he strongly favored."

Ellen was curious about how her mother felt about seeing her dad, even though she had never encouraged either one of her parents to see the other. "When is Dad coming back to see you? He told me he'd be out here for a few days, contacting Hollywood agents about a movie idea."

"He said he'd phone me and come back to see me. I think he wants to let me think more about what's really happened before he comes back to visit. He hinted at coming over just before I leave the hospital. I think he wanted to drive me home or help me."

Rene lay back against the pillows and asked Anson if his parents would be coming over Sunday afternoon.

"Yes, they asked us to check with you," Anson said. "They'd like to come over about three or three-thirty, if that's okay with you."

"That'll be fine. I do want to see them. Will you talk with them? Or maybe I'll call Esther." Rene looked at Anson, and he thought she might feel uncomfortable calling his mother.

"I'll have Mom call you when they're ready to leave the house," Anson replied. "That way, you'll know they're on their way."

Rene was feeling rather embarrassed about calling her friends, too. She hadn't called Bruce and Susan, but Ellen had called them on her behalf. She was expecting to hear from both Bruce and Susan on Sunday, if not today. She *hoped* they would call her.

Ellen went over to Rene's bed, put her arm around her mother's shoulders, and stroked her hair back. "We'll let you rest now, Mom, but would you like for me to bring some more things over for you? Any special robe or dress? You know, you'll probably be sitting up in a chair tomorrow when Dr. Clawson comes over."

Rene looked at Ellen and reached for her daughter's hand. "Ellen, you're very thoughtful. I do want some things, and I wrote them down before you came in. Will you have time to go by my apartment and pick them up? I've indicated where you can find them, and you have an emergency key, don't you? Do you suppose you could bring them by in the morning after your breakfast?"

"Sure, Rene," Anson said. "We'll take Laura for a ride and pick them up, and Ellen can run them up for you while I wait in the car with Laura. We'll be glad to do it. If you think of anything else you want, just call us. How about something to read?"

"No, Anson, they send the papers up. But thank you. You've been so helpful."

"Well," Anson said sincerely, "we owe you about ten favors for every one we can do for you. So let us do more," he said laughingly. He reached out for her hand and kissed it. "We have to be going now, and you need more rest."

"Goodbye, kids. Say hello to Laura for me. Esther must be having fun with her now."

Ellen smiled knowingly. "Yes, Mom, but she'll be ready for relief by the time we get home. Laura is pretty particular about things —maybe like her maternal grandfather."

Ellen and Rene laughed.

# 37

After Jonathan left Rene's hospital room on Saturday morning, he drove back to his hotel and phoned Susan in New York. It was three-fifteen in the afternoon, New York time, and since there were no classes on Saturday, he thought Susan might be home. She was. Before he could say more than 'Hello,' she asked if he was in Los Angeles and if he had seen her mother.

"Yes, I have. She seems to be recovering rapidly. If all goes well, she should return to her apartment Monday afternoon or Tuesday. The doctor has assured her that her foot will be completely okay."

"That's great news, Dad. Will it be all right for me to phone her now?"

"Yes, Susan, it certainly is all right. She'll welcome your call. She may sound tired, because she's taking medication, and she hasn't overcome all the aftereffects of facing the front end of a gun and being shot. Our visit was cordial. She seemed to be glad to see me and wants me to see her again."

"Daddy, did you tell her that you still care a lot for her? Because I know you do." Susan wanted to be sure her father's visit had been pleasant for her mother.

"Susan, she was so pleased with the large bouquet of roses I sent her, I believe they told her before I arrived that I care for her. We discussed lots of things, even the likelihood of her buying a condominium and decorating it from scratch, all by herself."

Then Jonathan got to the point. "But I called to find out if you had called her yet."

"No, Daddy, I haven't."

"I suggest you call her around nine-thirty or ten, your time, and she'll get the call right after her dinner. Ellen and Anson will be visiting her this afternoon."

"I sure want to talk to Mom, but I'll wait until her dinnertime. I won't say a thing about the shooting. And if she brings it up, I'll just ask her how her foot feels and when she'll be going back to her apartment. I'll tell her about my schoolwork and ask her to come see me when I get my MBA."

"That's just right, Susan. That's the way to put her accident in perspective and to let her know you're supportive."

But Susan was, in fact, concerned about both her parents.

"How are *you* feeling, Daddy? Of course, something like this may not surprise you, but I know it must hurt you," she said sympathetically.

"Honey, I appreciate your concern for me, but let's both just be concerned about your mother right now. She's lost her job and perhaps her career in academia. Of course, getting out of the academic environment may be a blessing to her. Handling public affairs is a task that demands so much patience, developing everybody's ideas and getting them used by the media."

"Okay, Daddy, I'll call Mom. And where can I reach you—at the hotel?"

"I'll be in and out, so I'll call you the first of the week."

"So long, Dad, and thanks for calling."

He hung up the phone and thought about calling Bruce. He was eager to talk to Bruce, but he decided to wait until seven-thirty that evening, which would be about eight-thirty Sunday morning in Tokyo. He could never quite remember the exact time differential.

Anyway, he wanted to make sure Susan and Bruce knew that their mother was emotionally and physically ready to receive calls. He also wanted to call two of their oldest friends, Arthur and Sybil Sonberg, and prompt them to call or visit Rene.

He looked up the Sonberg's number and dialed. Arthur answered, and Jonathan said in response, "If you're as late as usual for lunch, come over to the Bel Air Sands and get a free one."

"It could be no one but Jonathan," Arthur said happily. "Glad you're out here. I was just headed for the kitchen to make a martini. Now I'll wait and have one with you. Sybil is over at the Hillcrest Club having lunch with a group of her friends, so you called at a good time."

"If you're about to have a martini all by yourself, you do need company," Jonathan replied. "Let's eat outdoors here near the pool."

"Sure thing. I'll meet you in the lobby in ten minutes."

Jonathan had a benevolent purpose in having lunch with Arthur. He wanted to ask Arthur if he had seen the publicity on the shooting and to let him know that Rene was recovering rapidly. He hoped Arthur would ask about their visiting Rene. Jonathan wanted Rene to know that she still had friends who wouldn't ostracize her. He was concerned about the hesitancy of her co-workers at Southland to have any contact with her. But he believed that such picayunish attitudes would soon pass.

Jonathan could understand that Rene's friends at Southland felt they had to be concerned with maintaining good will with their superiors and co-workers. It didn't matter that many of them had envied Rene's popularity before she had been caught.

But Rene was no longer one of them and couldn't help them get good publicity for themselves or their departments. He knew Rene tried not to be judgmental of her friends. Now maybe she would notice how many of them were finding it impractical to be equally tolerant. Very few individuals are strong and independent enough to be judgmental and not fear being judged themselves.

Jonathan went down to the lobby to meet Arthur. The men greeted each other with smiles and a warm handshake.

"You always look the same. Don't you ever age?" Arthur said, as he greeted Jonathan enthusiastically.

"It isn't that I don't age, Arthur. It's simply a case of my being much younger than my contemporaries," he replied jokingly. "Take your case, for example. If one does nothing but bank residuals, write an occasional great song, play the piano, swim, and join friends at the Friars' Club—all those tough tasks—one ages faster. However, I admire the youthful enthusiasm you have, despite the above handicaps.

"What new movie are you working on now?" Jonathan asked as they walked across the lobby.

"There goes the old psychic sense again. If do have a new assignment for what should be a great movie—if you can predict success by the millions it's costing. I'll tell you more about it as I get farther into it. It's the first such assignment I've had in five years. They thought I was in retirement.

"Did Rene's being in the hospital bring you out? Have you seen her, and how is she?" Arthur asked.

"Yes," Jonathan replied. "I spent some time with Rene this morning. She's recovering rapidly. She should be back in her apartment by Monday or Tuesday. The doctor says her foot will heal perfectly. Did you see both the picture story and the *Chronicle* article?"

They walked on through the restaurant, and the hostess guided them to a nice table outdoors, a short distance from the pool. A waiter showed up immediately and took their order for martinis. As they sat down, Arthur responded to Jonathan's question.

"Yes, I saw both stories and heard the TV interview with the woman who shot Rene. I almost cried for Rene. I know she meant no harm to anyone, but that's the risk one runs when one is with someone else's spouse. It's done every day by lots of people, but Rene got caught.

"Of course, some spouses don't take infidelity seriously. How is Rene taking this whole thing?" Arthur inquired, sincerely concerned about her.

"Well, she knows she was wrong. She's been affected more emotionally than physically. She hated to disappoint her children and her friends. She hated to have to leave her job at the university. She's paid a high price, but she's coming through all right." Jonathan stated the case very unemotionally.

"Do they allow visitors yet? Sybil and I should go see her." Arthur had asked what Jonathan hoped he would ask.

"Yes, she's seeing non-family visitors tomorrow. Why don't you or Sybil phone her, maybe go see her Sunday about seven-thirty, after her hospital dinner? Anyway, I'm sure she'd be glad to see you and Sybil anytime. She's in Room 308A at UCLA Medical."

The waiter brought their drinks and left menus. Before looking at his menu, Arthur raised his drink in a toast to Rene's recovery and future happiness. They sat silently for a sip or two and then picked up the menus. After a few minutes, Jonathan motioned to the waiter, and they ordered.

The luncheon conversation covered many recollections, but the prime focus was on Arthur's new assignment. He was eager to be involved in a major task that would challenge him to organize his time and to try to surpass any of his previous achievements, although he didn't expect to win another Oscar.

Jonathan talked with Arthur briefly about his contacts with an agent in his search for a writer to sketch out a scenario for his *Dante's Masquerade* idea. It all sounded rather nebulous to Arthur until Jonathan explained that he would personally hire the writer and obtain outside financing for the production.

"I suppose you'll be coming out more often to follow through on the *Masquerade* script and to be near Rene while she read justs?" Arthur asked.

401

"Yes, but I don't want Rene to feel that she is the primary factor. I still want her to be free, but I also want her to know that I'm available to her, to help her find a condominium she'd want to buy, or to consult with her about her future activities in journalism, real estate, or whatever interests her."

Having the lunch was a pleasant interlude for the two old friends. They discussed small things. Arthur knew that Jonathan didn't want to talk about family matters any more. They agreed to get together again soon, and Arthur said that he and Sybil would phone Rene and arrange a time for them to visit at the hospital. They said goodbye, and Jonathan went back to his room.

During the afternoon he looked around the western part of Los Angeles, Westwood and Santa Monica to see what he could find in the way of a decent studio apartment that he could rent on a weekly basis. He returned to the hotel in time to have a cocktail and catch the news, and then it was time to call Bruce in Tokyo.

The phone call got through, and a very sleepy voice answered.

"So. I woke you up again. Sorry, son," Jonathan said. "Other than being sleepy, how are you?"

"Dad, let me shake my head and jump up and down a time or two. I want to be awake when I talk to you. Last time, I couldn't remember what we said."

There was a brief pause on the other end of the phone, and Jonathan smiled as he thought of his son trying to wake up quickly. Then Bruce was back on the phone.

"Now, tell me how Mother is. I take it you're calling from Los Angeles. Have you seen her?" Jonathan could tell that he had been worrying and hoping for a call.

"Bruce, I had a cordial meeting with your Mother. The doctor says she can leave the hospital Monday or Tuesday, and her foot will be just fine, with not even a scar."

"I know she'd like to hear from you. Susan is calling her about now—at seven or seven-thirty, our time, Saturday night. Can you call her soon, so you'll reach her before nine, our time? After nine she may be asleep."

"Sure will, Dad. I wondered if she could take calls, because I was going to try within an hour, anyway. Ellen gave me the number."

"Be sure to do that. She'll be very pleased. Have you heard from anyone but Ellen?"

"No, Dad, just the one call from her. She told me what hap-

402

pened. Thank you for helping Mother now, when she needs it so much. Are *you* doing okay?" There was concern in Bruce's voice.

"Yes, son, I'm fine. I'll be back in touch in a few days. Is all well with your work and health?"

"Going strong. Goodbye, Dad."

"Goodbye, Bruce."

As Jonathan hung up the phone he thought, so far, so good. Rene's welfare was of prime concern. Now he would call Ellen and find out how her meeting with Rene had gone. He dialed, and Ellen's pleasant voice responded immediately.

"Ellen, how come you're so handy to the phone? Is Laura asleep?"

"No, Dad, I'm sitting at my desk, going over some back letters, and Laura is nursing contentedly in my arms.

"I don't know all that you and Mom talked about, but I can assure you that your visit cheered her up considerably. She was surprised and pleased that you weren't reproachful.

"But the thing that seemed to Anson and me most helpful to her was your encouraging her to buy a condominium, to look to the future with confidence, and even to call the dentist," Ellen rushed on.

"I've talked to Bruce and Susan," Jonathan said, "and they'll join in our efforts to get your mother through this period fast enough that no resentments against life, no paranoia, will have a chance to get, shall I say, a 'foothold.' "

"Still playing with words, Dad! But that wasn't as bad as some." Ellen replied, laughing.

"Incidentally, Mom did call Dr. Clawson and found him interesting enough to ask him to see her at one-thirty tomorrow and to bring the pictures he took at the scene. He seemed happy she called and will see her tomorrow.

"But what are you doing? Mom said you were going to call and see her again, maybe Monday."

"Ellen, I'm going to look at studio apartment rentals. However, I may decide on a guest-hotel type of studio apartment."

"When are you coming out to see Laura again?"

"Well, of course, you and Anson are pressed for time right now and have little time to just visit. But I would like to come out Monday night, if I may. I want to see your mother late Monday afternoon. If Monday night is clear for you, I'll stop and bring a bucket of chicken this time."

"Monday night and chicken are okay. I appreciate your bringing ready-to-eat food, but I do take time to cook now and then. Just not as much as I used to.

"Anyway, I appreciate your wanting me to have as much time as possible free for Laura," she added.

"Ellen, I have in mind going back to Washington on Tuesday, by way of Chicago. I'll pack a carload of clothing and things and drive back to Los Angeles."

Just then Laura began to cry.

"From the cries I hear, I'd guess Laura has had enough to eat," Jonathan said. "I'll call you again and see you Monday evening for dinner.

"Goodbye, Ellen. Goodbye, Laura."

Laura was screaming loudly, and Ellen said hastily, "Goodbye, Dad."

Jonathan decided after his conversation with Ellen that he would wait until about ten the next morning to call Rene, after she had had time to read the papers. He thought it would be likely that no other calls would be coming in then. Now, he wanted her line clear for Susan's and Bruce's calls. He decided to go have a Mexican dinner.

The next morning he had his breakfast sent up to his room. He requested from, room service his standard order of scrambled eggs and bacon, English muffins, milk, orange juice, a small thermos of coffee, and the Sunday paper. He felt strange, like he was about to go home, but he wasn't sure where home was—maybe it would be Chicago again.

His breakfast was served out on the balcony, where he could enjoy his favorite panoramic view of the western area of Los Angeles. The weather was beautiful, clear and sunny. He was alone, but there seemed to be someone with him. He supposed everyone hallucinated once in a while—maybe hallucinations were endemic to southern California.

As soon as he finished breakfast, he called Rene. She answered after the third ring, speaking clearly but not very energetically. "Hello, this is Rene Barron."

"And this is Jonathan Barron, who is eager to know how and what Rene is doing," He greeted her warmly and cheerfully.

"Rene has been—happily—very busy," she replied. "After Ellen and Anson left yesterday afternoon, Susan called me around dinnertime. Then Bruce called from Tokyo. And just a few minutes ago, Sybil Sonberg called, said she saw the story in the paper, and wanted to know if I felt well enough to see them tonight after dinner. Sounds like I have an active social calendar, doesn't it?"

"It certainly does, but you didn't tell me if you called the dentist, your friendly neighborhood photographer," Jonathan said probingly.

Rene replied quickly, "Oh, yes, I called him, and I wasn't holding back information from you. I was saving him for last. Esther and Charlie are coming over around three this afternoon. I told Dr. Clawson that if he would be sure to bring all the pictures he took at the scene, I would see him at one-thirty today."

Rene seemed to be very pleased that people were paying attention to her, wanting to see her, despite all the bad publicity. This feeling she reflected pleased Jonathan, because in his opinion, it was much-needed therapy for her at this time.

"So, your curiosity got the best of you. How did Dr. Clawson sound over the phone?" He wanted Rene to talk and to feel optimistic again.

"Well, he had a very pleasant, deep, but soft baritone voice. About the same tone and clarity as yours, but his seemed a little softer. Maybe that's the voice he uses for the kind of women patients you described that dentists often have.

"Anyway," she continued, "he was very gracious and gentlemanly, very apologetic about the pictures. When are you coming over to see me again?"

Rene seemed to want to get off the subject of Dr. Clawson.

"I was thinking I'd come about four tomorrow. When will you start having the physical check-up and x-rays that Dr. Sukman suggested?"

"Oh, I'm glad you asked, because my nurse has me scheduled to start at eight-thirty tomorrow morning. She said I wouldn't be finished until two or three o'clock. Then the doctor will come to see me at three-thirty or four, the nurse estimated. You haven't met Dr. Sukman. Maybe if you come at four he'll still be in the hospital, and you can talk to him."

"I doubt that Dr. Sukman would care about seeing me," Jonathan responded casually. "You're the patient. But then, it might be good for me to meet him. Who knows, even I might need a doctor sometime."

They both laughed. They were truly enjoying talking to each other. It had been a long time since they had joked comfortably back and forth.

"Of course," he continued, "When I come to see you, a part of the deal is for you to tell me how your visit with Dr. Clawson turned out, the visit you'll have with him today."

"Jonathan, I'll do that, but do you know you really aren't all that perfect in your psychic or social-scientific guesses?" Rene chided.

"Oh, I'm often wrong. Did you find out that the dentist is a Baptist?" he replied.

"No, he *is* an Episcopalian, as you suspected, but you didn't tell me he was a *vestryman* in the Episcopal Church—St. Matthew's, in West Los Angeles," Rene kidded laughingly.

"That was an oversight. But you know how the smog can interfere with crystal ball gazing in southern California," he answered. "I'll have to keep that in mind the next time I predict something.

"So you want me to come by around three-thirty to four, Monday?"

"Yes, Jonathan, I'll be glad to see you again. Have luck in your apartment hunting," she said happily.

"And you keep on getting 'weller and weller.' So long."

# 38

On Monday afternoon, Jonathan went to see Rene earlier than originally planned, arriving at the hospital at three-fifteen. The nurse checked with Rene and told Jonathan he could go right in.

As he entered Rene's room, he said brightly, "Hello, young lady. You're looking mighty well. When did you start sitting up in the chair?"

"Yesterday," Rene said. "I've been back only a few minutes from my round of x-rays and tests. The doctor told me it was actually better for me to sit in a chair, instead of staying in bed all the time. You see, I can prop my foot up whenever I need to." She motioned to the ottoman to the left of her chair. "I'm really quite comfortable.

"You look dapper and cheerful. Did you find an apartment?" Rene asked, with an eagerness that suggested she hoped he had.

"Yes," he replied, "I found a residential hotel that rents beautifully furnished studio apartments on a weekly basis. I'll not be staying out here all the time but will go back and forth."

"When do you plan to move in?" she asked. "You'll have to go back to Washington and get more clothes and stuff, won't you? Will you drive back so you can have your own car here?"

"Well, I plan to leave for Washington tomorrow, spend a couple of days there, then drive back. So I should be back here and in my new apartment by Thursday of next week."

Jonathan was somewhat surprised by Rene's interest in him and in his coming to Los Angeles. He remembered, however, that before she became so angry with him last Christmas, she had suggested it might be nice if he lived in California, too.

"I think a studio apartment will be best for you now. At least it'll give you time to find out if you want to stay in California longer than a couple of months," Rene said. "Anyway, I think it's nice that you'll be here for a while, where you can see Laura more often."

"And you too, I hope," Jonathan said softly.

"Oh, let's see how things are after you come out," Rene said rather vaguely. "I do hope we can stay on friendly terms."

"Well," Jonathan said abruptly, "where's your doctor? Has he been around yet?"

He really didn't want to discuss what he and Rene might or might not do in regard to seeing one another, and he didn't think she did, either. He did want her to know that he wished to be her friend, available to her if she needed him. He loved her now, he thought, for a host of sentimental reasons.

He saw her reaching for the ottoman and went over to help. He lifted her feet to the center of the footstool. Her injured foot had only a small area bandage on it. As he moved back to his chair, Dr. Sukman came in.

"Dr. Sukman, this is Jonathan Barron, my husband of thirty years, now ex-husband, but still a helpful friend," Rene said graciously.

"Hello, Mr. Barron, nice of you to come out," Dr. Sukman said as he shook Jonathan's hand. "Our patient has been recovering rapidly, in spirit and body."

Jonathan started to leave, in deference to doctor-patient privacy, but Rene asked, "Is it all right for Jonathan to stay in the room now, Doctor?"

Dr. Sukman hesitated and then looked at Jonathan, who was standing by the door. He looked at Rene, who was smiling comfortably, and said, "Mrs. Barron, if you and Mr. Barron wish it that way, I think it's quite all right. Perhaps it is best that he stay.

"I have some unpleasant news for you. Mrs. Barron, we're not pleased with what your chest x-rays indicate. There seems to be a dark spot or lesion in your left lower lung."

Rene's smile faded rapidly, and Jonathan didn't move.

"As you know," Dr. Sukman continued, "we took you back to x-ray and made more detailed films. I'll be able to see those tomorrow."

For a moment, no one in the room said anything. Then Rene looked questioningly at Dr. Sukman and asked, "What do the x-rays tell you, Doctor?"

"Well, Mrs. Barron, they don't tell us enough." Dr. Sukman walked over to the window and then turned directly toward Rene. "But they hint at trouble. You've told me that you've been smoking a pack or more of cigarettes a day for some time now." He paused.

"And we do know that that kind of smoking can create danger signs."

Still speaking with objective curiosity, Rene asked, "What do these danger signs suggest? If the more detailed films indicate more or darker spots, what are we talking about then, Doctor?"

"Mrs. Barron, in such a case, we would want to look more closely, go to a bronchoscopic examination of the lesions. We have already sent sputum samples to the laboratory, and we'll get some indication from that examination by this time tomorrow. Until I get the sputum report and the additional x-rays, I'm unable to comment any further. What I do want to tell you now is that you should make arrangements to stay here for a few more days, maybe until the end of the week, at least."

"I conclude," Rene said calmly, "that there's a suspicion of lung cancer now, and you wish to determine if that's really the case and what can be done about it. You'd need some kind of biopsy before you could really tell, wouldn't you?"

"Yes, that might be called for," the doctor responded. "We'll have to wait until tomorrow's reports are in. As for a biopsy, there are different approaches to that problem, and we must know the exact situation before proceeding."

Then he added kindly, "I'm sorry, Mrs. Barron, to have to keep you here longer, but that's what we should do. Perhaps nothing of a serious nature will be discovered, but we must be certain. I'll come by about this same time tomorrow, or a little earlier.

"Now, let me take a look at that foot. The nurse says it's coming along fine."

Rene lifted her foot mechanically, just as the nurse came in. They took the bandage off. The wound was scarcely visible. The doctor felt the different areas of the foot and asked Rene to move her toes and stretch the foot slowly. Rene and the doctor both seemed pleased. The nurse put only a small bandage on her foot.

Dr. Sukman stood up and looked at Rene and at Jonathan, who was still standing beside the door. "If these x-rays had come up clear, you'd be going home tomorrow, Mrs. Barron. Your foot is doing fine."

He started for the door. "I'll see you tomorrow."

Turning to Jonathan, he said, "I'm glad to have met, you, Mr. Barron," and was out the door, on his way to another patient and another set of problems.

For a few minutes both Rene and Jonathan were silent, and he watched her, as she stared at the foot of the bed. He moved his chair over and sat next to her.

"I like your doctor," he said. "I think he's doing everything right. He told you all he knows, based on what he knows now."

She just looked at him, saying nothing.

"So, when are you going to tell me about your other doctor visitor?" Jonathan asked.

Rene looked puzzled; then she smiled and said, "Oh, you mean Gerald! Dr. Clawson. Yes, he came over promptly at one-thirty yesterday afternoon. He is a rather charming, attractive man, low-key in manner, but not as handsome and debonair as you—or Greg. I'll bet he's more even-tempered than either of you, though.

"He's a pretty big fellow," she continued, "six feet or more, probably weighs about two hundred pounds, but he looks muscular, not fat. I guess that dog-walking keeps his weight down, as well as giving him a chance to take pictures and meet people. He told me he's fifty-nine years old. He has all his hair. It's wavy brown and turning just a little gray. He likes to swim and bet me he could beat me at racquetball."

Jonathan laughed. "Other than these things, you didn't notice much about him, did you?"

"Yes, I noticed a lot about Dr. Clawson. He's almost the perfect prototype of the successful, intelligent, sociable 'nice' fellow that you thought would be right for me, in contrast to your being such an isolate. Perhaps I should have gone to the Episcopal church when you first suggested it months ago. But I've learned a lot. Facing that gun, I saw a full-color picture of myself and my life. You know, I think I *will* join St. Matthew's, but I'll not be looking for a lover."

Jonathan made no comment on Rene's declaration, because he believed she was finding her own way, maybe back to the Rene who had been his wife. So he simply pursued the subject of Clawson's visit and casually inquired, "Did he bring the rest of the pictures?"

"Oh, the pictures!" Rene exclaimed, as if she had totally forgotten them. "Yes, he did. And the negatives. They're there on the nightstand."

As Jonathan brought them to her, she said, "They're not very clear. The papers used the best one." She thumbed through the photos and said, "I'm glad this one showing me wrapping towels around Greg's foot wasn't used."

410

He leaned over her shoulder and looked, as she held one up to the light. "Jonathan, it shows fifteen or twenty people gathered around. I didn't remember seeing anyone except the police and ambulance people."

She handed the pictures to him, with the ones showing the crowd on top. He glanced through them and put them back on her bedside table.

"Did Clawson tell you anything about his family?" Jonathan asked. He was sure Rene would have asked about his family.

"Well, when he talked about his wife dying of cancer . . ." she stopped abruptly and then began again, " . . . it reminded me of the way you talked to me about Mindy's death when we were first married. Dr. Clawson's wife also had a breast removed and went through a long illness, determined not to give up. She was fifty-two when she died, about five years ago. They had no children. She had been very active in church affairs, clubs, League of Women Voters, and that sort of thing. She was a Sagittarius, too, like me, and only a year or so older than I am now when she died."

With that summary, Rene remained quiet for a few moments. But Jonathan thought she should talk about Clawson, because the whole idea of his appearing on the scene in such a rare incident seemed incomprehensible to her. Then Rene spoke up quickly, as if she had forgotten something she should have mentioned at once.

"It's interesting, Jonathan. He never really liked dentistry very much. He said he liked journalism and photography. But he's really more into real estate than anything else. He said he owns a forty-unit condominium out in Santa Monica near Ellen's place. I've seen it. It's very nice. Must be worth eight or ten million dollars. He also owns two or three small commercial buildings.

"The reason he told me about his real estate is that I told him I wanted to buy a condominium and that I used to be in real estate. He was very excited to learn that and offered to take a look at whatever I decided to buy and give me his opinion of its value, if I wanted him to.

"We had lots to talk about.

"He's a very nice, unassuming, and really quite modest man. He is definitely retiring from dentistry very soon. He said he's already brought in two good dentists, and he can leave anytime. He said if his wife had lived, he would already be retired. But he needed to stay busy, and many of his patients are also his friends."

411

"Rene, darling, I think it's a very good thing that Dr. Clawson came by," Jonathan said gently. "I think he wants to see you because you are you, but I think he feels an obligation to you, too. I believe he's sad about the pictures, and I think he was genuinely impressed by your coolness under fire, going up and calling the police and getting towels and attending to the other injured person. All that before attending to yourself. I think he perceived you to be a wonderful woman, notwithstanding the cause of the shooting.

"I think Clawson is right. And I think you became a different person at that moment. The shooting triggered, if I may use that word, a change that brought you back to the worthiness that has characterized your life."

She smiled at him and said softly, "Thank you so much. You have explained and forgiven so much in what you just said. Come over and kiss me, will you?"

"Very gladly," and he leaned over and kissed her warmly. He knelt beside her chair and held her hands and kissed her again. Then he got up and walked around the room, hesitantly. "I must be going, honey. And you should try to get a little rest."

"Jonathan," Rene said hastily, "you didn't let me tell you what a nice visit I had with Arthur and Sybil last evening. It was so thoughtful of them to come over. They surely think the world of you."

"That's nice. Arthur and Sybil have always been dear to me, too —to both of us." Jonathan moved toward the door. "I'll be leaving in the morning, but I'll be back next week to see you. Then I'll be around, off and on, for a while."

He turned suddenly at the door. "Oh, I almost forgot to ask. Isn't Dr. Clawson celebrating his birthday about now?"

"Jonathan, when Gerald came over yesterday, he said seeing me was his best birthday present," Rene said, shaking her head and gazing at Jonathan in wonder—as she had thirty years before, when they went to Jacques' for their very first lunch together and he had guessed her birthday.

He went back and kissed her again. "For you, I should have been a Gemini," he said softly. Then his voice grew stronger. "I'll see you next week."

"Goodbye, Jonathan. I hope we can always be friends."

He waved a kiss to her and walked down the hall to the elevator.

412

He was oblivious to all around him, thinking only of Rene and of what the doctor had said. This whole series of events was crazy. Here he was, twenty-three years older than Rene, and yet she was the sick one—maybe very sick.

He headed his car in the direction of Ellen's house and realized that he would arrive too early, since it was only about a quarter of six. Ellen wouldn't be home until six-thirty, after picking up Laura. There was a chicken place just a few blocks from Ellen's, so he decided to go park near the beach and look around for a while.

As he walked along the beach, he watched the sun lingering lazily over the waters. He and Mindy used to walk along this same Santa Monica beach. At Christmas he and Rene had parked up on the palisades and looked down at the beach. He was surrounded by memories here.

Very soon, it seemed, it was six-thirty. He was relieved to have the enforced break in his thoughts. He went back to his car, drove over to pick up a bucket of chicken with all the fixings, and went to Ellen's.

She opened the door for her father and immediately exchanged Laura for the chicken, taking it to the kitchen, where she would warm it in the microwave oven later when they were ready to eat.

Jonathan made a chair of his left hand and a back of the chair with his right and began gently swinging Laura to and fro in front of him in a porch-swing rhythm. Laura liked it for a while but readily went to her father when he came over. Anson threw her up and caught her—much more exciting, she indicated by her laughter.

According to Ellen's report on the day-care home, Laura was thriving in that environment, with so many things to do, including seeing other babies and small children. Ellen and Anson, of course, missed being with Laura more than she seemed to miss them. They all seemed to be doing well at home, although Ellen and Anson both worked during the day. Jonathan looked at the situation and contrasted it with the early home life of Ellen, Bruce, and Susan. He could see that both environments could work well, if the child had a great deal of love and good care.

"Dad," Ellen said, "why don't you make yourself a martini, and Anson will have a beer. Then tell us about your visit with Mom."

Ellen was eager to hear about her mother, although she had had a brief conversation with her at noon. At that time, Rene had

413

seemed quite pleased with her progress, and she had also mentioned that the Sonbergs had visited her and that Dr. Clawson had come by to bring the pictures.

"Well, you're pretty up-to-date," he said. "I'll get the martini and come back and relax a little."

Ellen noticed an unexpected reserve in her father's face as he left the room. "Dad, you seem to be very tense and rather sad. What's the matter?"

She picked up Laura and hurried down the hall.

"As soon as I change Laura, we need to talk."

Anson came into the kitchen for his beer and helped Jonathan with the ice. As they went into the living room, Anson inquired about Jonathan's apartment hunting and asked, "Do you really plan to come to California?" Anson had never thought that his father-in-law would want to live around Los Angeles, even for a few weeks.

"Yes, Anson, I'm going to try it, off and on, for a while. I want to renew some old professional acquaintances and find out if they think anything could be developed from my notion on a *Dante's Masquerade* story. At least, I want to persuade a good writer to give it a try."

Ellen came back holding Laura, who was peacefully depleting a bottle of milk. "What did you and Mom talk about today, Dad?" she asked.

"Oh, earlier this morning on the phone, she told me about her phone calls from Susan and Bruce. She was apparently delighted with her visit with Dr. Clawson. They share a common interest in journalism, real estate, racquetball, and other activities. I'm very pleased that she's found someone to get acquainted with through a variety of common interests.

"And more importantly, your mother seemed to like him personally. I think he makes good company for her while she's in the hospital. She'll need non-family visitors."

Laura cooed in her mother's arms, and no one said a word. Ellen and Anson waited for Jonathan to continue. He took a sip or two from his martini and decided that he would have to tell them what the doctor had found in Rene's x-rays.

"There is some concern about your mother's health. While I was there, Dr. Sukman came in. I was invited by Rene to stay to hear his report on her test results. First, her foot is doing well, as

**414**

predicted. But Dr. Sukman told us that the chest x-ray had revealed dark spots, lesions, in her left lung. He ordered more detailed x-rays made, and he'll get those back tomorrow. He also ordered sputum tests—he'll get those results tomorrow, too."

At first Ellen just sat, stunned. So did Anson. Laura played happily with her bottle. Then Ellen began to cry softly. "My God, Dad, does he think she might have lung cancer? How horrible!"

"Ellen," her father said gently, "one thing Dr. Sukman made very clear was that he doesn't know what her condition is at this time. That's why he's ordered more tests, a gradual, step-by-step search for the evidence of what may or may not be. He does know, however, that she must arrange to stay in the hospital a few more days."

Anson's voice trembled slightly as he said, "I judge from what you say that there *is* a likelihood of Rene's having cancer."

"Anson, I think Dr. Sukman is a very sound doctor. I don't believe he would use the term 'likelihood' in reference to cancer. He's following the steps that should be taken. And, of course, if these tests prove to be positive, showing there is evidence of malignancy, he still couldn't give us a final answer. There are several types of lung cancer. Survival may depend, too, upon the general physical condition of the patient. Rene has played so much racquetball lately, she should be in good shape. But Dr. Sukman may want to get a closer look at the lesions, using a bronchoscope."

Ellen, still slightly tearful, asked her father, "What do you think would happen if the tissue shows malignancy? Would her life be hopeless?"

"By no means, Ellen. They would probably operate and try to remove these coin lesions, as they're called, and all the affected areas, if any. You know, I had a brother who lived a wild, active life for forty years after he had one lung removed. Lungs are very efficient and adaptable. The problem would be whether or not the cancer had spread. And as I understand it, even if the doctors thought they had it all, they might recommend radiotherapy, chemotherapy, or other treatments for perhaps six months following the operation.

"Of course, I don't know what the doctors would elect to do. But I do know she has a very interested and very able doctor. And I know that medicine has made considerable progress in the treatment of the various manifestations of cancer."

415

Jonathan took another sip from his martini. Ellen and Anson sat quietly, seemingly lost in thought.

"Poor Mom," Ellen commented sorrowfully. "So many things at once."

"But, Ellen," her father emphasized, "let's look at Rene's situation this way. She may recover completely, may not have cancer at all. All the test results may be negative. Even with cancer, a successful operation may permit her to live out a normal lifetime."

"Dad, this occurrence of cancer in women you love—and I'm sure you still do love Mom—must be searing in its effect on you. I am sorry for you, as well as for Mom. I'm glad you're coming out here for a while. Did you have a forewarning of the possibilities confronting her?"

"Ellen, I don't get forewarnings. And we must not assume that she has cancer. We all have premonitions, presentiments, one might say, about many events. But I do sense that fate will not wreak further vengeance on your mother. I believe she's paid a big price already."

"What do you mean, Daddy? Do you really believe she might escape cancer?"

"All I can say now is that I believe Rene will eventually come through everything in good shape.

"As for Dr. Clawson, I paid no attention to the casual remark she made when I was teasing her, in a pleasant way, about this Episcopalian dentist showing up. She lay in bed, holding her hands together, staring at nothing, and said to me, 'You know, Jonathan, I'm no spring chicken any more, not even a summer chicken.' She wasn't thinking about lovers—she was thinking about life, her entire life.

"She was thinking about a future job and what she might do. I outlined things she could do, like writing feature stories, short stories, maybe even a novel. I urged her to buy a condominium. She may not have to make money, but she needs to work.

"Rene and Clawson should go into business together—he wants her journalism know-how, and she would enjoy promoting his real estate ventures. She was, you'll remember, a real estate appraiser, as well as a broker.

"Since Laura is snoozing now," he said, "do I have time for a little more martini and then some chicken?"

Ellen nodded, and Jonathan left the living room to refill his drink. He was very sad. They were all very sad. But there was nothing any of them could do except wait.

Anson jumped up and said, "I was hoping you'd want another half martini, a split, as you call it, because I want another beer." He turned to Ellen as she stood up with Laura in her arms.

"Ellen, shall I get a Tab or a Sprite for you?"

"Yes, thanks. I'll put Laura in her bed. She won't sleep long. We'll play with her after dinner."

When Ellen and Anson returned to the living room, Jonathan told them, "I'll be out here for Rene to call upon, if she needs me. But she has a good friend, potentially, in Clawson. I'll bet your mother will get so interested in his real estate and he in her journalism that she'll be too busy to need much from me except my faith and confidence in her."

Tears welled up in Ellen's eyes. "Oh, Daddy," she said, "I'm so pleased that you feel that way toward Mom. Of course, if she and Dr. Clawson become business partners, it shouldn't surprise you."

Jonathan seemed to have lessened Ellen's and Anson's pessimism about Rene's health and future. By the time they had finished their drinks, Jonathan found that he wasn't at all hungry and decided to go back to his hotel.

As he reached the front door, he turned and said, "Ellen, will you please try to see Rene and her doctor late tomorrow afternoon? I'll phone you tomorrow night to see what progress report Dr. Sukman might have had."

"Yes, Daddy, I'll do that. Where shall I try to reach you?"

"I'll call you after you get home, about eight o'clock, your time. I plan to stop off in Chicago on my way to Washington."

Jonathan shook hands with Anson and hugged his daughter.

"Tell Laura goodbye for me. And you two mustn't be gloomy about Rene. Have a positive attitude, so she'll catch your faith and enthusiasm for the future."

He put his hand on his son-in-law's shoulder and said, "Anson, thank you for all you've done for your family and for Rene."

"Goodbye, Jonathan," Anson said. "Have a good trip and take a little care of yourself. We'll keep up with Rene, so don't worry. We'll see you back here next week."

# 39

Jonathan left Los Angeles Tuesday morning at eleven and arrived in Chicago a few minutes past five. As soon as he got off the plane, he went to the nearest telephone and called to see if Katherine was home from her office yet. She was, so he took a taxi directly to her apartment. Because Katherine had seemed so pleased that he had arrived on schedule, Jonathan could scarcely keep from asking his driver to hurry. She would want to know about Rene's accident, and he would tell her. Based on what she had heard from Jonathan, Katherine liked Rene, Jonathan sensed, just as Rene had always liked Mindy, without ever having known her.

There had been no appropriate time yet for Jonathan to tell Rene about Katherine, but as soon as Rene was on solid ground, he would. As he rode along on Kennedy Expressway, he thought that when he was with Katherine, he was just about as happy as he could be. He considered the idea of complete happiness an illusion, harnessed to the notion of the perfectability of man. Fortunately for all humans, he thought, there are moments when joy transcends reality. He was thankful for the joy he had found with Katherine, but he knew that he would always be concerned about Rene's happiness, too.

The appearance of Dr. Clawson in Rene's life seemed to Jonathan to be predestined, as a few of his old Baptist friends might say. Rene could be a reward for Clawson, and Clawson could be the right friend, the right partner, for Rene's future. It is not so unusual, Jonathan had observed, for a man or a woman to meet a future spouse at a time when one or the other is at the nadir, the bleakest and lowest point in life. Love is nurtured by a need that sometimes creates the condition for an instant replay of one's life, a quick analysis of oneself. A woman suffering the physical and emotional consequences of a careless abortion may inspire an exceptionally compassionate man to help her achieve mental and physical health—and she, in turn, may become a great mother and loving wife. One's past need not consume one's future. Jonathan felt strongly that Rene would pull through her cancer scare and her emotional disturbances. As he got out of the taxi at Katherine's apartment building entrance, he was eagerly anticipating the happiness of being with her again.

Their greeting was a long, silent embrace accompanied by gentle kisses. Then Katherine opened her eyes and said, "We mustn't forget and leave your luggage in the hallway." She kissed him again to let him know she welcomed his lack of concern for such pedestrian but handy things as luggage. She picked up his briefcase, and Jonathan took his three-suiter and followed her to "his" bedroom.

"If you wouldn't mind unpacking later, Jonathan, I have some hot hors d'oeuvres ready. And last week, I found a new California white wine that I'd never heard of, but it's really good. Could I persuade you to try it tonight?" She looked at him with a smile that said, "I'm trying to wean you off martinis."

When they were settled comfortably in her library, a very cozy, spiritual sort of den, she poured the wine. It looked clear and cool. Their toast was too long and too much and too deep to express except with their eyes—eyes that seemed to say, "I'm so lucky to have found you at last." After a full drink of the new wine, he moved over to share the taste on Katherine's lips.

"So, tell me about Rene's accident," she said with concern and curiosity. Jonathan recounted the whole story, including the press reports and the appearance of the dentist-photographer, adding that he felt fairly optimistic about her future. Katherine wanted to prevent Jonathan from sliding into a gray-skies mood and said very softly, "Of course, you care very much for Rene and her future. That's the way it should be and the only way you could be. But you must realize that once you've done all you can, you must table not only the task but the memory, until the time comes when you can do more. Now, do you want to go out to dinner or stay here and we'll have a couple of three-hundred-calorie frozen dinners?"

"That's the kind of dinner I usually have at my place, but tonight let's see if we can get in at the Cape Cod Room. This wine calls for some tasty fish. I'll phone them." He remembered the number correctly and got reservations for two at eight-thirty. "How does eight-thirty suit you, Katherine?"

"That's fine. Since it's only about a five-minute walk, we'll have time to go to my room and rest together during the hour or more we have to wait. I'm so glad you thought of the Cape Cod Room, Jonathan." She kissed him warmly and led the way to her room.

"You're the mind reader in this family, Katherine," he said, almost falling down as he followed her, while taking off his coat.

"All I do is read the signs," Katherine replied laughingly. "But, honey, you needn't hurry so much. We have at least an hour."

The three-block walk to the Cape Cod Room was pleasant and invigorating. They expected to enjoy the dinner, and they did. Jonathan asked Katherine how her ethics program was moving along. She reported that it was going great, with increasing support from the bank's top management, including the directors. Katherine had found that in studying the factors involved in establishing a code of ethics and the means of implementing the code, she had become more involved in all areas of the bank's operations. The bank's president, Charles Andresen, had asked her to discuss with him one of his own special assignments, streamlining the bank's structure and staff. It appeared to Andresen that Katherine's work in ethics would directly relate to these changes.

"You know, Mrs. Brown," Andresen had told her, "we're going through so many changes in what banks can and can't do that one of the main obstacles to improving ethics is not with management. It's paradoxical that middle management and lower-echelon employees are harder to convince than the bosses of the pragmatic beneits of honesty and responsibility! Of course, I suppose that in any large, service-oriented, high-tech operation, it's as difficult to measure individual efficiency as it is to measure individual ethics. But, Mrs. Browne, I'm discovering that basic ethical attitudes may become the key to increasing productivity and profits."

Jonathan listened carefully and asked Katherine, "When did you say President Andresen will reach retirement age?"

"In three years. Why do you ask, Jonathan?"

"Well, in three years, during which period you'll get some corporate loan experience and increased participation in general administrative problems, you'll learn a great deal from the opportunities Mr. Andresen seems to be opening up for you. By the time he retires, you might be the logical presidential selection for your bank. In the meantime, you should take your vacations in London, Tokyo, Hong Kong, and other such places for international banking contacts. Further, a couple of nights a week in the University

420

of Chicago's graduate school might look good on your resume for a headhunter firm looking for a top financial officer."

"Lord, Jonathan, who else would take me from bed to the bank presidency and back to bed? But I like both ideas."

"Yes," Jonathan said, "your talents in all areas are far above the requirements."

They walked back to the apartment in plenty of time for Jonathan to phone Ellen to get her report on Rene. When they reached the apartment, Katherine attended to her own accumulated phone calls, using her private-line desk phone, and Jonathan went to his room to call Ellen.

"Hello, Dad. I've just arrived home from the hospital." Ellen's voice was on the edge of breaking. "Dr. Sukman says they'll have to operate on Mom. The operation is scheduled for Thursday morning. Until after the operation, I can't tell you any more."

"Ellen, I realize that the need for the operation is enough to cause anxiety. But the operation doesn't mean she has cancer. I haven't talked with Dr. Sukman, and he probably doesn't feel free to say much to you at this time. Actually, the decision to operate may simply indicate that they have to open up the chest to get at and remove one or two small lesions. These lesions may or may not be malignant. True, they often are. But good doctors don't say yes or no until they have conclusive evidence. Did Dr. Sukman tell you that your mother has cancer?"

"No, Dad, he actually didn't, but don't you think he was just waiting until after the operation?" Ellen remained very pessimistic.

"Ellen, you do realize that some lesions, for whatever reasons, prove to be negative for cancer, prove to be non-malignant. Didn't Dr. Sukman tell you that further tests would be made—tests on the exorcised lesions themselves?"

"Yes, he told me that, Dad. I'm to talk with him Friday for his final verdict." Ellen was speaking more normally.

"Well, my dear Ellen, let's wait and hope. For what it's worth, my guess is that your mother will be surprised as hell that she's escaped cancer. I think she'll soon be in good shape, looking for new career opportunities. And, by the way, please encourage Mother to have Dr. Clawson visit her. He's the best possible therapy for her. They have so much in common to talk about—real estate, photography, journalism. And I'll bet he won't let me outdo him on roses for Rene. Take care of Laura, and best wishes to

Anson. If you can talk with your mother tomorrow, please tell her I think she's going to love her new condominium in Santa Monica. I'll call you Friday evening on my way back to Los Angeles. One more thing, Ellen. Do you remember when I asked you why you were never frightened when I used to throw you high in the air and catch you? You said, 'I always knew you would catch me.' So, Ellen, let's have faith now. Goodbye."

"Goodbye, Daddy. Thank you for the hope. I love you."

Jonathan met Katherine in her library. She had finished her calls and had poured a small brandy for each of them—more symbol than substance. She handed him his brandy, joined him on the sofa, and waited for him to report on Rene. He told her of his conversation with Ellen.

"Jonathan, my dear, I'm glad you've passed along to Ellen your belief in her mother's recovery. And, of course, I believe you're right. She may indeed escape cancer. I think she'll live long and happily, maybe with Dr. Clawson.

"As strange as their first meeting was, I'll bet many husbands and wives have had stranger first meetings than they had. Now, you've had a busy day. After you've dressed for bed, come in and say good night to me. Okay?"

"How soon?" he asked.

"Ten minutes," she answered as she moved toward her bedroom.

Jonathan returned to Washington on Wednesday. He arranged with a secretary in the building to handle his mail and phone calls, forwarding them to him when requested. Then he began putting his stuff together and packed his car. When he left for Los Angeles the next morning, he wondered if his car needed heavier shock absorbers. It was really loaded. He didn't rush, but even so, he made it to Knoxville, Tennessee, the first night. He wanted to call Ellen at seven-thirty, her time, so he had his customary martini, read the *Knoxville News-Sentinel,* and enjoyed an excellent dinner until it was time to phone Ellen. She answered on the first ring.

"Oh, Dad, I'm so glad you called. Mom got through the operation in good shape, but it took longer than expected. The doctors removed two small lesions and sent them to the laboratory for testing. They found no evidence of malignancy. But Dr. Sukman said he couldn't give me a final report until tomorrow afternoon when he gets a full report. He seemed optimistic but said they would have to wait and see. If further examination proves the lesions are malignant, Mom will have to be operated on again to remove enough tissue to check spreading."

"Ellen, the doctors seem to be doing everything right. But we all may be quite surprised to find conclusive evidence that there is no malignancy, and she'll soon be well. She may be one of the few who beat the percentages. If she did have lung cancer, the chance for survival would be about one in ten. In any event, as of now, we can all look forward to her living a long time. But I'll phone you tomorrow and hope you'll then be able to report that Rene was 'shot' into the hospital before any cancer could get started. I think your mother will be a greater and more serene person. However, she's been through an experience that certainly can't be forgotten. Psychological recovery is often much slower than physical recovery.

"Will you send flowers to her now? Send a large vase of bright, mixed spring flowers. She'll like the gaiety and optimism they'll reflect. Then, too, when she receives the luscious roses that Dr. Clawson will send, she'll get the right message from both her friends—the roses will be more symbolic of her new future partnership."

"Dad, you're funny, but thoughtful. Thank you for all of us, including Mom. Talk with you tomorrow about the same time."

"Wait a minute, Ellen. With all the news about Mother, I forgot to ask how Laura and Anson are."

"They're okay and feeling good. Goodbye, Dad."

"So long, Ellen."

Jonathan drove on to Fort Smith, Arkansas, for his Friday evening stop. He drove an hour or so longer than he really wanted to, but that enabled him to have a brief dinner and to call Ellen without waiting. He reached her a little before seven-thirty, her time.

"Daddy, Daddy, I have wonderful, unbelievable news. On full examination of the lesions, they found no evidence of any sign of cancer, no malignancy! Isn't that great, just great?"

"Yes, Ellen, that is great news. Everyone should be very thankful indeed. I see a fine life ahead for Rene, and I'll bet Dr. Clawson will share it. Your mother has been so blessed by fate to have her life and health extended. When should I call her?"

"Why not call her tomorrow about noon? She'll be feeling

423

pretty sick for a while. She got the flowers. Just the way you hoped —roses from Clawson and bright, optimistic greetings from you. Dr. Sukman said she should be able to go home by Tuesday, but I'm going to suggest that she stay on in the hospital an extra day or so, if Dr. Sukman approves.

"Dad, why were you so confident Mom was going to recover fully? You even thought she might not have cancer."

"I had no premonition. I only had a belief that your mother deserved to come through, because for so many years she was a wonderful mother and wife. Now she has a chance to give to others some of her new understanding. I wish for her much happiness. I believe she'll now be able to live the life I had hoped for her when we divorced. I myself feel forgiven for the divorce, however well-intentioned I was."

"Daddy, what are you going to do, now that it appears you'll get your wish for Mom's future?"

"Ellen, I have met Dante's angel, Beatrice, and she's living in Chicago. I'll be seeing you soon. Goodbye."

"Goodbye, Daddy."

Jonathan wanted to call Katherine but doubted that she would be home on a Friday night. He knew she had a number of business-related social affairs to attend. He called anyway and was surprised when she answered.

"Katherine, you're probably busy, but can you talk to me a minute or two?"

"Yes, and gladly, Jonathan. I just returned from a cocktail party, which I left early—the hors d'oeuvres were like sawdust and so was much of the company. What has developed with Rene?"

"Rene came through the operation with no lesions or tissues showing any signs of malignancy—everything negative for cancer. Of course, the children are ecstatically happy. I'm happy, too, but I rather expected the favorable results, despite the low probabilities. She may now live the kind of life I had hoped for her."

"It's amazing, Jonathan. I'm so glad for all of you. And I'm glad for myself, too, because I know you'll be happier now and free of a responsibility you kept holding as yours alone."

"Katherine, I don't have premonitions regarding you, except that I think you'll achieve your professional ambitions, plus some well-earned honors. I have no premonition regarding us—it's too subjective a contemplation to permit my senses to work. But from here on, my greatest wish is to be with you, to help you if I can, to serve you as Dante would have served his Beatrice. And to love you without limits."

"How did you know my middle name is Beatrice?" Katherine replied. "But lucky for you, I'm no angel. Jonathan, I do want to see you. I've an idea. It's both personal and business. It may be a crazy idea, but I'd like to share it with you. Where will you be on Friday, July 2?"

"I plan to be in Los Angeles, but I'll be wherever you want me to be, if you're there." Jonathan was rather puzzled, but where Katherine was concerned, he was agreeable to anything. "Where do you want me to be?"

"Well, I'd like to see you at my apartment during the lunch hour on July 2. Then, if you could stand being with me on through July 5, I'd very much like you to. My children won't be here for the July 4 holiday week-end. I'd like to stay in Chicago, if you could be here."

"Katherine, I'll be at your apartment at twelve noon on July 2. And please don't change your mind about letting me stay with you over the July 4 week-end. Being with you for several days—all in a row—what a gift from the heavens! Oh, Lord, Katherine, tell me I heard you correctly."

She laughed. "My dear, wonderful Jonathan, with all my love, I declare you heard me correctly, and I'm going to be very happy to see you. Now, goodbye, and drive very carefully."

"I'm too excited to drive ten feet now. But I'll be okay by morning. Goodbye, Katherine."

"Goodbye, dear."

What a wonderful July 4 week-end for him to anticipate by the minute. Whatever Katherine had in mind was fine, so long as the occasion meant seeing and being with her three or four whole twenty-four-hour days. He had often thought that if he had not known the wonders of Mindy and Rene, he would not be capable of wanting Katherine so very much now.

With Rene's health outlook good and a new friend in her new life, Jonathan felt strangely free, free. Tomorrow he would call his old Chicago florist and ask him to send Katherine a very special arrangement of flowers every Tuesday and Friday. He hoped she would understand how totally hers he had now become.

Jonathan arrived in Los Angeles in the early afternoon on Monday. He had driven from Washington at a pace that was reasonable, for him. The apartment he had selected was a studio unit in a hotel where he had phone service and inside parking. As soon as he had registered, he moved everything from his car to his apartment and then called Ellen at her office.

"Hello, Ellen. I'm in town and in my apartment. How's your mother?"

"Welcome back to California, Dad. Mom is recovering satisfactorily, but slowly. She's had the usual post-operational discomfort, but not too much. You can call her now, and she can see visitors. She was pleased with your messages that I passed along to her. She did say that she would advise others not to wait until they were 'shot' into a hospital before getting their physical check-ups. Go ahead and call her, and call me tonight, will you?"

"I'll do both, Ellen. Talk to you later." Jonathan was eager to talk with Rene.

"Rene, this is your commuting Californian speaking. I understand things are going pretty well with you?"

"Oh, hello, Jonathan. I'm glad you're back. When are you coming over?"

"Just waiting for an invitation. When would you like for me to come over?"

"How about tomorrow morning at ten? By that time, I should be stronger and feel better and maybe look better."

"Ten tomorrow it is," Jonathan said with enthusiasm.

"Wait a minute, Jonathan, before we hang up. I don't know if you personally picked out the refreshing bouquet of spring flowers, but they're just what the doctor ordered. They're a real pick-me-up picture. Thank you."

"When I see you in the morning, maybe they'll brighten me up for you and I'll feel 'there is sunshine in my soul today,' as the old hymn goes. Have a good night."

"Good night, Jonathan."

The next morning when he went to see Rene, Jonathan was dressed in the spirit of southern California. He wore light tan gabardine slacks, a silky-nylon shirt with tailored open collar, light cream-colored jacket, and beige-tan Italian shoes. He wanted to reflect the feeling of the spring bouquet and surprise Rene with the signs of his new life-style.

"Oh my!" Rene exclaimed as he entered the room. "If you're my former husband, please come over and kiss me."

Jonathan quickly complied and commented, "You look okay, so you must be okay. How are you feeling? Any pain?"

"A little, but the doctor says I'm doing very well and that I'm very lucky. He was here just a few minutes ago. Ellen told me before my operation that you were convinced that I'd beat all odds and come through with no cancer. Crazy as it seems, Jonathan, I still have such faith in you that I went to the operating room with no fear. When I asked Ellen why you were so optimistic, she said you had told her that fate had punished me enough. She said you believed that I deserved to live because I'd been such a good mother and wife for so many years. Jonathan, I know that you're not the fate you often speak of, but I can't help believing that your faith and your desire for me to come through must have had a lot to do with my escape."

"Thank you, my dear, dear Rene. But I suggest that you thank God, your good doctors, and your generally good health. Now you must reward everyone, including your very devoted children. You must be what we all know you can be. Do you remember when you once asked me why I wished to marry you and I emphasized your great personal discipline and perserverence? You've demonstrated that ability before, and you can do it again."

"Jonathan, I believe my future life will be all that you hoped it would be when we separated. Strangely, I love you now more than ever, as a friend and counselor. You're too remote for us ever to be lovers again. Maybe it's because I know so much more now than I did when we separated. I guess I'm what one could call a bornagain Rene. I'm going to make everyone who ever knew me as proud of me as they've ever been, maybe more so, especially you and my children." Rene was crying, but her smile showed only tears of joy. "And, Jonathan, the very first Sunday that I'm well enough, I'm going with Gerald to his Episcopal church. I hope to become a member."

"You're a wonderful person, Rene, and I deeply appreciate your continuing love. Your plans for the future sound great." He got up and walked around the room and suddenly asked, "Who the hell sent you better flowers than I did? There must be two dozen roses in this big vase," he said, lifting it from the table.

"So, you finally had to ask about my garden of roses. Gerald sent them to me. I think he's as crazy about flowers as you are."

"And crazy about you," Jonathan interposed.

"Jonathan, Gerald has been a very good friend. He's going to take me around to help me find a condominium to buy—just as soon as the doctor says it's okay for me to move about. Gerald is coming over this afternoon to bring multiple-listing sheets showing pictures and descriptions of a half-dozen places he's already checked out. He loves real estate. He's like you—he has an uncanny way of knowing the market values of properties. I'm glad he's going to help me look around. I think he knows every building in the Santa Monica area. Gerald and I would make a great team in real estate—just as you and I did when you were about his age."

"So you already have a chauffeur, one that knows the market. I think I'll try to get my movie script off the ground, now that you'll not need a chauffeur and shopper." Jonathan spoke teasingly to Rene.

"Well, Gerald just came along. And ain't that the truth! Funny how friends first meet," Rene said more to herself than to Jonathan. "I wish someone would come along and share some of your worries. I think Gerald and I may open up an office to deal with real estate and real estate promotions. I may even write a real estate column and do features stories on some of the more interesting real estate buildings and developments."

"Well, well," Jonathan said with a little sigh of resignation. "I used to think I moved fast into different businesses, but here you are, hardly off the operating table, and you and your partner have almost opened up a business."

"That's what we'll talk about this afternoon when Gerald visits me. We may call our firm Barron & Clawson Enterprises. Our office will be in, or close to, Santa Monica."

"Well, since you're moving right along, I think I'll go to Chicago and visit my banker there. Maybe I could call you again Thursday morning before I leave Thursday afternoon. I have a noon appointment in Chicago on Friday and don't want to risk being late for it." He recognized that he was talking in a way his old friends in Arkansas would have described as going all the way around the house to get in the front door.

"Who's your banker in Chicago? I thought your friend Whitten died." Rene was just mildly curious.

"I'm going to be doing some business with City National Bank. It's a very progressive bank, and my personal contact there is a very smart banker, a vice-president, Katherine Browne."

"If she's that smart, she must be very experienced. How old is she, fifty-five or sixty?" Rene's curiosity was still just about another professional woman.

"Rene, Katherine Browne is fifty-two. She's not only smart but very, very attractive. She got a divorce several years before we did. She has two grown daughters, both successful and happily married —one lives in Denver and the other in Hartford. I just met Katherine a few months ago. She and Barbara Ballinger were sorority sisters in college, and Barbara invited me to have lunch with her and Katherine because Katherine's in charge of developing a code of ethics for her bank."

Rene was really interested, but pleasantly so. "What is Katherine's sorority?"

"When I met her, I guessed Delta Gamma, and I happened to guess right."

"That's a good sign, Jonathan. All the DG's I've known have been worthwhile women, first-class. How well do you know Mrs. Browne? Do you know her personally as well as professionally?" Rene wanted to get to the heart of the matter now.

"Rene, surprisingly, Katherine seems to like me, personally and professionally. She's reasonably comfortable financially—has a large Lake Shore Drive condominium. She prefers that I stay there when I'm in Chicago, which is becoming a happy habit. I can give Katherine no greater compliment than to say that she continues the tradition of my wonderful wives, Mindy and Rene. But we don't even think about marriage. We just love being together. And we share ambitions, *her* ambition to become the chief executive officer of her big bank. And my ambition to help her, if possible, and to be with her as much as possible—but I'll not let my wanting to be with her interfere with her ambitions. I once had a smart and beautiful wife whom I encouraged to leave me so she could live on her own and then marry a good man, a happy, sociable man more her own age. I wanted her to find that man and be happy, knowing that I could never be really happy until she was, until my dream for her was fulfilled. Katherine is also much younger than I. I don't wish to marry Katherine—*for her sake,* not mine. But Rene, Katherine Browne is to me what the angel, Beatrice, was to Dante. Katherine is a strong, glorious, beautiful angel who has been sent by fate to fetch me out of the purgatory in which I have been living, especially since we separated."

Rene looked at Jonathan. She began to cry softly. "Jonathan, I'm so glad for you, so very glad. I'll bet your friend fate has brought you to Katherine for the tenderness and understanding that I always wished I had had more of to give you. From the way you look and the way you sound when you speak her name, I'd guess that Katherine must be all that Mindy and I wanted to be to you. Mindy's short life limited her enormous benefits to you, and I just did the best I could. Now, God willing, you have a chance to be as happy as I think I shall be. And Katherine must be very smart. She'll benefit so much from being with you. I know, I know. Yes, I certainly want you to be happy because, like you, I can never be as happy as I want to be if you aren't, too."

Jonathan went over to Rene, and they kissed, as they both wept tears of joy and hope.

"Isn't it wonderful, Jonathan, that you and I may have enjoyed one another at just the time in our lives that we needed each other most?" Rene asked. "And now we may be lucky enough to merge our pasts with our futures—in Katherine and Gerald. But now all this is just talk between you and me. We'll both have to see how our new friendships and other relationships develop."

"I can't imagine any person getting more pleasure from another's love and friendship than I already get when I'm with Katherine," Jonathan declared. "I think that's the way your friendship, as you build it, will develop with Gerald. And your observation about the timing of the harmony that existed between you and me is a very perceptive one. Sometimes a man and a woman don't adjust synchronously to the winds of change, especially cultural change. But fortunately for most people, there's a wide range of time and circumstance that permits changes to occur in tandem."

"Jonathan, let's remain friends so that we can challenge one another to make the very best of these opportunities life seems willing to give us." Rene spoke very earnestly.

"Rene, it's a deal. And let's make Katherine and Gerald the prime beneficiaries of our challenge to one another."

Jonathan left Rene's bedside and went over to the vase of roses. "Yes," he said, "things are really coming up roses for you. I guess you have a new florist now."

430

"Yes, but remember, Jonathan. Roses are for lovers. Spring flowers are for bright greetings from old friends."

"I'd better leave you now so you can get plenty of rest and some lunch and be feeling good when your new business partner arrives. You'll certainly feel at home looking at multiple-listing sheets on real estate for sale. I'll call you Thursday morning. Who will take you home if the doctor says you can go on Thursday?"

"Ellen and Anson have insisted on that duty. Gerald offered, but he yielded to Ellen. They have a larger, four-door car now. I'll probably go home Thursday, but phone me here or at home, will you? Now, goodbye, Mr. Good Fate. I'll bet your friend Katherine will soon be having more fun and flowers than any banker in the history of Chicago."

He went over and kissed her goodbye and said, "So long, my friend."

Jonathan called Ellen at her office, but her secretary said she would be at a meeting outside the office for most of the day. Rarely did Ellen take time out for a social lunch. So he went alone to a Westwood cafe patronized by a young crowd, not just students. After lunch he called an agent he had known for years and made an appointment for Wednesday afternoon to discuss finding a writer to explore the *Dante's Masquerade* idea. He returned to his apartment to finish organizing his things and to wait impatiently until it was four o'clock, six o'clock in Chicago. Four o'clock finally arrived, and he phoned. Katherine answered, out of breath.

"Oh, Jonathan I was just on my way out to represent the bank at a Chamber of Commerce dinner, but I always have a minute or two for you. How's Rene?"

"Rene is doing very well, mentally and physically. I'm calling to tell you that I'll be coming in Thursday night so I won't have to take an early Friday morning plane and risk being late for our noon date. Since our lunch date is a business one, I'd feel better if I just checked in at the Drake this time."

"Jonathan, I'd like nothing better than for you to come to my apartment, but my aunt will be staying with me. She'll be at our Friday meeting. And please know that I'll be restless Thursday evening, knowing you're so close but not close enough. Goodbye, darling, until Friday noon."

"So long, Katherine."

Jonathan was curious. He was glad to hear that it was her aunt staying with Katherine, but why would her aunt be a part of what now appeared to be a business lunch? He could just vaguely get a signal. He might like the proposal to be discussed Friday. And he liked the fact that a member of her family was going to be there. He wasn't sure, but he thought there was a logical possibility that he would be pleased with Katherine's idea—and obviously time was of the essence in the deal. Why figure it out, he thought; if Katherine wanted it, he would.

Ellen called him and said she would be a little late getting home for dinner but asked Jonathan to go out about six-thirty, when Anson and Laura would be home. Yes, if he wanted to bring an assortment of carry-out Chinese foods, it would be welcome, because she really wouldn't have much time to help make dinner.

After the dinner at Ellen's, she and Anson were eager to find out about his visit with Rene. Jonathan gave such an optimistic, glowing report about Rene's health and future and Dr. Clawson that Ellen didn't wait very long before she asked her father about "Dante's Beatrice," his new friend in Chicago. Ellen hadn't seen her father so youthfully enthusiastic in years. She wanted to know all about Katherine: what color her eyes were, her month of birth, what type of clothes she wore, and whether she was really as pretty and smart and kind as he said, or if he was just dreaming. Ellen and Anson checked out Jonathan and Katherine as though they were a romantic college couple.

"Dad, I think you and Mom know that you're both very lucky— each of you wanting happiness, but each knowing the other must be happy, too. From the way you describe Mom's reaction, I think she feels almost as good about your meeting and knowing Katherine as she does about her prospects of good health and a serious relationship with Dr. Clawson. I like the way they're planning to be in business and aren't even talking about an affair or marriage. Do you think you and Katherine might possibly marry, Dad?"

"No, Ellen. It wouldn't be fair to Katherine, any more than my holding on to your mother would have been fair to her. But I'm going to make every effort to be with Katherine as much as she'll let me—or can justify—considering that we both want a great career for her."

"Well, then," Ellen went on, "why don't you move to Chicago so you can see her more often?"

"Ellen, you've always made too much sense. Keep in mind that

I'm an older man and she is much younger, very beautiful and very smart." Jonathan thought that that was the last word, but Ellen said, "That's just why she wants you, Dad, and can get you. Our family has so much to be thankful for. It's so great that Mom came through with no trace of cancer."

"Ellen, once fortune has given us a chance, we must work to make things go well. Good night, folks. I'm going back to my apartment to have pleasant dreams—like Laura's having now."

"Good night, Dad. Thanks for everything."

The Wednesday afternoon appointment with his talent agency friend was cordial, but talent agents hear so many dreams, they know that most will never survive getting out of bed. Yet, they wouldn't be agents if some dreams didn't turn into commissions. This agent, Oscar Lindstrom, thought he could find a writer for Jonathan—a writer who, for a fair fee, could help shape up a story on the *Dante's Masquerade* idea. He would talk with the writer to see if his current assignments would permit his taking on another assignement. Lindstrom said he would be back in touch with Jonathan in a few days. If the writer was available, he and Jonathan could plan a preliminary meeting about the story.

On Thursday morning Jonathan phoned Rene at the hospital. She was doing so well the doctor thought she could go home. Jonathan told her that he would be returning to California in a week or ten days, and he knew she would have all the help she needed.

He told her to take her time getting well, to buy a condominium that she could readily sell if she decided to move again, and to go ahead with plans to develop Barron & Clawson Enterprises. "You're a highly intelligent and impressive businesswoman," he told her. "It's time for you to own your own business or have a partnership."

"Jonathan, it makes me feel good to hear you say that. I've actually been wanting to be a part of my own business. I was getting a little tired of the academic bureaucracy and bureaucrats. I think Gerald and I will make a very good team."

"Gerald is a lot smarter guy in real estate than I ever was," Jonathan quickly stated. "And you're a much better business promoter than you were years ago. If you ever sell stock in Barron & Clawson, let the family in first.

"Incidentally, have Ellen and Anson met Dr. Clawson?" he asked.

"Oh, yes, they have. They think he's a very fine fellow. Actually, Ellen and Anson treat Gerald like an old friend, something they never did with any other male friend of mine that they met. Gerald and Anson seem like buddies. They talk about things just like Anson does with his dad."

"Rene, your kids are very wise. Anyway, if you need to talk with me, just call my Washington number. The secretarial desk will always have my current phone number, despite my moving about so much.

"I hope to see you soon, swimming around in Ellen's pool."

Rene responded happily, "Goodbye, now. Have a good time in Chicago."

# 40

At long last, seemingly weeks to Jonathan, he arrived at Katherine's apartment at noon on Friday. The desk clerk phoned Mrs. Browne to advise her that a Mr. Barron was in the lobby and said to Jonathan, "Mrs. Browne requests that you come right up. She's on the ninth floor, apartment number 940." Jonathan smiled to himself, hoping that this new desk clerk would soon know him as well as the old ones did.

Katherine was in her doorway, waiting for him. She looked glorious. All Jonathan could think of to say was, "Hello." She kissed him lightly but warmly and led him into her library-den and introduced him to Mrs. David Findlay, her Aunt Mary. Jonathan was indeed pleased to meet Mrs. Findlay, a tall, dignified, and quite attractive woman of seventy-eight or eighty. She greeted Jonathan with a bright smile and asked him to be seated next to her, explaining that she had a slight hearing problem. Jonathan understood. Katherine immediately excused herself to check on her luncheon preparations. And, as usual, Jonathan wanted to know more about the woman he had just met.

"Mrs. Findlay, where do you live now—in Chicago, or have you long since left for Florida?"

"Mr. Barron, I'm glad you asked, because I lived in Chicago for many years. My husband was a professor of comparative literature at the University of Chicago. We used to live in this building, but since his death almost three years ago, I've been living in Naples, Florida, where I have many friends, including an old college classmate. I found it difficult to live in our apartment here after David's sudden death, following a heart attack, so I leased the apartment to a professor friend and his wife and moved to Naples.

"Katherine tells me you live in Washington, but you're thinking about moving, maybe to California. She says Chicago used to be your hometown."

"Yes, I do live in Washington, but it really doesn't make much difference to me where I live. I'll be in California for a month or two, and then I may move somewhere other than Washington. But I like to hear you talk. Your accent reflects the beautiful countryside of Ireland."

"Oh, I guess my husband liked my accent when we were courting," Aunt Mary said demurely, "and I just kept it going for him." She smiled softly, but a little mischievously.

Katherine returned with a tray which held three crystal glasses of white wine and some very thin cheese slices. As she served the wine, she said, "It seems that you and Aunt Mary are getting along so well, I don't even need to tell you why I wanted you to be here and meet her. I've already warned Aunt Mary to be careful of her thoughts, as you might pick them up."

"Oh, Jonathan and I were just getting started. He likes my 'touch' of Ireland. But, Jonathan, I hadn't gotten around to telling you that our professor friend to whom we rented our apartment now wants to retire to Santa Fe, New Mexico, and write. His wife has been bothered with arthritis, especially in her knees, and they believe the high altitude of Santa Fe will bring relief. They're both troubled by arthritis. Some of their friends also live out around Santa Fe and Taos. It seems there are a number of immigrants from Boston, New York, and Chicago who go to Santa Fe to indulge themselves in the arts without having to be serious about it. The professor and his wife are moving out August 1."

"And who will be leasing your apartment then, Mrs. Findlay, or do you wish to sell it?" Jonathan wanted Aunt Mary to keep talking, before Katherine could take over.

"Well, Jonathan, I really have to rent it. You see, David requested in his will that the apartment be bequeathed to me, along with all his other assets, and stipulated that it not be sold during my lifetime. David loved me very much, but he knew that I've always handled money rather loosely, especially when it comes to helping out friends. He wanted to make sure I didn't sell the apartment, that I'd have a place to live or at least have some rental income."

Katherine could wait no longer. "Jonathan, you've spoiled my sales pitch. You and Aunt Mary have become such instant friends that about all there is for me to say now is that there are, of course, lots of people, many undesirable, who would like to lease an apartment in this building. I asked Aunt Mary to meet you before we even let anyone else consider renting it. Now, if Aunt Mary approves of you as a tenant, let's go look at the place. Aunt Mary, do you think Jonathan might be an acceptable tenant for you?"

"Katherine, I knew before hand that if you approved of Jonathan, I would. But aside from your recommendation, I not only approve of Jonathan but would like to visit more with him. I think he and David would have had a grand time discussing anything and everything. Shall we go look at the apartment now, Jonathan? I especially want to show you how David converted one of the bedrooms into what I think is a beautiful library."

"I'm eager to go," Jonathan said as he extended his hand to help Aunt Mary up from the sofa. Katherine just smiled and jingled the apartment keys.

They went out the door to the elevators. Jonathan pushed the "seven" button. Katherine looked at him, wondering if Aunt Mary had told him the apartment was on the seventh floor. She made no comment, except to explain that the present tenants had gone to northern Wisconsin for the holiday week-end and had given Katherine permission to show the apartment. Jonathan turned to the right when they got off the elevator, and Katherine said, "I'll open the apartment door for you, since I have the keys." She quickly led the way to the apartment, so that just in case Jonathan guessed the apartment number as he had the floor, Aunt Mary wouldn't think he had been there before.

The apartment pleased Jonathan. The bedroom that Professor Findlay had converted into a library was beautiful and functional, with ash shelving running from floor to ceiling around the entire room, except for doors and windows. Under all the shelving were twenty-seven-inch-high closed cabinets with light bronze door handles. The top of the cabinets extended about eight inches from the shelving, providing a working table surface, where one could remove and examine books. The lightly stained, natural-grained ash was very attractive, making the library bright and inviting. Before seeing the rest of the apartment, Jonathan said to Mrs. Findlay, "As I look at this library, I can tell you that your husband and I would have had much in common. I had exactly the same type of library in our Winnetka home. I used ash, just like this, and the same design for shelves and cabinets. But let's look around. All the rugs seem to be in good shape and in a good color."

The library-bedroom had a walk-in closet and a bathroom with a combination tub and shower. The master bedroom was much larger than most condominium bedrooms, with an extra-large walk-in closet. The master bathroom was roomy, with a separate stall shower, and the bathroom fixtures were of the highest quality. The kitchen was large enough for a comfortable breakfast table.

Jonathan stopped his tour and said, "I hope your apartment likes me as well as I like it. No need to go further. What length of lease do you wish, and what rent does the present tenant pay?" He addressed his questions more to Katherine than to Aunt Mary.

"Would a two-year lease be okay with you, Jonathan, with an option to renew? Professor Jacobson, who is renting it now, has been paying a little under what I think the market is." Katherine looked at Aunt Mary for approval, and she smiled and nodded.

"Katherine, I don't want to frighten Aunt Mary by having her think I'm prescient or engaging in any of that guesstimate stuff, but within the past two months I've considered moving to Chicago, and I checked sale prices and rental prices on condominiums, especially two-bedroom, two-bath units. So I'd say, Aunt Mary, you should be getting a hundred dollars a month more than what your present tenant is probably paying you. If you and Katherine would like for me to lease your apartment for two years with that price increase, I'll be glad to do so, with an option to renew, based on the going lease rate at that time, plus a right of first refusal should the apartment be put on the market for sale for whatever reason.

"I think Aunt Mary can use the extra twelve hundred dollars a year income, and in case she needs a little extra money now, to catch up on expenses, without having to borrow from these high-priced banks, I'll pay her three months' rent in advance."

Aunt Mary, without waiting for Katherine to speak, said, "That's fine, very fine with me, Jonathan."

Katherine smiled. "Well, it looks as if you and Aunt Mary don't need any help to agree. So, I agree."

"And, Katherine," Jonathan continued, "if you don't have a standard lease form available, I'll be disappointed and surprised."

"By the strangest coincidence, Jonathan, I do have the lease forms on hand. And I think we should go up and have our lunch and sign the lease now. Then I can go back to the office, and Aunt Mary, now that she's personally approved the tenant, can fly back to Florida."

Aunt Mary was very happy. On the way up to Katherine's apartment, she asked, "Jonathan, how many books will you be bringing with you? I ask, because the shelves will hold about fourteen or fifteen hundred."

"Aunt Mary, a few months ago I gave the Ethics Group library several hundred books. I'll bring only about eight hundred. Why do you ask?"

"Well, Jonathan, I think you and David would not only have liked each other, but you'd probably have liked many of the same books. I forgot to tell you that there's a large storage room that goes with the apartment, and that's where we stored a thousand of David's books, including some of the very best American, French, and English literature. I'm so pleased that you're going to live in our apartment that I want to give you a key to all the special steel files in which the books are locked. You can choose the books you want, to fill out your library."

"Aunt Mary, may I kiss you for such thoughtfulness?"

"Jonathan, if Katherine has no objection, you may kiss me for any reason."

Katherine laughed and said, "Jonathan, it runs in the family."

After Jonathan signed the lease and gave Aunt Mary his check for the three months' rental, he whispered to Katherine that being on the seventh floor placed him just two flights from paradise. She answered discreetly, "You may want to use the elevators on some occasions, to conserve all your energy."

Aunt Mary had her bag all packed, so after lunch Jonathan carried it over to the Walton Street entrance of the Drake hotel, where she caught the airport bus to O'Hare for her flight to Naples. Katherine took a taxi to her office.

As she got into the cab, she said, "Everything is wonderful, wonderful. I'll meet you at the apartment at six. Please be early."

Rene had no complications whatsoever following her operation on Thursday morning. Dr. Sukman said she could go home sooner, but he advised her to remain in the hospital a full week. Rene agreed and made arrangements with Ellen and Anson to pick her up at four-thirty the following Thursday afternoon.

When they arrived at the apartment, Anson's mother, Esther, greeted them, proudly presenting a newly cleaned and vacuumed apartment and two big vases of flowers—lovely roses from Gerald and a colorful assortment of spring flowers from Jonathan. When Esther told Rene she had come to stay with her until they caught

439

up on their talking, Anson observed with a grin that surely Rene would be more than recovered before then.

Ellen and Anson and Esther were doing their best to make Rene feel glad to be home, but as Rene reclined on her living room sofa, she found that she hated the place. It had been just two weeks since she and Greg had left that very room to go to dinner, but now the whole place seemed to belong to some other woman. Rene wanted to leave as soon as she could.

The first thing she did was to call Gerald, and after thanking him for the roses, she asked if he could take her to look at one of the condominiums they had discussed in the hospital, when he had brought descriptive listing sheets on a half dozen places. She wanted to go and look at them Saturday.

"Rene, I'll be very happy to show you three good condominiums out of the group we talked about. One of them I believe you'll like, and they've given me a first refusal on it for ten days, just to give you a chance to see it. But Rene, dear, do ask Dr. Sukman if it'll be all right for you to go out Saturday. If he says it's okay, I'll be at your place at nine-thirty Saturday morning, and we'll go condo shopping."

"Gerald, you're so kind. I hope you understand why I want to move as soon as possible. This apartment I'm in belonged to a woman who no longer exists."

In Chicago, Jonathan thought that no two people could have enjoyed a July 4, stay-in-town, holiday week-end more completely, so interwoven in mind, body, and soul, than he and Katherine did. They went down and looked at Jonathan's apartment and thought about where things should go. They became curious about Uncle David's locked files of books, so using the keys Aunt Mary had already given him, Jonathan and Katherine had fun skimming through the titles, occasionally stopping to read a paragraph or a page in one good book or another. Uncle David had a great collection. They walked up Lake Michigan's struggling beach that survived each year's battle with ice, wind, and waves. They walked through Lincoln Park, talking about politics, business, books, trees, and whatever else came to mind. Back in Katherine's apartment, they watched TV talk shows, sports features, news, and Lincoln Center live specials. They read the newspapers and exchanged comments. They ate and drank selectively—and made love exquisitely.

They had decided to eat only at places within walking distance, and there were plenty, most of them not crowded because of the holiday exodus. To Jonathan, his days with Katherine represented a joyful fulfillment he had never expected to experience again. He hoped that Katherine was one-tenth as pleased as he.

Katherine recognized Jonathan's great devotion to her, and she wanted him to know that she enjoyed many pleasures and benefits from being with him, too. "I may not be able to tell you in all the words and ways that you tell me, but Jonathan, I love you very much. I respect you very much. I enjoy traveling the world of ideas with you. You are undoubtedly helping me to gain a perspective and understanding of business and the world that my competitors, male or female, can't get from any one source. You're an inspiring mentor and an exciting lover.

"So many of today's women," she continued, "have become so capable that contemporary men, with few exceptions, aren't able to equal them, much less encompass them intellectually, spiritually, and physically. Yet, as smart and mature as many of the women are that I'm now meeting, some still cherish that vestigial notion that 'Someday my prince will come.' I tell them that to obtain such a prince, they may have to adopt a frog and help him change into a prince. The qualities a woman admires and appreciates in a man are often the characteristics some other woman or women have patiently helped him to acquire—and vice versa— though less often, because not as many men pay that much attention to their women.

"Jonathan," Katherine continued, "you and I may be the rare ones who can enjoy the best of two worlds. But I want you to know, age factors notwithstanding, that if you ever really want me to marry you, I will. Now you know how much I appreciate and love you." She smiled warmly and reached out to put her hand on his. Jonathan appeared slightly bewildered.

The setting for Katherine's statement was a window table in the revolving restaurant on the thirty-third floor, atop the Holiday Inn's Lake Shore Drive hotel. For a while, Jonathan seemed to be a little stunned. He stared at the lovely, sensuous lips from which the news had come. He looked at Katherine's deep, hazel brown eyes that glistened from the glow of the quick mind that focused them. He traced her dark, beautifully shaped eyebrows. He looked at her pretty nose as if he had just discovered its slight Irish tilt.

He looked with adoring approval at her soft, lush, uniformly dark hair, so perfectly styled for a stately, intelligent, absolutely beautiful woman. Katherine watched Jonathan as he seemed to absorb her totally. Finally, she asked with a confident, smiling curiosity, "Well?"

Jonathan came back to earth. She was so beautiful, so tenderly caring, and she had said she loved him enough to marry him. "I'm still adrift in a dream world filled with nothing but beauty—your presence. What you've just told me honors me, incredibly. How satisfying, how wonderful for me to be loved so much by you—beautiful, strong, and lovely as you are. I think you know, as I do, that we have mysteriously loved one another since that moment after our lunch with Barbara when you wrote your home phone number on the back of your business card. But to hear you speak that love exceeds all my hopes for this life of mine. My love for you, my admiration of you, borders on total worship. It makes me feel that I've found a new life and entered another world.

"But when one is both a lover and a mentor," he continued quietly, "his responsibilities as a mentor to the one he loves exceeds the ineffable—how else can I say it?—joy of being loved. However indescribably desirable marriage to you would be for me, it might not be best for you. Your willingness to marry me, however, emphasizes that you put love first, which inspires me to put your future first.

"But looking at you and knowing you love me so much does make me damn near crazy enough to jump on top of this table and yell, 'Drinks on the house! An angel loves me!' "

Katherine laughed. "Oh, Jonathan, I wish I had a tape of all that you've been saying. No one would ever believe that such a remote man is so totally un-remote. There are a lot of reasons I love you, and you've just demonstrated one—you're an intriguing human being.

"Fate, in the name of Barbara Ballinger, brought us together, and we do have a good thing going. But I'll not give fate or chance or anyone credit for my holding Aunt Mary's apartment for you. That's one of the smartest deals I've made in a while—maybe in a decade or so. Yet, all it took was love and common sense."

"You know, Katherine, there's something about your Aunt Mary's apartment that makes it the most wonderful place for me in all the world—it's only forty-six seconds from you. No wonder the real estate people keep emphasizing the importance of location when they sell properties! I hope the professor moves out before the first of August.

"Where we sit now, Katherine, represents a memorable place in my life. It's where you said you loved me enough to marry me. Let's order champagne, just for us, not for the house, and stay here for dinner."

"This has been an important moment for me, too," Katherine responded. "Do you realize that I never, never, never expected to love another man enough to tell him I'd marry him? I may now be going around and around, but the next time our apartment building comes into view, I'll say again, 'I love you.' Let's do have more champagne and dinner here. After all, we're on a holiday."

"Now, Katherine, you're invading my pun territory." Jonathan never dreamed he could be so happy again, so in love. And Katherine seemed quite happy, too. Whoever said love was only for the young?

From Chicago, Jonathan went to his Virginia apartment, and his first call was to his real estate broker friend who seemed to sell or lease most of the condominiums in his building. "No trouble at all, Jonathan," the broker said. "We have a waiting list of people wanting to lease units in your building. We'll have a good tenant in there by August 1. You want a two-year lease?"

"Yes, two years," Jonathan confirmed. "To a good tenant, I'll give a first refusal to extend the lease, should I wish to lease it longer."

Then he called the family-owned moving company that had handled his move so well when he moved to McLean. The mover said he could come in and pack on July 30 and be in Chicago the afternoon of August 1. He arranged with the real estate broker's secretary to handle all the new change-of-address notifications and planned to return to his apartment for a final check when the movers came in. He could discontinue his McLean phone at that time. By Friday, he was back in Los Angeles.

After he checked into his Los Angeles apartment, he called Ellen to find out when he could see her.

"Oh, Dad, why not come out Sunday afternoon and stay for dinner? Have you called Mom yet? She'd probably like to hear from you just to tell you what a beautiful condominium she and

443

Gerald found. She's getting along very well, but I'll bet she'd like to bring you up to date on what she and Gerald have planned for their business enterprises."

"Okay, I'll call your mother and congratulate her. And I'll see you Sunday afternoon. Maybe Anson and Laura and I can watch TV together. She should know all about baseball, now that's she's over nine months old. See you Sunday, Ellen."

Jonathan called Rene right away. She answered the phone in a voice that suggested her bright, enthusiastic mood. "How's friend Jonathan? Did you enjoy Chicago?"

"Yes, indeed, Rene. You sound great, but no wonder. Ellen said you've already found a condominium. Where is it and when do you move in?" Jonathan kept the conversation on a light and friendly business basis.

"I'm going to be out of this place and into my new corner unit by August 1. Gerald found it for me, or rather we went together to look at several he had checked out and thought were worth looking at. Actually, I picked the one I bought because it's in the best location, in the fine residential and apartment area in the north part of Santa Monica. I'll bet I could sell it at a profit the day I move in. So how's your banking business in Chicago?"

"Rene, everything there is going great, just as it is for you here. You and I are again very lucky people. I, too, am moving August 1—back to Chicago. I'm leasing my apartment in McLean, and I've already leased one in Chicago. It's three blocks from the Drake, but another reason I like the location is that it's in the same building where Katherine lives, two floors down. Her widowed aunt owns it. Her aunt's husband was a professor of comparative literature, like John Elliott, the fellow we like so much in Church City. Katherine's Uncle David converted one of the bedrooms into a library with built-in ash shelving, like we had in our Winnetka home. There's room for fifteen hundred books! But I'd like to hear how your business plans are moving."

"They're coming along very well. We're planning our office layout and looking at furniture. Our office will be located on the east edge of Santa Monica, not far from Century City. You'll be among the first to get one of our business cards."

"Well, Rene, when you and Gerald decide to go public with Barron & Clawson Enterprises, I'll bet every member of your family will buy stock. Are you going to consider me a family member?"

"Oh, we'll always let you be an ex-officio family member. Jonathan, I've always respected your judgment of people, and I appreciate your continued confidence in me and your confidence in Gerald."

"That's a good 'goodbye' statement to hear. Keep being healthy and positive in your faith in all good things. Goodbye, dear."

"Goodbye, Jonathan."

Jonathan's Sunday visit with Ellen and her family was very pleasant. She and Anson were very happy with the way things were developing for Rene and felt proud of their direct encouragement and support of Rene and Gerald. Jonathan was pleased with their romance watching, too.

"But, Dad, Mom just doesn't seem to want another lover, another man, even though she and Gerald see each other every weekday and Sunday, too. Mom likes St. Matthew's Episcopal Church; she'll make many friends there. She goes to church every Sunday. Do you think she'll ever marry Gerald or any other man?"

"Sure she will, Ellen. It's taken her a little while to accept a man in her life, to think of having a lover and a husband again. But Gerald understands that. He's the perfect mate for her, as well as being a good business partner. Incidentally, in that connection, do you remember how much both you and your mother wanted to visit the Greek Islands? You were both so nuts about the trip, you wanted to go together."

"I remember, Dad. I'd still like to go. Why?" Ellen asked.

"I was thinking that the Greek Islands might still represent to your mother an unfulfilled wish. You know, it would be a great place for a honeymoon. I'll bet Gerald would like to see these travel folders that I brought for you." He reached into his inside jacket pocket and handed them to Ellen.

"You can pass them along and tell Gerald how much your mother wanted to visit the Greek Island area. You know, if she's so straight-laced now, church every Sunday and all that, she might want to go with Gerald to the Islands—but not unless she's married to him."

"You're right," Ellen said thoughtfully. "I'll look these over for me and Anson and then pass them along to Gerald or Mom—or to both of them sometime when they're over here. And, Dad, I won't tell who gave them to me. I appreciate you more all the time, not only because you're my dad but also because you continue to care about Mom. You always seem to want happiness for her."

"This is a good time for me to exit. But before I go, I might tell you that your mother said she made such a good buy on her new condominium that she could sell it at a profit the day she moves. If she ever does get married, she should try to persuade Gerald to combine the two second-floor corner apartments facing the ocean in the building he owns. I went by there, just to look at his building. It's very nice. But even when Rene was young, she preferred all the rooms on one floor, including the big family room with fireplace. Who knows, Gerald may have this arrangement in mind for himself, anyway. I'm sure he doesn't want to continue living in Rene's old neighborhood. He's changed, as Rene has.

"Incidentally, I didn't tell you that I'm moving to Chicago on August 1."

"You are!" Ellen exclaimed. "That's great, Dad. But are you sure you won't miss Washington?"

"Ellen, I like the location of the apartment I've leased in Chicago. It's in the same building where Katherine Browne lives. I've told you a little about my favorite banker. Actually, I'll be on the seventh floor, and Katherine is on the ninth—just forty-six seconds away from me, via the stairway. And do you know, as pretty as she is, as obviously intelligent as she is—her business success attests to that—well, she's said she loves me very much, and I love her. Rene and I may have been lucky enough to have known one another when we needed each other most. Now she has in Gerald the kind of man I believed could make the rest of her life very happy —the kind of man she needs. And you can't believe how much Katherine and I need one another—I, ten times more than she, however."

"Oh, Daddy, I never thought that your deep depression and sadness of the past few years, especially since you and Mom separated, could ever be so completely eliminated."

"The old saying used to be, 'Never underestimate the power of a woman,'" Jonathan said. "For me, the greatest joy is the deep love of a woman. Of course, history has recorded the power of love, the benefits, the paradise that only love can make possible. Katherine is to me what Beatrice was to Dante. She has brought me out of purgatory into paradise—which is forty-six seconds from where I'll be living beginning August 1."

"But, Dad, if Katherine loves you so much and you love her, why don't you two get married?"

446

"Ellen, Katherine offered marriage to me, but I love her far too much to take advantage of that offer. I once loved another woman far too much to ask her to sacrifice all her chances to be on her own. I hoped she would marry the perfect man for her new life. I believe Dr. Clawson came along, as he was meant to."

"I understand, Daddy." Ellen kissed him goodbye, saying, "I love you very much."

He and Anson shook hands just as Laura woke up, and her demands were loud and clear.

On October 3 the business section of the Chicago Sunday newspapers carried a story stating that Katherine Browne had been elected a Senior Vice-President of City National Bank. Coincidentally, on that same date, the business section of the Los Angeles Sunday newspapers had a story on the establishment of Barron & Clawson Enterprises. Both the Chicago and Los Angeles papers featured pictures of the women executives referred to in the respective news articles.

On November 15, Jonathan received a letter from Rene, on the new Barron & Clawson Enterprises letterhead, telling him that she and Gerald were to be married in a private ceremony at St. Matthew's Episcopal Church on November 20 at noon. They had already received the bishop's approval. Only Ellen and Anson would be in attendance. Immediately following the wedding, Ellen and Anson would take them to the airport. They would fly to Rome and Athens and would then spend three weeks in the Greek Islands. In her letter, Rene asked, "Don't you think the Greek Islands will be a nice place for us to honeymoon? The travel agent said the nights might be a little nippy, but the November days are usually sunny and bright. You know me, I like the idea of getting the finest accommodations at half price, with the usual tourist families and children not around."

Jonathan phoned Rene to thank her for her letter and to wish much happiness and success and good health for her and Gerald. "I believe you're each getting a great partner in marriage, in life," he added.

He also told her that he would be flying to Australia on November 20. Katherine had already departed for Sydney but would stop en route in Tokyo, Hong Kong, Singapore, and Djakarta to meet with bankers and business leaders, because of City National's increasing activity in the Pacific Rim countries. In Sydney, Katherine

447

would conclude her business meetings and would join Jonathan for a three-week vacation in Australia and New Zealand.

"Just think, Jonathan," Rene said, "after a delay of forty years or more, you're finally going to Australia. But with Katherine there with you, I'll bet you'll feel the reward was worth the wait. We wish you and Katherine a joyful journey together. Your old fate has certainly reached way out to bring happiness to us."

"Well, you waited a long time for your trip to the Greek Islands, and I hope your wait will be rewarded with a glorious honeymoon. Goodbye, Rene, and best wishes forever."

"Goodbye, Jonathan, and best wishes forever."